A FIELD GUIDE TO THE
National Parks
OF EAST AFRICA

other books in the same series

A FIELD GUIDE TO THE BIRDS OF EAST AFRICA *John Williams and Norman Arlott*

A FIELD GUIDE TO THE LARGER MAMMALS OF AFRICA
Jean Dorst and Pierre Dandelot

A FIELD GUIDE TO THE MAMMALS OF AFRICA AND MADAGASCAR
T. Haltenorth and H. Diller

A FIELD GUIDE TO THE BUTTERFLIES OF AFRICA *John Williams*

A FIELD GUIDE TO THE SNAKES OF SOUTHERN AFRICA *V. F. M. FitzSimons*

A FIELD GUIDE TO THE TREES OF SOUTHERN AFRICA *Eve Palmer*

A FIELD GUIDE TO THE BIRDS OF SOUTHERN AFRICA *O. P. M. Prozesky*

A FIELD GUIDE TO THE BIRDS OF WEST AFRICA *W. Serle and G. Morel*

A FIELD GUIDE TO THE SEABIRDS OF SOUTH AFRICA AND THE WORLD
G. S. Tuck and Hermann Heinzel

THE MAMMALS OF RHODESIA, ZAMBIA AND MALAWI: A Handbook
Reay H. N. Smithers

THE BIRDS OF ZAMBIA *C. W. Benson, R. K. Brooke, Michael P. Stuart Irwin*

THE BIRDS OF SEYCHELLES AND THE OUTLYING ISLANDS *Malcolm Penny*

A FIELD GUIDE TO THE BIRDS OF BRITAIN AND EUROPE
Roger Peterson, Guy Mountfort and P. A. D. Hollom

A FIELD GUIDE TO THE BUTTERFLIES OF BRITAIN AND EUROPE
N. D. Riley and L. G. Higgins

A FIELD GUIDE TO THE TREES OF BRITAIN AND NORTHERN EUROPE
Alan Mitchell

A FIELD GUIDE TO THE REPTILES AND AMPHIBIANS OF BRITAIN AND EUROPE
N. Arnold, J. A. Burton and D. W. Ovenden

A FIELD GUIDE TO THE INSECTS OF BRITAIN AND NORTHERN EUROPE
Michael Chinery

A FIELD GUIDE TO THE LAND SNAILS OF BRITAIN AND NORTH-WEST EUROPE
Michael Kerney, Robert Cameron and Gordon Riley

A FIELD GUIDE TO THE NESTS, EGGS AND NESTLINGS OF BRITISH AND EUROPEAN BIRDS *Colin Harrison*

BIRDS OF THE WEST INDIES *James Bond*

THE SEA SHELLS OF THE WEST INDIES *Michael Humphrey*

A GUIDE TO SEABIRDS ON THE OCEAN ROUTES *G. S. Tuck*

A FIELD GUIDE TO THE

National Parks

OF EAST AFRICA

John G. Williams

with 24 colour plates and
5 black and white plates
by Norman Arlott and
Rena Fennessy

COLLINS
Grafton Street, London

William Collins Sons & Co Ltd
London · Glasgow · Sydney · Auckland
Toronto · Johannesburg

First published 1967 with paintings by Rena Fenessy

Reprinted 1984
Reprinted 1986 (twice)
Reprinted 1988 (twice)
Reprinted 1991
ISBN 0 00 219215 2

Filmset by Jolly and Barber Ltd, Rugby

Printed in Hong Kong by South China Printing Co.

Contents

UGANDA 129

PART 2

The Mammals of East Africa 161

PART 3

The Commoner Birds of East Africa 233

Key to Maps in Part 1

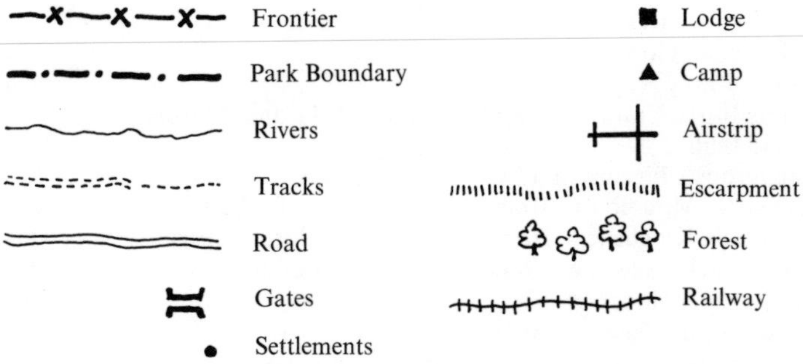

Plates

Mammals *painted by Rena Fennessy*

Birds *painted by Norman Arlott*

Introduction

A Field Guide to the National Parks of East Africa has two main aims. The first of these is to assist the user in identifying the mammals and birds to be seen in the faunal reserves, and secondly it is a reference guide to help in planning an East African holiday to the best possible advantage. In this context the author will always be pleased to meet or hear from naturalist visitors and to advise on itineraries.

This Field Guide is divided into three sections. In the first the National Parks, Game Reserves and other areas of special zoological importance and tourist appeal are detailed, each with a list of its characteristic mammals and birds. The second section is a guide to the mammals of East Africa, mainly the larger and more commonly observed smaller species, with their diagnostic field characters and distributions. The last section is a field guide to the commoner East African birds, species most likely to be encountered in the National Parks. The presentation of both the mammal and bird sections is in systematic order.

It is the author's pleasure to record his deep appreciation and gratitude to the Directors and Staff of the National Parks and Game Departments in Kenya, Tanzania and Uganda, and to numerous professional tour leaders in those countries, without whose active co-operation this book would not have been written. He also extends his warmest thanks to friends in Africa and overseas who have assisted in many ways. The author is especially indebted to Mr Norman Arlott, the talented young British artist who has so successfully illustrated the birds and to Mrs R. M. Fennessy of Kenya who painted the mammals. Their work greatly enhances the value of this book.

Kenya, Tanzania and Uganda are unique: no other region in the world has so much to offer the visitor. I hope that readers take away with them unforgettable memories of African wildlife, and that their experiences foment a growing concern for wildlife conservation throughout the world.

JOHN G. WILLIAMS

Introduction

[illegible]

PART 1

The National Parks, Game Reserves and other faunal areas

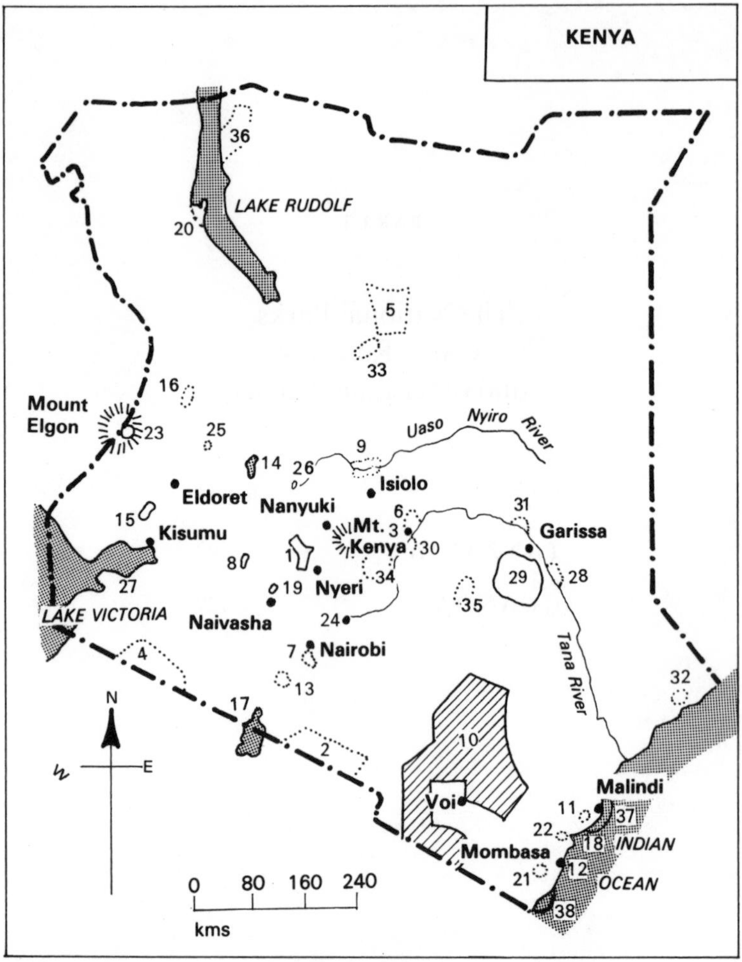

1	Aberdare NP	14	Lake Baringo	28	Arawale GR
2	Amboseli NP	15	Kakamega Forest	29	Boni GR
3	Mt Kenya NP	16	Kongelai Escarpment	30	Kora GR
4	Masai-Mara GR	17	Lake Magadi	31	Rahole GR
5	Marsabit NR	18	Mida Creek	32	Dodori NR
6	Meru NP	19	Lake Naivasha	33	Losai NR
7	Nairobi NP	20	Ferguson's Gulf	34	Mwea NR
8	Lake Nakuru NP	21	Shimba Hills NR	35	Ngai Ndethya NR
9	Samburu-Buffalo Springs-Shaba GR	22	Sokoke-Arabuku Forest	36	Sibiloi NR
10	Tsavo NP	23	Mt Elgon NP	37	Malindi and Watamu Marine NPs
11	Gedi NP	24	Ol Doinyo Sabuk NP	38	Kisite-Mpungut Marine NP
12	Fort Jesus NP	25	Saiwa Swamp NP		
13	Olorgesailie NP	26	Lake Bogoria NR		
		27	Lambwe Valley GR		

KENYA

Kenya boasts 16 major faunal reserves designated as National Parks, National Reserves and Game Reserves administered through the Game Department of Kenya and by County Councils. These are Aberdare National Park, Amboseli National Park, Mount Elgon National Park, Mount Kenya National Park, Meru National Park, Nairobi National Park, Lake Nakuru National Park, Ol Doinyo Sebuk National Park, Saiwa Swamp National Park, Tsavo National Park, Lake Boria (Hannington) National Reserve, Lambwe Valley Game Reserve, Marsabit National Reserve, Masai Mara Game Reserve, Samburu-Buffalo Springs-Shaba National Reserves and Shimba Hills National Reserve. In addition other faunal areas are in process of development. These include four Game Reserves in the Tana River-Garissa region, Arawale, Boni, Kora and Rahole, the Dodori National Reserve on the Dodori River near the coast in eastern Lamu district, Losai National Reserve in the Marsabit district, Mwea National Reserve in the Embu district, Ngai Ndethya National Reserve in the Kitui district of Eastern Province and the new Sigiloi National Reserve in the Northern Frontier Province along the north-eastern shores of Lake Turkana (Rudolf).

The distinction between a National Park and a Reserve, broadly speaking, is that in the former complete protection of fauna and flora is the paramount purpose and human utilisation of the land is precluded. In the Reserves preservation of wildlife is a primary purpose but human activities such as the grazing of cattle are sometimes allowed. It is fitting to pay homage to the pastoral tribes, peoples who have lived in harmony with wildlife from time immemorial, and to their wise Councils who now have set aside these Game Reserves where their wildlife heritage may be preserved.

In addition to the faunal National Parks there are three other Parks which are mainly of historical and archaeological importance. These are:

Fort Jesus National Park which protects the seventeenth-century Portuguese fort at Mombasa, overlooking the Indian Ocean.

Gedi National Park which protects one of the most outstanding thirteenth-century ruined Arab cities.

Olorgesailie National Park, in the Great Rift Valley, which preserves a Pleistocene living-site of hand-axe man, with his artifacts and associated prehistoric mammal fossils exhibited *in situ*.

These National Parks are also not without their zoological interest, which will be detailed later in this section.

Lastly there are the three Marine National Parks, two, Malindi Marine National Park and Watamu National Park, both established in 1968, on the Kenya north coast, and the Kisite-Mpungut Marine National Park, opened in 1973, incorporating three islets off Shimoni, Kenya south coast. The establishment of a fourth Marine National Park, to be sited amongst islands of the Kiunga Archipelago immediately south of Kenya-Somali border is under consideration.

ABERDARE NATIONAL PARK

The Aberdare National Park, established in 1950, comprises an area of 590sq km (228sq miles). This includes the moorlands and part of the forest of the Aberdare Mountains, for the most part over 3,000m (10,000ft). The famous Treetops Hotel, 19km (12 miles) from Nyeri, is situated in a salient of the Park which extends down the eastern side of the range to the lower edge of the forest.

The second forest lodge in the Aberdare National Park is the Ark, also accessible from Nyeri, via the Aberdares Country Club. This lodge, sited in the forest above a swampy glade, water hole and salt lick is the most likely place in Kenya from which to see Bongo, these large and handsome forest antelopes being frequent visitors. Leopard sightings are also not infrequent.

The Park is readily accessible from Nyeri and Naro Moru on the eastern side, the road crossing the Park and connecting with the road from Naivasha and North Kinangop on the west.

The Aberdare Mountains are part of the central highlands of Kenya, running roughly north-south between Nairobi and Thomson's Falls. In altitude the range rises to some 3,930m (12,900ft). The mountain slopes, especially on the eastern and western flanks, are covered with heavy forest with tree ferns in places giving way to a bamboo-hargenia zone at higher levels.

Deep ravines cut through the forested inclines, through which hidden trout streams flow and waterfalls cascade down hundreds of feet of rock face. Above the forest stretch miles of open moorlands, broken by lichen-covered rocky outcrops, hills and crags, thickets of giant heath and tussock-grass bogs.

To appreciate the full glory of this very beautiful Park, camping is recommended at one of the several approved sites. The hour or so immediately following dawn is the most rewarding time to look for game, and it is then that one has the best chance of suddenly coming upon that shy and elusive animal the Bongo. The upper bamboo zone and hypericum scrub is its favourite habitat.

In the forest are Red Duiker, Suni, Bushbuck – some of the old males on the Aberdares are nearly black – Elephant, Buffalo, Giant Forest Hog, Leopard – all black examples have been recorded – and Colobus monkey.

Eland occur on the open moorlands. The moorland thickets are the home of Bush Duiker and Black-fronted Duiker, and Black Rhino are by no means rare. The Aberdare moorlands is a good locality for Serval, and both the normal spotted and melanistic animals may be seen.

Bird life is abundant and varied. Perhaps the most conspicuous group is

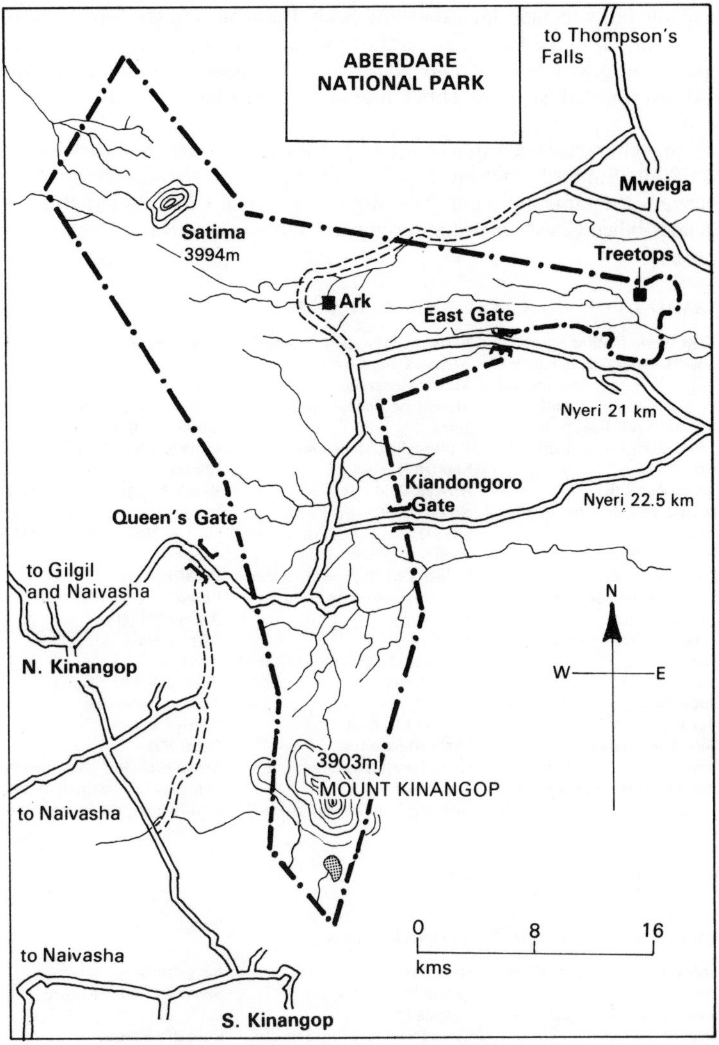

the sunbirds. Four species may be seen – Tacazze Sunbird, brilliant metallic violet and bronze with a black belly; Golden-winged Sunbird, scintillating coppery-bronze with golden yellow edged wings and tail; the emerald green Malachite Sunbird, and the tiny Double-collared Sunbird with metallic green upperparts and throat and scarlet chest band.

Game birds include Jackson's and Scaly Francolins in the forest and the very local Montane Francolin on the moorlands. Birds of prey are specially interesting and Crowned and Ayres' Hawk Eagles, Mountain Buzzard, Rufous-breasted Sparrow Hawk and African Goshawk are usually to be seen.

Some characteristic birds of the higher moorlands are the Scarlet-tufted Malachite Sunbird – but much rarer here than in the alpine zone of Mount Kenya – the tame and confiding Mountain or Hill Chat, Augur Buzzard, Slender-billed Chestnut-wing Starling and White-naped Raven.

MAMMALS OF ABERDARE NATIONAL PARK

Giant White-toothed Shrew
Mole Shrew Mainly in bamboo zone, where they burrow just below surface of ground
Rousette Fruit Bat In caves in forest: attracted to fruiting fig trees
Hollow-faced Bat
Banana Bat or **African Pipistrelle**
Greater Galago
Black-faced Vervet
Blue or **Sykes' Monkey**
Olive Baboon
Black and White Colobus
Hunting Dog Probably spasmodic visitors
Black-backed or **Silver-backed Jackal**
Side-striped Jackal
Zorilla
Clawless Otter Not uncommon along trout streams, but rarely seen. Feeds on fresh-water crabs
African Civet
Bush or **Large-spotted Genet**
African Palm Civet
Marsh Mongoose
Slender or **Black-tipped Mongoose**
White-tailed Mongoose
Spotted Hyaena
African Wild Cat
Serval Not uncommon on moorlands: melanistic examples sometimes seen
Golden Cat Reputed to occur, but not yet confirmed
Lion Rare
Leopard
Ant Bear Occurs at lower levels
Tree Hyrax
Rock Hyrax
African Elephant
Black Rhinoceros
Giant Forest Hog Often seen at Treetops
Bush Pig Common but shy: not often seen
Blue Duiker
Bush Duiker
Klipspringer
Suni
Steinbok
Common Waterbuck
Bohor Reedbuck
Chanler's Reedbuck
Impala
Bongo Found mainly in upper bamboo zone; very shy and elusive. Has been recorded at Treetops
Bushbuck
Eland
African Buffalo
African Hare
Porcupine
Bush Squirrel
African Dormouse
Crested Rat
Giant Rat
Kenya Mole Rat Their presence indicated by the earth mounds thrown up by the animals whilst digging

BIRDS OF ABERDARE NATIONAL PARK

Little Grebe Recorded at Treetops
Long-tailed Cormorant Treetops
Black-headed Heron Treetops
Yellow-billed Egret Treetops
Little Egret
Buff-backed Heron or **Cattle Egret**
Hamerkop
Wood Ibis or **Yellow-billed Stork** Treetops
Sacred Ibis Treetops
Hadada Ibis
Green Ibis A rare forest species. Frequents swampy glades in forest
Yellow-billed Duck Treetops
African Black Duck On streams in forest
Garganey Teal Treetops
Red-billed Duck Treetops
Egyptian Goose Treetops
Secretary Bird Recorded on moorlands
Ruppell's Vulture
White-backed Vulture
Hooded Vulture
Peregrine
Lanner
European Kestrel
Lesser Kestrel

Cuckoo Falcon An uncommon species in forest
European Black Kite
African Black Kite
Black-shouldered Kite Spasmodic visitor to moorlands
Verreaux's Eagle
Steppe Eagle
Ayres' Hawk Eagle Sometimes seen soaring above forest
Crowned Hawk Eagle Uncommon in forest
Long-crested Eagle
Lammergeyer Rare visitor. Not known to breed
Steppe Buzzard In some years a common winter visitor; in other years seldom seen
Mountain Buzzard Not uncommon in forest
Augur Buzzard
Rufous-breasted Sparrow Hawk
Great Sparrow Hawk
African Goshawk
Montagu's Harrier Winter visitor and passage migrant to moorlands
Pallid Harrier Winter visitor and passage migrant to moorlands
European Marsh Harrier Winter visitor. Rare
Montane Francolin Scrub and moorlands above forest
Scaly Francolin Forest species
Jackson's Francolin Forest and bamboo zones
Cape Quail Uncommon on moorlands
African Crake Spasmodic visitor moorlands. Rarely seen
African Finfoot Rare. Streams at lower altitudes
Crowned Crane Treetops
Black-winged Plover Spasmodic visitor to moorlands
European Common Snipe
Great Snipe Mainly passage migrant April/May in moorland bogs
Jack Snipe Rare winter visitor. High altitude bogs
Ruff Treetops
Green Sandpiper Winter visitor. Mountain streams
Wood Sandpiper Treetops
Greenshank Treetops
Marsh Sandpiper Treetops
Olive Pigeon Forest. Common
Bronze-naped Pigeon Forest
Pink-breasted Dove
Red-eyed Dove
Ring-necked Dove Treetops
Laughing Dove Treetops
Tambourine Dove
Emerald-spotted Wood Dove
Lemon Dove Rare. Forest at lower levels
Green Pigeon
Red-chested Cuckoo Treetops
Emerald Cuckoo Treetops, and low level forest
Didric Cuckoo
Klaas' Cuckoo
White-browed Coucal Treetops
Hartlaub's Turaco Not uncommon in forest
Red-headed Parrot Forest
European Roller Uncommon passage migrant. Treetops
Lilac-breasted Roller Treetops
Broad-billed Roller Lower level forest
Pied Kingfisher Treetops
Giant Kingfisher On forest streams. Feeds largely on freshwater crabs
Malachite Kingfisher Treetops
European Bee-eater Uncommon visitor. Treetops
Cinnamon-chested Bee-eater Forest glades
Silvery-cheeked Hornbill Forest
Crowned Hornbill Treetops
Ground Hornbill Treetops
White-headed Wood Hoopoe Forest
Cape Grass Owl Swampy hollows on moorlands
African Marsh Owl Moorlands
Mackinder's Eagle Owl Crags and cliffs above forest
Spotted Eagle Owl
Verreaux's Eagle Owl Treetops
European Nightjar Migrant. Treetops
Abyssinian Nightjar
Pennant-wing Nightjar Rare visitor. Treetops
Speckled Mousebird Treetops
Narina's Trogon Forest
Bar-tailed Trogon Forest
Golden-rumped Tinkerbird Treetops
Greater Honeyguide Treetops. Uncommon
Fine-banded Woodpecker Forest
Nyanza Swift
Alpine Swift
Mottled Swift
Mountain Wagtail Forest streams
Red-capped Lark Moorlands
Blue-headed Wagtail and races Moorlands on spring migration
Richard's Pipit
Red-throated Pipit
Sharpe's Longclaw Moorlands
Yellow-vented Bulbul Treetops
Fischer's Greenbul Treetops
Olive-brested Mountain Greenbul
Yellow-whiskered Greenbul
European Spotted Flycatcher Treetops. Migrant
Dusky Flycatcher Treetops
White-eyed Slaty Flycatcher Treetops
Mountain Yellow Flycatcher
Chin-spot Flycatcher Treetops
Paradise Flycatcher Treetops
Olive Thrush
Abyssinian Ground Thrush Bamboo zone
European Common Wheatear
Isabelline Wheatear
Pied Wheatear
Capped Wheatear Uncommon. Moorlands
Hill or **Mountain Chat** Alpine zone
Stonechat
Ruppell's Robin Chat
Robin Chat
White-starred Bush Robin Common in bamboo zone
Blackcap Warbler Treetops
European Sedge Warbler Treetops
Cinnamon Bracken Warbler
Greater Swamp Warbler Treetops
European Willow Warbler
Brown Woodland Warbler
Grey Apalis
Black-breasted Apalis

Chestnut-throated Apalis
Grey-backed Camaroptera
Wing-snapping Cisticola Alpine grasslands
Hunter's Cisticola Common in moorland thickets
Tinkling Cisticola Moorland bogs
European Swallow
African Sand Martin
African Rock Martin
Black Rough-wing Swallow
White-headed Rough-wing Swallow
Purple-throated Cuckoo Shrike
Grey Cuckoo Shrike
Drongo Treetops
Fiscal Shrike Treetops
Tropical Boubou Forest
Black-backed Puff-back Treetops
Black-fronted Bush Shrike Forest trees and creepers
Doherty's Bush Shrike Lower forest: frequents undergrowth
White-breasted Tit
Black-headed Oriole
Black-winged Montane Oriole High level forest
Pied Crow Treetops
White-naped Raven
Violet-backed Starling Treetops
Sharpe's Starling
Blue-eared Glossy Starling Treetops
Slender-billed Chestnut-wing Starling Alpine moorlands and waterfalls, below which it nests
Superb Starling Treetops
Red-billed Oxpecker Treetops
Kikuyu White-eye
Malachite Sunbird
Scarlet-tufted Malachite Sunbird High moorlands
Tacazze Sunbird
Bronzy Sunbird Treetops
Golden-winged Sunbird
Variable Sunbird Treetops
Eastern Double-collared Sunbird
Northern Double-collared Sunbird Treetops
Amethyst Sunbird Treetops
Scarlet-chested Sunbird Treetops
Olive Sunbird Lower altitudes in forest
Collared Sunbird
Spectacled Weaver Treetops
Reichenow's Weaver
Brown-capped Weaver Forest
Red-naped Widow-bird Treetops
Long-tailed Widow-bird Open bushy moorland
Bronze Mannikin Treetops
Grey-headed Negro Finch Treetops
Abyssinian Crimson-wing Common in bamboo zone
Yellow-bellied Waxbill
Waxbill Treetops
Black-headed Waxbill Forest glades
Red-cheeked Cordon-bleu
Brimstone Canary
Yellow-crowned Canary Upper edges of forest and bamboo zone
Thick-billed Seed-eater Forest undergrowth
Oriole Finch Forest. Uncommon
African Citril Treetops
Golden-breasted Bunting

AMBOSELI NATIONAL PARK

Amboseli is justly famous both for its big game – elephants, lions and cheetahs are the main attractions – and for its great scenic beauty.

The 3,810sq km (1,259sq miles) of this National Park and Game Reserve embody five main wildlife habitats, plus a generally dry lake-bed, Lake Amboseli, from which it takes its name. These are open plains; extensive stands of yellow-barked acacia woodland; rocky, lava strewn thorn-bush country; swamps and marshes; and at the western end of the Reserve, above Namanga, the massif of Oldoinyo Orok rising to over 2,760m (8.300ft) and still for the most part zoologically unexplored.

The landscape is everywhere dominated by the glistening, majestic snow-cap of Kilimanjaro immediately to the south – Africa's highest mountain (5,894m–19,340ft) – a fitting back-drop to a wild region where the pastoral Masai and their cattle have lived in harmony with wild creatures for many a century.

Amboseli may be reached from Nairobi by two main routes. The first is to Athi River and thence along the main Kajiado-Namanga-Arusha road, turning left through the National Park main gate at Namanga to Ol Tukai Lodge, 75km (47 miles) on. Total distance from Nairobi is 240km (150

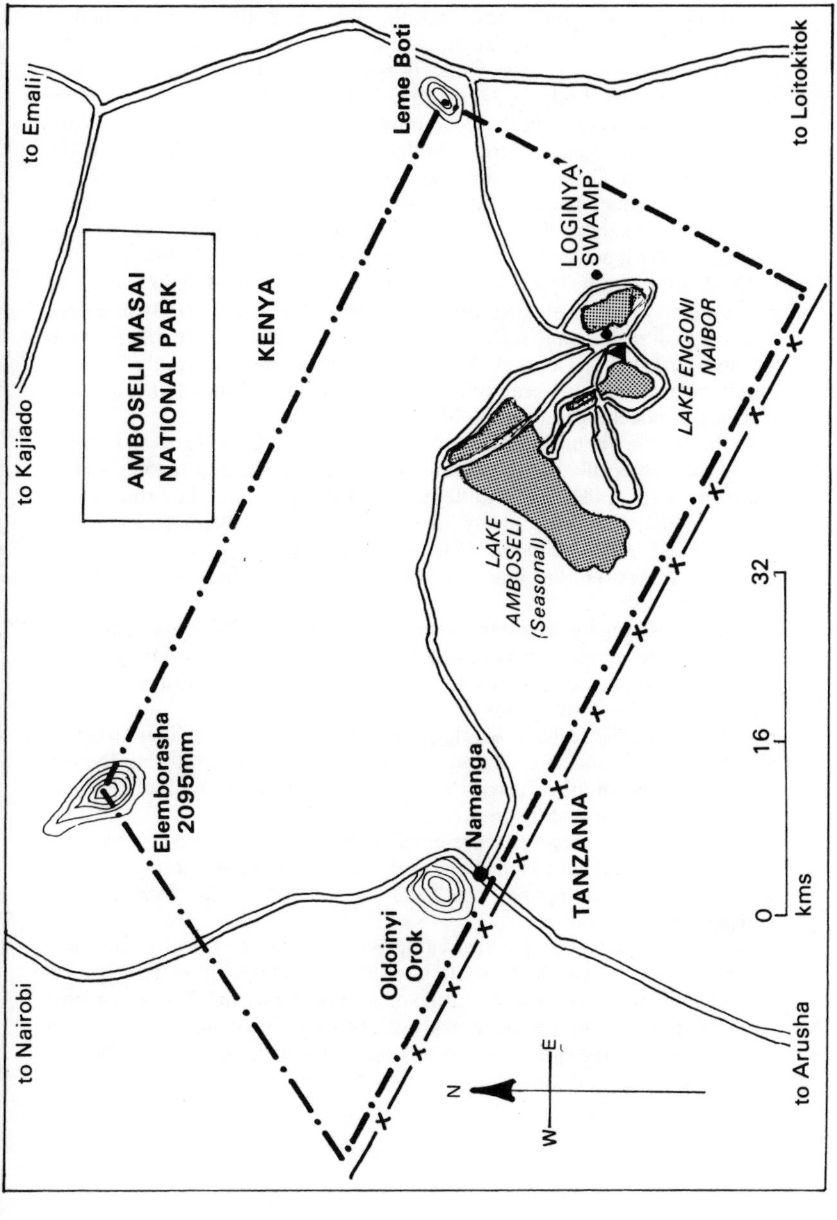
AMBOSELI MASAI
NATIONAL PARK
KENYA
TANZANIA
to Emali
to Kajiado
to Nairobi
to Loitokitok
to Arusha
Leme Boti
LOGINYA SWAMP
LAKE ENGONI NAIBOR
LAKE AMBOSELI (Seasonal)
Elemborasha 2095mm
Namanga
Oldoinyi Orok
0
16
32
kms
N
W
E

miles). The second route is from Nairobi along the main Mombasa road to some 16km (10 miles) past Emali, then branching right and following the main Loitokitok road: approximately 64km (40 miles) along this road it forks right and the Lodge is 32km (20 miles) farther on. Total mileage from Nairobi is 228km (142 miles). Accommodation is available at Amboseli New Lodge, Ol Tukai Lodge, Serena Lodge, Ol Tukai Tented Camp and the Namanga Hotel. Camp sites are also available.

The main game-viewing area of Amboseli lies in the eastern half of the Park, in the vicinity of Ol Tukai Lodge and lakes Engoni Naibor and Loginya. Here a network of roads and tracks opens up a wild life paradise.

Elephant, Lion, Leopard, Cheetah, Masai Giraffe and Buffalo may all be encountered during a single morning's drive of about 90km (50–60 miles), together with plains game such as Common Zebra, Eland, Coke's Hartebeest, White-bearded Gnu, Common Waterbuck, Thomson's and Grant's Gazelles and Impala. Black Rhino can still be seen occasionally although they are now rare due to poaching in the mid-1970s.

In the dry bush country towards Namanga, and in the arid area en route to Emali, two especially interesting antelopes may be found: the long-necked Gerenuk – often called the 'Giraffe-necked Antelope' – and the Fringe-eared Oryx. Smaller mammals always in evidence include Black-faced Vervet Monkey and Yellow Baboon, Black-backed Jackals, Spotted Hyaena and Bat-eared Foxes. The last may often be seen basking in the sun outside their dens on the open plains.

Bird life is equally abundant, especially in the vicinity of the lakes and swamps where a great variety of water birds may be seen. That rarity in East Africa, the Madagascar Squacco Heron, turns up at fairly regular intervals and the plover with the habits of a lily-trotter, the Long-toed Lapwing, is a resident in small numbers. Sandgrouse of three species, Yellow-throated, Chestnut-bellied and Black-faced, water in their hundreds during the dry season, announcing their arrival at their favourite drinking place with far-carrying gutteral sounding flock calls.

Birds of prey are very well represented. Including the six species of vultures no less than 47 different kinds have been recorded from Amboseli, amongst which are two great rarities, the Taita Falcon and the Southern Banded Harrier Eagle.

Around the lodges and tented camp, visitors will see flocks of a yellow weaver-bird with a patch of chestnut on the nape. This is the extremely local Taveta Golden Weaver, which outside of Amboseli may rightly be considered a rare bird. But the bird which quickly draws attention to itself on account of its brilliant plumage and fearless behaviour – it will alight on your table and partake of bread and cake crumbs – is the Superb Starling.

MAMMALS OF AMBOSELI NATIONAL PARK

Spectacled Elephant Shrew Generally frequents low bush at edge of acacia woodland
Short-snouted Elephant Shrew Inhabits open plains where patches of low bush exist
East African Hedgehog
Giant White-toothed Shrew
Rousette Fruit Bat Attracted to fruiting fig trees
Epauletted Fruit Bat Attracted to fruiting fig trees
White-bellied Tomb Bat
Hollow-faced Bat
False Vampire Bat Colonies often found in disused Masai huts
Yellow-winged Bat Hangs in acacia trees and bushes by day
Lander's Horseshoe Bat
Lesser Leaf-nosed Bat
Banana Bat or **African Pipistrelle**
Yellow-bellied Bat
Angola Free-tailed Bat Inhabits roofs of huts and lodges
White-bellied Free-tailed Bat
Bush Baby Frequents acacia woodland
Black-faced Vervet Monkey
Blue or **Sykes' Monkey**
Yellow Baboon
Hunting Dog
Golden Jackal The rarest of the jackals at Amboseli
Black-backed or **Silver-backed Jackal**
Side-striped Jackal
Bat-eared Fox Often seen basking outside holes on open plains
Zorilla Seen usually at dusk
Ratel or **Honey Badger** Rarely seen
African Civet
Neumann's or **Small-spotted Genet**
Bush or **Large-spotted Genet**
Marsh Mongoose
Dwarf Mongoose
Large Grey Mongoose
Slender or **Black-tipped Mongoose**
White-tailed Mongoose
Banded Mongoose
Aard-wolf Rarely seen: nocturnal
Spotted Hyaena
Striped Hyaena Rare
Cheetah
Caracal
African Wild Cat
Serval
Lion
Leopard
Ant Bear Nocturnal: rarely seen
Tree Hyrax
Rock Hyrax
African Elephant
Black Rhinoceros
Burchell's or **Common Zebra**
Hippopotamus
Warthog
Masai Giraffe
Coke's Hartebeest or **Kongoni**
White-bearded Gnu or **Wildebeest**
Red Duiker Much rarer than Bush Duiker
Bush Duiker
Klipspringer
Steinbok
Kirk's Dik-Dik
Common Waterbuck
Bohor Reedbuck
Impala
Thomson's Gazelle
Grant's Gazelle
Gerenuk
Fringe-eared Oryx
Bushbuck
Lesser Kudu
Eland
African Buffalo
African Hare
Porcupine Nocturnal: seldom seen
Striped Ground Squirrel
Unstriped Ground Squirrel
Bush Squirrel
Spring Hare
African Dormouse
Kenya Mole Rat

BIRDS OF AMBOSELI NATIONAL PARK

Masai Ostrich Not uncommon on the plains
Little Grebe
White-necked Cormorant Uncommon visitor
Long-tailed Cormorant
African Darter
White Pelican
Pink-backed Pelican Spasmodic visitors in varying numbers
Grey Heron
Black-headed Heron
Goliath Heron
Purple Heron
Great White Egret
Yellow-billed Egret
Little Egret
Buff-backed Heron or **Cattle Egret**
Rufous-bellied Heron
Squacco Heron
Madagascar Squacco Heron A non-breeding visitor in small numbers. Generally observed in Loginya swamps
Green-backed Heron
Night Heron
Little Bittern
Dwarf Bittern (The best place to look for herons and egrets is in the swamps below Observation Hill and along the edges of Loginya swamp east of Ol Tukai Lodge.)
Hamerkop
White Stork Winter visitor and passage migrant in flocks of varying numbers
European Black Stork Rare winter visitor
Woolly-necked Stork Rare visitor
Abdim's Stork Spasmodic visitor, sometimes in large flocks. Plains
Open-bill Stork Visitor in small numbers

Saddle-bill Stork Resident in small numbers. Usually seen in Loginya Swamp
Marabou Stork
Wood Ibis or **Yellow-billed Stork**
Sacred Ibis
Hadada Ibis
Glossy Ibis Rare visitor
African Spoonbill
Greater Flamingo
Lesser Flamingo Flamingos occur as vagrants, never in large numbers
White-backed Duck
African Pochard
Tufted Duck Rare winter visitor
European Shoveler
Yellow-billed Duck
Garganey Teal
Hottentot Teal
Red-billed Duck
European Pintail
White-faced Tree Duck Uncommon visitor
Fulvous Tree Duck
Knob-billed Duck
Egyptian Goose
Spur-winged Goose
Secretary Bird
Ruppell's Vulture
White-backed Vulture
Nubian or **Lappet-faced Vulture**
White-headed Vulture
Egyptian Vulture
Hooded Vulture
Peregrine Visitor in small numbers
Lanner Visitor in small numbers, but commoner than Peregrine
Taita Falcon Rare visitor. Has habit of perching high in dead acacia trees
European Hobby Uncommon spring passage migrant
European Kestrel Winter visitor
Greater or **White-eyed Kestrel** Resident in small numbers, mainly Namanga area
Lesser Kestrel Winter visitor and passage migrant
Pygmy Falcon Most frequent acacia bush country towards Namanga
European Black Kite
African Black Kite
Black-shouldered Kite
Bat Hawk Occurs near Namanga. Probably overlooked on account of its crepuscular habits
Honey Buzzard Rare visitor, usually in April/May
Steppe Eagle Winter visitor in small numbers. Perches on ground on open plains
Tawny Eagle
Wahlberg's Eagle
African Hawk Eagle
Booted Eagle Rare winter visitor
Martial Eagle
Crowned Hawk Eagle Recorded a few times: usually immature birds
Long-crested Eagle
Lizard Buzzard
Brown Harrier Eagle
Black-chested Harrier Eagle
Southern Banded Harrier Eagle Single record of pair in acacia woodland south of Observation Hill
Grasshopper Buzzard Non-breeding visitor. Mainly in bush country on Emali road
Bateleur
African Fish Eagle
Steppe Buzzard Winter visitor in varying numbers
Augur Buzzard
Little Sparrow Hawk
Shikra
Gabar Goshawk
Pale Chanting Goshawk
Montagu's Harrier
Pallid Harrier
European Marsh Harrier
African Marsh Harrier
Harrier Hawk
Osprey Rare visitor
Coqui Francolin
Crested Francolin
Shelley's (Greywing) Francolin
Yellow-necked Spurfowl
Harlequin Quail
Helmeted Guinea-fowl
Vulturine Guinea-fowl
Kaffir Rail Sometimes seen in swamp near Simek Causeway
Black Crake
Moorhen
Red-knobbed Coot
Crowned Crane
Kori Bustard
Jackson's Bustard Plains. The rarest of the Amboseli bustards
White-bellied Bustard
Buff-crested Bustard Not uncommon in dry bush country
Black-bellied Bustard
Hartlaub's Bustard
Spotted Stone Curlew
Water Dikkop
African Jacana
Ringed Plover
Little Ringed Plover
Kittlitz's Plover
Three-banded Plover
Caspian Plover Winter visitor in flocks. Open plains
Grey Plover Rare winter visitor
Crowned Plover
Senegal Plover Rare visitor in small numbers. Open plains
Blacksmith Plover
Long-toed Lapwing Swamps. Walks on floating aquatic vegetation in manner of jacana
Avocet
Black-winged Stilt
Painted Snipe
European Common Snipe
African Snipe
Curlew Sandpiper
Little Stint
Ruff
Common Sandpiper
Green Sandpiper
Wood Sandpiper
Spotted Redshank Winter visitor in small numbers
Marsh Sandpiper
Greenshank
Temminck's Courser Often attracted to recently burned grassland
Two-banded Courser Open plains
Heuglin's Courser Uncommon. Bush country
Pratincole
Gull-billed Tern Uncommon visitor
White-winged Black Tern
Button Quail

Chestnut-bellied Sandgrouse
Black-faced Sandgrouse
Yellow-throated Sandgrouse In flocks on open grassy plains
Speckled Pigeon
Red-eyed Dove
Mourning Dove
Ring-necked Dove
Laughing Dove
Namaqua Dove
Tambourine Dove
Emerald-spotted Wood Dove
Green Pigeon
Cuckoo
Red-chested Cuckoo
Black Cuckoo
Great-spotted Cuckoo
Levaillant's Cuckoo
Black and White Cuckoo
Emerald Cuckoo
Didric Cuckoo
Klaas' Cuckoo
Blue-headed Coucal
White-browed Coucal
White-bellied Go-away-bird
Orange-bellied Parrot
Brown Parrot
European Roller Sometimes abundant on spring migration
Lilac-breasted Roller
Rufous-crowned Roller
Broad-billed Roller
Pied Kingfisher
Giant Kingfisher Uncommon
Malachite Kingfisher
Pygmy Kingfisher In scrub and acacia woodland
Grey-headed Kingfisher
Striped Kingfisher
European Bee-eater
Madagascar Bee-eater Visitor
Blue-cheeked Bee-eater Uncommon migrant visitor
White-throated Bee-eater
Little Bee-eater
Grey Hornbill
Red-billed Hornbill
Yellow-billed Hornbill
Von der Decken's Hornbill
Crowned Hornbill
Ground Hornbill
European Hoopoe
African Hoopoe
Green Wood Hoopoe
Scimitar-bill
Abyssinian Scimitar-bill
African Marsh Owl
African Scops Owl
White-faced Scops Owl
Pearl-spotted Owlet
Spotted Eagle Owl
Verreaux's Eagle Owl
European Nightjar
Dusky Nightjar
Plain Nightjar
Long-tailed Nightjar
Speckled Mousebird
Blue-naped Mousebird
Brown-throated Barbet
Spotted-flanked Barbet
Red-fronted Barbet
Red-fronted Tinkerbird
Red and Yellow Barbet
D'Arnaud's Barbet
Greater Honeyguide
Scaly-throated Honeyguide
Lesser Honeyguide
Wahlberg's Honeyguide
Nubian Woodpecker
Cardinal Woodpecker
Bearded Woodpecker
Grey Woodpecker
Nyanza Swift
Mottled Swift
Little Swift
White-rumped Swift
Horus Swift
Palm Swift
Singing Bush Lark
Northern White-tailed Lark
Flappet Lark
Fawn-coloured Lark
Pink-breasted Lark Confined to arid bush areas
Fischer's Sparrow Lark
Red-capped Lark
African Pied Wagtail
Blue-headed and **Yellow Wagtails** Flocks of various races pass through on spring migration
Long-billed Pipit
Richard's Pipit
Yellow-throated Longclaw
Black-lored Babbler
Northern Pied Babbler
Rufous Chatterer
Yellow-vented Bulbul
Northern Brownbul
European Spotted Flycatcher
Dusky Flycatcher
Grey Flycatcher
South African Black Flycatcher
Silverbird
Chin-spot Flycatcher
Black-throated Wattle-eye
Paradise Flycatcher
Olive Thrush
Bare-eyed Thrush Occurs in arid bush country
European Rock Thrush
European Common Wheatear
Isabelline Wheatear
Pied Wheatear
Schalow's Wheatear Found near Namanga
Capped Wheatear
Cliff Chat Occurs on Oldoinyo Orok
Anteater Chat
European Whinchat
White-browed Robin Chat
Red-capped Robin Chat
Robin Chat
Spotted Morning Warbler
Red-back Scrub Robin
White-winged Scrub Robin
White-throated Robin Single record near Ol Tukai: may be overlooked
European Nightingale Winter visitor in small numbers
Thrush Nightingale or **Sprosser** Winter visitor, commoner than nightingale
European Whitethroat
Garden Warbler
Blackcap Warbler
Barred Warbler
Great Reed Warbler Passage migrant in spring
European Sedge Warbler
Greater Swamp Warbler Resident in small numbers
European Willow Warbler
Grey Wren Warbler
Black-breasted Apalis
Red-faced Apalis Occurs in arid bush areas
Grey-capped Warbler
Buff-bellied Warbler
Crombec
Red-faced Crombec
Banded Tit-warbler
Yellow-bellied Eremomela
Grey-backed Camaroptera
Pectoral-patch Cisticola
Rattling Cisticola

Winding Cisticola
Tawny-flanked Prinia
European Swallow
Angola Swallow
Wire-tailed Swallow
Red-rumped Swallow
Mosque Swallow
Striped Swallow
Grey-rumped Swallow
European Sand Martin
African Sand Martin
Banded Martin
African Rock Martin Occurs near Namanga
Black Rough-wing Swallow
White-headed Rough-wing Swallow
Black Cuckoo Shrike
Drongo
Straight-crested Helmet Shrike
White-crowned Shrike
Northern Brubru
Grey-backed Fiscal
Lesser Grey Shrike Passage migrant late March/April
Fiscal Shrike Namanga area
Taita Fiscal Dry bush country
Long-tailed Fiscal
Red-backed Shrike
Red-tailed Shrike
Slate-coloured Boubou
Tropical Boubou Undergrowth in acacia woodland
Black-backed Puff-back
Black-headed Tchagra
Brown-headed Tchagra
Sulphur-breasted Bush Shrike
Grey-headed Bush Shrike
Rosy-patched Shrike
Grey Tit
White-breasted Tit
Red-throated Tit
African Penduline Tit
European Golden Oriole
African Golden Oriole
Black-headed Oriole
Pied Crow
White-naped Raven
Wattled Starling Often perch on zebra in manner of oxpeckers
Violet-backed Starling
Blue-eared Glossy Starling
Ruppell's Long-tailed Starling
Red-winged Starling Namanga area
Fischer's Starling
Hildebrandt's Starling
Superb Starling
Red-billed Oxpecker
Yellow White-eye
Bronzy Sunbird Namanga area
Beautiful Sunbird (black-bellied race)
Mariqua Sunbird
Variable Sunbird
Amethyst Sunbird Mainly in Namanga area
Scarlet-chested Sunbird Mainly in Namanga area
Hunter's Sunbird Mainly in dry bush in eastern section
Olive Sunbird Occurs around Namanga
Collared Sunbird
Kenya Violet-backed Sunbird
Buffalo Weaver
White-headed Buffalo Weaver
White-browed Sparrow Weaver
Grey-headed Social Weaver
Rufous Sparrow
Swahili Sparrow
Parrot-billed Sparrow
Chestnut Sparrow
Yellow-spotted Petronia
Speckled-fronted Weaver
Layard's Black-headed Weaver
Speke's Weaver
Masked Weaver
Vitelline Masked Weaver
Chestnut Weaver
Taveta Golden Weaver
Black-necked Weaver
Spectacled Weaver
Holub's Golden Weaver
Reichenow's Weaver Near Namanga
Grosbeak Weaver Swamps
Red-headed Weaver
Red-billed Quelea
Cardinal Quelea
Yellow Bishop
Yellow-crowned Bishop Spasmodic in appearance: turns up in swampy hollows in years when heavy rains have fallen
Fan-tailed Widow-bird
White-winged Widow-bird
Bronze Mannikin
Silverbill
Grey-headed Silver-bill Frequents dry acacia bush
Cut-throat
Quail Finch Frequents marshy spots on open plains
Parasitic Weaver Spasmodic in appearance: occurs only in seasons of heavy rains
Green-winged Pytilia
African Fire Finch Common around Namanga
Jameson's Fire Finch
Red-billed Fire Finch
Yellow-bellied Waxbill
Waxbill
Crimson-rumped Waxbill
Black-cheeked Waxbill
Black-faced Waxbill
Red-cheeked Cordon-bleu
Blue-capped Cordon-bleu
Purple Grenadier
Indigo-bird
Pin-tailed Whydah
Steel-blue Whydah Dry bush country near Namanga
Fischer's Straw-tailed Whydah
Paradise Whydah
Yellow-fronted Canary
White-bellied Canary
Brimstone Canary
Kenya Grosbeak Canary
Yellow-rumped Seed-eater
Streaky Seed-eater
Golden-breasted Bunting
Cinnamon-breasted Rock Bunting

MOUNT ELGON NATIONAL PARK

Although covering an area of only 108sq km (42sq miles), the Mount Elgon National Park in western Kenya includes within its boundaries a variety of habitats from savannah woodland and montane forest to alpine moorlands. The forests on Mount Elgon are among the most impressive in Kenya with gigantic Podocarpus trees and majestic stands of Juniper and Elgon Olive.

The entrance to the Park is 27km (17 miles) from Kitale, via the Endebess road, and is well signposted. Accommodation with all facilities is available at the Mount Elgon Lodge, sited near the main entrance.

Big game mammals commonly encountered include Elephant, Buffalo and Leopard. Black Rhinoceros are also reputed to occur. Among other species are the rare Golden Cat which may be encountered in the higher altitude forest or on the moorlands, the Black-fronted Duiker, again found mainly in the forest or where moorlands and forest meet, and the black and white Colobus Monkey. The Mount Elgon Golden Mole is common in the sub-alpine zone.

Birdlife is much in evidence. Some of the caves in the forest a few miles from the main gate hold nesting colonies of the Scarce Swift; Doherty's Bush Shrike is often heard and seen in the forest undergrowth and sunbirds are extremely common when the flowers at which they feed are in bloom. Forest birds of prey including Crowned Eagle, Ayres' Hawk Eagle, Rufous-breasted Sparrow Hawk, African Hobby and Mountain Buzzard may be seen, but the most common falcon on Mount Elgon is the Lanner Falcon.

Mount Elgon is a famous botanical locality with a great wealth of Afro-alpine flowers on the moorlands. Both terrestrial and epiphytic orchids are common. The peak flowering season is during June and July but flowers of some sort are to be found abundantly throughout the year.

MAMMALS OF THE MOUNT ELGON NATIONAL PARK

Golden Mole
Rousette Fruit Bat
Blue Monkey
Brazza Monkey
Olive Baboon
Black and White Colobus
African Civet
Palm Civet
Large-spotted Genet
Spotted Hyaena
African Wild Cat
Golden Cat
Leopard
Tree Hyrax
Rock Hyrax
African Elephant
Black Rhinoceros (status uncertain)
Giant Forest Hog
Bush Pig
Black-fronted Duiker
Bush Duiker
Suni
Bushbuck
African Buffalo
Porcupine
Scaly-tailed Flying Squirrel
African Dormouse
Crested Rat
Bush Squirrel
Mole Rat

BIRDS OF MOUNT ELGON NATIONAL PARK

Hamerkop
African Black Duck
Lammergeyer
Harrier Hawk
Bateleur
Great Sparrow Hawk
African Goshawk
Rufous-breasted Sparrow Hawk
Little Sparrow Hawk
Lizard Buzzard
Augur Buzzard
Steppe Buzzard

Mountain Buzzard
Long-crested Eagle
Crowned Eagle
Ayres' Hawk Eagle
Tawny Eagle
Verreaux's Eagle
Wahlberg's Eagle
Black Kite
Honey Buzzard
Cuckoo Falcon
Lanner
Peregrine
African Hobby
European Hobby
Lesser Kestrel
Kestrel
Montane Francolin
Scaly Francolin
Cape Quail
Black-winged Plover
Green Sandpiper
Common Sandpiper
African Snipe
Olive Pigeon
Red-eyed Dove
Dusky Turtle Dove
Tambourine Dove
Blue-spotted Wood Dove
Green Pigeon
Red-fronted Parrot
Hartlaub's Turaco
Ross' Turaco
Eastern Grey Plantain-eater
Red-chested Cuckoo
Klaas' Cuckoo
Emerald Cuckoo
Blue-headed Coucal
White-browed Coucal
Spotted Eagle Owl
Red-chested Owlet
African Wood Owl
Abyssinian Nightjar
Alpine Swift
Mottled Swift
African Swift
Scarce Swift
Speckled Mousebird
Narina's Trogon
Bar-tailed Trogon
European Bee-eater
Cinnamon-chested Bee-eater
White-headed Wood Hoopoe
Crowned Hornbill
Black and White-casqued Hornbill
Double-toothed Barbet
Grey-throated Barbet
Moustached Green Tinkerbird
Golden-rumped Tinkerbird
Yellow-billed Barbet
Scaly-throated Honeyguide
Greater Honeyguide
Lesser Honeyguide
Thick-billed Honeyguide
Fine-banded Woodpecker
Cardinal Woodpecker
Grey Woodpecker
African Sand Martin
Angola Swallow
Red-rumped Swallow
Striped Swallow
African Rock Martin
Black Roughwing Swallow
White-headed Roughwing Swallow
Mountain Wagtail
African Pied Wagtail
Grey Cuckoo Shrike
Black Cuckoo Shrike
Red-shouldered Cuckoo Shrike
Yellow-vented Bulbul
Yellow-whiskered Greenbul
Olive-breasted Mountain Greenbul
Puff-back Shrike
Luhder's Bush Shrike
Tropical Boubou
Doherty's Bush Shrike
Mackinnon's Shrike
Stonechat
Hill Chat
Equatorial Akalat
White-starred Bush Robin
Robin Chat
Blue-shouldered Robin Chat
Snowy-headed Robin Chat
Olive Thrush
Abyssinian Ground Thrush
Abyssinian Hill Babbler
Cinnamon Bracken Warbler
Mountain Yellow Flycatcher
Blackcap Warbler
Willow Warbler
Chiffchaff
Brown Woodland Warbler
Hunter's Cisticola
Chubb's Cisticola
White-chinned Prinia
Banded Prinia
Black-collared Apalis
Black-throated Apalis
Chestnut-throated Apalis
Grey-capped Warbler
Grey-backed Camaroptera
Spotted Flycatcher
Dusky Flycatcher
White-eyed Slaty Flycatcher
Black Flycatcher
Blue Flycatcher
Paradise Flycatcher
White-breasted Tit
Spotted Creeper
Olive Sunbird
Green-headed Sunbird
Scarlet-chested Sunbird
Variable Sunbird
Eastern Double-collared Sunbird
Northern Double-collared Sunbird
Malachite Sunbird
Bronzy Sunbird
Golden-winged Sunbird
Collared Sunbird
Yellow White-eye
Brimstone Canary
African Citril
Streaky Seed-eater
Thick-billed Seed-eater
Oriole Finch
Abyssinian Crimsonwing
Grey-headed Negro-finch
Red-headed Bluebill
Yellow-bellied Waxbill
Black-headed Waxbill
Common Waxbill
Black and White Mannikin
Bronze Mannikin
Grosbeak Weaver
Reichenow's Weaver
Black-headed Weaver
Dark-backed Weaver
Spectacled Weaver
Black-billed Weaver
Brown-capped Weaver
Red-headed Malimbe
Yellow Bishop
Grey-headed Sparrow
Stuhlmann's Starling
Waller's Chestnut-wing Starling
Red-wing Starling
Slender-billed Chestnutwing Starling
Splendid Glossy Starling
Blue-eared Glossy Starling
Violet-backed Starling
Sharpe's Starling
African Golden Oriole

Black-headed Oriole	**Pied Crow**	**White-necked Raven**
Drongo	**Cape Rook**	

MOUNT KENYA NATIONAL PARK

The Mount Kenya National Park was established in 1949 and covers an area of 588sq km (227sq miles), the park boundary being the 3,364m (11,000ft) contour. It comprises small sections of the higher forest and bamboo-hypericum zone, alpine moorlands, glaciers, tarns and glacial moraines. It is dominated by the twin peaks of the mountain, Batian (5,200m–17,058ft) and Nelion (5,188m–17,022ft).

The visitor to the Mount Kenya National Park does not need to be an experienced mountaineer, and access to the alpine moorlands is easy via the Sirimon Track which branches to the right off the main Nanyuki-Isiolo road several kilometres north of Nanyuki: but a four-wheel-drive vehicle is necessary to negotiate the rough surface and steep inclines. The trail passes through magnificent stands of juniper and podocarpus before reaching the high altitude bamboo forest with mighty gorges, sylvan glades and trout streams. Elephant and Buffalo are common, and Black Rhino exist but are not often seen. In the early morning there are always Bushbuck and Bush Duiker in evidence and the expectation of Leopard and the elusive Bongo if one is very lucky.

Another road of access is via a turning off the Nyeri-Nanyuki road near Naro Moru. This easy track is now the most used access to the Park but it ends at the upper level of the forest, after which one proceeds on foot. There are lodge huts at its highest point, suitable for those carrying their own bedding and food. Mountain Lodge sited at a little over 2,134m (7,000ft) in the Mt Kenya forest, is an outstanding attraction. It is reached via a sign-posted access road near Nyeri, off the main Nyeri-Nanyuki road. Several mammals can be seen here which are encountered rarely elsewhere, such as Bush Pig, Giant Forest Hog (also easily seen at Treetops and the Ark), Large-spotted Genet, Tree Hyrax, Greater Galago, White-tailed, Swamp, Black-tipped and Large Grey Mongooses. Elephant, Black Rhinoceros, Buffalo, Bush Buck, Red Duiker, Suni and Defassa Waterbuck are common and Leopard may be seen sometimes. Birds seen from the lodge include Green Ibis, African Black Duck, Ayres' Hawk Eagle, Rufous-breasted and Great Sparrow Hawks, Scaly Francolin, Silvery-cheeked Hornbill, Hartlaub's Turaco, Red-headed Parrot, Bronze-naped Pigeon, Mackinder's Eagle Owl, Ruppell's Robin Chat and various Sunbirds to name but a few.

Birds are not over abundant in the forest, but sometimes Ayres' Hawk Eagle and the Crowned Hawk Eagle may be seen soaring over their hunting grounds. The Red-headed Parrot and Hartlaub's Turaco frequent fruiting podocarpus trees, whilst two forest francolins, Jackson's Francolin and Scaly Francolin, scuttle away into the undergrowth as your vehicle approaches. The rare Mount Kenya race of the Green Ibis feeds in marshy

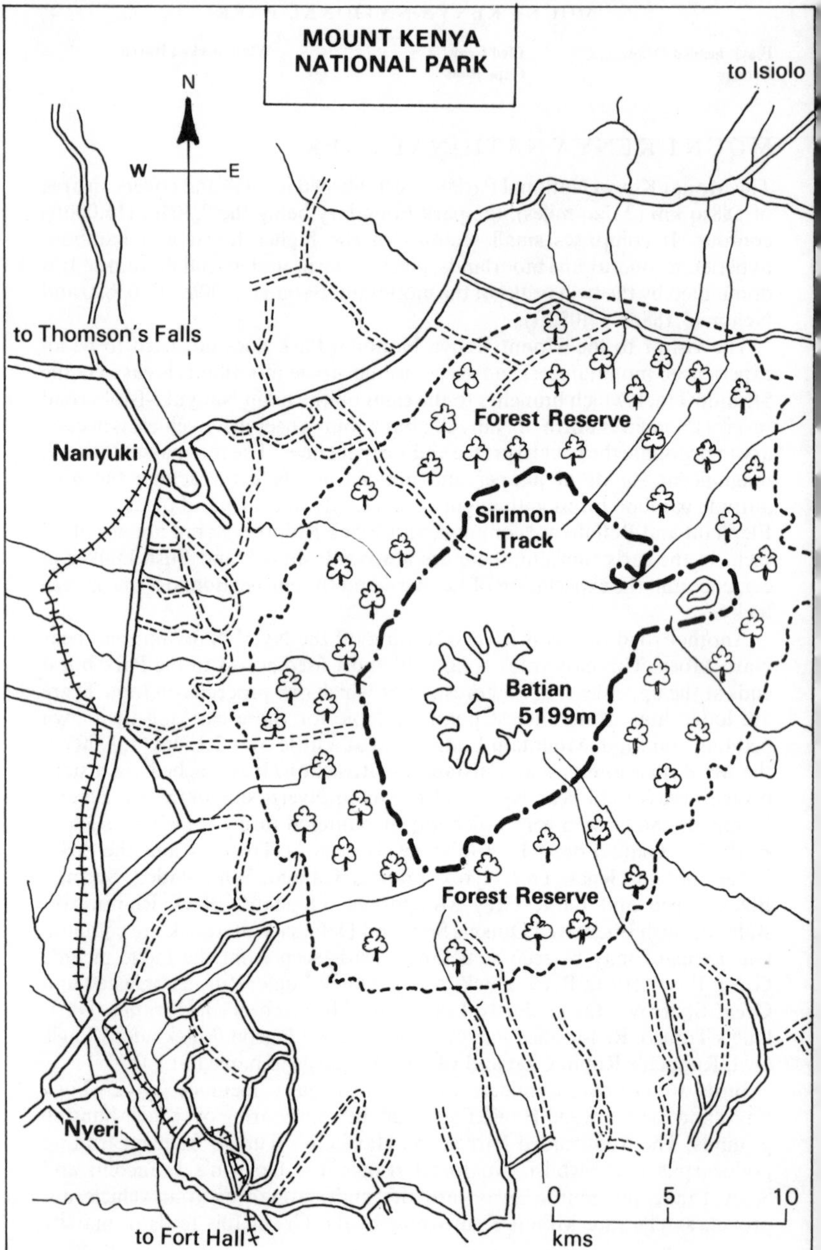
MOUNT KENYA
NATIONAL PARK
N
W
E
to Isiolo
to Thomson's Falls
Nanyuki
Forest Reserve
Sirimon
Track
Batian
5199m
Forest Reserve
Nyeri
to Fort Hall
0
5
10
kms

forest glades and another great rarity, the Abyssinian Long-eared Owl, has been recorded from the high forest near the Sirimon Track.

The high altitude forest merges into the bamboo zone, and this in turn changes into hypericum scrub before the moorlands are reached. When in flower the hypericum trees are a glory of golden yellow blossoms and alive with brightly hued sunbirds.

Two interesting small mammals live in this zone. Here and there in the glades there are large 'mole hills' thrown up by some fossorial animal – the giant Mount Kenya Mole Rat. In more shady places, and especially where moss grows on the ground, slightly raised earth outlines the tunnels of another burrower: it is the Mount Kenya Mole Shrew, a species known only from this mountain although a closely related form occurs on the Aberdare range.

The flora of the alpine moorlands of Mount Kenya is outstanding with its giant Senecios, Lobelias and Heaths and many colourful true alpines. Two species of giant Lobelias are common, the narrow, feathery-leafed *Lobelia telekii* and the broad leafed *Lobelia keniensis*. Scarlet-tufted Malachite Sunbirds feed at the half-hidden blossoms and Slender-billed Chestnut-wing Starlings search the plant for the thin-shelled snails which make their home there. Among the smaller plants are a tiny mauve crocus-like flower, *Romulea keniensis*, two terrestrial orchids, a *Disa* and a *Habenaria*, and an orange flowered gladiolus, *Gladiolus watsonioides*.

The most interesting larger mammal on the Mount Kenya moorlands is the Black-fronted Duiker, which is local but by no means rare. Among the birds are the Montane Francolin, the tame, almost robin-like Mountain Chat and the finest of East African owls, Mackinder's Eagle Owl. Alpine Swifts nest on certain crags, often associated with a much rarer species the Scarce Swift.

Expeditions on the mountain, using mules as pack animals, are organised by a firm specialising in mountain safaris, and if you are a mountaineer use of the alpine huts can be booked through the Mountain Club of Kenya. For the visitor who just wishes to spend a day or so on the mountain, first class hotel accommodation is available in and near Nanyuki, 198km (123 miles) north of Nairobi, or in Nyeri, 257km (160 miles) north of Nairobi.

MAMMALS OF MOUNT KENYA NATIONAL PARK

Mole Shrew Burrows just below surface of ground in bamboo zone

Banana Bat or **African Pipistrelle** Recorded from high level forest

Sykes' Monkey Occurs in forest just below bamboo zone

Olive Baboon

Black and White Colobus

Hunting Dog

Black-backed or **Silver-backed Jackal**

Side-striped Jackal

Clawless Otter In streams in forest

African Civet

Bush or **Large-spotted Genet**

Slender or **Black-tipped Mongoose**

Spotted Hyaena

African Wild Cat

Serval

Lion Reputed to occur at times, but no recent records

Leopard

Tree Hyrax

Rock Hyrax
African Elephant In forest
Black Rhinoceros In forest
Burchell's or **Common Zebra**
Giant Forest Hog
Bush Pig
Red Duiker In forest
Black-fronted Duiker In bamboo zone and on moorlands
Bush Duiker
Klipspringer
Suni
Chanler's Reedbuck Reputed to occur
Bongo Extremely shy and seldom seen: mainly in upper levels of forest and in bamboo zone
Bushbuck
African Buffalo In forest
African Hare
Porcupine
African Dormouse
Crested Rat
Mt Kenya Mole Rat

BIRDS OF MOUNT KENYA NATIONAL PARK

Hamerkop At Waterholes
White Stork Once recorded on alpine moorlands
Green Ibis Occurs in meadows bordering mountain streams in forest. Rare
African Black Duck Occurs on mountain streams and tarns
Secretary Bird Has been recorded on moorlands. Rare
Ruppell's Vulture
Peregrine
Lanner
European Kestrel
Lesser Kestrel Occurs in small numbers on moorlands during migration
Cuckoo Falcon In forest
European Black Kite
African Black Kite Probably migrants. Occur spasmodically on moorlands and above forest
Verreaux's Eagle
Steppe Eagle
Ayres' Hawk Eagle In forest
Crowned Hawk Eagle In forest
Long-crested Eagle
Lammergeyer Seen from time to time and may nest
Steppe Buzzard
Eastern Steppe Buzzard Rare
Mountain Buzzard
Augur Buzzard
Rufus-breasted Sparrow Hawk Occurs in forest and bamboo zone
Great Sparrow Hawk
African Goshawk
Montagu's Harrier
Pallid Harrier
European Marsh Harrier The three harriers occur on the moorlands during migration: rare at other times
Montane Francolin On moorlands
Scaly Francolin
Jackson's Francolin
Cape Quail
Black-winged Plover Uncommon visitor to moorlands
European Common Snipe
Great Snipe Mainly on spring migration
African Snipe
Jack Snipe Rare winter visitor and passage migrant
Green Sandpiper
Greenshank
Olive Pigeon Forest species
Bronze-naped Pigeon
Pink-breasted Dove
Red-eyed Dove
Lemon Dove
Green Pigeon
Red-chested Cuckoo
Emerald Cuckoo
Klaas' Cuckoo
Hartlaub's Turaco In forest
Red-headed Parrot In forest
Giant Kingfisher On forest streams
Grey-headed Kingfisher On forest streams
Cinnamon-chested Bee-eater In forest
Silvery-cheeked Hornbill In forest
Crowned Hornbill
White-headed Wood Hoopoe
Cape Grass Owl In marshy hollows on moorlands
Abyssinian Long-eared Owl Occurs rarely in both upper forest and bamboo zone, and in thickets on moorlands
African Marsh Owl Moorlands
African Wood Owl In forest
Mackinder's Eagle Owl Occurs along cliffs on moorlands: several pairs live in Teleki Valley
Abyssinian Nightjar
Golden-rumped Tinkerbird
Fine-banded Woodpecker
Nyanza Swift
Scarce Swift Probably nests in crags on alpine moorlands
Alpine Swift
Mottled Swift
Mountain Wagtail Occurs on streams
European Grey Wagtail
Well's Wagtail At waterholes
Red-throated Pipit
Abyssinian Hill Babbler
Yellow-vented Bulbul
Olive-breasted Mountain Greenbul
Yellow-whiskered Greenbul
Dusky Flycatcher
White-eyed Slaty Flycatcher
Mountain Yellow Flycatcher
Black-throated Wattle-eye
Paradise Flycatcher
Olive Thrush
Orange Ground Thrush Occurs mainly on eastern side of mountain
Abyssinian Ground Thrush
European Rock Thrush Uncommon migrant
Little Rock Thrush
European Common Wheatear
Capped Wheatear
Hill or **Mountain Chat**
Stonechat

Ruppell's Robin Chat
Robin Chat
White-starred Bush Robin Common in bamboo zone
Blackcap Warbler
Cinnamon Bracken Warbler
European Willow Warbler
Brown Woodland Warbler
Grey Apalis
Black-throated Apalis
Chestnut-throated Apalis
Hunter's Cisticola
European Swallow Uncommon on migration
African Sand Martin
African Rock Martin
Black Rough-wing Swallow
White-headed Rough-wing Swallow
Tropical Boubou Sometimes reaches upper levels of forest
White-breasted Tit
Black-winged Montane Oriole
White-naped Raven
Sharpe's Starling
Slender-billed Chestnut-wing Starling
Kenrick's Starling
Kikuyu White-eye
Malachite Sunbird
Scarlet-tufted Malachite Sunbird
Tacazze Sunbird
Golden-winged Sunbird
Eastern Double-collared Sunbird
Reichenow's Weaver
Spectacled Weaver Bred at lodge in 1977
Brown-capped Weaver
Grey-headed Negro Finch
Abyssinian Crimson-wing Common in bamboo zone
Yellow-bellied Waxbill
Black-headed Waxbill
Yellow-crowned Canary
Streaky Seed-eater
Thick-billed Seed-eater
Oriole Finch

MASAI MARA NATIONAL RESERVE

The Mara Game Reserve, as it was originally known, an area of some 1,812sq km (700sq miles), was established in 1961. Its southern boundary is contiguous with Tanzania's Serengeti National Park, and it is divided into two sections. The inner reserve of 518sq km (200sq miles) has been developed on the lines of a National Park, no intrusion of human settlement being allowed, while the outer remains an undeveloped area where local Masai are permitted to pasture their cattle but which is otherwise undisturbed.

The Mara country is world famous for its vast assemblages of plains game together with their associated predators. It is perhaps the only region left in Kenya where the visitor may see animals in the same super-abundance as existed a century ago.

The Reserve extends from the edge of the Loita Hills in the east to the Mara Triangle and the base of the Siria Escarpment in the west. The inner section, with its network of roads specially constructed for game watching, embraces the area around the Keekorok Lodge and westwards to the Mara River.

Everything is big in Mara. It is a country of breath-taking vistas, a panorama of vast rolling plains and rounded hills, of intermittent groves of acacia woodlands and dense thickets of scrub. The whole is bisected by the Mara River and its tributaries which are margined by luxuriant riverine forest. And in every direction, there are the seemingly endless herds of game animals.

Mara possesses the largest population of lions to be found in Kenya, although poisoning by farmers along the western border has reduced the number of Black-maned Lions. It also boasts large herds of Topi and a small population of Roan Antelope, animals not found in many other Kenya National Parks or Reserves (although more common in Lambwe Valley and the Shimba Hills). Elephants are fairly common and the traveller may sometimes be held up by 'elephants on the road'.

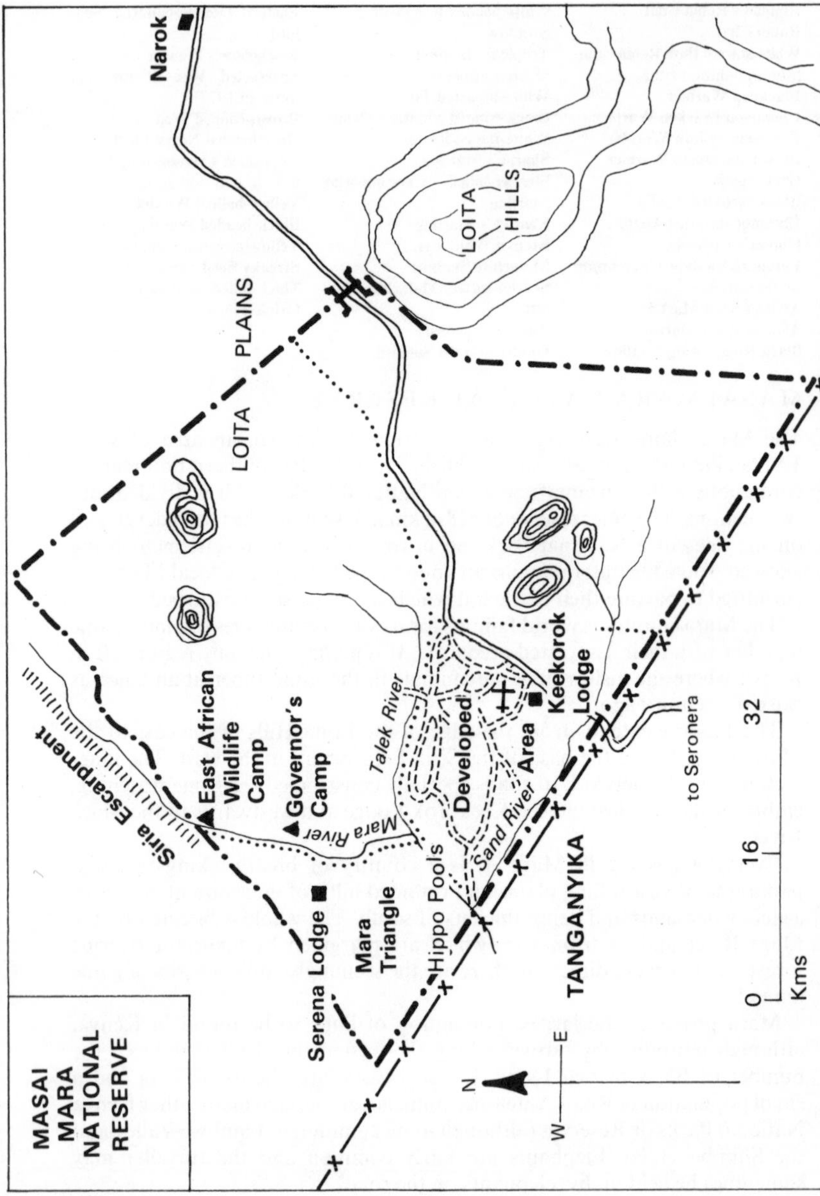
MASAI
MARA
NATIONAL
RESERVE
Narok
LOITA
HILLS
LOITA PLAINS
East African
Wildlife
Camp
Governor's
Camp
Mara River
Talek River
Developed
Area
Keekorok
Lodge
Sand River
Hippo Pools
Mara
Triangle
Serena Lodge
Siria Escarpment
TANGANYIKA
to Seronera
0
16
32
Kms
N
E
W

Among the great variety of large beasts are Buffalo, Black Rhino (which may be seen more easily than at Amboseli or Tsavo), and Hippopotamus. The hippo-viewing platform on the Mara River near the Mara Serena Lodge is probably the best place in Kenya for seeing hippo. Other mammals include Leopard, Cheetah, Common Zebra, Coke's Hartebeest, White-bearded Gnu, Oribi, Warthog, and Thomson's and Grant's Gazelles.

The bird life of Mara is as profuse as its mammalian fauna. The red-winged Schalow's Turaco with its attenuated white-tipped crest is common along the numerous wooded watercourses, and in the more extensive riverine forest there is also Ross' Turaco. The Mara River is also the home of the great orange-buff Pel's Fishing Owl and of flocks of wary Crested Guinea-fowl.

On the open plains there is a variety of bustards including the large Jackson's Bustard and the black-bellied Hartlaub's Bustard. The latter during nuptial display soars high in the air, then with rigid wings descends slowly to earth like a pricked balloon. Ground Hornbills are one of the most spectacular birds of the open plains and more easily seen in the Mara than elsewhere in Kenya.

Birds of prey are abundant, and no less than 53 different species have so far been recorded. Secretary Birds are a common sight as they stalk sedately over the grasslands, and in the sky there are always vultures and that effortless flier the Bateleur.

Accommodation in Masai Mara National Reserve is at Keekorok Lodge, which is 265km (165 miles) from Nairobi on a road quite negotiable by saloon cars. The route is via the Nairobi-Naivasha road, turning left at 56km (35 miles); thence to Narok, 103km (64 miles), and then 106km (66 miles) to the Lodge through some of the best game country in Kenya. In the undeveloped part of the Reserve a limited number of camp sites are available, but the numbers of campers allowed into the reserve is strictly limited to avoid disturbance to the game, and there are tented camps near the eastern entrance and elsewhere.

In addition there is the Mara Serena Lodge, sited on high ground in the west of the Park overlooking the Mara River and two luxury camps sited on the eastern bank of the Mara River. These are the East African Wildlife Safari Camp near the old Mara bridge and the Governor's Camp some miles further downstream.

MAMMALS OF MASAI MARA NATIONAL RESERVE

Spectacled Elephant Shrew
East African Hedgehog
Giant White-toothed Shrew
Straw-coloured Fruit Bat
Rousette Fruit Bat
Epauletted Fruit Bat
Pale-bellied Fruit Bat
Hollow-faced Bat
False Vampire Bat
Yellow-winged Bat
Lander's Horseshoe Bat
Lesser Leaf-nosed Bat
Banana Bat or **African Pipistrelle**
Yellow-bellied Bat
Angola Free-tailed Bat
White-bellied Free-tailed Bat
Greater Galago
Bush Baby
Black-faced Vervet Monkey
Blue or **Sykes' Monkey**
Red-tailed or **White-nosed Monkey**
Patas Monkey

Olive Baboon
Black and White Colobus
Lesser Ground Pangolin
Hunting Dog
Golden Jackal
Black-backed or **Silver-backed Jackal**
Side-striped Jackal
Bat-eared Fox
Zorilla
Ratel or **Honey Badger**
Clawless Otter
African Civet
Neumann's or **Small-spotted Genet**
Bush or **Large-spotted Genet**
African Palm Civet
Marsh Mongoose
Dwarf Mongoose
Large Grey Mongoose
Slender or **Black-tipped Mongoose**
White-tailed Mongoose
Banded Mongoose
Aard-wolf
Spotted Hyaena
Striped Hyaena
Cheetah
African Wild Cat
Serval
Lion
Leopard
Ant Bear
Tree Hyrax
Rock Hyrax
African Elephant
Black Rhinoceros
Burchell's or **Common Zebra**
Hippopotamus
Giant Forest Hog
Warthog
Bush Pig
Masai Giraffe
Coke's Hartebeest or **Kongoni**
White-bearded Gnu or **Wildebeest**
Topi
Red Duiker
Blue Duiker
Bush Duiker
Klipspringer
Suni
Oribi
Steinbok
Kirk's Dik-Dik
Defassa Waterbuck
Bohor Reedbuck
Impala
Thomson's Gazelle
Grant's Gazelle Some examples approach the race *robertsi* with outward growing horns
Roan Antelope
Bushbuck
Eland
African Buffalo
African Hare
Cane Rat
Porcupine
Striped Ground Squirrel
Unstriped Ground Squirrel
Bush Squirrel
Giant Forest Squirrel
Spring Hare
African Dormouse
Kenya Mole Rat

BIRDS OF MASAI MARA NATIONAL RESERVE

Masai Ostrich
Little Grebe
Long-tailed Cormorant
African Darter
Black-headed Heron
Yellow-billed Egret
Little Egret
Buff-backed Heron or **Cattle Egret**
Squacco Heron
Green-backed Heron Not uncommon on well-wooded rivers
Night Heron
Hamerkop
White Stork
European Black Stork Single birds recorded most years
Woolly-necked Stork Rare
Abdim's Stork Numbers vary greatly
Open-bill Stork Uncommon
Saddle-bill Stork
Marabou Stork
Wood Ibis or **Yellow-billed Stork**
Sacred Ibis
Hadada Ibis
African Black Duck
Garganey Teal
Hottentot Teal
Red-billed Duck
Knob-billed Duck
Egyptian Goose
Spur-winged Goose
Secretary Bird
Ruppell's Vulture
White-backed Vulture
Nubian or **Lappet-faced Vulture**
White-headed Vulture
Egyptian Vulture
Hooded Vulture
Peregrine
Lanner
European Hobby Mainly spring passage migrant
African Hobby Rare
European Kestrel
Greater or **White-eyed Kestrel** Occurs on open plains with scattered thorn trees
Lesser Kestrel
Grey Kestrel
Pygmy Falcon
Cuckoo Falcon Occurs in thick riverine forest. Uncommon
European Black Kite
African Black Kite
Black-shouldered Kite
Bat Hawk Recorded on the Mara River, hunting bats over the water, and near Keekorok Lodge
Honey Buzzard Rare winter visitor
Steppe Eagle
Tawny Eagle
Wahlberg's Eagle
African Hawk Eagle Rare resident
Booted Eagle Rare winter visitor
Martial Eagle Occurs in open country with scattered trees
Crowned Hawk-eagle Occurs in riverine forest
Long-crested Eagle
Lizard Buzzard
Brown Harrier Eagle

Black-chested Harrier Eagle
Banded Harrier Eagle One record from Mara River
Bateleur
African Fish Eagle
Lammergeyer Rare visitor
Steppe Buzzard
Augur Buzzard
Little Sparrow Hawk
Ovampo Sparrow Hawk Rare: two records only
Great Sparrow Hawk
Shikra
African Goshawk Mainly in riverine forest
Gabar Goshawk
Pale Chanting Goshawk
Dark Chanting Goshawk
Montagu's Harrier
Pallid Harrier
European Marsh Harrier
African Marsh Harrier Uncommon visitor
Harrier Hawk
Osprey Rare: a few records from the Mara River
Coqui Francolin
Crested Francolin
Shelley's (Grey-wing) Francolin
Hildebrandt's Francolin Common around Keekorok Lodge
Scaly Francolin Forest
Yellow-necked Spurfowl
Cape Quail
Harlequin Quail
Blue Quail Uncommon and local. Mainly in western area of Reserve
Helmeted Guinea-fowl
Crested Guinea-fowl In thick riverine forest. Uncommon
European Corn Crake Uncommon passage migrant
African Crake Occurs in long grass. Uncommon
Black Crake
White-spotted Pygmy Crake Recorded in forest along Mara River
African Finfoot
Crowned Crane
Kori Bustard
Jackson's Bustard
White-bellied Bustard
Black-bellied Bustard Rarer than Hartlaub's Bustard
Hartlaub's Bustard
Spotted Stone Curlew
Water Dikkop Occurs along all the rivers. Mainly nocturnal
African Jacana
Little Ringed Plover Uncommon migrant
Kittlitz's Plover
Three-banded Plover
Caspian Plover Numbers vary from year to year. Sometimes present in large flocks on open plains
Crowned Plover
Senegal Plover
Black-winged Plover Uncommon visitor
Blacksmith Plover
Brown-chested Wattled Plover Recorded but not confirmed: probably rare visitor. Often associates with Senegal Plover on open plains
Wattled Plover Uncommon
Avocet Vagrant in years of heavy rains
Black-winged Stilt Uncommon
Painted Snipe
European Common Snipe
Great Snipe Spring migrant in small numbers
African Snipe
Ruff
Common Sandpiper
Green Sandpiper Found on rivers and streams
Wood Sandpiper
Temminck's Courser
Two-banded Courser
Heuglin's Courser
Bronze-winged Courser
Pratincole
Button Quail
Chestnut-bellied Sandgrouse
Black-faced Sandgrouse
Yellow-throated Sandgrouse
Speckled Pigeon
Olive Pigeon In riverine forest. Uncommon
Red-eyed Dove
Mourning Dove
Ring-necked Dove
Laughing Dove
Namaqua Dove
Tambourine Dove
Blue-spotted Wood Dove Mainly in western part of Reserve
Emerald-spotted Wood Dove
Green Pigeon
European Cuckoo
African Cuckoo
Red-chested Cuckoo
Black Cuckoo
Great-spotted Cuckoo
Levaillant's Cuckoo
Black and White Cuckoo
Emerald Cuckoo
Didric Cuckoo
Klaas' Cuckoo
Blue-headed Coucal
Senegal Coucal In western areas of Reserve. Uncommon in bush country
White-browed Coucal
Green Coucal or **Yellow-bill** Lives in creeper festooned trees in riverine forest
Schalow's Turaco Not uncommon in riverine forest
Ross's Turaco Recorded in riverine forest along Mara River
Eastern Grey Plaintain-eater
White-bellied Go-away-bird
Bare-faced Go-away-bird
Brown Parrot
European Roller
Lilac-breasted Roller
Rufous-crowned Roller
Broad-billed Roller
Pied Kingfisher
Giant Kingfisher Recorded on Mara River
Malachite Kingfisher
Pygmy Kingfisher
Woodland Kingfisher
Brown-hooded Kingfisher
Grey-headed Kingfisher
Striped Kingfisher
European Bee-eater
Madagascar Bee-eater Uncommon visitor in small numbers
Blue-cheeked Bee-eater Winter visitor and passage migrant. Often associated with European Bee-eater
White-throated Bee-eater
Little Bee-eater
Cinnamon-chested Bee-eater Forested areas
Blue-breasted Bee-eater

White-fronted Bee-eater
Black and White-casqued Hornbill
Grey Hornbill
Red-billed Hornbill
Von der Decken's Hornbill
Crowned Hornbill
Ground Hornbill
European Hoopoe Uncommon passage migrant
African Hoopoe
Green Wood Hoopoe
Scimitar-bill
Abyssinian Scimitar-bill
African Marsh Owl
African Wood Owl
African Scops Owl
White-faced Scops Owl
Pearl-spotted Owlet
Spotted Eagle Owl
Verreaux's Eagle Owl
Pel's Fishing Owl Recorded from the Mara River. Rare
European Nightjar
Dusky Nightjar
Freckled Nightjar Frequents rocky outcrops
Plain Nightjar
White-tailed Nightjar Uncommon. Frequents marshy places
Gaboon Nightjar
Pennant-wing Nightjar Uncommon migrant August/September
Long-tailed Nightjar
Speckled Mousebird
Blue-naped Mousebird
Narina's Trogon Inhabits riverine forest. Not uncommon
Double-toothed Barbet Frequents fruiting fig trees
Black-billed Barbet Uncommon. Mainly in western parts of Reserve
White-headed Barbet
Brown-throated Barbet
Spotted-flanked Barbet
Red-fronted Barbet Inhabits acacia woodland
Grey-throated Barbet
Yellow-spotted Barbet Rare. In forest along Mara River
Red-fronted Tinkerbird
Lemon-rumped Tinkerbird
Red and Yellow Barbet
D'Arnaud's Barbet
Yellow-billed Barbet In forest along Mara River
Greater Honeyguide Common. Bird often attracted by knocking a short length of wood against a tree trunk
Scaly-throated Honeyguide
Lesser Honeyguide
Wahlberg's Honeyguide Inhabits acacia bush
Cassin's Honeyguide Inhabits riverine forest
Nubian Woodpecker
Cardinal Woodpecker
Brown-backed Woodpecker
Bearded Woodpecker
Grey Woodpecker
Red-breasted Wryneck Often found in Euphorbia trees
Nyanza Swift
Mottled Swift
Little Swift
White-rumped Swift
Palm Swift
Boehm's Spinetail One record from country towards Sand River
African Broadbill Occurs in forest along Mara River. Not common
Singing Bush Lark
Northern White-tailed Lark
Redwing Bush Lark
Rufous-naped Lark
Flappet Lark
Fawn-coloured Lark
Fischer's Sparrow Lark
Red-capped Lark
African Pied Wagtail
Mountain Wagtail
Well's Wagtail
European Grey Wagtail
Blue-headed Wagtail and races Common winter visitors and passage migrants
Long-billed Pipit
Plain-backed Pipit
Richard's Pipit
Tree Pipit
Red-throated Pipit
Yellow-throated Longclaw
Pangani Longclaw
Rosy-breasted Longclaw On open plains
Arrow-marked Babbler
Black-lored Babbler
Northern Pied Babbler
Rufous Chatterer
Yellow-vented Bulbul
Bristle-bill In riverine forest along Mara River
Fischer's Greenbul
Yellow-whiskered Greenbul
European Spotted Flycatcher
Dusky Flycatcher
Ashy Flycatcher
Pale Flycatcher
Grey Flycatcher
White-eyed Slaty Flycatcher
Black Flycatcher
Silverbird
Chin-spot Flycatcher
Wattle-eye Flycatcher
Paradise Flycatcher
African Thrush
European Rock Thrush
European Common Wheatear
Isabelline Wheatear
Pied Wheatear
Schalow's Wheatear
Capped Wheatear
Red-tailed Chat
Sooty Chat
Anteater Chat
European Whinchat
White-browed Robin Chat
Red-capped Robin Chat
Robin Chat
Spotted Morning Warbler
White-winged Scrub Robin
European Nightingale
Sprosser
European Whitethroat
Garden Warbler
Blackcap Warbler
European Sedge Warbler
European Willow Warbler
Fan-tailed Warbler
Black-breasted Apalis
Grey-capped Warbler
Buff-bellied Warbler
Crombec
Red-faced Crombec
Banded Tit-warbler
Brown Tit-warbler
Yellow-bellied Eremomela
Grey-backed Camaroptera
Pectoral-patch Cisticola
Rattling Cisticola
Singing Cisticola
Winding Cisticola
Stout Cisticola

Tawny-flanked Prinia
Moustached Warbler
European Swallow
Angola Swallow
Blue Swallow
Wire-tailed Swallow
Red-rumped Swallow
Grey-rumped Swallow
European Sand Martin
African Sand Martin
European House Martin
Banded Martin
African Rock Martin
Black Rough-wing Swallow
White-headed Rough-wing Swallow
Black Cuckoo Shrike
Grey Cuckoo Shrike
Drongo
Straight-crested Helmet Shrike
Grey-crested Helmet Shrike
White-crowned Shrike
Northern Brubru
Grey-backed Fiscal
Lesser Grey Shrike Spring migrant
Fiscal Shrike
Long-tailed Fiscal
Red-backed Shrike
Red-tailed Shrike
Black-headed Gonolek
Slate-coloured Boubou
Tropical Boubou
Black-backed Puff-back
Puff-back Shrike
Black-headed Tchagra
Brown-headed Tchagra
Blackcap Bush Shrike
Sulphur-breasted Bush Shrike
Grey-headed Bush Shrike
Rosy-patched Shrike
Yellow White-eye
Bronzy Sunbird
Little Purple-banded Sunbird Recorded from near Mara River
Mariqua Sunbird
Variable Sunbird
Amethyst Sunbird
Scarlet-chested Sunbird
Green-headed Sunbird Recorded in riverine forest along Mara River
Olive Sunbird
Collared Sunbird
Buffalo Weaver
White-headed Buffalo Weaver
White-browed Sparrow Weaver
Grey-headed Social Weaver
Rufous Sparrow
Grey-headed Sparrow
Chestnut Sparrow
Yellow-spotted Petronia
Speckled-fronted Weaver
Black-headed Weaver
Masked Weaver
Vitelline Masked Weaver
Little Weaver
Chestnut Weaver
Black-necked Weaver
Spectacled Weaver
Holub's Golden Weaver
Vieillot's Black Weaver
Black-billed Weaver Uncommon in riverine forest
Reichenow's Weaver
Grosbeak Weaver
Red-headed Weaver
Red-billed Quelea
Red-headed Quelea Uncommon and local. Mainly in western area of Reserve
Cardinal Quelea
Red Bishop
Black-winged Bishop
Yellow Bishop
Fan-tailed Widow-bird
White-winged Widow-bird
Red-naped Widow-bird
Jackson's Widow-bird
Bronze Mannikin
Black and White Mannikin
Silverbill
Grey-headed Silverbill
Grey-headed Negro Finch
Cut-throat
Quail Finch
Parasitic Weaver Rare: very few records
Green-backed Twin-spot Occurs in riverine forest. Shy and easily overlooked
Green-winged Pytilia
African Fire Finch
Red-billed Fire Finch
Yellow-bellied Waxbill
Waxbill
Crimson-rumped Waxbill
Red-cheeked Cordon-bleu
Purple Grenadier
Indigo-bird
Pin-tailed Whydah
Paradise Whydah
Yellow-fronted Canary
White-bellied Canary
Brimstone Canary
Yellow-rumped Seed-eater
Streaky Seed-eater
Golden-breasted Bunting
Cinnamon-breasted Rock Bunting
Grey Tit
White-breasted Tit
Red-throated Tit
African Penduline Tit
European Golden Oriole
African Golden Oriole
Black-headed Oriole
Wattled Starling
Violet-backed Starling
Blue-eared Glossy Starling
Ruppell's Long-tailed Starling
Hildebrandt's Starling
Superb Starling
Yellow-billed Oxpecker
Red-billed Oxpecker
Pied Crow
Cape Rook
White-naped Raven

MERU NATIONAL PARK

The Meru National Park, an area of some 1,813sq km (700sq miles) to the north-east of Mount Kenya, possesses several special attractions for the visitor. Firstly it is part of the domain made famous by Elsa the lioness, whose association with this wild and lovely country is well known through

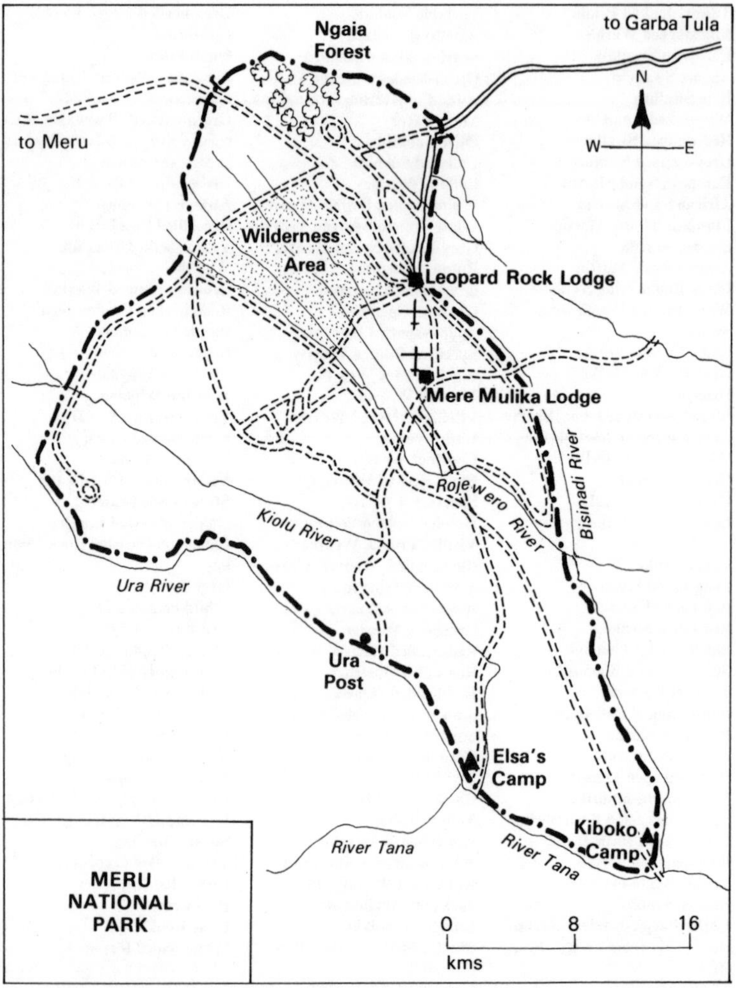

Joy Adamson's books. An excursion to Elsa's camp on the Ura River in the south of the Park is well worth while.

Secondly, a section of the Park has been designated as a wilderness area, in which there are no roads. The energetic visitor who would explore must proceed on foot, escorted by an experienced ranger guide and with porters to carry camping equipment and food. Such an expedition furnishes the opportunity to experience the pleasures, and perhaps some of the hazards, of a foot safari as it was at the beginning of the century. Approaching elephant, rhino and buffalo under these conditions is a very different proposition to viewing the animals from the safety of a motor vehicle.

The third novelty Meru has to offer is its introduced White Rhinos – the only Park or Reserve in Kenya to possess these animals.

Meru National Park ranges from 1,036m (3,400ft) in the foothills of the Nyambeni range, its northern boundary, to less than 3,040m (1,000ft) on the Tana River in the south-eastern sector. The area is well watered, the main rivers being the Rojerwero, Ura and Tana; all three are margined by dense riverine forest or magnificent stands of dom and raphia palms. Most of the Park is covered by bush of varying densities, Combretum bush prevailing in the northern section and Commiphora in the south. The north-eastern quadrant is open dom palm country, grassland and acacia woods, and in the extreme north there is a small patch of rain forest, an outlier of the Ngaia forest.

A well-planned network of roads ensures excellent game-viewing and big game often includes Elephant, Black Rhinoceros, Hippopotamus, plentiful in the Rojerwero and Tana Rivers, Reticulated Giraffe, Grevy's and Common Zebra, Grant's Gazelle, Lesser Kudu and Gerenuk. Lion, Leopard and Cheetah may be found and Beisa Oryx are quite plentiful. In addition to game viewing on land, a motor boat suitable for four passengers plus crew is available for anyone wishing to explore the country from the rivers. This is perhaps the best way to locate the shy African Finfoot, a very elusive bird to seek from the river banks.

Birds are abundant and colourful. In dom palm areas the Red-necked Falcon is often to be seen. There are at least three species of Coursers, but one, Heuglin's Courser, is seldom observed on account of its nocturnal habits. Pel's Fishing Owl occurs on the Tana River and campers in this part of the Park should listen for its loud cry; an unforgettable sound. Those remarkable birds the honeyguides are represented by four species, and the rare Brown-backed Woodpecker frequents fig trees along the rivers. The resplendent Golden-breasted Starling is often encountered in flocks, but is usually shy and difficult to approach.

In the acacia woodlands along some of the rivers lives the smallest of the long-tailed Sunbirds, the diminutive Smaller Black-bellied Sunbird, which gathers insects and nectar from the branches of red-flowered parasitic Loranthus growing in the trees.

Accommodation in Meru includes Meru Mulika Lodge with full hotel facilities, and the Leopard Rock Bandas and Bwathongen Bandas. The latter are near the Park Headquarters, and can be booked through the Game Warden. These provide shelter, beds and cooking facilities only. Meru Mulika Lodge is sited a few miles from the main gate, overlooking a large swamp which is a favoured haunt of elephant and buffalo. Leopard Rock Lodge is farther north near the rocky outcrop from which it takes its name.

In addition there are camp sites, near the Leopard Rock and in the south on the Tana River.

There are two routes to the Meru Park from Nairobi. The first is the main road via Nyeri, Nanyuki and Meru: the second is via the Embu-Meru road, from which a new access road now forms the best approach to the Park via the Ura gate.

From Meru there is also a dry-weather route through Mathara and Kangeta towards Maua. After Kangeta and some three miles along the Maua road a left turn on to the Kinna road leads to the National Park gate, where instructions will be given on how to reach Leopard Rock or Meru Mulika Lodge. The road from Meru is well signposted.

In addition to access by road the visitor can fly to airstrips at Leopard Rock Lodge and Meru Mulika Lodge.

MAMMALS OF MERU NATIONAL PARK

Spectacled Elephant Shrew
East African Hedgehog
Giant White-toothed Shrew
Rousette Fruit Bat
Epauletted Fruit Bat
Pale-bellied Fruit Bat
White-bellied Tomb Bat
Hollow-faced Bat
False Vampire Bat
Yellow-winged Bat Hangs in acacia thickets during day
Lander's Horseshoe Bat
Lesser Leaf-nosed Bat
Banana Bat or **African Pipistrelle**
Yellow-bellied Bat
Angola Free-tailed Bat
White-bellied Free-tailed Bat
Flat-headed Free-tailed Bat Not yet recorded but certain to occur
Greater Galago
Bush Baby
Black-faced Vervet
Blue or **Sykes' Monkey**
Patas Monkey
Olive Baboon
Lesser Ground Pangolin Rare
Hunting Dog Spasmodic visitor
Black-backed or **Silver-backed Jackal**
Side-striped Jackal
Zorilla
Ratel or **Honey Badger**
Clawless Otter
African Civet
Neumann's or **Small-spotted Genet**
Bush or **Large-spotted Genet**
Marsh Mongoose
Dwarf Mongoose
Large Grey Mongoose
Banded Mongoose
Aard-wolf
Spotted Hyaena
Striped Hyaena
Cheetah
Caracal
African Wild Cat
Serval
Lion
Leopard
Ant Bear
Tree Hyrax
Rock Hyrax
African Elephant
Black Rhinoceros
Square-lipped or **White Rhinoceros** Introduced animals
Grevy's Zebra
Burchell's or **Common Zebra**
Hippopotamus
Warthog
Bush Pig
Reticulated Giraffe
Coke's Hartebeest or **Kongoni**
Blue Duiker
Bush Duiker
Suni
Oribi
Steinbok
Kirk's Dik-Dik
Common Waterbuck
Bohor Reedbuck
Impala
Grant's Gazelle
Gerenuk
Beisa Oryx
Bushbuck
Lesser Kudu
Eland
African Buffalo
African Hare
Cane Rat
Porcupine
Striped Ground Squirrel
Unstriped Ground Squirrel
Bush Squirrel
East African Red Squirrel Riverine woodland along Tana River
Spring Hare
African Dormouse
Giant Rat
Naked Mole Rat

BIRDS OF MERU NATIONAL PARK

Somali Ostrich
Little Grebe
Long-tailed Cormorant
African Darter
Black-headed Heron
Buff-backed Heron or **Cattle Egret**
Great White Egret Swamp – Meru Mulika Lodge

Green-backed Heron Along rivers
Hamerkop
White Stork Spasmodic visitor
Abdim's Stork Uncommon visitor
Marabou Stork
Saddlebill Stork Swamp – Meru Mulika Lodge
Wood Ibis or **Yellow-billed Stork**
Sacred Ibis Uncommon
Hadada Ibis
African Black Duck
Egyptian Goose
Secretary Bird
Ruppell's Vulture
White-backed Vulture
Nubian or **Lappet-faced Vulture**
White-headed Vulture
Egyptian Vulture
Hooded Vulture
Lanner
Red-necked Falcon Associated with palms. Recorded from north-eastern sector of Reserve
European Kestrel
Lesser Kestrel
Pygmy Falcon
European Black Kite
African Black Kite
Black-shouldered Kite
Steppe Eagle
Tawny Eagle
Wahlberg's Eagle
African Hawk Eagle
Martial Eagle
Long-crested Eagle
Lizard Buzzard
Brown Harrier Eagle
Black-chested Harrier Eagle
Grasshopper Buzzard
Bateleur
Augur Buzzard
African Fish Eagle
Palm-nut Vulture
Steppe Buzzard Uncommon winter visitor
Little Sparrow Hawk
Shikra
Gabar Goshawk
Pale Chanting Goshawk
Montagu's Harrier
Pallid Harrier
European Marsh Harrier The three harriers are most frequent during spring migration
Harrier Hawk
Crested Francolin
Yellow-necked Spurfowl
Harlequin Quail
Helmeted Guinea-fowl
Kenya Crested Guinea-fowl
Vulturine Guinea-fowl
Kaffir Rail
Black Crake
African Finfoot On thickly wooded rivers and streams
Crowned Crane
Kori Bustard
White-bellied Bustard
Buff-crested Bustard
Spotted Stone Curlew
Water Dikkop
African Jacana
Little Ringed Plover
Kittlitz's Plover
Three-banded Plover
Caspian Plover
Crowned Plover
Senegal Plover
Blackhead Plover
Painted Snipe Rare
Ruff
Common Sandpiper
Green Sandpiper
Wood Sandpiper
Temminck's Courser Uncommon visitor
Two-banded Courser
Heuglin's Courser Largely nocturnal: rests in thick bush during the day
Button Quail
Chestnut-bellied Sandgrouse
Black-faced Sandgrouse
Lichtenstein's Sandgrouse
Speckled Pigeon
Red-eyed Dove
Mourning Dove
Ring-necked Dove
Laughing Dove
Namaqua Dove
Emerald-spotted Wood Dove
Green Pigeon
European Cuckoo Occurs mainly on spring migration
African Cuckoo
Red-chested Cuckoo
Black Cuckoo
Great Spotted Cuckoo
Black and White Cuckoo
Didric Cuckoo
Klaas' Cuckoo
White-browed Coucal
White-bellied Go-away-bird
Orange-bellied Parrot
Brown Parrot
European Roller
Lilac-breasted Roller
Rufous-crowned Roller
Broad-billed Roller
Pied Kingfisher
Giant Kingfisher Rare
Malachite Kingfisher
Pygmy Kingfisher
Brown-hooded Kingfisher Occurs mainly in riverine woodland
Grey-headed Kingfisher
Striped Kingfisher
European Bee-eater
Madagascar Bee-eater
Blue-cheeked Bee-eater Uncommon spring migrant
White-throated Bee-eater
Little Bee-eater
Somali Bee-eater
Grey Hornbill
Red-billed Hornbill
Yellow-billed Hornbill
Von der Decken's Hornbill
Crowned Hornbill
European Hoopoe Uncommon spring migrant
African Hoopoe
Green Wood Hoopoe
Violet Wood Hoopoe Found mainly on the Tana River
Scimitar-bill
Abyssinian Scimitar-bill
African Marsh Owl
African Scops Owl
White-faced Scops Owl
Pearl-spotted Owlet
Barred Owlet
Verreaux's Eagle Owl
Pel's Fishing Owl Occurs along the Tana and Rojerwero Rivers
European Nightjar
Dusky Nightjar
Donaldson-Smith's Nightjar
Nubian Nightjar
Plain Nightjar
Long-tailed Nightjar
Speckled Mousebird
Blue-naped Mousebird
Narina's Trogon

Brown-throated Barbet
Spotted-flanked Barbet
Red-fronted Barbet
Red-fronted Tinkerbird
Red and Yellow Barbet
D'Arnaud's Barbet
Greater Honeyguide
Scaly-throated Honeyguide
Lesser Honeyguide
Wahlberg's Honeyguide
Nubian Woodpecker
Cardinal Woodpecker
Brown-backed Woodpecker The rarest of the Meru Park Woodpeckers
Bearded Woodpecker
Nyanza Swift
Mottled Swift
Little Swift
White-rumped Swift
Palm Swift
Singing Bush Lark
Northern White-tailed Lark
Redwing Bush Lark
Flappet Lark
Fawn-coloured Lark
Pink-breasted Lark
Chestnut-backed Sparrow Lark
Chestnut-headed Sparrow Lark
Fischer's Sparrow Lark
Red-capped Lark
African Pied Wagtail
Blue-headed Wagtail Various races occur on spring migration
Richard's Pipit
Yellow-throated Longclaw
Scaly Babbler Occurs along Tana River. Rare
Northern Pied Babbler
Rufous Chatterer
Yellow-vented Bulbul
Northern Brownbul
European Spotted Flycatcher
Dusky Flycatcher
Ashy Flycatcher
Grey Flycatcher
South African Black Flycatcher
Chin-spot Flycatcher
Pygmy Puff-back Flycatcher
Black-throated Wattle-eye
Paradise Flycatcher
Bare-eyed Thrush
European Rock Thrush
European Common Wheatear
Isabelline Wheatear
Pied Wheatear
Capped Wheatear
White-browed Robin Chat
Red-capped Robin Chat
Stonechat
Morning Warbler Associated with stands of palms
Spotted Morning Warbler
Red-backed Scrub Robin
European Nightingale
Thrush Nightingale or **Sprosser**
Garden Warbler
Blackcap Warbler
Barred Warbler
Olive-tree Warbler
Great Reed Warbler Uncommon passage migrant in spring
European Marsh Warbler Spring passage migrant
European Sedge Warbler
European Willow Warbler
Grey Wren Warbler
Black-breasted Apalis
Red-faced Apalis
Grey-capped Warbler Occurs in riverine thickets
Buff-bellied Warbler
Crombec
Banded Tit-warbler
Yellow-bellied Eremomela
Grey-backed Camaroptera
Rattling Cisticola
Winding Cisticola
Tiny Cisticola
Ashy Cisticola
European Swallow
Angola Swallow
Wire-tailed Swallow
Red-rumped Swallow
Striped Swallow
European Sand Martin
African Sand Martin
Banded Martin
Black Cuckoo Shrike
Drongo
Straight-crested Helmet Shrike
Chestnut-fronted Shrike
White-crowned Shrike
Northern Brubru
Lesser Grey Shrike Spring passage migrant
Fiscal Shrike
Teita Fiscal
Long-tailed Fiscal
Red-backed Shrike
Red-tailed Shrike
Slate-coloured Boubou
Tropical Boubou
Black-backed Puff-back
Puff-back Shrike
Black-headed Tchagra
Brown-headed Tchagra
Three-streaked Tchagra
Sulphur-breasted Bush Shrike
Grey-headed Bush Shrike
Rosy-patched Shrike
Grey Tit
Mouse-coloured Penduline Tit
European Golden Oriole
Black-headed Oriole
White-naped Raven
Fan-tailed Raven
Wattled Starling
Violet-backed Starling
Blue-eared Glossy Starling
Ruppell's Long-tailed Starling
Golden-breasted Starling
Fischer's Starling
Hildebrandt's Starling
Superb Starling
Red-billed Oxpecker
Yellow White-eye
Smaller Black-bellied Sunbird
Mariqua Sunbird
Variable Sunbird
Hunter's Sunbird
Collared Sunbird
Kenya Violet-backed Sunbird
Buffalo Weaver
White-headed Buffalo Weaver
White-browed Sparrow Weaver
Grey-headed Social Weaver
Black-capped Social Weaver
Rufous Sparrow
Parrot-billed Sparrow
Chestnut Sparrow
Yellow-spotted Petronia
Speckle-fronted Weaver
Layard's Black-headed Weaver
Masked Weaver
Vitelline Masked Weaver
Chestnut Weaver
Black-necked Weaver
Spectacled Weaver
Golden Weaver
Grosbeak Weaver
Red-headed Weaver
Red-billed Quelea
Cardinal Quelea
Red Bishop
Yellow Bishop
White-winged Widow-bird
Bronze Mannikin

Grey-headed Silverbill
Cut-throat
Green-winged Pytilia
African Fire Finch
Jameson's Fire Finch
Red-billed Fire Finch
Waxbill
Red-cheeked Cordon-bleu
Purple Grenadier
Indigo-bird
Pin-tailed Whydah
Steel-blue Whydah
Fischer's Straw-tailed Whydah
Paradise Whydah
Yellow-fronted Canary
Yellow-rumped Seed-eater
Somali Golden-breasted Bunting
Cinnamon-breasted Rock Bunting
Pied Crow

NAIROBI NATIONAL PARK

Nairobi National Park is unique. Nowhere else in the world does there exist a wild life reserve with such a variety of animals and birds so close to a major city. Only four miles separate the centre of Nairobi from the Park where game animals, and the large carnivores which prey upon them, exist today in the splendour of half a century ago.

The area of Nairobi National Park is a little over forty-four square miles. Though of such small dimensions compared with other faunal reserves in East and Central Africa, Nairobi Park possesses a diversity of environments. Each of these has its own special animals and birds. Over much of the Park open plains country predominates, with or without scattered acacia bush. There is a section of highland forest in which crotons, Kenya olive, muhugu, ekebergia, markhamia and Cape chestnut are some of the characteristic trees; and a permanent river with fringing riverine forest mainly Yellow-barked Acacia, *Acacia xanthophloea*, the 'fever tree' of the early explorers. Also there are stretches of broken bush country and deep, rocky valleys and gorges with scrub and long grass. The comparatively recent construction of dams has added a further type of habitat, favourable to certain birds previously uncommon or even unrecorded.

The main entrance to Nairobi National Park is off the Langata Road, Nairobi, and thence along a road which traverses a sector of forest before reaching the expanse of plains beyond. Anywhere in the Park an abundance of animal and bird life can be seen throughout the day, but the ideal time for a visit is shortly after dawn. At that hour there is a good chance of seeing some of the nocturnal species, not usually encountered, before they disappear into their daytime hideouts.

It is perhaps unnecessary to suggest that the visitor to the Nairobi National Park – and this applies equally to parks elsewhere in East and Central Africa – should proceed slowly, with frequent stops to scan the immediate surroundings through binoculars. Many of the rarely-seen animals may be discovered in apparently deserted places by dint of slow progess and diligent searching.

The large game animals are obviously Nairobi Park's main attraction and many such may be seen, from Lion, Leopard and Cheetah to Masai Giraffe, Zebra and Hippo. Black Rhino are not uncommon, especially along forest margins. Elephants are not found in the Park but Buffalo which were

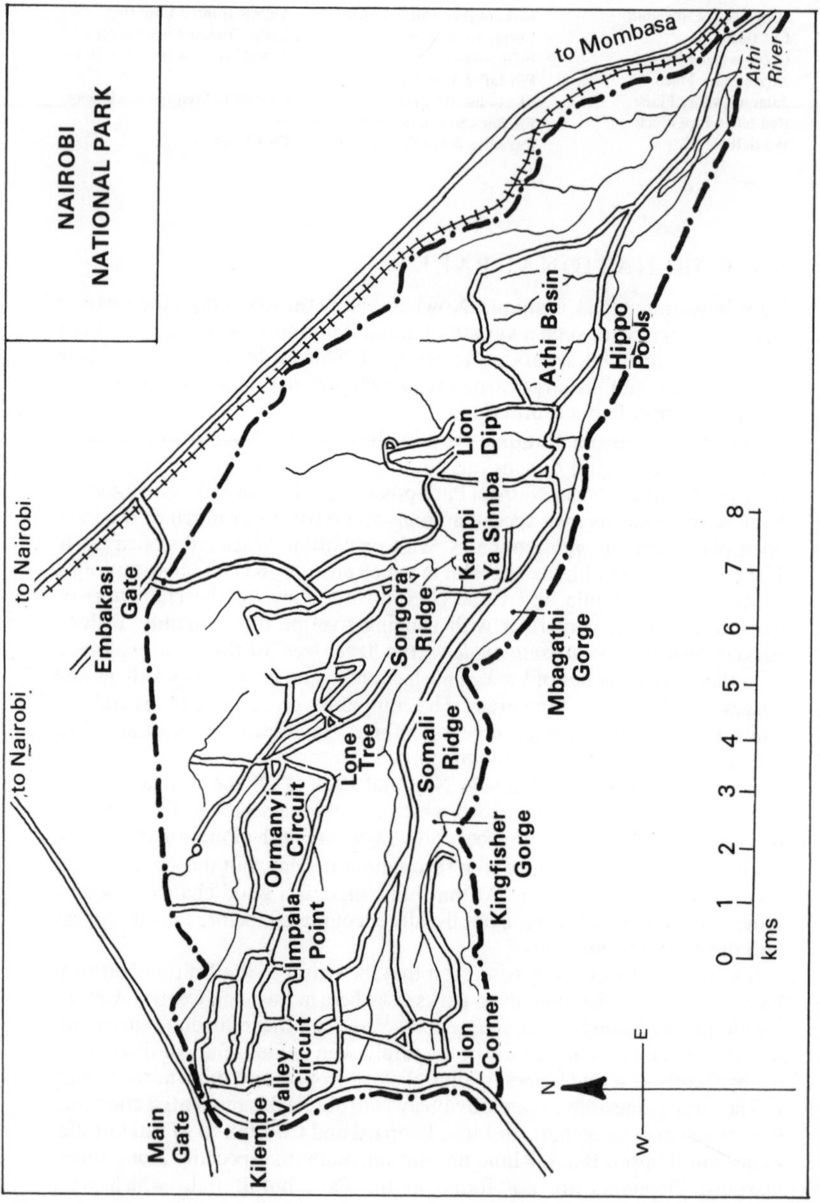
NAIROBI NATIONAL PARK
to Nairobi
to Nairobi
to Mombasa
Embakasi Gate
Main Gate
Kilembe Valley
Circuit
Impala Point
Ormanyi Circuit
Lone Tree
Songora Ridge
Kampi Ya Simba
Lion Dip
Athi Basin
Hippo Pools
Athi River
Somali Ridge
Kingfisher Gorge
Mbagathi Gorge
Lion Corner
0 1 2 3 4 5 6 7 8
kms
N
E
W

introduced, are now common, and great herds can often be seen. Masai Giraffe are also common.

It is among the ungulates that the greatest abundance of animals is found. Impala, Coke's Hartebeest (usually called Kongoni), Wildebeest and Eland can all be considered common, as also Thomson's Gazelle and Grant's Gazelle. These two species may be distinguished at all ages by the extent of white on the buttocks: in Thomson's Gazelle the white stops below the root of the tail; in Grant's Gazelle the white extends above the base of the tail and on to the rump.

The variety of bird life in Nairobi National Park may be gauged by the fact that more species of birds have been observed there than have been recorded in the British Isles. But birds are not always present in very large numbers. Much depends on the season of the year – northern migrants pass through during late March and in April; on whether rains have been plentiful or poor, recent or remote; and upon the availability of food for both insectivorous and frugivorous birds and of suitable prey for raptorials.

Birds of prey are much in evidence, from the stately Secretary Bird – two or three pairs nest and are resident – to Martial, Crowned, Tawny and Bateleur Eagles, six species of vultures and a variety of buzzards and hawks. The Augur Buzzard, identified by its red tail and chequered black and white wing patch, is the most common raptor. During March and early April many Montagu's, European Marsh and Pallid Harriers may be seen moving northwards in loose parties, and flocks of migrating Common and Lesser Kestrels are also in evidence.

That associate of vultures, king of the scavenging birds, the Marabou Stork is common around the Park dams and is extremely tame and confiding. They often rest on their tarsi in a most comical, clown-like manner.

Game birds are represented by Helmeted Guinea-fowl and Yellow-necked Spurfowl which are common in open country alongside Shelley's (Greywing) Francolin, and by Scaly Francolins in the forest area. In some years Harlequin Quails are extremely abundant in the grasslands and their far-carrying 'pleet, pleet, pleet, pleet' can be heard on all sides. The larger Cape Quail is an uncommon visitor.

Two endemic African bird families, the Turacos and the Mousebirds, are represented by Hartlaub's Turaco – a pigeon-sized bird with a long broad tail, mainly green and blue-black plumage and vivid red flight feathers – and by the Speckled and Blue-naped Mousebirds or Colies. Mousebirds are drab coloured, very long-tailed birds of gregarious habits. The blue-naped species has a patch of turquoise-blue on the back of the head and long, wire-like tail feathers. It occurs in acacia country while the Speckled Mousebird keeps to bush near the forest edge.

The largest living bird in the world, the Ostrich, is common on the plains. During the nesting season the male's neck and thighs take on a bright pink hue. Other large birds often encountered are the Crowned Crane, Kori Bustard, Ground Hornbill, European White Stork, Abdim's Stork, Egyptian

Goose, Black-necked Heron – seen more frequently on dry land, where it accounts for many rodents, than in swampy places – and the Wood Ibis or Yellow-billed Stork.

Sunbirds are much in evidence when the flowers they visit are in blossom. They favour especially the bushy, orange-flowered Leonotis and a greenish-yellow crotolaria bush. Among the commoner species are Bronzy, Variable, Malachite, Amethyst, Collared and the gem-like black-bellied Beautiful Sunbird. Weaver-birds and their allies are also well represented. The commonest species are the black-backed Reichenow's Weaver and the mottled-backed Speke's Weaver. The former nest singly while the latter builds colonies in isolated acacia trees.

In the more bushy grasslands the Red-naped Widow-bird is numerous and in years of good grass the related Jackson's Widow-bird appears, the male of which constructs dancing rings in the grass wherein to perform to the female.

MAMMALS OF NAIROBI NATIONAL PARK

Short-snouted Elephant Shrew
East African Hedgehog
Giant White-toothed Shrew
Rousette Fruit Bat
Epauletted Fruit Bat
White-bellied Tomb Bat
Hollow-faced Bat
False Vampire Bat
Yellow-winged Bat
Lander's Horseshoe Bat
Banana Bat or **African Pipistrelle**
Yellow-bellied Bat
Angola Free-tailed Bat
White-bellied Free-tailed Bat
Greater Galago
Bush Baby
Black-faced Vervet Monkey
Sykes' Monkey
Olive Baboon
Black and White Colobus Occurs in adjacent Ngong Hills forest
Hunting Dog
Black-backed or **Silver-backed Jackal**
Side-striped Jackal
Bat-eared Fox
Zorilla
Ratel or **Honey Badger**
Clawless Otter Recorded at Hippo Pools at dusk
African Civet
Neumann's or **Small-spotted Genet**
Bush or **Large-spotted Genet** Melanistic examples sometimes occur
African Palm Civet
Marsh Mongoose
Dwarf Mongoose
Slender or **Black-tipped Mongoose**
White-tailed Mongoose
Aard-wolf Rare
Spotted Hyaena
Striped Hyaena Rare
Cheetah
Caracal
African Wild Cat
Serval
Lion
Leopard
Ant Bear
Tree Hyrax
Rock Hyrax
Black Rhinoceros
Burchell's or **Common Zebra**
Hippopotamus
Warthog
Masai Giraffe
Coke's Hartebeest or **Kongoni**
White-bearded Gnu or **Wildebeest**
Bush Duiker
Klipspringer
Suni
Steinbok
Kirk's Dik-dik
Common Waterbuck
Defassa Waterbuck (Animals showing intermediate characters between Common and Defassa Waterbuck have been recorded)
Bohor Reedbuck
Chanler's Reedbuck A small herd exists in the Sosian Gorge
Impala
Thomson's Gazelle
Grant's Gazelle
Bushbuck
Eland
African Buffalo Introduced animals
African Hare
Cane Rat
Porcupine
Striped Ground Squirrel
Bush Squirrel
Spring Hare
African Dormouse
Giant Rat
Kenya Mole Rat

BIRDS OF NAIROBI NATIONAL PARK

Masai Ostrich
Little Grebe
White-necked Cormorant
Long-tailed Cormorant
White Pelican
Pink-backed Pelican Pelicans are visitors in small numbers
Grey Heron
Black-headed Heron Common
Goliath Heron Uncommon
Purple Heron Uncommon
Great White Egret Uncommon
Yellow-billed Egret
Little Egret
Buff-backed Heron or **Cattle Egret**
Squacco Heron
Green-backed Heron Occurs along Athi River
Night Heron May be heard flying over at dusk, but rarely seen in Park
Dwarf Bittern A nocturnal species which is rarely seen: has been picked up dead in Park after striking wires
Hamerkop
White Stork Spasmodic visitor. Sometimes in large flocks
European Black Stork Single birds recorded from time to time
Abdim's Stork Spasmodic visitor
Open-bill Stork Uncommon
Saddle-bill Stork Two records
Marabou Stork
Wood Ibis or **Yellow-billed Stork**
Sacred Ibis
Hadada Ibis
African Spoonbill
Greater Flamingo
Lesser Flamingo Flamingos turn up from time to time as stragglers on dams
White-backed Duck
African Pochard
European Shoveler
Yellow-billed Duck
African Black Duck A few residents on Athi River
Garganey Teal
Hottentot Teal
Red-billed Duck
European Pintail
Fulvous Tree Duck
Knob-billed Duck
Egyptian Goose
Spur-winged Goose Uncommon visitor
Secretary Bird
Ruppell's Vulture
White-backed Vulture
Nubian or **Lappet-faced Vulture**
White-headed Vulture
Egyptian Vulture
Hooded Vulture
Peregrine Rare visitor
Lanner
European Hobby Mainly passage migrant in late April
European Kestrel
Greater or **White-eyed Kestrel** Uncommon resident. Plains
Lesser Kestrel
Cuckoo Falcon Resident small numbers, forest area
European Black Kite
African Black Kite
Black-shouldered Kite
Honey Buzzard Uncommon winter visitor and migrant
Steppe Eagle
Tawny Eagle
Wahlberg's Eagle Uncommon visitor
Ayres' Hawk Eagle Single record, forest area
Martial Eagle
Crowned Hawk Eagle
Long-crested Eagle
Lizard Buzzard
Brown Harrier Eagle Uncommon visitor
Black-chested Harrier Eagle
Bateleur
African Fish Eagle Sometimes seen Athi River
Lammergeyer Rare visitor
Steppe Buzzard
Augur Buzzard
Little Sparrow Hawk Uncommon. Resident in forest
Ovampo Sparrow Hawk Rare resident
Great Sparrow Hawk Uncommon resident, forest
African Goshawk
Gabar Goshawk
Pale Chanting Goshawk
Montagu's Harrier
Pallid Harrier
European Marsh Harrier
African Marsh Harrier
Harrier Hawk
Osprey Rare visitor
Shelley's (Greywing) Francolin
Scaly Francolin Occurs in forest
Yellow-necked Spurfowl
Cape Quail
Harlequin Quail
Helmeted Guinea-fowl
European Corn Crake Probably common migrant but not often seen
African Crake Occurs in thick cover near dams. Rarely seen.
Black Crake Common on dams and along Athi River
Striped Crake Probably occurs on dams as species recorded several times in Nairobi
Purple Gallinule Straggler
Moorhen
Lesser Moorhen Rare
Red-knobbed Coot Uncommon visitor
African Finfoot Rare resident, Athi River
Crowned Crane
Kori Bustard
White-bellied Bustard
Hartlaub's Bustard
Spotted Stone Curlew
African Jacana
Ringed Plover
Little Ringed Plover
Kittlitz's Plover
Three-banded Plover
Caspian Plover Winter visitor in small flocks. Frequents short-grassed open plains
Crowned Plover
Black-winged Plover
Blacksmith Plover
Avocet Uncommon visitor
Black-winged Stilt
Painted Snipe
European Common Snipe
Great Snipe Uncommon spring migrant

African Snipe
Curlew Sandpiper
Little Stint
Ruff
Common Sandpiper
Green Sandpiper
Wood Sandpiper
Spotted Redshank Uncommon winter visitor
Marsh Sandpiper
Greenshank
Temminck's Courser
Pratincole Uncommon visitor
Button Quail Spasmodic visitor
Black-faced Sandgrouse
Yellow-throated Sandgrouse
Speckled Pigeon
Olive Pigeon
Pink-breasted Dove
Red-eyed Dove
Ring-necked Dove
Laughing Dove
Namaqua Dove
Tambourine Dove
Emerald-spotted Wood Dove
Green Pigeon
European Cuckoo Mainly spring migrant
African Cuckoo
Red-chested Cuckoo
Black Cuckoo
Great-spotted Cuckoo
Black and White Cuckoo
Emerald Cuckoo
Didric Cuckoo
Klaas' Cuckoo Mainly in forest area
White-browed Coucal
Hartlaub's Turaco
White-bellied Go-away-bird
European Roller
Lilac-breasted Roller
Rufous-crowned Roller
Broad-billed Roller
Pied Kingfisher
Giant Kingfisher Occurs along Athi River
Malachite Kingfisher
Pygmy Kingfisher
Grey-headed Kingfisher
Striped Kingfisher
European Bee-eater
White-throated Bee-eater
Little Bee-eater
Cinnamon-chested Bee-eater Occurs in forest
White-fronted Bee-eater
Silvery-cheeked Hornbill
Grey Hornbill
Red-billed Hornbill
Von der Decken's Hornbill
Crowned Hornbill Mainly in forest area
Ground Hornbill Uncommon
European Hoopoe
African Hoopoe Uncommon. Acacia country
Green Wood Hoopoe
White-headed Wood Hoopoe
Abyssinian Scimitar-bill
African Barn Owl Uncommon resident
African Marsh Owl
African Wood Owl Occurs in forest area
Pearl-spotted Owlet
Spotted Eagle Owl
Verreaux's Eagle Owl
European Nightjar
Dusky Nightjar
Plain Nightjar Uncommon visitor
Abyssinian Nightjar
Long-tailed Nightjar
Speckled Mousebird
Blue-naped Mousebird
Narina's Trogon Uncommon resident, forest area
White-headed Barbet
Spotted-flanked Barbet
Red-fronted Barbet
Red-fronted Tinkerbird
Golden-rumped Tinkerbird Occurs forest area
Red and Yellow Barbet
D'Arnaud's Barbet
Greater Honeyguide Best located by its call, a loud and distinct 'weet-ear, weet-ear' repeated over and over again
Scaly-throated Honeyguide Rare
Lesser Honeyguide
Wahlberg's Honeyguide Occurs acacia woodland
Zambezi Honeyguide Occurs forest area
Nubian Woodpecker
Cardinal Woodpecker
Bearded Woodpecker
Grey Woodpecker
Nyanza Swift
Mottled Swift
Little Swift
White-rumped Swift
Horus Swift Uncommon visitor
Northern White-tailed Lark Inhabits long grass
Rufous-naped Lark
Fawn-coloured Lark Uncommon
Short-tailed Lark Occurs on plains near Athi River
Fischer's Sparrow Lark
Red-capped Lark
African Pied Wagtail
Well's Wagtail
Blue-headed Wagtail and races Winter visitor and passage migrant. Common
Long-billed Pipit
Richard's Pipit
Tree Pipit
Red-throated Pipit
Yellow-throated Longclaw
Pangani Longclaw
Rosy-breasted Longclaw
Black-lored Babbler
Northern Pied Babbler
Yellow-vented Bulbul
Fischer's Greenbul
Yellow-whiskered Greenbul
European Spotted Flycatcher
Dusky Flycatcher
Grey Flycatcher
White-eyed Slaty Flycatcher
South African Black Flycatcher
Chin-spot Flycatcher
Paradise Flycatcher
Olive Thrush
European Rock Thrush
European Common Wheatear
Isabelline Wheatear
Pied Wheatear
Schalow's Wheatear
Capped Wheatear
Anteater Chat
Stonechat
European Whinchat
White-browed Robin Chat
Ruppell's Robin Chat Occurs in forest
Robin Chat
White-winged Scrub Robin
European Nightingale
Thrush Nightingale or **Sprosser**
Garden Warbler

Blackcap Warbler
European Sedge Warbler
Greater Swamp Warbler
European Willow Warbler
Grey Apalis Occurs in forest
Black-headed Apalis Occurs in forest
Black-breasted Apalis
Grey-capped Warbler
Buff-bellied Warbler
Crombec
Red-faced Crombec
Banded Tit-warbler
Yellow-bellied Eremomela
Grey-backed Camaroptera
Pectoral-patch Cisticola
Rattling Cisticola
Singing Cisticola
Winding Cisticola
Stout Cisticola
Tawny-flanked Prinia
European Swallow
Angola Swallow
Wire-tailed Swallow
Red-rumped Swallow
Striped Swallow
European Sand Martin
African Sand Martin
Banded Martin
African Rock Martin
European House Martin
Black Rough-wing Swallow
White-headed Rough-wing Swallow
Black Cuckoo Shrike
Grey Cuckoo Shrike
Drongo
Retz's Red-billed Shrike
White-crowned Shrike
Northern Brubru
Grey-backed Fiscal
Lesser Grey Shrike
Fiscal Shrike
Teita Fiscal
Long-tailed Fiscal
Red-backed Shrike
Red-tailed Shrike
Slate-coloured Boubou
Tropical Boubou
Black-backed Puff-back
Black-headed Tchagra
Brown-headed Tchagra
Sulphur-breasted Bush Shrike
White-breasted Tit
Red-throated Tit Uncommon
African Penduline Tit
European Golden Oriole
African Golden Oriole
Black-headed Oriole
Pied Crow
White-naped Raven
Wattled Starling
Violet-backed Starling
Blue-eared Glossy Starling
Red-winged Starling
Hildebrandt's Starling
Superb Starling
Yellow-billed Oxpecker Rare
Red-billed Oxpecker
Yellow White-eye
Kikuyu White-eye
Malachite Sunbird
Bronzy Sunbird
Beautiful Sunbird (black-bellied race)
Variable Sunbird
Amethyst Sunbird
Scarlet-chested Sunbird
Collared Sunbird
Kenya Violet-backed Sunbird
Buffalo Weaver Uncommon visitor
White-browed Sparrow Weaver
Grey-headed Social Weaver
Rufous Sparrow
Parrot-billed Sparrow Uncommon
Chestnut Sparrow
Yellow-spotted Petronia
Speke's Weaver
Masked Weaver
Vitelline Masked Weaver
Chestnut Weaver
Black-necked Weaver
Spectacled Weaver
Holub's Golden Weaver
Reichenow's Weaver
Brown-capped Weaver
Grosbeak Weaver
Red-billed Quelea
Cardinal Quelea
Yellow Bishop
White-winged Widow-bird
Red-naped Widow-bird
Jackson's Widow-bird
Bronze Mannikin
Rufous-backed Mannikin
Cut-throat
Quail Finch
Parasitic Weaver Rare
Green-winged Pytilia
African Fire Finch
Red-billed Fire Finch
Yellow-bellied Waxbill
Waxbill
Crimson-rumped Waxbill
Red-cheeked Cordon-bleu
Purple Grenadier
Indigo-bird
Pin-tailed Whydah
White-bellied Canary
Brimstone Canary
Yellow-rumped Seed-eater
Streaky Seed-eater
Golden-breasted Bunting
Cinnamon-breasted Rock Bunting

LAKE NAKURU NATIONAL PARK

Lake Nakuru, the world-famous haunt of flamingos, is a shallow alkaline lake in Kenya's Rift Valley, some 62sq km (24sq miles) in extent, immediately south of Nakuru township. A first-class tarmac highway connects Nairobi with Nakuru, the 156-km (97-mile) road link passing down the forested Kikuyu Escarpment with fine views over the Kedong Valley and Mounts Suswa and Longonot, then north-westwards past Lakes Naivasha and

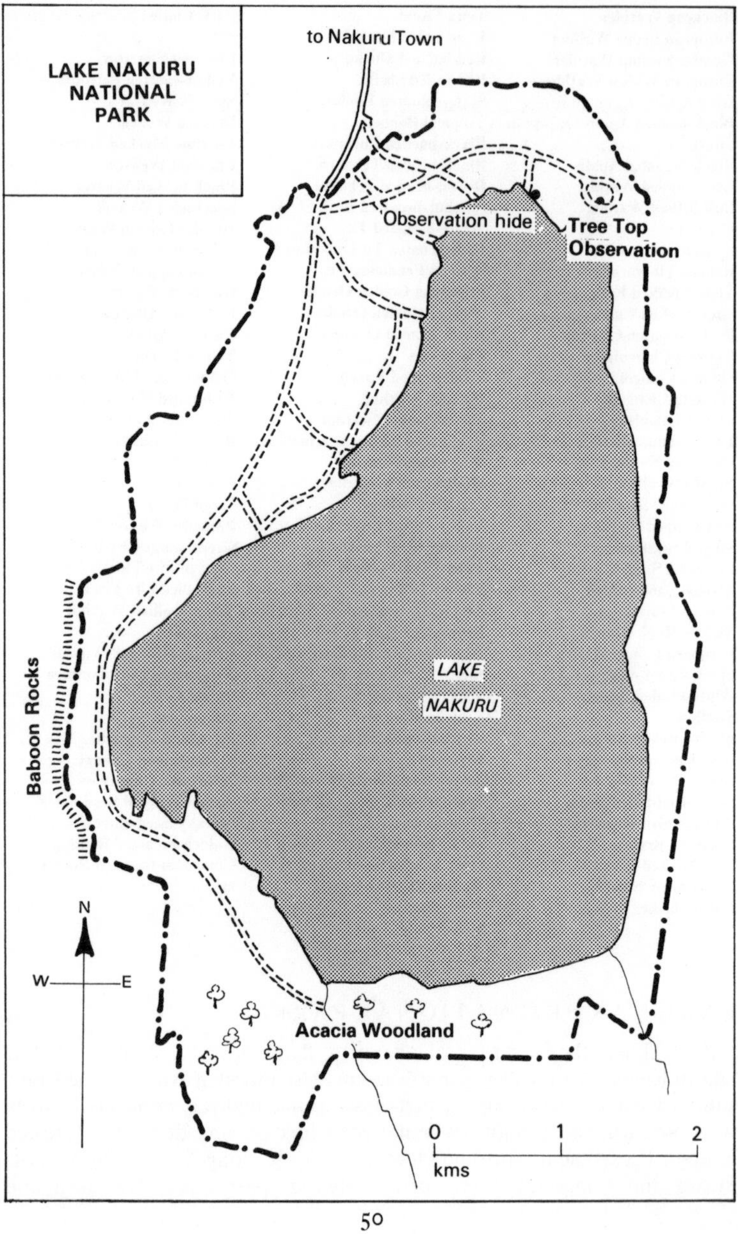
LAKE NAKURU
NATIONAL
PARK
to Nakuru Town
Observation hide
Tree Top
Observation
LAKE
NAKURU
Baboon Rocks
N
W
E
Acacia Woodland
0
1
2
kms

Elmenteita. From Nakuru the route to the lake is well signposted. Visitors to Lake Nakuru National Park may stay in hotels in Nakuru, at the Lake Nakuru Lodge, converted from a farmhouse at the southern edge of the Park, or at Lion Hill Camp, which provides full service.

The National Park comprises the lake and its surrounds. The landscape is picturesque, areas of sedge, marsh and grasslands alternating with rocky cliffs and outcrops, stretches of yellow-barked acacia woodland and on the eastern perimeter rocky hillsides covered with a forest of grotesque-looking Euphorbia trees – all set against a background of hilly, broken country.

The Park was created in 1960 chiefly as a bird sanctuary. At times vast concentrations of more than a million flamingos live on the lake, forming what the famous ornithologist, Roger Tory Peterson, has described as 'the most fabulous bird spectacle in the world'. But flamingos are unpredictable creatures, and not always to be found on Lake Nakuru in such vast numbers. The lake water-levels derive from rainfall, and the inflow of the tiny Njoro River fluctuates greatly. As conditions and food supplies alter, so do the numbers of flamingos present. However, even when the flamingo population is at low ebb there is always a wealth of bird-life to be observed on Lake Nakuru, both water-birds and those species which favour the habitats surrounding the lake. At present, nearly four hundred species have been recorded within the area of the Park. White Pelicans can be seen in large numbers at the southern end of the Lake and on the north-eastern shore, where they come to wash, and where hides and viewing platforms have been erected. These birds have increased considerably since the alkaline-tolerant fish, *Talapia grahami* was introduced into the lake by the present writer and have now become a spectacular feature of the Park.

Although Lake Nakuru National Park is primarily a bird sanctuary, the number of animals to be encountered is not inconsiderable. A small herd of Hippopotamus lives among the reeds in the north-eastern corner, where springs have created a series of hippo pools. The lake shore is a good place to observe Bohor Reedbuck; these animals are often flushed from high grass or sedge in which they sleep during the day. In recent years there has been a marked increase in the numbers of Bohor Reedbuck and of Defassa Waterbuck in the Park. Bushbuck may be seen at the edge of the acacia woodland, especially at dawn and towards dusk. Lake Nakuru is the home of a very rare bat, the Long-eared Leaf-nosed Bat (*Hipposideros megalotis*), a tiny orange-buff species with ears half the length of its body.

During 1977 an experiment was carried out to introduce a small herd of Rothschild's Giraffe into the Lake Nakuru National Park. The animals came from the Soy area of western Kenya where the future of these giraffe is uncertain. Latest reports indicate that the experiment is a success.

Both Lesser and Greater Flamingos occur abundantly as non-breeding visitors on Lake Nakuru, the former vastly the more numerous. There is a great variety of other water birds including two interesting ducks, the Cape Wigeon, a lover of brackish waters, and the stiff-tailed Maccoa Duck.

Several species of plovers are resident, Blacksmith Plover, Spurwing Plover, Crowned Plover, Kittlitz's Plover and Three-banded Plover; and many northern-breeding shore birds occur along the margins of the lake as winter visitors. During the spring migration their numbers are augmented by passage migrants, many of which are in full summer plumage. Among these are flocks of Little Stints, Curlew Sandpipers, Marsh Sandpipers and Greenshanks, smaller parties of Wood and Green Sandpipers and sometimes a few Black-tailed Godwits.

Birds of prey are always much in evidence, including five species of vultures, Lanner, Long-crested Eagle, Augur Buzzard, Brown and Black-chested Harrier Eagles, Fish Eagle, Gabar Goshawk and Harrier Hawk. During the winter months and on migration further species appear, the following being common: European and Lesser Kestrels, European Black Kite, Steppe Eagle, Steppe Buzzard, and Montagu's, Pallid and European Marsh Harriers. The line of cliffs known as 'Baboon Rocks', which rise above the western shore, is the home of a pair of majestic black Verreaux's Eagles.

In the acacia woodlands contiguous to the lake birds are numerous and the following species are characteristic: Red-chested Cuckoo, Levaillant's Cuckoo, Emerald Cuckoo, Didric Cuckoo, Lilac-breasted Roller, Grey-headed Kingfisher, Little Bee-eater, African Hoopoe, Pearl-spotted Owlet, Verreaux's Eagle Owl, Greater Honeyguide, Grey Woodpecker, Rattling Cisticola, Grey-capped Warbler, White-browed Robin-chat, Black Cuckoo Shrike, Drongo, Grey-backed Fiscal, Tropical Boubou, White-breasted Tit, Blue-eared and Superb Starlings, Bronzy and Variable Sunbirds, Speke's Weaver and Red-cheeked Cordon-bleu.

MAMMALS OF LAKE NAKURU NATIONAL PARK

Spectacled Elephant Shrew
Giant White-toothed Shrew
Rousette Fruit Bat
Epauletted Fruit Bat
White-bellied Tomb Bat
Hollow-faced Bat
False Vampire Bat
Yellow-winged Bat
Lander's Horseshoe Bat
Lesser Leaf-nosed Bat
Long-eared Leaf-nosed Bat
African Trident Bat
African Mouse-eared Bat
Banana Bat or **African Pipistrelle**
Yellow-bellied Bat
Angola Free-tailed Bat
Bush Baby
Black-faced Vervet Monkey
Blue or **Sykes' Monkey**
Olive Baboon
Black and White Colobus
Lesser Ground Pangolin Rare
Hunting Dog Very uncommon visitor
Black-backed or **Silver-backed Jackal**
Side-striped Jackal
Bat-eared Fox
Zorilla
Ratel or **Honey Badger** Rare
African Civet
Neumann's or **Small-spotted Genet**
Bush or **Large-spotted Genet**
Marsh Mongoose
Dwarf Mongoose
Slender or **Black-tipped Mongoose**
White-tailed Mongoose
Aard-wolf Rare
Spotted Hyaena
Cheetah Rare
African Wild Cat
Serval
Leopard Rare
Ant Bear
Tree Hyrax
Rock Hyrax
Burchell's or **Common Zebra**
Hippopotamus
Rothschild's Giraffe Introduced
Bush Duiker
Klipspringer
Steinbok
Kirk's Dik-dik
Defassa Waterbuck
Bohor Reedbuck
Chanler's Reedbuck
Impala
Thomson's Gazelle
Grant's Gazelle
Bushbuck

Eland
African Buffalo Rare
African Hare
Cane Rat
Porcupine
Bush Squirrel
Spring Hare
African Dormouse
Giant Rat
Kenya Mole Rat

BIRDS OF LAKE NAKURU NATIONAL PARK

Great-crested Grebe
Black-necked Grebe
Little Grebe
White-necked Cormorant
Long-tailed Cormorant
African Darter
White Pelican
Pink-backed Pelican
Grey Heron
Black-headed Heron
Goliath Heron Rare visitor
Purple Heron Recorded a few times near Hippo pools
Great White Egret
Yellow-billed Egret
Little Egret
Reef Heron Two examples in dark plumage phase were present on lake in late 1965 and early 1966
Buff-backed Heron or **Cattle Egret**
Squacco Heron
Green-backed Heron Recorded mouth of Njoro River
Night Heron
Little Bittern Uncommon
Dwarf Bittern Rare
Hamerkop
White Stork Spasmodic visitor and passage migrant
European Black Stork Rare winter visitor
Abdim's Stork Uncommon visitor
Saddle-bill Stork Uncommon
Marabou Stork
Wood Ibis or **Yellow-billed Stork**
Sacred Ibis
Hadada Ibis
Glossy Ibis
African Spoonbill
Greater Flamingo
Lesser Flamingo
Maccoa Duck
African Pochard
Tufted Duck Uncommon winter visitor
European Shoveler
Yellow-billed Duck Uncommon
Garganey Teal
Cape Wigeon Common resident
Hottentot Teal
Red-billed Duck
Gadwall Rare winter visitor
European Wigeon Uncommon winter visitor
European Teal Rare winter visitor
European Pintail
White-faced Tree Duck Uncommon
Fulvous Tree Duck
Knob-billed Duck
Egyptian Goose
Spur-wing Goose Uncommon
Secretary Bird
Ruppell's Vulture
White-backed Vulture
Nubian or **Lappet-faced Vulture**
White-headed Vulture
Egyptian Vulture
Hooded Vulture Vultures are spasmodic visitors in small numbers
Peregrine Uncommon
Lanner
European Hobby Mainly spring passage migrant
African Hobby Rare
European Kestrel
Greater or **White-eyed Kestrel**
Lesser Kestrel
European Black Kite
African Black Kite
Black-shouldered Kite
Bat Hawk Rare
Honey Buzzard Uncommon winter visitor and passage migrant
Verreaux's Eagle Pair resident on Baboon Rock cliffs
Steppe Eagle
Tawny Eagle
Wahlberg's Eagle
Booted Eagle Rare winter visitor
Martial Eagle Uncommon visitor
Long-crested Eagle
Lizard Buzzard
Brown Harrier Eagle
Black-chested Harrier Eagle
Bateleur
African Fish Eagle
Steppe Buzzard
Augur Buzzard
Little Sparrow Hawk Occurs in acacia belt on western side of lake
Great Sparrow Hawk
African Goshawk
Gabar Goshawk
Montagu's Harrier
Pallid Harrier
European Marsh Harrier
African Marsh Harrier
Harrier Hawk
Coqui Francolin
Hildebrandt's Francolin
Yellow-necked Spurfowl
Cape Quail
Harlequin Quail
Helmeted Guinea-fowl
Kaffir Rail Recorded at Hippo pools
European Corn Crake Uncommon migrant
African Crake
Black Crake Occurs at Hippo pools
Purple Gallinule Uncommon
Allen's Gallinule One record
Moorhen
Lesser Moorhen Uncommon
Red-knobbed Coot
Crowned Crane
Jackson's Bustard Rare
White-bellied Bustard
Spotted Stone Curlew
Ringed Plover
Little Ringed Plover
Kittlitz's Plover
Three-banded Plover

Caspian Plover Uncommon visitor
Grey Plover
Crowned Plover
Black-winged Plover
Spurwing Plover
Blacksmith Plover
Avocet
Black-winged Stilt
Painted Snipe
European Common Snipe
Great Snipe
African Snipe
Curlew Sandpiper
Little Stint
Temminck's Stint Uncommon winter visitor
Ruff
Common Sandpiper
Green Sandpiper
Wood Sandpiper
Redshank Rare winter visitor
Spotted Redshank Uncommon winter visitor
Marsh Sandpiper
Greenshank
Black-tailed Godwit Uncommon winter visitor
Curlew Uncommon winter visitor
Temminck's Courser
Pratincole
Lesser Black-backed Gull Winter visitor in small numbers
Grey-headed Gull
Gull-billed Tern
White-winged Black Tern
Whiskered Tern
African Skimmer Spasmodic visitor in small numbers
Button Quail
Speckled Pigeon
Pink-breasted Dove
Red-eyed Dove
Ring-necked Dove
Laughing Dove
Namaqua Dove
Tambourine Dove
Emerald-spotted Wood Dove
Green Pigeon
European Cuckoo
African Cuckoo
Red-chested Cuckoo
Black Cuckoo
Great Spotted Cuckoo
Levaillant's Cuckoo
Black and White Cuckoo
Emerald Cuckoo
Didric Cuckoo
Klaas' Cuckoo
White-browed Coucal
Green Coucal or **Yellow-bill**
European Roller
Lilac-breasted Roller
Rufous-crowned Roller
Broad-billed Roller
Pied Kingfisher
Half-collared Kingfisher Rare
Malachite Kingfisher
Pygmy Kingfisher
Grey-headed Kingfisher
Striped Kingfisher
European Bee-eater
Blue-cheeked Bee-eater Uncommon passage migrant
White-throated Bee-eater
Little Bee-eater
White-fronted Bee-eater
Grey Hornbill
Red-billed Hornbill
Crowned Hornbill
Ground Hornbill
European Hoopoe Uncommon passage migrant
African Hoopoe
Green Wood Hoopoe
Scimitar-bill
African Barn Owl
Cape Grass Owl Rare
African Marsh Owl
African Wood Owl
African Scops Owl
White-faced Scops Owl Rare
Pearl-spotted Owlet
Spotted Eagle Owl
Verreaux's Eagle Owl
European Nightjar
Plain Nightjar
Abyssinian Nightjar
Pennant-wing Nightjar Uncommon migrant July/September
Long-tailed Nightjar
Speckled Mousebird
Narina's Trogon In dense acacia woodland on western shores of lake
Spotted-flanked Barbet
Red-fronted Barbet
Red-fronted Tinkerbird
D'Arnaud's Barbet
Greater Honeyguide
Scaly-throated Honeyguide
Lesser Honeyguide
Wahlberg's Honeyguide
Nubian Woodpecker
Cardinal Woodpecker
Brown-backed Woodpecker
Bearded Woodpecker
Grey Woodpecker
Red-breasted Wryneck
Nyanza Swift
Mottled Swift
Little Swift
White-rumped Swift
Horus Swift
Northern White-tailed Lark
Rufous-naped Lark
Fawn-coloured Lark
Fischer's Sparrow Lark
Red-capped Lark
African Pied Wagtail
Wells' Wagtail
Blue-headed Wagtail and races
Long-billed Pipit
Sandy Plain-backed Pipit
Richard's Pipit
Tree Pipit
Red-throated Pipit
Yellow-throated Longclaw
Rosy-breasted Longclaw Uncommon
Black-lored Babbler
Yellow-vented Bulbul
European Spotted Flycatcher
Dusky Flycatcher
Ashy Flycatcher
Grey Flycatcher
White-eyed Slaty Flycatcher
South African Black Flycatcher
Chin-spot Flycatcher
Black-throated Wattle-eye
Paradise Flycatcher
Olive Thrush
European Rock Thrush
European Common Wheatear
Isabelline Wheatear
Pied Wheatear
Schalow's Wheatear
Capped Wheatear
Cliff Chat Occurs on Baboon Rocks cliff
Anteater Chat
Stonechat
European Whinchat Uncommon winter visitor and passage migrant
White-browed Robin Chat
Robin Chat
White-winged Scrub Robin
White-throated Robin Rare winter visitor

Thrush Nightingale or **Sprosser**
European Whitethroat
Garden Warbler
Blackcap Warbler
European Sedge Warbler
Greater Swamp Warbler
European Willow Warbler
Grey Wren Warbler
Black-breasted Apalis
Grey-capped Warbler
Buff-bellied Warbler
Red-faced Crombec
Banded Tit-warbler
Brown Tit-warbler
Yellow-bellied Eremomela
Grey-backed Camaroptera
Pectoral-patch Cisticola
Rattling Cisticola
Singing Cisticola
Winding Cisticola
Stout Cisticola
Tinkling Cisticola
Tawny-flanked Prinia
European Swallow
Angola Swallow
Wire-tailed Swallow
Red-rumped Swallow
Mosque Swallow
Striped Swallow
Grey-rumped Swallow
European Sand Martin
African Sand Martin
Banded Martin
African Rock Martin
European House Martin Uncommon migrant
Black Rough-wing Swallow
White-headed Rough-wing Swallow
Black Cuckoo Shrike
Grey Cuckoo Shrike
Drongo
Grey-crested Helmet Shrike Uncommon
White-crowned Shrike
Northern Brubru
Grey-backed Fiscal
Lesser Grey Shrike Spring passage migrant
Fiscal Shrike
Red-backed Shrike
Red-tailed Shrike
Slate-coloured Boubou
Tropical Boubou
Black-backed Puff-back
Puff-back Shrike
Black-headed Tchagra
Brown-headed Tchagra
Sulphur-breasted Bush Shrike
Grey-headed Bush Shrike
White-breasted Tit
Red-throated Tit
Mouse-coloured Penduline Tit
European Golden Oriole
African Golden Oriole
Black-headed Oriole
Pied Crow
Cape Rook
White-naped Raven
Wattled Starling
Violet-backed Starling
Blue-eared Glossy Starling
Red-wing Starling
Superb Starling
Red-billed Oxpecker
Yellow White-eye
Malachite Sunbird Uncommon visitor
Bronzy Sunbird
Beautiful Sunbird Uncommon visitor
Golden-winged Sunbird
Mariqua Sunbird
Variable Sunbird
Amethyst Sunbird
Scarlet-chested Sunbird
Collared Sunbird
Spotted Creeper Rare
Buffalo Weaver
White-browed Sparrow Weaver
Rufous Sparrow
Grey-headed Sparrow
Parrot-billed Sparrow
Chestnut Sparrow
Speckle-fronted Weaver
Speke's Weaver
Masked Weaver
Viteline Masked Weaver
Chestnut Weaver
Spectacled Weaver
Holub's Golden Weaver
Reichenow's Weaver
Red-billed Quelea
Cardinal Quelea
Yellow Bishop
White-winged Widow-bird
Red-naped Widow-bird
Jackson's Widow-bird
Bronze Mannikin
Rufous-backed Mannikin Uncommon
Silverbill
Grey-headed Silverbill
Cut-throat
Quail Finch
Green-winged Pytilia
African Fire Finch
Red-billed Fire Finch
Yellow-bellied Waxbill
Waxbill
Crimson-rumped Waxbill
Black-cheeked Waxbill
Red-cheeked Cordon-bleu
Purple Grenadier
Indigo-bird
Pin-tailed Whydah
Paradise Whydah Uncommon
Yellow-fronted Canary
Brimstone Canary
Yellow-rumped Seed-eater
Streaky Seed-eater
African Citril
Golden-breasted Bunting
Cinnamon-breasted Rock Bunting

OL DOINYO SABUK NATIONAL PARK

Ol Doinyo Sabuk mountain rises a few miles to the south-east of Thika township, 77km (48 miles) north of Nairobi. This is a recently developed National Park, although gazetted in 1967. It comprises the forested slopes and ravines and the summit of the mountain which rises to a little over

2,134m (7,000ft). Its principal attraction is the scenic views to be had from its open top on a clear day.

Big game is not plentiful, Buffalo and Bushbuck being the main species. Black Rhinoceros and Leopard occurred in the forest until recent years and may still exist. Sykes' Monkeys and Black-faced Vervets are common.

Access is from Thika via Doinyo market which is some three miles from the entrance gate. The track through the forest is rough and steep and a powerful car or a four-wheel-drive vehicle is necessary to reach the top, especially after rain.

Forest birds are common and species such as Ayres' Hawk Eagle, Great Sparrow Hawk, African Goshawk, Olive Pigeon, Lemon Dove, Emerald Cuckoo, Hartlaub's Turaco, Cinnamon-chested Bee-eater, Narina's Trogon, White-eyed Slaty Flycatcher, Black-throated Apalis, Ruppell's Robin Chat, White-starred Bush Robin, Grey Cuckoo Shrike, Malachite Sunbird, Bronzy Sunbird, Golden-winged Sunbird, Variable Sunbird, Eastern Double-collared Sunbird, Amethyst Sunbird, Collared Sunbird, Brown-capped Weaver, Abyssinian Crimsonwing and Thick-billed Seed-eater may be seen.

At certain times of the year, usually after the start of the rains, butterflies are noticeably abundant, including species of Swallowtails and Charaxes. The relatively rare *Charaxes nandina* is sometimes common on Ol Doinyo Sabuk.

SAIWA SWAMP NATIONAL PARK

This is one of the smallest National Parks in Kenya, covering an area of only 15.5sq km (6sq miles). It lies 22km (14 miles) east of Kitale on a well signposted road. The Park was created specially to protect a small population of the semi-aquatic Sitatunga antelope and encloses the swamp fed by the Saiwa River together with its fringing belts of rain forest.

The Sitatunga living in this swamp number approximately 40 animals. They may be viewed and photographed from several tree hides which have been constructed along the western margin.

Besides the Sitatunga other mammals of note include the white-bearded, gnome-like Brazza Monkey, the nocturnal Potto, Spotted-necked Otter and the Giant Forest Squirrel. Leopards have been recorded but are probably spasmodic visitors.

Birds are abundant and specially noticeable. Among the Turacos are Eastern Grey Plaintain-eater, Bare-faced Go-away-bird, Great Blue Turaco and Ross' Turaco. Narina's Trogon is not uncommon within the forest, and Double-toothed, Grey-headed and Black-billed Barbets are frequent along the forest margins. Hartlaub's Marsh Widow-bird and Yellow-billed Shrike occur in marshy grassland and bush near the forest. Other special birds include the following:

African Marsh Harrier
Harrier Hawk
Banded Harrier Eagle
Great Sparrow Hawk
Ovampo Sparrow Hawk
Lizard Buzzard
Crowned Eagle
Fish Eagle
Bat Hawk
Grey Kestrel
Red-wing Francolin
Harlequin Quail
Crowned Crane
Kaffir Rail
Green Sandpiper
Olive Pigeon
Tambourine Dove
Blue-spotted Wood Dove
Green Pigeon
Brown Parrot
African Cuckoo
Emerald Cuckoo
Green Coucal
Black Coucal
Blue-headed Coucal
Cape Grass Owl
African Marsh Owl
White-tailed Nightjar
Giant Kingfisher
Pied Kingfisher
Malachite Kingfisher
Woodland Kingfisher
Striped Kingfisher
Grey-headed Kingfisher
Little Bee-eater
Cinnamon-chested Bee-eater
Broad-billed Roller
Crowned Hornbill
Black and White-casqued Hornbill
Ground Hornbill
Lesser Honeyguide
Cassin's Honeyguide
Cardinal Woodpecker
Brown-backed Woodpecker
Rufous-chested Swallow
Mosque Swallow
Red-rumped Swallow
Joyful Greenbul
Bristle-bill
Luhder's Bush Shrike
Grey-headed Bush Shrike
Sulphur-breasted Bush Shrike
Sooty Chat
Blue-shouldered Robin Chat
Snowy-headed Robin Chat
African Thrush
Abyssinian Hill Babbler
Fan-tailed Warbler
Little Rush Warbler
Grey-capped Warbler
Black Flycatcher
Silverbird
Blue Flycatcher
Paradise Flycatcher
African Penduline Tit
Spotted Creeper
Green-headed Sunbird
Scarlet-chested Sunbird
Olive-bellied Sunbird
Mariqua Sunbird
Coppery Sunbird
Grey-headed Negro-finch
Yellow-bellied Waxbill
Black-crowned Waxbill
African Firefinch
Red-billed Firefinch
Black and White Mannikin
Grosbeak Weaver
Holub's Golden Weaver
Black-headed Weaver
Vieillot's Black Weaver
Dark-backed Weaver
Spectacled Weaver
Black-necked Weaver
Brown-capped Weaver
Fan-tailed Widow-bird
Yellow Bishop
Black-winged Bishop
Yellow-shouldered Widow-bird
Splendid Glossy Starling
Lesser Blue-eared Glossy Starling

TSAVO NATIONAL PARK

The Tsavo National Park, a vast arid region of 20,807sq km (8,034sq miles), is Kenya's largest wildlife stronghold. The Park comprises a diversity of habitats, open plains alternating with savannah bush and semi-desert scrub; acacia woodlands; rocky ridges and outcrops, and more extensive ranges and isolated hills; belts of riverine vegetation; palm thickets; and on the Chyulu Hills extension area, mountain forest. A section of Lake Jipe is included in the extreme south-west of the Park, an extremely rich bird locality where Pygmy Geese and Black Heron are common.

The Park, which lies roughly half-way between the coast and Nairobi, is bisected by the main Nairobi-Mombasa road and railway. This is designated as the Tsavo Road and Railway National Reserve. That portion lying north and east of the road is designated Tsavo Park East; that to the south and west, Tsavo Park West. The Park is watered by two permanent rivers, the Tsavo River which flows through Tsavo Park West and the Athi River which crosses a corner of Tsavo Park East. The two unite above Lugard Falls to become the Galana River. The Voi River, to the south, is not permanent.

Mainly on account of the difficult waterless nature of much of the terrain,

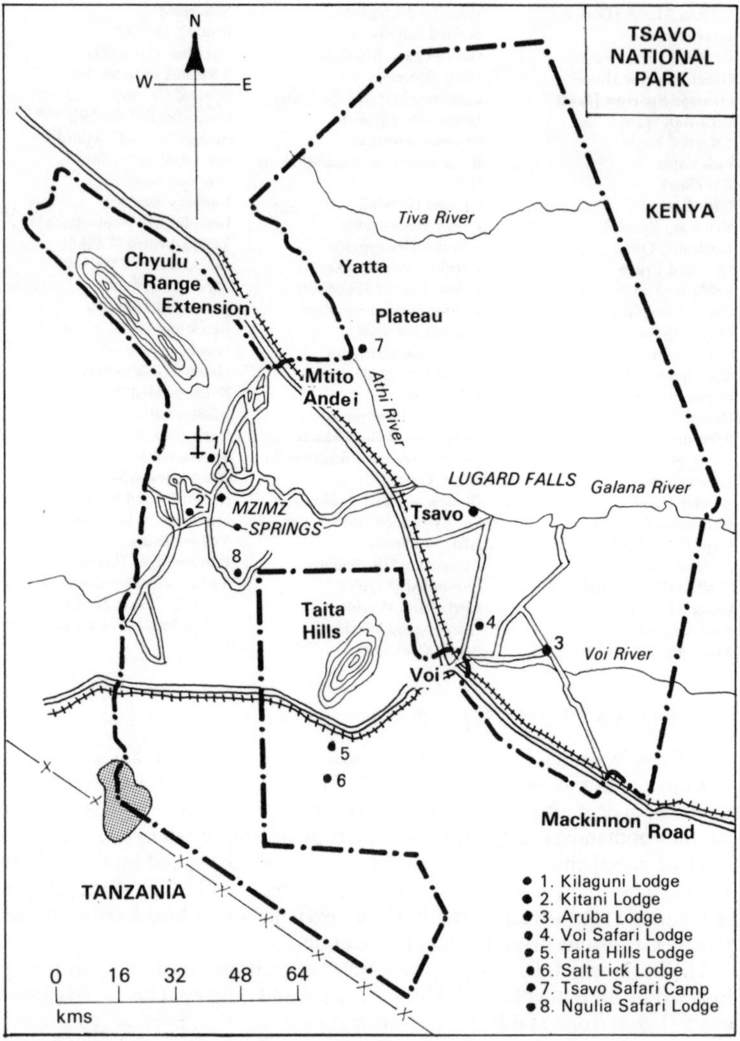

parts of the Park have not yet been developed for visitors. These include the uninhabited scrub desert north of the Galana River.

Most of the Park is made up of basement gneisses and schists, but part of the western sector is of recent volcanic origin, including the Chyulu Hills extension. Here may be seen many lava flows and cones, such as Shitani, near Kilaguni Lodge, which is a perfect example of a recent volcano. This volcanic zone also contains the famous Mzima Springs, where some 50 million gallons of sparkling crystal-clear water gush out daily from below a lava ridge. Hippopotamus and shoals of Barbel live in the springs and provide a dramatic spectacle. The water is so clear that every action of these huge aquatic beasts under the water, and of their attendant piscine scavengers, may be watched from the lookouts or through the plate-glass windows of the submerged observation chamber.

Downstream from the springs is a dense and luxuriant stand of wild date palms and Raphia palms, the latter with immense fronds of up to 9m (30ft) long. It is not unusual to spot the rare and elusive African Finfoot swimming between the fronds where these touch the water.

One of the other great spectacles of Tsavo Park, perhaps its greatest, is Mudanda Rock between Voi and Manyani. This 1½km-long outcrop is a water catchment area which supplies a natural dam at its base. In the dry season hundreds of elephants come to drink and bathe. From a safe vantage point just above the water visitors may have the luck to sit and watch the activities of the great beasts below them. A similar elephant spectacle may also be observed at Aruba Dam.

The Lugard Falls on the Galana River, 40km (25 miles) from Voi, are remarkable for the fantastic shapes of the water-worn rocks. The river disappears into a rocky gorge so narrow in one part that it is possible to stand astride the cleft with the Falls immediately below.

At present there is a network of over 800km (500 miles) of roadways in the Tsavo Park, passing through much of the best game viewing areas and following the rivers where there is the greatest concentration of game during the dry season. Specially rewarding circuits are those along the Galana River from Lugard Falls to Sobo, southwards to Aruba and then north-west to Mudanda Rock; and from Kilaguni Lodge to Tsavo Gate, along a stretch of the Tsavo River.

Elephants in large herds are the number one attraction at Tsavo. For those who like to indulge in game watching without effort, what could be pleasanter than to recline in a comfortable chair on the veranda of Kilaguni Lodge, a cold drink at hand, and watch the elephants take their refreshment from the waterhole 90m (100yd) or so away.

Tsavo is also a good place to see one of our most beautiful antelopes, the Lesser Kudu with spiral horns and white striped coat. Whilst you may come across these graceful animals almost anywhere, the dry bush along the Galana River is their favourite haunt. Other animals likely to be encountered are Buffalo, Common Waterbuck, Eland, Gerenuk, Fringe-eared Oryx, Impala and Masai Giraffe. Black Rhinoceros, once numerous, are now less frequently seen.

Birdlife is legion in the Park and the visitor is constantly meeting with new species. One of the most conspicuous is the White-headed Buffalo Weaver, brownish-black and white with a startling vivid red rump when it flies. Starlings are numerous, including the brilliantly plumaged Golden-breasted Starling and the rare but duller Fischer's Starling. Hornbills are another prevalent group of birds, eight species occur in the Park. Birds of prey, Bustards, Sunbirds and Weaver-birds are other families well represented. Hole-nesting birds – Starlings, Parrots, Barbets and Rollers – are often associated with the thick-trunked Baobab trees which are such a feature of the landscape.

Accommodation in the Tsavo National Park includes Kilaguni Lodge, 35km (22 miles) from Mtito Andei, with full catering facilities and amenities. Some 32km (20 miles) from Kilaguni, at the end of the Ngulia Valley is the Ngulia Safari Lodge, also with all facilities. Nearby mist-netting is used to catch palearctic migrant birds for ringing. Just outside the southern boundary of the Park, south of the Taita Hills, are the Taita Hills Lodge and the nearby Salt Lick Lodge from which one can sometimes watch an elephant display at the water-holes there. One of Africa's rarest birds, the Taita Falcon, sometimes visits these water-holes whilst hunting its avian prey.

Voi Safari Lodge, sited on top of one of the hills near the main entrance gate to Tsavo East at Voi, also offers full amenities. Further west there is a luxury camp operated by Tsavo Safaris on the Athi River, with an access road from Mtito Andei.

Self-service accommodation is available at Kitani Lodge, Ngulia Self-service Bandas and Murka Lodge in Tsavo West, and at Aruba Lodge in Tsavo East, 35km (22 miles) from Voi. There are Bandas and a camp site with water at Lake Jipe, where a boat is also available. In addition there are camp sites with showers, toilets and drinking water at Tsavo East and West, Mtito Andei Gate, Chyulu Gate, Voi Gate and Buchumu Gate. They are sometimes used by film companies and booking is recommended. Outside the Park accommodation is available at hotels at Mtito Andei and at Voi. Main roads connect Tsavo National Park with Nairobi and Mombasa, and for those who travel by air there are landing fields at Kilaguni Lodge, Aruba and elsewhere.

MAMMALS OF TSAVO NATIONAL PARK

Spectacled Elephant Shrew
East African Hedgehog
Giant White-toothed Shrew
Rousette Fruit Bat
Epauletted Fruit Bat
Pale-bellied Fruit Bat
White-bellied Tomb Bat
Hollow-faced Bat
False Vampire Bat
Yellow-winged Bat
Lander's Horseshoe Bat
Lesser Leaf-nosed Bat
Giant Leaf-nosed Bat Recorded from Galana River
African Trident Bat Recorded from Kilaguni Lodge
Banana Bat or **African Pipistrelle**
Yellow-bellied Bat
Angola Free-tailed Bat
White-bellied Free-tailed Bat
Flat-headed Free-tailed Bat
Greater Galago
Bush Baby
Black-faced Vervet Monkey
Blue or **Sykes' Monkey**
Yellow Baboon
Lesser Ground Pangolin
Hunting Dog
Golden Jackal
Black-backed or **Silver-backed Jackal**
Side-striped Jackal
Bat-eared Fox
Zorilla
Ratel or **Honey Badger**
Clawless Otter
African Civet

Neumann's or **Small-spotted Genet**
Bush or **Large-spotted Genet**
African Palm Civet
Marsh Mongoose
Dwarf Mongoose
Large Grey Mongoose
Slender or **Black-tipped Mongoose**
White-tailed Mongoose
Banded Mongoose
Aard-wolf
Spotted Hyaena
Striped Hyaena
Cheetah
Caracal
African Wild Cat
Serval
Lion
Leopard
Ant Bear
Tree Hyrax
Rock Hyrax
African Elephant
Black Rhinoceros
Grevy's Zebra Reputed to occur in extreme north of Park
Burchell's or **Common Zebra**
Warthog
Masai Giraffe
Coke's Hartebeest or **Kongoni**
Hunter's Hartebeest or **Hirola** Introduced into Park, present status not known
Red Duiker
Blue Duiker
Bush Duiker
Klipspringer
Suni
Steinbok
Kirk's Dik-dik
Common Waterbuck
Bohor Reedbuck
Impala
Grant's Gazelle
Gerenuk
Fringe-eared Oryx
Bushbuck
Lesser Kudu
Eland
African Buffalo
African Hare
Cane Rat
Porcupine
Striped Ground Squirrel
Unstriped Ground Squirrel
Bush Squirrel
East African Red Squirrel
Spring Hare
African Dormouse
Giant Rat
Kenya Mole Rat
Naked Mole Rat

BIRDS OF TSAVO NATIONAL PARK

Masai Ostrich Occurs mainly south of the Galana River
Somali Ostrich Occurs mainly north of the Galana River
Little Grebe Recorded from Aruba and Tsavo River
Long-tailed Cormorant
African Darter
White Pelican
Pink-backed Pelican Pelicans occur from time to time on larger dams
Grey Heron
Black-headed Heron
Goliath Heron
Purple Heron Recorded from Tsavo River
Great White Egret
Yellow-billed Egret
Black Heron Lake Jipe
Little Egret
Buff-backed Heron or **Cattle Egret**
Squacco Heron
Madagascar Squacco Heron Recorded from Mzima Springs
Green-backed Heron Occurs on rivers
Night Heron
White-backed Night Heron Probably occurs Lake Jipe on southern border
Little Bittern
Dwarf Bittern
Hamerkop
White Stork
European Black Stork Rare winter visitor
Woolly-necked Stork
Abdim's Stork
Open-bill Stork
Saddle-bill Stork
Marabou Stork
Wood Ibis or **Yellow-billed Stork**
Sacred Ibis
Hadada Ibis
Glossy Ibis Rare visitor
African Spoonbill Uncommon visitor to dams
European Shoveler
Yellow-billed Duck
African Black Duck Recorded from Tsavo and Athi Rivers
Garganey Teal
Hottentot Teal
Red-billed Duck
European Pintail
White-faced Tree Duck
Fulvous Tree Duck
Pygmy Goose Lake Jipe
Knob-billed Duck
Egyptian Goose
Spur-winged Goose
Secretary Bird
Ruppell's Vulture
White-backed Vulture
Nubian or **Lappet-faced Vulture**
White-headed Vulture
Egyptian Vulture
Hooded Vulture
Peregrine Uncommon
Lanner
Taita Falcon Rare: has been recorded in the Voi area
European Hobby Occurs mainly as spring passage migrant
African Hobby Recorded from near Chyulu Hills
Sooty Falcon Recorded during autumn migration along the Galana River
Eastern Red-footed Falcon Very uncommon: a few to be seen amongst flocks of migrating Lesser Kestrels in spring
Red-necked Falcon Occurs along Tsavo and Galana Rivers
European Kestrel
African Kestrel
Greater or **White-eyed Kestrel**
Lesser Kestrel

Grey Kestrel Uncommon. Occurs along rivers
Pygmy Falcon
Cuckoo Falcon Uncommon. Occurs in forest and well-wooded areas
European Black Kite
African Black Kite
Black-shouldered Kite
Bat Hawk Not uncommon in the Voi area
Honey Buzzard Uncommon winter visitor and passage migrant
Verreaux's Eagle Rare
Steppe Eagle
Tawny Eagle
Wahlberg's Eagle
African Hawk Eagle
Ayres' Hawk Eagle
Booted Eagle Rare winter visitor
Martial Eagle
Crowned Hawk Eagle Occurs in the Chyulu Hills forest
Long-crested Eagle
Lizard Buzzard
Brown Harrier Eagle
Black-chested Harrier Eagle
Lesser Spotted Eagle Rare winter visitor
Grasshopper Buzzard Common visitor between November and March
Bateleur
African Fish Eagle
Palm-nut Vulture
Lammergeyer Rare visitor
Steppe Buzzard Winter visitor in varying numbers
Augur Buzzard Occurs in Chyulu Hills
Little Sparrow Hawk
Ovampo Sparrow Hawk Uncommon. Usually found in vicinity of baobab trees
Great Sparrow Hawk
Shikra
African Goshawk
Gabar Goshawk
Pale Chanting Goshawk
Montagu's Harrier
Pallid Harrier
European Marsh Harrier
African Marsh Harrier Rare
Harrier Hawk
Osprey Rare visitor
Coqui Francolin
Crested Francolin
Shelley's (Greywing) Francolin
Scaly Francolin Occurs on Chyulu Hills
Yellow-necked Spurfowl
Cape Quail
Harlequin Quail
Stone Partridge Reputed to occur on rocky hills north of the Galana River, but not confirmed
Helmeted Guinea-fowl
Kenya Crested Guinea-fowl
Vulturine Guinea-fowl
Kaffir Rail Rarely seen
European Corn Crake Passage migrant, seldom seen
Black Crake
Moorhen
Red-knobbed Coot Uncommon
African Finfoot
Crowned Crane
Kori Bustard
Jackson's Bustard Rare
White-bellied Bustard
Buff-crested Bustard
Black-bellied Bustard
Hartlaub's Bustard
Spotted Stone Curlew
Water Dikkop
African Jacana
Ringed Plover
Little Ringed Plover
Kittlitz's Plover
Three-banded Plover
Caspian Plover Winter visitor. Frequents open plains
Crowned Plover
Senegal Plover
Blacksmith Plover
Blackhead Plover
Avocet
Black-winged Stilt
Painted Snipe
European Common Snipe
Great Snipe
African Snipe
Curlew Sandpiper
Little Stint
Ruff
Common Sandpiper
Green Sandpiper
Wood Sandpiper
Marsh Sandpiper
Greenshank
Temminck's Courser
Two-banded Courser
Heuglin's Courser
Bronze-winged Courser
Pratincole
Button Quail
Chestnut-bellied Sandgrouse
Black-faced Sandgrouse
Yellow-throated Sandgrouse
Speckled Pigeon
Olive Pigeon
Bronze-naped Pigeon
Red-eyed Dove
Mourning Dove
Ring-necked Dove
Laughing Dove
Namaqua Dove
Tambourine Dove
Emerald-spotted Wood Dove
Green Pigeon
European Cuckoo
African Cuckoo
Red-chested Cuckoo
Black Cuckoo
Great-spotted Cuckoo
Levaillant's Cuckoo
Black and White Cuckoo
Emerald Cuckoo
Didric Cuckoo
Klaas' Cuckoo
White-browed Coucal
Hartlaub's Turaco Occurs in forest on Chyulu Hills
Violet-crested Turaco Rare
White-bellied Go-away-bird
Orange-bellied Parrot
Brown Parrot
European Roller
Lilac-breasted Roller
Rufous-crowned Roller
Broad-billed Roller
Pied Kingfisher
Giant Kingfisher
Half-collared Kingfisher Rare
Malachite Kingfisher
Pygmy Kingfisher
Brown-hooded Kingfisher
Grey-headed Kingfisher
Striped Kingfisher
European Bee-eater
Madagascar Bee-eater
Blue-cheeked Bee-eater
Carmine Bee-eater
White-throated Bee-eater
Little Bee-eater
Trumpeter Hornbill
Silvery-cheeked Hornbill

Grey Hornbill
Red-billed Hornbill
Yellow-billed Hornbill
Von der Decken's Hornbill
Crowned Hornbill
Ground Hornbill
European Hoopoe
Senegal Hoopoe Occurs mainly north of the Galana River
African Hoopoe
Green Wood Hoopoe
Violet Wood Hoopoe Recorded from the Galana River
Scimitar-bill
Abyssinian Scimitar-bill
African Barn Owl
African Marsh Owl
African Wood Owl
African Scops Owl
White-faced Scops Owl
Pearl-spotted Owlet
Barred Owlet
Spotted Eagle Owl
Verreaux's Eagle Owl
Pel's Fishing Owl Not yet recorded but should occur along the Tsavo and Galana Rivers
European Nightjar
Dusky Nightjar
Donaldson-Smith's Nightjar
Nubian Nightjar
Freckled Nightjar
Plain Nightjar
Long-tailed Nightjar
Speckled Mousebird
White-headed Mousebird Uncommon
Blue-naped Mousebird
Narina's Trogon In Chyulu forest and in riverine forest
Black-collared Barbet
Brown-breasted Barbet
Brown-throated Barbet
Spotted-flanked Barbet
Red-fronted Tinkerbird
Golden-rumped Tinkerbird
Red and Yellow Barbet
D'Arnaud's Barbet
Greater Honeyguide
Scaly-throated Honeyguide
Lesser Honeyguide
Wahlberg's Honeyguide
Nubian Woodpecker
Golden-tailed Woodpecker Recorded near Voi
Cardinal Woodpecker
Bearded Woodpecker
Grey Woodpecker
Nyanza Swift
Mottled Swift
Little Swift
White-rumped Swift
Palm Swift
Mottled-throated Spinetail
Boehm's Spinetail Frequents rocky hills near Mtito Andei
Singing Bush Lark
Northern White-tailed Lark
Redwing Bush Lark
Flappet Lark
Fawn-coloured Lark
Pink-breasted Lark
Chestnut-backed Sparrow Lark
Fischer's Sparrow Lark
Red-capped Lark
European White Wagtail Rare visitor
African Pied Wagtail
Wells' Wagtail Uncommon
Blue-headed Wagtail and races
Long-billed Pipit
Richard's Pipit
Tree Pipit
Red-throated Pipit Uncommon spring passage migrant
Striped Pipit Frequents bushy slopes of hills
Golden Pipit
Yellow-throated Longclaw
Pangani Longclaw
Rosy-breasted Longclaw Uncommon. Inhabits open plains
Arrow-marked Babbler
Northern Pied Babbler
Rufous Chatterer
Scaly Chatterer Occurs mainly north of Galana River
Abyssinian Hill Babbler Occurs in Chyulu Hills forest
Yellow-vented Bulbul
Northern Brownbul
Fischer's Greenbul
Yellow-whiskered Greenbul
European Spotted Flycatcher
Dusky Flycatcher
Ashy Flycatcher
Pale Flycatcher
Grey Flycatcher
Little Grey Flycatcher Recorded from north of Galana River
White-eyed Slaty Flycatcher Chyulu Hills
South African Black Flycatcher
Silverbird
Yellow Flycatcher
Chin-spot Flycatcher
Pygmy Puff-back Flycatcher
Black-throated Wattle-eye
Paradise Flycatcher
Olive Thrush
Bare-eyed Thrush
European Rock Thrush
European Common Wheatear
Isabelline Wheatear
Pied Wheatear
Capped Wheatear
Cliff Chat
Anteater Chat Chyulu Hills
Stonechat Chyulu Hills
European Whinchat
White-browed Robin Chat
Red-capped Robin Chat
Robin Chat
Morning Warbler Frequents palm thickets
Spotted Morning Warbler
Red-backed Scrub Robin
White-winged Scrub Robin
Eastern Bearded Scrub Robin
White-throated Robin Rare winter visitor
European Nightingale
Thrush Nightingale or **Sprosser**
European Whitethroat
Garden Warbler
Blackcap Warbler
Barred Warbler Sometimes common on spring migration
Olive-tree Warbler
Great Reed Warbler Uncommon passage migrant
European Marsh Warbler
European Sedge Warbler
Greater Swamp Warbler
European Willow Warbler
Brown Woodland Warbler Occurs in forest on Chyulu Hills
Grey Wren Warbler
Fan-tailed Warbler
Black-breasted Apalis
Red-faced Apalis
Grey-capped Warbler
Buff-bellied Warbler
River Warbler
Crombec
Banded Tit-warbler
Yellow-bellied Eremomela
Grey-backed Camaroptera
Pectoral-patch Cisticola
Rattling Cisticola

Singing Cisticola
Winding Cisticola
Stout Cisticola
Croaking Cisticola
Tiny Cisticola
Ashy Cisticola
Tawny-flanked Prinia
African moustached Warbler
European Swallow
Angola Swallow
Ethiopian Swallow Uncommon
Wire-tailed Swallow
Red-rumped Swallow
Mosque Swallow
Striped Swallow
Grey-rumped Swallow
European Sand Martin
African Sand Martin
Banded Martin
African Rock Martin
Black Rough-wing Swallow
White-headed Rough-wing Swallow
Black Cuckoo Shrike
Grey Cuckoo Shrike Chyulu Hills forest
Drongo
Straight-crested Helmet Shrike
Retz's Red-billed Shrike
White-crowned Shrike
Northern Brubru
Grey-backed Fiscal
Lesser Grey Shrike
Fiscal Shrike
Taita Fiscal
Long-tailed Fiscal
Red-backed Shrike
Red-tailed Shrike
Slate-coloured Boubou
Tropical Boubou
Red-naped Bush Shrike Occurs in dry bush country near Galana River
Black-backed Puff-back
Black-headed Tchagra
Brown-headed Tchagra
Three-streaked Tchagra
Blackcap Bush Tchagra
Sulphur-breasted Bush Shrike
Four-coloured Bush Shrike
Grey-headed Bush Shrike
Rosy-patched Shrike
Nicator Occurs in acacia forest near Voi
Grey Tit
White-breasted Tit
African Penduline Tit
Mouse-coloured Penduline Tit
European Golden Oriole
African Golden Oriole
Black-headed Oriole
Pied Crow
White-naped Raven
Fan-tailed Raven
Wattled Starling
Violet-backed Starling
Abbott's Starling Recorded Chyulu Hills forest
Blue-eared Glossy Starling
Black-breasted Glossy Starling
Ruppell's Long-tailed Starling
Golden-breasted Starling
Red-wing Starling
Fischer's Starling
Hildebrandt's Starling
Shelley's Starling
Superb Starling
Yellow-billed Oxpecker
Red-billed Oxpecker
Yellow White-eye
Bronzy Sunbird
Beautiful Sunbird (black-bellied race)
Smaller Black-bellied Sunbird Inhabits acacia trees near rivers
Little Purple-banded Sunbird
Violet-breasted Sunbird
Mariqua Sunbird
Variable Sunbird
Eastern Double-collared Sunbird Chyulu Hills forest
Amethyst Sunbird
Scarlet-chested Sunbird Chyulu Hills
Hunter's Sunbird
Olive Sunbird
Collared Sunbird
Kenya Violet-backed Sunbird
Buffalo Weaver
White-headed Buffalo Weaver
White-browed Sparrow Weaver
Grey-headed Social Weaver
Black-capped Social Weaver
Rufous Sparrow
Swahili Sparrow
Parrot-billed Sparrow
Chestnut Sparrow
Yellow-spotted Petronia
Speckle-fronted Weaver
Layard's Black-headed Weaver
Masked Weaver
Vitelline Masked Weaver
Chestnut Weaver
Golden Palm Weaver
Black-necked Weaver
Spectacled Weaver
Golden Weaver
Holub's Golden Weaver
Reichenow's Weaver Chyulu Hills
Grosbeak Weaver
Red-headed Weaver
Red-billed Quelea
Red-headed Quelea
Cardinal Quelea
Red Bishop
Zanzibar Red Bishop
Black-winged Bishop
Yellow Bishop
Fire-fronted Bishop
Fan-tailed Widow-bird
White-winged Widow-bird
Red-collared Widow-bird
Bronze Mannikin
Rufous-backed Mannikin
Silverbill
Greyheaded Silverbill
Cut-throat
Quail Finch
Parasitic Weaver
Peters' Twin-spot Occurs in dense cover: easily overlooked
Green-winged Pytilia
African Fire Finch
Jameson's Fire Finch
Red-billed Fire Finch
Yellow-bellied Waxbill
Waxbill
Black-cheeked Waxbill
Red-cheeked Cordon-bleu
Blue-capped Cordon-bleu
Purple Grenadier
Indigo-bird
Pin-tailed Whydah
Steel-blue Whydah
Fischer's Straw-tailed Whydah
Paradise Whydah
Yellow-fronted Canary
White-bellied Canary
Brimstone Canary
Kenya Grosbeak Canary
Yellow-rumped Seed-eater
Streaky Seed-eater
Golden-breasted Bunting
Somali Golden-breated Bunting
Cinnamon-breasted Rock Bunting

SIBILOI NATIONAL PARK

Although designated as a National Park, Sibiloi at present does not have facilities for visiting tourists as exist in other National Parks in Kenya. Visitors must be prepared to camp and to be entirely self-sufficient. The Park covers an area of approximately 2,486sq km (960sq miles) situated along the north-eastern shores of Lake Turkana (Rudolf) and is adjacent to the Ethiopian frontier. The terrain is lake shore, dry semi-desert bush and near desert country. The Park is specially important as the site of fossil remains of early man and associated fauna. Many important discoveries in this field have been made in recent years by Mr Richard Leakey, Director of Kenya's National Museum.

A comprehensive faunal survey of the Park has yet to be undertaken, but preliminary reports suggest that the birdlife especially is of great interest. Large mammals include Tiang (Topi), Common Zebra, Reticulated Giraffe, Grant's Gazelle, Lion and Cheetah. Golden Jackals also occur near Alia Bay. Access is usually by air although Sibiloi can be reached through North Horr from Marsabit and there is a very rough track skirting the eastern shores of Lake Turkana northwards from Loiyangalani, passable only by four-wheel-drive vehicles. Adequate stocks of fuel and water must be carried. The Park is waterless, apart from the alkaline waters of the Lake, and it is essential to be self-contained in water if travelling overland. Deaths have occurred in this area due to lack of adequate supplies of water. Enquiries and applications for permission to visit Sibiloi should be addressed to the Warden, Sibiloi National Park, P.O. Box 162, Nanyuki, Kenya.

National Parks of Historical and Archaeological Interest

GEDI NATIONAL PARK

The Gedi National Park, situated on the Kenya coast 19km (12 miles) south of Malindi, is a ruined city of Islamic origin dating from the thirteenth century. The Great Mosque, portions of the palace and other dwellings have been partly restored, and deep wells cleared of vegetation which formerly choked them. An information centre displays some of the more spectacular finds which have been made and sets out what is known of the city's history.

The Gedi ruins are set in the midst of tall coastal forest and have much of interest to the naturalist, especially the colony of the uncommon Mottled-throated Spinetail, a swift which nests in the disused wells. The following interesting mammals and birds may be seen.

MAMMALS OF GEDI NATIONAL PARK

Yellow-rumped Elephant Shrew
Epauletted Fruit Bat
False Vampire Bat
Greater Galago
Bush Baby
Sykes' Monkey
Black-faced Vervet Monkey
Yellow Baboon
Black and White Colobus
Dwarf Mongoose
Red Duiker
Blue Duiker
Zanzibar Duiker
Suni
Bush Squirrel

BIRDS OF GEDI NATIONAL PARK

Cuckoo Falcon
Crowned Hawk Eagle
Southern Banded Harrier Eagle
Little Sparrow Hawk
Kenya Crested Guinea-fowl
Green Pigeon
Fischer's Turaco
Brown-headed Parrot
Trumpeter Hornbill
Silvery-cheeked Hornbill
Crowned Hornbill
Narina's Trogon
Mottled-throated Spinetail
Boehm's Spinetail
African Pitta
Scaly Babbler
East Coast Akalat
Eastern Bearded Scrub Robin
Retz's Red-billed Shrike
Chestnut-fronted Shrike
Zanzibar Puff-back Shrike
Nicator
Black-breasted Glossy Starling
Mouse-coloured Sunbird
Plain-backed Sunbird
Dark-backed Weaver
Peters' Twin-spot
Spotted Ground Thrush

FORT JESUS NATIONAL PARK

Fort Jesus, a seventeenth century Portuguese fort overlooking the Indian Ocean at Mombasa, was designated a National Park in 1958. Much reconstruction work has been carried out and a historical museum established, in which displays illustrate the culture of the coast from the thirteenth to the nineteenth century.

Two birds of special note may be seen at the Fort. During the day the Indian House Crow is common and at dusk the Bat Hawk is often observed.

OLORGESAILIE NATIONAL PARK

Olorgesailie National Park is a 21-hectare (52-acre) prehistoric living site of hand-axe man, 67km (42 miles) from Nairobi on the Nairobi-Magadi road. It has been developed as a field museum with hand axes and other tools preserved *in situ*, together with fossils of associated extinct mammals.

The site was developed during the early 1940s by the famous Kenya prehistorian Dr L. S. B. Leakey and Mrs Leakey. Later excavations in 1962–63 have revealed parts of a number of camps and living floors at different levels, and these are now exhibited exactly as they were uncovered. Olorgesailie has been acclaimed as one of the most important sites of this period of culture in the world.

In addition to its archaeological importance, Olorgesailie and the country surrounding the site is of great zoological interest. The following notable mammals and birds occur there.

MAMMALS OF OLORGESAILIE NATIONAL PARK

Spectacled Elephant Shrew
Olive Baboon
Ratel or **Honey Badger**
African Civet
Neumann's or **Small-spotted**
Genet
Aard-wolf
Striped Hyaena
Caracal
Lion
Leopard
Black Rhinoceros
Klipspringer

BIRDS OF OLORGESAILIE NATIONAL PARK

Lanner
African Hawk Eagle
Martial Eagle
Gabar Goshawk
Pale Chanting Goshawk
Buff-crested Bustard
Two-banded Courser
Heuglin's Courser
Button Quail
Black-faced Sandgrouse
White-throated Bee-eater
Wahlberg's Honeyguide
Beautiful Sunbird (Black-bellied race)
Steel-blue Whydah
Fischer's Straw-tailed Whydah
Paradise Whydah

Marine National Parks

Kenya possesses three Marine National Parks, two sited on the north coast at Watamu and Malindi, 112 and 128km (70 and 80 miles) north of Mombasa. Their combined area is 19sq km (7½sq miles). On the Kenya south coast is the slightly smaller Kisite-Mpunguti Marine National Park situated off Wasin Island, Shimoni near the Tanzania border and 83km (52 miles) south of Mombasa.

The best time to visit the Marine National Parks is during the dry seasons, January-March and June-October – if the weather is 'normal'. During the rains silt is brought down by the Sabaki River north of Malindi which affects visibility over the reefs in the northern Reserves. In the southern Marine Park the water becomes too rough for snorkeling during the rains. It should be pointed out that although snorkeling is permitted in the Marine Parks it is an offence to disturb the marine life in any way or to collect sea shells. At low water 80–100 species of fish can be seen around every distinct reef or sandbank.

Outside the Marine National Parks is a buffer zone designated as Marine National Reserve. This extends along the coast from a point just south of Malindi town to a point just south of the entrance to Mida Creek. A 30-metre (100-foot) wide strip above high water mark is included in the Reserve which extends seawards to the three-mile (4.5km) territorial limit. The area covered is 214sq km (82½sq miles).

MALINDI AND WATAMU MARINE NATIONAL PARKS

It is convenient to treat both these Parks as one unit as they are incorporated in the same Marine National Reserve. A visit in a glass-bottomed boat over the coral gardens, as they are called, is a highlight of any holiday visit to Kenya. The best time to make the trip is at low tide when visibility is at its best. To float slowly over the coral beds is an unforgettable experience, with its ever changing panorama of strange branched corals, brilliantly coloured marine fishes, often of bizarre shapes, spiny sea urchins, brightly hued sea slugs (nudibranchs), crabs and star-fish. If you decide to snorkel you will find this is even more thrilling than watching through a glass-bottomed boat.

Whale Island, off the entrance to Mida Creek, is the nesting ground of Roseate and some Bridled Terns from June to September, when they should not be disturbed. Razor sharp rocks and rough seas help protect them from visitors. Shore birds are common along the beaches, especially Sanderlings, Curlew Sandpipers, Little Stints, Whimbrel and Greenshanks and three species of Plovers, Grey, Great Sand and Mongolian Sand. In late April, just before they migrate, birds in full breeding plumage may be observed.

Terns and gulls which are often common non-breeding visitors include Swift, Lesser Crested and Saunders' Little Terns and the Sooty or Hemprich's Gull.

KISITE MPUNGUTI MARINE NATIONAL PARK

Three islands lie within the boundaries of this Marine National Park, one of which, Kisite Island, is or was the breeding ground of colonies of Roseate and Sooty Terns. Before the Park was established these colonies were raided frequently so that in recent years relatively few birds have appeared during May to September. It is hoped that with protection the colonies will eventually build up to their original size.

Access to this Marine National Park is in boats which can be hired from the nearby Pemba Channel Fishing Club. The coral gardens surrounding Kisite Island afford the best snorkeling.

National Reserves

MARSABIT NATIONAL RESERVE

Marsabit National Reserve, an area of some 2,070sq km (800sq miles) in Kenya's Northern Region, consists of a forested mountain which rises like an oasis in the midst of a desert wilderness, a spectacular group of volcanic craters of which Gof Bongoli is the largest and most dramatic, foothills of rugged grandeur and black lava desert which boasts an impressive list of rare and little-known birds.

Apart from the fascination of visiting a wild and remote region which is still 'off the map' to most visitors, the great attractions at Marsabit are its Elephants and its Greater Kudu. This Reserve is one of the very few places

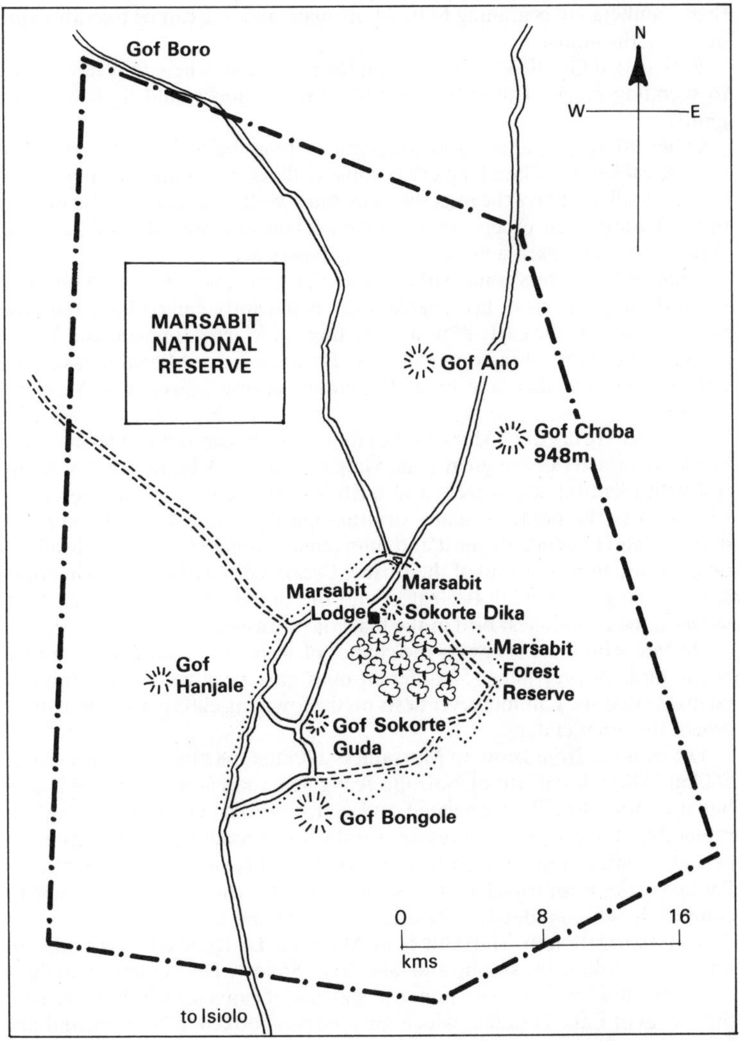

where there is still a possibility of seeing elephant with tusks of 45kg (100lb) and over though they keep mainly to the forest and are difficult to locate. Prior to 1960 Greater Kudu also were abundant on Marsabit, but in that year they were greatly reduced by an outbreak of rinderpest. Now, however, their numbers are beginning to build up again and one can be tolerably sure of seeing the animals.

Reticulated Giraffe are common on the mountain, where they have taken to spending much of their time in the forest – a most unlikely habitat for giraffe.

Other interesting animals at Marsabit include the Striped Hyaena – the maniac cackle of its laughing cry is spine-chilling if you are under canvas – and its smaller relative the insectivorous Aard-wolf. The Caracal also occurs, but is seldom seen except on a nocturnal trip into the edge of the Dida Galgalla desert – itself a most rewarding experience.

Some of the craters come within the forest zone, and one, which fills with water during seasons of favourable rains, is the aptly named Lake Paradise made famous by the early films and writings of Martin Johnson and Vivien de Wattville. Most of the water-birds so far recorded at Marsabit have been observed around this lake or at the crater swamp adjacent to Marsabit Lodge.

Immediately north of Marsabit lies that most inhospitable of terrains, the black lava wastes of the great Dida Galgalla desert. A buffer zone of sandy soil with plentiful acacia trees and bush lies between it and the mountain. This area is the home of many ornithological rarities, from the majestic black-faced Heuglin's Bustard and immaculate Somali Ostrich to Swallow-tailed Kites, most graceful of their tribe, Cream-coloured Coursers in abundance, pale green Somali Bee-eaters and the supposedly rare Masked Lark which is the commonest bird in the black lava wastes.

On Marsabit there is always the chance of seeing something really special in the birds of prey line – 52 different ones have been recorded – and it is probable that the Lammergeyer nests on the towering cliffs of Gof Bongoli or one of the other craters.

The distance from Isiolo to Marsabit is 270km (168 miles), in other words 560km (348 miles) north of Nairobi. A big new road now reaches Marsabit but it is often heavily corrugated and a strong four-wheel drive vehicle is preferable, and even more necessary for the forest roads off the main road. A permit to enter the area must be obtained from Provincial Headquarters at Isiolo; parties must travel in at least two suitable vehicles, and they must be completely self-contained as regards fuel, water and food.

Accommodation at Marsabit is at Marsabit Lodge sited at the edge of forest overlooking the swamp and lake in the Sokorte Dika crater. Also there are camp sites for those who prefer to stay under canvas, including one near the shores of Lake Paradise, which must be pre-booked in Nairobi, and one just outside the town which requires no booking.

MAMMALS OF MARSABIT NATIONAL RESERVE

Spectacled Elephant Shrew In dry scrub at lower altitudes
East African Hedgehog
Rousette Fruit Bat
Epauletted Fruit Bat
Pale-bellied Fruit Bat
White-bellied Tomb Bat
Hollow-faced Bat
False Vampire Bat

Yellow-winged Bat In acacia thickets
Lander's Horseshoe Bat
Lesser Leaf-nosed Bat
Banana Bat or **African Pipistrelle**
Yellow-bellied Bat
Angola Free-tailed Bat
White-bellied Free-tailed Bat
Black-faced Vervet Monkey
Blue or **Sykes' Monkey**
Patas Monkey Reputed to occur but not confirmed
Olive Baboon
Black and White Colobus Reputed to occur, but no recent records
Lesser Ground Pangolin
Hunting Dog
Golden Jackal
Black-backed or **Silver-backed Jackal**
Side-striped Jackal
Bat-eared Fox
Zorilla
Ratel or **Honey Badger**
African Civet
Neumann's or **Small-spotted Genet**
Bush or **Large-spotted Genet**
Dwarf Mongoose
Large Grey Mongoose
Slender or **Black-tipped Mongoose**
White-tailed Mongoose
Banded Mongoose
Aard-wolf
Spotted Hyaena
Striped Hyaena
Cheetah Uncommon
Caracal
African Wild Cat
Serval
Lion
Leopard
Ant Bear
African Elephant
Black Rhinoceros
Grevy's Zebra
Warthog
Reticulated Giraffe
Bush Duiker
Klipspringer
Suni
Guenther's Dik-Dik
Grant's Gazelle The race *petersi* in which fawn body colour extends to root of tail; horns almost parallel
Gerenuk
Beisa Oryx
Bushbuck
Greater Kudu
Lesser Kudu
African Buffalo
African Hare
Porcupine
Striped Ground Squirrel
Unstriped Ground Squirrel
Bush Squirrel
East African Red Squirrel Reputed to occur but not confirmed
Spring Hare reputed to occur but not confirmed
African Dormouse
Giant Rat
Kenya Mole Rat A mole rat of unknown species occurs on Marsabit
Naked Mole Rat

BIRDS OF MARSABIT NATIONAL RESERVE

Somali Ostrich
Little Grebe Recorded on Lake Paradise
Purple Heron Recorded on Lake Paradise
Buff-backed Heron or **Cattle Egret**
Squacco Heron
White Stork
European Black Stork
Abdim's Stork
Saddle-bill Stork Rare
Marabou Stork
Wood Ibis or **Yellow-billed Stork**
Sacred Ibis
Hadada Ibis
Maccoa Duck
African Pochard Spasmodic visitor
European Shoveler
Yellow-billed Duck
Garganey Teal
Hottentot Teal
Red-billed Duck
European Pintail
Fulvous Tree Duck
Knob-billed Duck
Egyptian Goose
Spur-wing Goose The numbers of water birds at Marsabit depend on the water level in Lake Paradise: during the occasional years of heavy rains wild-fowl occur commonly
Secretary Bird Rare
Ruppell's Vulture
White-backed Vulture
Nubian or **Lappet-faced Vulture**
White-headed Vulture
Egyptian Vulture
Hooded Vulture
Peregrine
Lanner
European Hobby Spring migrant
Eastern Red-footed Falcon Occurs on spring migration in small numbers. Usually associated with migrating Lesser Kestrels
European Kestrel
African Kestrel Resident in small numbers
Greater or **White-eyed Kestrel**
Fox Kestrel Uncommon visitor
Lesser Kestrel
Pygmy Falcon
Swallow-tailed Kite Spasmodic visitor. Sometimes nests at edge of Dida Galgalla desert north of Marsabit
European Black Kite
African Black Kite
Black-shouldered Kite
Honey Buzzard Uncommon on spring migration
Steppe Eagle
Tawny Eagle The very pale cream-coloured phase occurs
African Hawk Eagle
Booted Eagle Uncommon migrant and winter visitor
Martial Eagle

Crowned Hawk Eagle Reputed to occur but not confirmed
Long-crested Eagle
Lizard Buzzard
Brown Harrier Eagle
Black-chested Harrier Eagle
Spotted Eagle Rare visitor
Lesser Spotted Eagle Rare visitor
Grasshopper Buzzard
Bateleur
Lammergeyer Uncommon, but may breed in the cliffs of Gof Bongoli
Steppe Buzzard
Mountain Buzzard Resident in small numbers
Long-legged Buzzard Rare visitor
Augur Buzzard
Rufous-breasted Sparrow Hawk
Great Sparrow Hawk
Shikra
African Goshawk
Gabar Goshawk
Pale Chanting Goshawk
Montagu's Harrier
Pallid Harrier
European Marsh Harrier
Harrier Hawk
Crested Francolin
Scaly Francolin
Yellow-necked Spurfowl
Harlequin Quail
Stone Partridge
Helmeted Guinea-fowl
Vulturine Guinea-fowl
European Corn Crake Uncommon spring migrant
Crowned Crane
Kori Bustard
Heuglin's Bustard Rare on Marsabit, but common in the Dida Galgalla desert immediately to the north
Buff-crested Bustard
Hartlaub's Bustard
European Stone Curlew Rare winter visitor
Senegal Stone Curlew
Spotted Stone Curlew
Caspian Plover
Crowned Plover
Spurwing Plover Lake Paradise
Blackhead Plover
Black-winged Stilt
Ruff Uncommon visitor to Lake Paradise
Common Sandpiper Lake Paradise
Wood Sandpiper Lake Paradise
Greenshank Uncommon visitor to Lake Paradise
Cream-coloured Courser
Temminck's Courser Much less common than the Cream-coloured Courser
Heuglin's Courser
Bronze-winged Courser
Pratincole Uncommon visitor to Lake Paradise
Button Quail
Chestnut-bellied Sandgrouse
Black-faced Sandgrouse
Lichtenstein's Sandgrouse
Speckled Pigeon
Olive Pigeon
Pink-breasted Dove
Red-eyed Dove
Mourning Dove
Ring-necked Dove
Laughing Dove
Namaqua Dove
Tambourine Dove
Emerald-spotted Wood Dove
Bruce's Green Pigeon
European Cuckoo Spring migrant
African Cuckoo
Red-chested Cuckoo
Black Cuckoo
Great Spotted Cuckoo
Black and White Cuckoo
Emerald Cuckoo
Didric Cuckoo
Klaas' Cuckoo
Blue-headed Coucal
White-browed Coucal
Hartlaub's Turaco
White-bellied Go-away-bird
European Roller
Lilac-breasted Roller
Rufous-crowned Roller
Broad-billed Roller
Pygmy Kingfisher
Grey-headed Kingfisher
Striped Kingfisher
European Bee-eater
Madagascar Bee-eater
Blue-cheeked Bee-eater
Carmine Bee-eater Spasmodic visitor, sometimes common
White-throated Bee-eater
Little Bee-eater
Cinnamon-chested Bee-eater
Somali Bee-eater Common in the Dida Galgalla desert north of Marsabit
Grey Hornbill
Red-billed Hornbill
Yellow-billed Hornbill Uncommon
Von der Decken's Hornbill
Crowned Hornbill
Abyssinian Ground Hornbill
European Hoopoe
Senegal Hoopoe
Green Wood Hoopoe
Abyssinian Scimitar-bill
African Barn Owl
African Scops Owl
White-faced Scops Owl
Pearl-spotted Owlet
Barred Owlet
Spotted Eagle Owl
Verreaux's Eagle Owl
European Nightjar
Dusky Nightjar
Donaldson-Smith's Nightjar
Nubian Nightjar
Freckled Nightjar Associated with rocky outcrops
Star-spotted Nightjar This little-known species is common on Marsabit
Plain Nightjar
Abyssinian Nightjar
Standard-wing Nightjar Uncommon visitor. A few may breed
Pennant-wing Nightjar One record
Long-tailed Nightjar
Speckled Mousebird
Blue-naped Mousebird
Narina's Trogon Resident in small numbers
Brown-throated Barbet
Red-fronted Barbet
Red-fronted Tinkerbird
Red and Yellow Barbet
D'Arnaud's Barbet
Greater Honeyguide
Scaly-throated Honeyguide
Lesser Honeyguide
Nubian Woodpecker
Cardinal Woodpecker
Bearded Woodpecker

Nyanza Swift
Scarce Swift
Alpine Swift
Mottled Swift
Little Swift
White-rumped Swift
Palm Swift
Williams' Bush Lark
Redwing Bush Lark
Flappet Lark
Fawn-coloured Lark
Pink-breasted Lark
Crested Lark Occurs commonly in sandy areas
Short-crested Lark Found in lava country
Short-tailed Lark
Chestnut-backed Sparrow Lark
Chestnut-headed Sparrow Lark
Fischer's Sparrow Lark
Red-capped Lark
Masked Lark Occurs both on Marsabit and commonly in Dida Galgalla desert
European White Wagtail Uncommon winter visitor
African Pied Wagtail
Blue-headed Wagtail and races. Common winter visitor and spring migrant
Long-billed Pipit
Richard's Pipit
Tree Pipit
Red-throated Pipit Spring migrant, often associated with Blue-headed Wagtails
Yellow-throated Longclaw
Rufous Chatterer
Abyssinian Hill Babbler
Yellow-vented Bulbul
Northern Brownbul
Fischer's Greenbul
Yellow-whiskered Greenbul
European Spotted Flycatcher
Dusky Flycatcher
Pale Flycatcher
Grey Flycatcher
White-eyed Slaty Flycatcher
Black-throated Wattle-eye
Paradise Flycatcher
Olive Thrush
European Rock Thrush
Little Rock Thrush
European Common Wheatear
Isabelline Wheatear
Pied Wheatear
Capped Wheatear
Cliff Chat
Stonechat
European Whinchat
White-browed Robin Chat
Ruppell's Robin Chat
Red-capped Robin Chat
Robin Chat
Spotted Morning Warbler
White-winged Scrub Robin
White-throated Robin Winter visitor in small numbers
European Nightingale
Thrush Nightingale or **Sprosser**
European Whitethroat
Garden Warbler
Blackcap Warbler
Barred Warbler
European Sedge Warbler
European Willow Warbler
Brown Woodland Warbler
Grey Wren Warbler
Grey Apalis
Black-breasted Apalis
Grey-capped Warbler
Crombec
Banded Tit-warbler
Yellow-bellied Eremomela
Yellow-vented Eremomela
Grey-backed Camaroptera
Rattling Cisticola
Ashy Cisticola
European Swallow
Ethiopian Swallow
Wire-tailed Swallow
Red-rumped Swallow
Mosque Swallow
Striped Swallow
European Sand Martin
African Sand Martin
Banded Martin
African Rock Martin
Black Rough-wing Swallow
Grey Cuckoo-shrike
Drongo
Retz's Red-billed Shrike
White-crowned Shrike
Northern Brubru
Lesser Grey Shrike Passage migrant, commonest in spring
Fiscal Shrike
Somali Fiscal
Teita Fiscal
Red-backed Shrike
Red-tailed Shrike
Slate-coloured Boubou
Tropical Boubou
Black-headed Tchagra
Three-streaked Tchagra
Sulphur-breasted Bush Shrike
Grey-headed Bush Shrike
Rosy-patched Shrike
Grey Tit
White-breasted Tit
Mouse-coloured Penduline Tit
European Golden Oriole
Black-headed Oriole
Dwarf or **Lesser Brown-necked Raven**
Cape Rook
White-naped Raven
Fan-tailed Raven
Wattled Starling
Violet-backed Starling
Ruppell's Long-tailed Starling
Golden-breasted Starling Occurs in bush country
Bristle-crowned Starling
Superb Starling
Yellow-billed Oxpecker
Red-billed Oxpecker
Yellow White-eye
Variable Sunbird
Eastern Double-collared Sunbird
Amethyst Sunbird
Hunter's Sunbird
Olive Sunbird
Collared Sunbird
Kenya Violet-backed Sunbird
Buffalo Weaver
White-headed Buffalo Weaver
White-browed Sparrow Weaver
Donaldson-Smith's Sparrow Weaver
Grey-headed Social Weaver
Rufous Sparrow
Swahili Sparrow
Chestnut Sparrow
Yellow-spotted Petronia
Speckle-fronted Weaver
Masked Weaver
Chestnut Weaver
Black-necked Weaver
Spectacled Weaver
Reichenow's Weaver
Brown-capped Weaver
Red-headed Weaver
Red-billed Quelea
Cardinal Quelea
Yellow Bishop
Bronze Mannikin

Silverbill
Grey-headed Negro Finch
Cut-throat
Green-winged Pytilia
Red-billed Fire Finch
Yellow-bellied Waxbill
Waxbill
Red-cheeked Cordon-bleu
Blue-capped Cordon-bleu
Purple Grenadier
Indigo-bird
Pin-tailed Whydah
Steel-blue Whydah
Fischer's Straw-tailed Whydah
Paradise Whydah
Yellow-fronted Canary
Brimstone Canary
Streaky Seed-eater
Somali Golden-breasted Bunting
Cinnamon-breasted Rock Bunting

SAMBURU-BUFFALO SPRINGS-SHABA NATIONAL RESERVES

The Samburu Game Reserves are the most accessible of the Northern Frontier faunal sanctuaries, 343km (213 miles) from Nairobi, 53km (33 miles) north of Isiolo township, over good roads. For those who prefer to travel by air there is a landing strip near the Samburu Lodge.

The Samburu Reserve covers an area of 104sq km (40sq miles) on the northern bank of the Uaso Nyiro River, with a river frontage of 16km (10 miles). The adjoining Buffalo Springs Reserve of 194sq km (75sq miles) lies on the southern bank of the same 16-km (10-mile) stretch. A bridge across the Uaso Nyiro a couple of miles upstream of the Samburu Lodge connects the two Reserves, and it is convenient to treat them as a single unit, together with the recently created Shaba Reserve. This third faunal area covers some 130sq km (50sq miles), also with its border along the southern bank of the Uaso Nyiro River, immediately east of the Buffalo Springs Reserve.

In addition to the rugged splendour of its landscape the very name 'Northern Frontier Province' conjures up an atmosphere of mystery and adventure. It is indeed a vast and little visited region, where travelling, even nowadays, is tough and where the nomadic tribes have changed little over the centuries. The three Reserves provide a worthy introduction to this most colourful part of Kenya.

Permanent water available from the 32km (20 miles) of river ensures that an abundance of wildlife exists in the Reserves at all times. The main attractions are Reticulated Giraffe, Grevy's Zebra, Beisa Oryx, the blue-necked Somali Ostrich and crocodiles in the river. Elephant are plentiful and Black Rhinoceros, Lion, Leopard, Cheetah, Gerenuk, Buffalo and the two species of hyaenas are to be seen. Among the smaller mammals the Ground Squirrel is abundant and tame.

For such a relatively small area the bird life is strikingly numerous and colourful; there is no difficulty in seeing well over a hundred species of birds in a single day. Perhaps the most impressive sight is the immense flocks of Helmeted and Vulturine Guinea-fowls which make their way each afternoon to the river-bank to drink, the latter resplendent with white-streaked necks and brilliant blue underparts.

Buffalo Springs, in the Reserve of that name, with its pools and streams of fresh water, is the drinking place in the dry season for literally thousands of sandgrouse and doves, in addition to a galaxy of smaller birds.

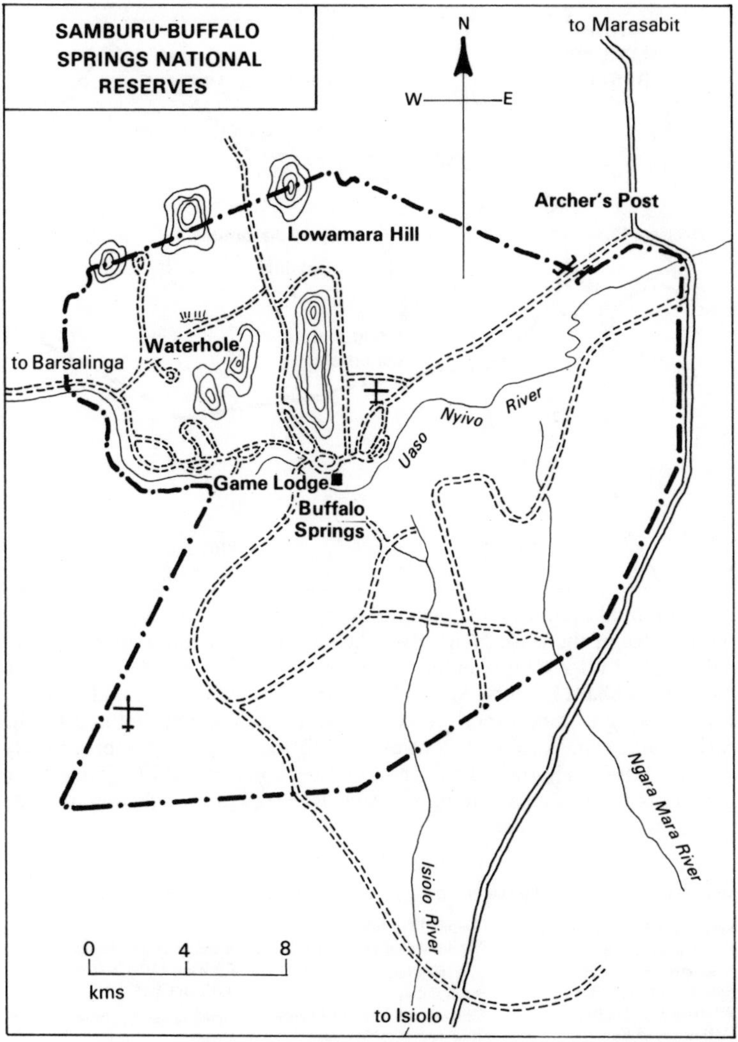

The tiny Pygmy Falcon is common, the males blue-grey and white, the females with a mahogany-brown mantle. At a distance, when perched high in some acacia tree, they distinctly resemble shrikes. The giant amongst eagles the Martial Eagle is often seen, usually perched high on some vantage point, alert for dik-dik or guinea-fowl.

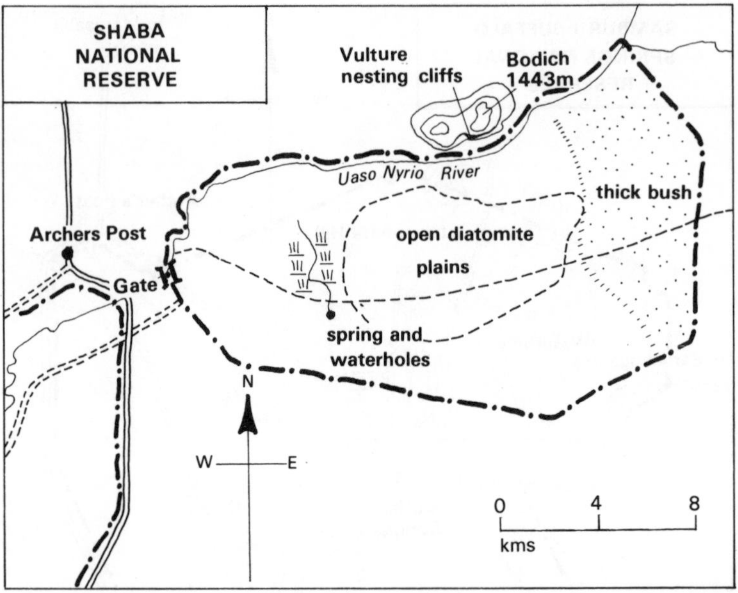

Accommodation with all amenities is at the Samburu Game Lodge, sited on the edge of the Uaso Nyiro River below giant Newtonia trees and dom palms. The Lodge is built on the camp site of one of the most famous of the old time elephant hunters, Arthur Newmann. The visitor may find it fitting, whilst taking a 'sundowner', to contemplate the austerity endured by the early hunters and explorers contrasted with the comfort of a present-day safari! At Buffalo Springs there is now another comfortable Lodge and there are camping sites available in all three Reserves, although they provide neither water or facilities.

MAMMALS OF SAMBURU-BUFFALO SPRINGS-SHABA RESERVES

Spectacled Elephant Shrew
Rousette Fruit Bat
Epauletted Fruit Bat
Pale-bellied Fruit Bat
White-bellied Tomb Bat
Hollow-faced Bat
False Vampire Bat
Yellow-winged Bat
Lander's Horseshoe Bat
Lesser Leaf-nosed Bat
Banana Bat or **African Pipistrelle**
Yellow-bellied Bat
Angola Free-tailed Bat
White-bellied Free-tailed Bat
Greater Galago
Bush Baby
Black-faced Vervet Monkey
Blue or **Sykes' Monkey**
Olive Baboon
Hunting Dog
Golden Jackal
Black-backed or **Silver-backed Jackal**
Side-striped Jackal
Bat-eared Fox
Zorilla
Ratel or **Honey Badger**
Clawless Otter Rare
African Civet
Neumann's or **Small-spotted Genet**
Bush or **Large-spotted Genet**
Marsh Mongoose
Dwarf Mongoose
Large Grey Mongoose
Slender or **Black-tipped Mongoose**
White-tailed Mongoose

Banded Mongoose
Aard-wolf
Spotted Hyaena
Striped Hyaena
Cheetah
Caracal
African Wild Cat
Serval
Lion
Leopard
Tree Hyrax
Rock Hyrax
African Elephant
Black Rhinoceros
Grevy's Zebra
Burchell's or **Common Zebra**
Hippopotamus
Warthog
Reticulated Giraffe
Red Duiker
Blue Duiker
Bush Duiker
Klipspringer
Steinbok
Kirk's Dik-dik
Guenther's Dik-dik
Common Waterbuck Intermediates between Common and Defassa Waterbucks have been recorded on Uaso Nyiro River
Impala
Grant's Gazelle
Gerenuk
Beisa Oryx
Bushbuck
Lesser Kudu
Eland
African Buffalo
African Hare
Porcupine
Striped Ground Squirrel
Unstriped Ground Squirrel
Bush Squirrel
East African Red Squirrel
Spring Hare
African Dormouse
Naked Mole Rat

BIRDS OF SAMBURU-BUFFALO SPRINGS-SHABA RESERVES

Somali Ostrich
Little Grebe
Long-tailed Cormorant
African Darter
Grey Heron
Black-headed Heron
Goliath Heron
Great White Egret
Little Egret
Buff-backed Heron or **Cattle Egret**
Green-backed Heron
Night Heron
Hamerkop
White Stork Rare visitor
Woolly-necked Stork Uncommon visitor
Abdim's Stork Spasmodic visitor: sometimes in flocks
Open-bill Stork Single record
Saddle-bill Stork Uncommon
Marabou Stork
Wood Ibis or **Yellow-billed Stork**
Sacred Ibis
Hadada Ibis
Egyptian Goose
Secretary Bird
Ruppell's Vulture
White-backed Vulture
Nubian or **Lappet-faced Vulture**
White-headed Vulture
Egyptian Vulture
Hooded Vulture
Peregrine
Lanner
European Hobby Spring passage migrant
Red-necked Falcon Rare
European Kestrel
Greater or **White-eyed Kestrel**
Lesser Kestrel
Pygmy Falcon
Swallow-tailed Kite Rare visitor
European Black Kite
African Black Kite
Black-shouldered Kite
Bat Hawk One recorded near Samburu Lodge
Honey Buzzard Rare visitor
Verreaux's Eagle
Steppe Eagle
Tawny Eagle
Wahlberg's Eagle
African Hawk Eagle Rare
Booted Eagle Rare visitor
Martial Eagle
Long-crested Hawk Eagle
Lizard Buzzard
Brown Harrier Eagle
Black-chested Harrier Eagle
Lesser Spotted Eagle Rare winter visitor
Grasshopper Buzzard Uncommon visitor
Bateleur
African Fish Eagle
Lammergeyer Rare visitor
Steppe Buzzard
Little Sparrow Hawk
Shikra
Gabar Goshawk
Pale Chanting Goshawk
Montagu's Harrier
Pallid Harrier
European Marsh Harrier
Harrier Hawk
Osprey Rare visitor
Crested Francolin
Yellow-necked Spurfowl
Harlequin Quail
Stone Partridge Occurs on rocky hills
Helmeted Guinea-fowl
Vulturine Guinea-fowl
Crowned Crane Uncommon visitor
Kori Bustard
Heuglin's Bustard Uncommon
Buff-crested Bustard
Spotted Stone Curlew
Water Dikkop
Little Ringed Plover
Three-banded Plover
Caspian Plover Rare visitor
Crowned Plover
Senegal Plover Uncommon visitor
Blackhead Plover Mainly nocturnal: often on airstrip at dusk
Common Sandpiper
Green Sandpiper
Greenshank
Cream-coloured Courser
Temminck's Courser
Two-banded Courser
Heuglin's Courser
Bronze-winged Courser
Pratincole Uncommon
Button Quail
Chestnut-bellied Sandgrouse
Black-faced Sandgrouse
Lichtenstein's Sandgrouse
Speckled Pigeon

Red-eyed Dove
Mourning Dove
Ring-necked Dove
Laughing Dove
Namaqua Dove
Tambourine Dove
Emerald-spotted Wood Dove
Green Pigeon
European Cuckoo
African Cuckoo
Red-chested Cuckoo
Black Cuckoo
Great-spotted Cuckoo Uncommon
Levaillant's Cuckoo
Black and White Cuckoo
Emerald Cuckoo
Didric Cuckoo
Klaas' Cuckoo
White-browed Coucal
White-bellied Go-away-bird
Orange-bellied Parrot Uncommon
Brown Parrot
European Roller
Lilac-breasted Roller
Rufous-crowned Roller
Broad-billed Roller
Pied Kingfisher
Giant Kingfisher
Half-collared Kingfisher Rare
Malachite Kingfisher
Pygmy Kingfisher
Brown-hooded Kingfisher Uncommon along river
Grey-headed Kingfisher
Striped Kingfisher
European Bee-eater Mainly spring passage migrant
Madagascar Bee-eater
Blue-cheeked Bee-eater Uncommon migrant
Carmine Bee-eater Occasional visitor
White-throated Bee-eater
Little Bee-eater
Somali Bee-eater
Grey Hornbill
Red-billed Hornbill
Yellow-billed Hornbill Uncommon
Von der Decken's Hornbill
Crowned Hornbill
European Hoopoe Mainly spring migrant
African Hoopoe
Green Wood Hoopoe
Scimitar-bill
Abyssinian Scimitar-bill
African Barn Owl Single record
African Marsh Owl
African Scops Owl
White-faced Scops Owl
Pearl-spotted Owlet
Spotted Eagle Owl
Verreaux's Eagle Owl
European Nightjar
Dusky Nightjar
Donaldson-Smith's Nightjar
Nubian Nightjar Uncommon
Freckled Nightjar Associated with rocky outcrops
Plain Nightjar
Pennat-wing Nightjar Uncommon visitor, July/September
Long-tailed Nightjar
Speckled Mousebird
White-headed Mousebird Usually found in flowering acacia bushes: feeds on blossoms
Blue-naped Mousebird
Narina's Trogon Rare in riverine woodland
Brown-breasted Barbet Uncommon. Frequents fruiting fig trees along river
Brown-throated Barbet
Spotted-flanked Barbet
Red-fronted Barbet
Red-fronted Tinkerbird
Red and Yellow Barbet
D'Arnaud's Barbet
Greater Honeyguide
Lesser Honeyguide
Nubian Woodpecker
Cardinal Woodpecker
Bearded Woodpecker
Grey Woodpecker
Nyanza Swift
Mottled Swift
Little Swift
White-rumped Swift
Palm Swift
Singing Bush Lark
Northern White-tailed Lark These two larks appear after good rains when there is long grass
Redwing Bush Lark
Flappet Lark
Fawn-coloured Lark Frequents open bush country
Pink-breasted Lark
Chestnut-backed Sparrow Lark
Chestnut-headed Sparrow Lark
Fischer's Sparrow Lark
Red-capped Lark
African Pied Wagtail
Blue-headed Wagtail and races Mainly on passage migration
Long-billed Pipit
Richard's Pipit
Golden Pipit Uncommon
Little Tawny Pipit
Yellow-throated Longclaw
Arrow-marked Babbler
Rufous Chatterer
Yellow-vented Bulbul
Northern Brownbul
European Spotted Flycatcher
Dusky Flycatcher
Ashy Flycatcher
Pale Flycatcher
Grey Flycatcher
South African Black Flycatcher
Silverbird Uncommon
Chin-spot Flycatcher
Pygmy Puff-back Flycatcher
Black-throated Wattle-eye
Paradise Flycatcher
Olive Thrush
Bare-eyed Thrush
European Rock Thrush
European Common Wheatear
Isabelline Wheatear
Pied Wheatear
Capped Wheatear
European Whinchat Uncommon migrant
White-browed Robin Chat
Red-capped Chat
Robin Chat
Spotted Morning Warbler
Red-backed Scrub Robin
White-winged Scrub Robin
White-throated Robin Rare winter visitor
European Nightingale
Thrush Nightingale or **Sprosser**
Garden Warbler
Blackcap Warbler
Barred Warbler
Olive-tree Warbler
European Sedge Warbler
European Willow Warbler
Grey Wren Warbler
Black-breasted Apalis
Red-faced Apalis

Buff-bellied Warbler
Crombec
Banded Tit-warbler
Yellow-bellied Eremomela
Yellow-vented Eremomela
Grey-backed Camaroptera
Pectoral-patch Cisticola
Rattling Cisticola
Tiny Cisticola
Ashy Cisticola
Tawny-flanked Prinia
European Swallow
Angola Swallow
Ethiopian Swallow Uncommon
Wire-tailed Swallow
Red-rumped Swallow
Striped Swallow
Grey-rumped Swallow Uncommon
European Sand Martin
African Sand Martin
Banded Martin
African Rock Martin
Black Rough-wing Swallow Uncommon visitor
Black Cuckoo Shrike
Drongo
White-crowned Shrike
Northern Brubru
Lesser Grey Shrike Mainly spring passage migrant
Somali Fiscal Rare visitor
Taita Fiscal
Long-tailed Fiscal
Red-backed Shrike
Red-tailed Shrike
Slate-coloured Boubou
Tropical Boubou
Black-backed Puff-back
Black-headed Tchagra
Three-streaked Tchagra
Sulphur-breasted Bush Shrike
Grey-headed Bush Shrike
Rosy-patched Shrike
Grey Tit
White-breasted Tit
Mouse-coloured Penduline Tit
European Golden Oriole Mainly spring passage migrant
Black-headed Oriole
Dwarf or **Lesser Brown-necked Raven**
White-naped Raven
Fan-tailed Raven
Wattled Starling
Violet-backed Starling Spasmodic visitor
Magpie Starling Uncommon visitor in small numbers
Blue-eared Starling
Black-breasted Glossy Starling Uncommon visitor
Ruppell's Long-tailed Starling
Bristle-crowned Starling
Golden-breasted Starling
Hildebrandt's Starling
Superb Starling
Yellow-billed Oxpecker
Red-billed Oxpecker
Yellow White-eye
Smaller Black-bellied Sunbird Rare
Shining Sunbird Rare visitor
Mariqua Sunbird
Variable Sunbird
Hunter's Sunbird
Collared Sunbird
Kenya Violet-backed Sunbird
Buffalo Weaver
White-headed Buffalo Weaver
White-browed Sparrow Weaver
Donaldson-Smith's Sparrow Weaver
Grey-headed Social Weaver
Black-capped Social Weaver
Rufous Sparrow
Grey-headed Sparrow
Swahili Sparrow
Chestnut Sparrow
Yellow-spotted Petronia
Speckle-fronted Weaver
Layard's Black-headed Weaver
Masked Weaver
Vitelline Masked Weaver
Chestnut Weaver
Black-necked Weaver
Spectacled Weaver
Golden Weaver
Red-headed Weaver
Red-billed Quelea
Cardinal Quelea
Yellow Bishop
Fire-fronted Bishop Appears in years of heavy rains when there is abundant grass
White-winged Widow-bird Spasmodic visitor
Bronze Mannikin
Silverbill
Grey-headed Silverbill
Cut-throat
Green-winged Pytilia
African Fire Finch
Jameson's Fire Finch
Red-billed Fire Finch
Waxbill
Blue-faced Waxbill
Red-cheeked Cordon-bleu
Blue-capped Cordon-bleu
Purple Grenadier
Indigo-bird
Pin-tailed Whydah
Steel-blue Whydah
Fischer's Straw-tailed Whydah
Paradise Whydah
Yellow-fronted Canary
White-bellied Canary
Yellow-rumped Seed-eater
Somali Golden-breasted Bunting
Cinnamon-breasted Rock Bunting

SHIMBA HILLS NATIONAL RESERVE

The Shimba Hills National Reserve near Kwale, 56km (35 miles) south of Mombasa and within easy range of the Kenya south coast holiday resorts, is famous for its Sable Antelopes – the only reserve in which these animals occur. The Shimba Hills Reserve embraces an area of upwards of 310sq km (120sq miles).

The Reserve is at an altitude of 300–400m (1,000–1,300ft) and comprises rolling park-like country, open grasslands alternating with majestic stands of coastal rain forest. Besides the Sable Antelope, which are relatively tame and

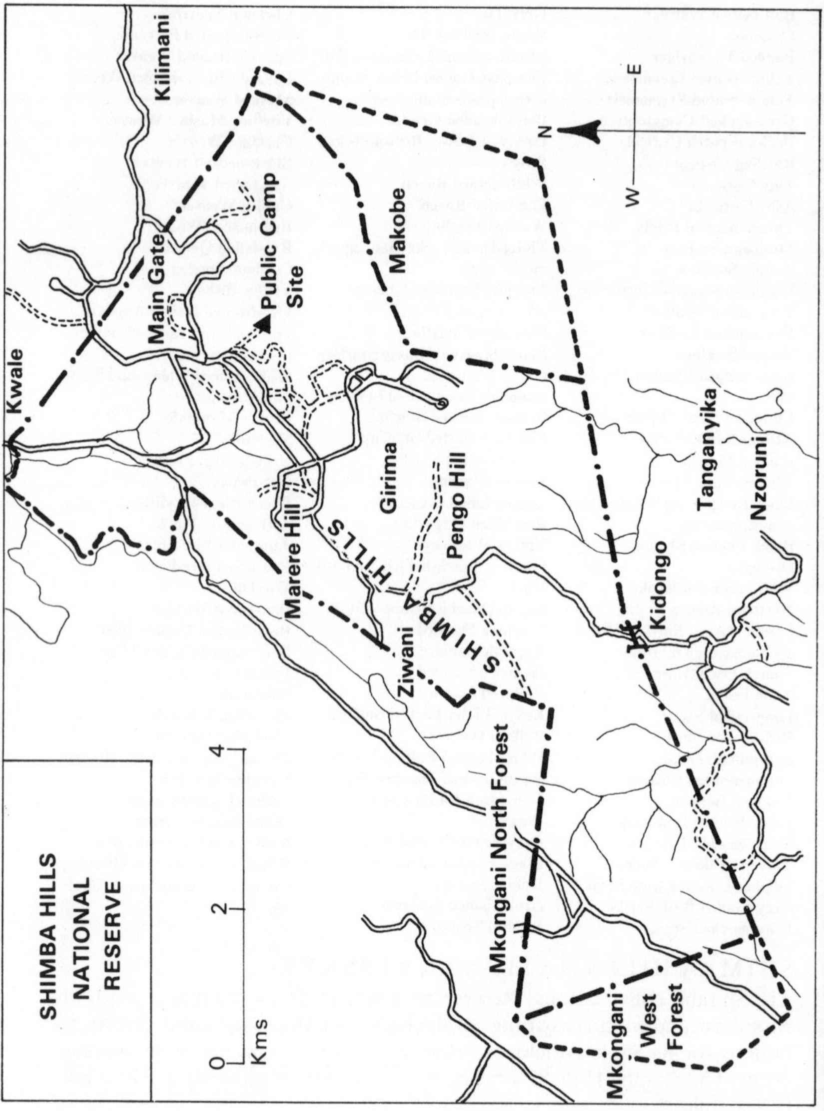
SHIMBA HILLS NATIONAL RESERVE
0
2
4
Kms
Kwale
Main Gate
Kilimani
Public Camp Site
Makobe
W
E
N
Girima
Pengo Hill
Marere Hill
SHIMBA HILLS
Ziwani
Mkongani North Forest
Mkongani West Forest
Kidongo
Tanganyika
Nzoruni

easy to photograph, Roan Antelope have been re-introduced and it is now possible to see groups of up to a dozen Roan and much larger herds of Sable. Buffalo are also common. Elephant, Lion and Leopard also occur but are not often seen although their spoor is obvious. Other noteworthy mammals are:

Knob-bristled Elephant Shrew
Black and Red Elephant Shrew
Greater Galago
Bush Baby
Black-faced Vervet Monkey
Sykes' Monkey
Coastal Black and White Colobus
Serval
Red Duiker
Blue Duiker
Bush Duiker
Suni
Bushbuck

Birds are not quite so common as in some other Reserves but during Spring migration, late March and early April, some spectacular concentrations of Palearctic migrants may be observed. These include days when the whole Reserve seems to be alive with European and Lesser Cuckoos and European Golden Orioles. Other migrants which occur spasmodically in numbers include Honey Buzzard, European Hobby and Red-backed Shrike. Some other birds which are characteristic of the Shimba Hills include the following:

Cuckoo Falcon
African Hawk Eagle
Crowned Hawk Eagle
Southern Banded Harrier Eagle
Palm-nut Vulture
Red-necked Spurfowl
Kenya Crested Guineafowl
Blue Quail
Fischer's Turaco
Black-breasted Bustard
Carmine Bee-eater
European Bee-eater
Trumpeter Hornbill
Silvery-cheeked Hornbill
Crowned Hornbill
Narina's Trogon
Black-collared Barbet
Brown-breasted Barbet
Green Barbet
White-eared Barbet
Green Tinkerbird
Greater Honeyguide
Scaly-throated Honeyguide
Lesser Honeyguide
Little Spotted Woodpecker
Golden-tailed Woodpecker
Mottled-throated Spinetail
Boehm's Spinetail
African Broadbill
African Pitta
Yellow-throated Longclaw
Pangani Longclaw
Flappet Lark
Little Yellow Flycatcher
East Coast Akalat
Croaking Cisticola
Black-headed Apalis
Spotted Ground Thrush
Drongo
Square-tailed Drongo
Retz's Red-billed Shrike
Chestnut-fronted Shrike
Zanzibar Puff-back Shrike
Four-coloured Bush Shrike
Nicator
Green-headed Oriole
African Golden Oriole
Black-headed Oriole
Black-breasted Starling
Violet-backed Starling
Plain-backed Sunbird
Uluguru Violet-backed Sunbird
Dark-backed Weaver
Zanzibar Red Bishop
Black-winged Bishop
Peters' Twinspot
Green-backed Twinspot

The Shimba Hills Reserve, in addition to its fauna, is very rich botanically. Two of Kenya's most beautiful terrestrial orchids flower there during April, *Eulophia livingstoniana* and *E. cucullata*. During July and August another member of the same genus, *E. wakefieldii* with green and yellow flowers, may be found blooming.

LAKE BOGORIA (HANNINGTON) NATIONAL RESERVE

Lake Bogoria, known previously as Lake Hannington, in Kenya's Rift Valley is a region of great scenic beauty. To the east steep hills descend abruptly to the lake shore, whilst along the western shores, which are flatter, are a series of spectacular hot springs. The Reserve includes the entire lake and its immediate surrounds and is some 114sq km (44sq miles) in area. A recently constructed access road, skirting Solai, runs to the lake from Nakuru, a distance of a little under 64km (40 miles). The route is adequately sign-posted. Camp sites are available in several places around the lake, otherwise the visitor should stay at one of the hotels in Nakuru, at Island Camp, Lake Baringo or at Lake Baringo Lodge. The Island Camp organises trips to Lake Bogoria (including the use of a boat), and to other places in the region.

The Lake Bogoria area is best known for its Greater Kudu, to be seen mainly along the eastern shores, and for the very large concentrations of Lesser and Greater Flamingos which often frequent the lake.

Mammals so far recorded from Lake Bogoria include the following:

Rufous Spectacled Elephant Shrew
Epauletted Fruit Bat
Yellow-winged Bat
White-bellied Free-tailed Bat
Bush Baby
Black-faced Vervet Monkey
Olive Baboon
Black-backed Jackal
Bat-eared Fox
African Civet
Small-spotted Genet
Dwarf Mongoose
White-tailed Mongoose
Banded Mongoose
Aard Wolf
Spotted Hyaena
Cheetah (rare)
Caracal
African Wild Cat
Rock Hyrax
Warthog
Coke's Hartebeest
Bush Duiker
Klipspringer
Steinbok
Kirk's Dikdik
Bohor Reedbuck
Chanler's Mountain Reedbuck
Impala
Grant's Gazelle
Gerenuk
Greater Kudu
African Buffalo
African Hare
Porcupine
Unstriped Ground Squirrel
Bush Squirrel
Spring Hare
Naked Mole Rat

BIRDS OF LAKE BOGORIA NATIONAL RESERVE

Black-necked Grebe
Great Crested Grebe
Little Grebe
White Pelican
Pink-backed Pelican
White-necked Cormorant
Night Heron
Great White Egret
Yellow-billed Egret
Goliath Heron
Purple Heron
Yellow-billed Stork
African Spoonbill
Greater Flamingo
Lesser Flamingo
White-faced Tree Duck
Egyptian Goose
Spur-winged Goose
Cape Wigeon
Garganey Teal
Maccoa Duck
Bateleur
Dark Chanting Goshawk
Gabar Goshawk
Augur Buzzard
Tawny Eagle
Verreaux's Eagle
Fish Eagle
Black Kite
Black-shouldered Kite
Swallow-tailed Kite (rare)
Lanner
Hildebrandt's Francolin
Crowned Crane
Red-knobbed Coot
Painted Snipe
Spur-winged Plover
Blackhead Plover
Kittlitz's Plover
Three-banded Plover
Marsh Sandpiper
Black-tailed Godwit
Black-winged Stilt
Avocet
Water Dikkop
Heuglin's Courser
Pratincole
Grey-headed Gull
Chestnut-bellied Sandgrouse
Speckled Pigeon
White-bellied Go-away-bird
Great Spotted Cuckoo
Black and White Cuckoo
Levaillant's Cuckoo
Spotted Eagle Owl
Plain Nightjar
Mottled Swift
Nyanza Swift
Horus Swift
Blue-naped Mousebird
Pied Kingfisher
Striped Kingfisher
Grey-headed Kingfisher
Madagascar Bee-eater
White-throated Bee-eater
Little Bee-eater

White-fronted Bee-eater
European Roller
Rufous-crowned Roller
Hoopoe
Green Wood Hoopoe
Grey Hornbill
Jackson's Hornbill
Crowned Hornbill
Hemprich's Hornbill
Abyssinian Ground Hornbill
Brown-throated Barbet
Spotted Flanked Barbet
Red-fronted Barbet
Red-fronted Tinkerbird
D'Arnaud's Barbet
Red and Yellow Barbet
Wahlberg's Honeyguide
Nubian Woodpecker
Cardinal Woodpecker
Grey Woodpecker
Bearded Woodpecker
Fawn-coloured Lark
Grey-rumped Swallow
African Rock Martin
White-crowned Shrike
Northern Brubru
Three-streaked Tchagra
Rosy-patched Shrike
Slate-coloured Boubou
Sulphur-breasted Bush Shrike
Capped Wheatear
Cliff Chat
Red-backed Scrub Robin
Spotted Morning Warbler
Rufous Chatterer
Crombec
Banded Tit Warbler
Pygmy Puff-back
Grey Tit
Mouse-coloured Penduline Tit
Variable Sunbird
Mariqua Sunbird
Beautiful Sunbird
Kenya Violet-backed Sunbird
Green-winged Pytilia
Purple Grenadier
Red-cheeked Cordon-bleu
Blue-capped Cordon-bleu
Cut-throat
Silverbill
Grey-headed Silverbill
Fischer's Straw-tailed Whydah
Steel-blue Whydah
Paradise Whydah
Little Weaver
Masked Weaver
Vitelline Masked Weaver
Yellow-crowned Bishop
White-headed Buffalo Weaver
White-browed Sparrow Weaver
Bristle-crowned Starling
Ruppell's Long-tailed Starling
Magpie Starling
Wattled Starling
Yellow-billed Oxpecker
Red-billed Oxpecker
Fan-tailed Raven
Cape Rook
White-necked Raven

LAMBWE VALLEY GAME RESERVE

The Lambwe Valley Game Reserve in South Nyanza covers an area of approximately 194sq km (75sq miles) near the town of Homa Bay on Winam Gulf, Lake Victoria. Access is via the Kisumu-Homa Bay road, a distance of 140km (87 miles). The Reserve was created to help to preserve the small population of Roan Antelope living there. The terrain is mainly rolling savannah country with some open woodland. Roan Antelope, Oribi and Jackson's Hartebeest can all be seen here more easily than elsewhere in Kenya. Otherwise the Reserve's main interest is in its birdlife. Among the less common species which have been recorded are the following:

Rufous-bellied Heron
Abdim's Stork
Woolly-necked Stork
Saddle-billed Stork
Openbill Stork
African Spoonbill
White-faced Tree Duck
African Marsh Harrier
Beaudouin's Harrier Eagle
Banded Harrier Eagle
Grey Kestrel
Painted Snipe
Long-toed Lapwing
Senegal Plover
Wattled Plover
Bare-faced Go-away-bird
Eastern Grey Plantain-eater
Levaillant's Cuckoo
Senegal Coucal
White-tailed Nightjar
Woodland Kingfisher
Blue-cheeked Bee-eater
Black-billed Barbet
Yellow-fronted Tinkerbird
Red-breasted Wryneck
Flappet Lark
Blue Swallow
Rufous-chested Swallow
Black-headed Gonolek
Red-tailed Chat
Sooty Chat
African Thrush
African Moustached Warbler
Black Flycatcher
Silverbird
Mariqua Sunbird
Coppery Sunbird
Red-chested Sunbird
Beautiful Sunbird
Black-bellied Firefinch
Zebra Waxbill
Quail-finch
Fan-tailed Widow-bird
Black Bishop
Hartlaub's Marsh Widow-bird
Black-winged Bishop
Red Bishop
Lesser Blue-eared Starling

THE TANA RIVER RESERVES

Of the four Reserves in various stages of development in the Garissa-Tana River region, Arawale, Boni, Kora and Rahole, the first is the most important.

Arawale Game Reserve covers an area of approximately 1,165sq km (450sq miles) and is sited 77km (48 miles) south of Garissa along the eastern side of the river, with a river frontage of 48km (30 miles), its western border. To the east its border is the Garissa-Lamu road. This Reserve has been created mainly for the protection of the rare Hunter's Antelope. Elephant are still common in the area as are other species of Northern Frontier game animals. Birdlife is abundant and varied. Species so far recorded include the following:

Woolly-necked Stork
Openbill Stork
Harrier Hawk
Black-chested Harrier Eagle
Brown Harrier Eagle
Little Sparrow Hawk
Ovampo Sparrow Hawk
Grasshopper Buzzard
Martial Eagle
African Hawk Eagle
Bat Hawk
Pygmy Falcon
Lanner
African Finfoot
Buff-crested Bustard
Blackhead Plover
Water Dikkop
Cream-coloured Courser
Heuglin's Courser
Orange-bellied Parrot
Great Spotted Cuckoo
African Cuckoo
Green Coucal
Scops Owl
White-faced Scops Owl
Pel's Fishing Owl
Barred Owlet
Nubian Nightjar
Donaldson-Smith's Nightjar
Narina's Trogon
White-throated Bee-eater
Violet Wood Hoopoe
Greater Honeyguide
Scaly-throated Honeyguide
Wahlberg's Honeyguide
Collared Lark (on red soil)
Golden Pipit
Retz's Red-billed Shrike
Pringle's Puff-back Shrike
Eastern Bearded Scrub Robin
White-throated Robin
Scaly Babbler
Tana River Cisticola
Hunter's Sunbird
Violet-breasted Sunbird
Smaller Black-bellied Sunbird
Paradise Whydah
Golden Palm Weaver
Magpie Starling
Shelley's Starling
African Golden Oriole

Boni National Reserve, gazetted in 1976, will cover an area of nearly 2,590sq km (1,000sq miles) in little-visited country south-east of Garissa. At present this Reserve is inaccessible until access roads are constructed and is reached across country only in dry weather in four-wheel-drive vehicles. Its fauna remains to be investigated.

Kora Game Reserve on the Tana River, some 322km (200 miles) from Nairobi via Thika and Ngomeni, lies east of Meru National Park with its eastern boundary along the Tana River. Wilderness trails, cut through riverine forest, are being developed. The fauna is similar to that of the Meru National Park. There is an airstrip located along the eastern border, adjacent to the river. Camp sites are available.

Rahole National Reserve, north-west of Garissa, is at present inaccessible until roads have been built. It can be reached only in the dry season in four-wheel-drive vehicles. This Reserve is being developed mainly to illustrate the co-existence of wildlife with the nomadic tribes who live in this area.

Up to date information on road conditions and the feasibility of visiting these Reserves may be obtained from the Game Warden, P.O. Box 58, Garissa, Kenya.

DODORI NATIONAL RESERVE

Dodori National Reserve in eastern Lamu district of Coast Province covers an area of approximately 1,295sq km (500sq miles) in the Dodori River Valley, north of Lamu. At present it is accessible only in the dry season in four-wheel-drive vehicles. The Reserve has been established to give protection to the small population of Topi living in the area. The habitats vary from coastal forest to open savannah woodland and grassland. Its avifauna has yet to be investigated in detail, but it is rich in birds of prey and during Spring migration many Palearctic migrants may be observed. Birds already noted include Palmnut Vulture, Southern Banded Harrier Eagle, Honey Buzzard (sometimes common on Spring migration), Brown-hooded Kingfisher, European and Carmine Bee-eaters, Brown-breasted Barbet and Violet-breasted Sunbird.

Up to date information on accessibility and feasibility of visiting this Reserve may be had from safari tour operators at Malindi, Kenya.

LOSAI NATIONAL RESERVE

Losai National Reserve, gazetted in 1976, is adjacent to Marsabit National Reserve and is being developed to give protection to Elephant, Lion, Greater Kudu, Lesser Kudu and Gerenuk occurring outside the boundaries of the Marsabit Reserve. It is accessible at present only in the dry season in four-wheel-drive vehicles. Its fauna is similar to that of the drier areas of the Marsabit Reserve. Up to date information on the feasibility of visiting the area may be had from the Warden, Losai National Reserve, P.O. Marsabit, via Isiolo, Kenya.

MWEA NATIONAL RESERVE

Mwea National Reserve, gazetted in 1976, is a small faunal area of approximately 104sq km (40sq miles) and is sited in Embu district within easy range of Embu township. Accommodation is available at hotels in Embu. It is an important locality for birds, being rich in birds of prey and when access roads are constructed will have appeal for visiting ornithologists. The adjacent Mwea rice growing area attracts large numbers of water-birds and waders. Information on development progress may be had from the Warden, Mwea National Reserve, P.O. Box 264, Embu, Kenya.

NGAI NDETHYA NATIONAL RESERVE

This Reserve in the Kitui district of Eastern Province, gazetted in 1976, is being developed as a wildlife refuge for Elephant, Lesser Kudu and Buffalo. It covers an area of about 310sq km (120sq miles) with rocky hills alternating with woodland, bush and savannah country. Access is via Kitui township with accommodation there for those prepared to accept rather rudimentary hotel facilities. Camp sites are also available in the Reserve. Birdlife is abundant. Information on development progress is supplied by the Warden, Ngai Ndethya National Reserve, P.O. Box 149, Machakos, Kenya.

Important Faunal Areas outside National Parks and Game Reserves

Not all of Kenya's wildlife exists within the boundaries of National Parks and Game Reserves. The following are some localities of special interest to the naturalist.

LAKE BARINGO. Lake Baringo, one of Kenya's Rift Valley lakes, north of Nakuru, possesses two major ornithological attractions. These are Gibraltar Island with the largest nesting colony of Goliath Herons in East Africa, and the escarpment immediately west of Campi ya Samaki on the western side of the lake, the home of Verreaux's Eagle, the rare Bristle-crowned Starling and Hemprich's Hornbill. Birds generally are abundant in the acacia woodland bordering the lake and include Curly-crested Helmet Shrikes, Silverbird, Grey-headed Silverbill, Grey-headed Bush Shrike, Northern Masked Weaver and West Nile Red Bishop.

First class accommodation with all facilities may be had at the Lake Baringo Lodge or at the luxury Island Camp on Ol Kokwa Island in Lake Baringo. Many people enjoy water-ski-ing on the lake in spite of the crocodiles and hippo!

KAKAMEGA FOREST. The Kakamega Forest lying east of Kakamega township is an area of immense ornithological interest. The forest is West African in character and many birds occur there that are not found elsewhere in Kenya. Characteristic species include the following:

Bat Hawk
Crowned Hawk Eagle
Ross's Turaco
Great Blue Turaco
Eastern Grey Plantain-eater
Grey Parrot
Blue-headed Bee-eater
Black and White-casqued Hornbill
Red-chested Owlet
Narina's Trogon
Bar-tailed Trogon
Double-toothed Barbet
Grey-throated Barbet
Yellow-spotted Barbet
Moustached Green Tinkerbird
Speckled Barbet
Thick-billed Honeyguide
Cassin's Honeyguide
Brown-eared Woodpecker
Buff-spotted Woodpecker
Yellow-crested Woodpecker
Sabine's Spinetail
African Broadbill
Bristle-bill
Honeyguide Greenbul
Joyful Greenbul

Shrike Flycatcher
Wattle-eye Flycatcher
Chestnut Wattle-eye
Jameson's Wattle-eye
Yellow-bellied Wattle-eye
Black-headed Paradise Flycatcher
Blue-shouldered Robin Chat
Equatorial Akalat
Brown-chested Alethe
Uganda Woodland Warbler
Black-faced Rufous Warbler
Petit's Cuckoo Shrike
Velvet-mantled Drongo
Square-tailed Drongo
Mackinnon's Grey Shrike
Pink-footed Puff-back Shrike
Doherty's Bush Shrike
Grey-green Bush Shrike
Dusky Tit
Waller's Chestnut-wing Starling
Stuhlmann's Starling
Orange-tufted Sunbird
Green-throated Sunbird
Blue-throated Brown Sunbird
Grey-chinned Sunbird
Green Hylia
Dark-backed Weaver
Vieillot's Black Weaver
Brown-capped Weaver
Yellow-mantled Weaver
Red-headed Malimbe
Red-headed Blue-bill
Oriole Finch

KONGELAI ESCARPMENT. The Kongelai Escarpment immediately north of Kapenguria is an easy day's trip from Kitale. Around Kapenguria at 2,286m (7,500ft) the Spotted Creeper is fairly numerous and is often a member of a mixed bird party with various tits, orioles, flycatchers and weavers. The Escarpment road, which drops to 1,371m (4,500ft) at the Suam River, is an extremely rich bird locality with some 300 species recorded. Special species include White-crested Turaco, Eastern Grey Plaintain-eater, Senegal Coucal, Yellow-billed Shrike, Stone Partridge, Lesser Blue-eared Starling, Curly-crested Helmet Shrike and Jackson's Hornbill.

LAKE MAGADI. This is a shallow alkaline lake in southern Kenya just north of the Tanzanian border and 113km (70 miles) from Nairobi. Water birds are abundant including the Chestnut-banded Sand Plover which is not found elsewhere in Kenya. The road to Magadi passes over the south-eastern end of the Ngong Hills at 2,134m (7,000ft), and then drops in a series of 'steps' down the eastern wall of the Rift Valley until the 610m (2,000ft) level at the lake is reached. As Magadi is a concession area permission to visit the lake should be obtained from the Magadi Soda Company.

Some of the more interesting mammals and birds found in this area are listed below:

Short-snouted Elephant Shrew
Black-faced Vervet Monkey
Olive Baboon
Bat-eared Fox
Zorilla
Ratel or **Honey Badger**
African Civet
Neumann's or **Small-spotted Genet**
Aard-wolf
Spotted Hyaena
Striped Hyaena
Cheetah
Caracal
African Wild Cat
Lion
Leopard
Ant Bear
Rock Hyrax
Black Rhinoceros
Common Zebra
Warthog
Masai Giraffe
Coke's Hartebeest
White-bearded Gnu
Bush Duiker
Klipspringer
Steinbok
Kirk's Dik-dik
Impala
Grant's Gazelle
Gerenuk
Fringe-eared Oryx
Porcupine
Striped Ground Squirrel
Bush Squirrel

Masai Ostrich
White Pelican
Pink-backed Pelican
Grey Heron
Goliath Heron
Little Egret
Dwarf Bittern Breeds in the fresh water swamps immediately south of Magadi

Saddle-bill Stork
African Spoonbill
Greater Flamingo
Lesser Flamingo Usually in very large numbers at southern end of lake. Breeding recorded
Cape Wigeon
Peregrine
Lanner
African Hawk Eagle
Brown Harrier Eagle
Pale Chanting Goshawk
Kori Bustard
White-bellied Bustard
Buff-crested Bustard
Spotted Stone Curlew
Chestnut-banded Sand Plover
Painted Snipe
Two-banded Courser
Temminck's Courser
Heuglin's Courser
Bronze-winged Courser
Pratincole
White-bellied Go-away-bird
Singing Bush Lark
Rosy-patched Shrike
Beautiful Sunbird (black-bellied race)
Kenya Violet-backed Sunbird
Steel-blue Whydah
Fischer's Straw-tailed Whydah
Paradise Whydah
Kenya Grosbeak Canary

MIDA CREEK. Mida Creek is a vast expanse of almost land-locked tidal mudflats a few miles south of Gedi National Park, and is one of the best localities in East Africa wherein to study the spring migration of waders. Here from late March until early May, migrating flocks of Little Stints, Curlew Sandpipers, Sanderlings, Turnstones, Greenshanks, Terek Sandpipers, Whimbrels, Curlews, Great and Mongolian Sand Plovers and Grey Plovers assemble briefly in their flight northwards. Many are in the full glory of their breeding plumage.

The belt of mangrove swamp which fringes this tidal basin offers ideal concealment from which to watch or photograph shore birds at close quarters. Besides the northern migrants Mida Creek is also one of the few places on the Kenya coast where Crab Plovers may be seen. Other interesting birds to be encountered are Osprey, Caspian Tern, Sooty Gull, and Lesser Crested Tern: whilst the mangrove trees offer perches for Carmine, Madagascar and European Bee-eaters.

LAKE NAIVASHA AND HELL'S GATE. Fresh-water Lake Naivasha, only 80km (50 miles) from Nairobi, is a bird-watcher's paradise. It is also the most beautiful of Kenya's Rift Valley lakes with its fringing banks of feathery-headed papyrus, secluded lagoons and channels, blue water-lilies and the Crescent Island Wildlife Sanctuary. Waterbirds exist in great variety and abundance.

Fish Eagles and Ospreys are resident, herons and egrets are well represented, Lily-trotters, Purple Gallinules, Red-knobbed Coots and Black Crakes are common. African Marsh Harriers and the three migrant harriers are often seen sailing just above the reed beds, hunting the little *Hyperolius* tree-frogs which form the bulk of their diet.

Some 13km (8 miles) south-east of Lake Naivasha are the towering cliffs of the Hell's Gate gorge, with their resident pair of Lammergeyers, several Verreaux's Eagles, colonies of Ruppell's Vultures and other notable birds.

In addition to its birds the following mammals are also found at Naivasha and Hell's Gate:

Black-faced Vervet Monkey
Olive Baboon
Black-backed and **Side-striped Jackals**
Bat-eared Fox
Zorilla

Clawless Otter
African Civet
Small-spotted Genet
Large-spotted Genet
Marsh Mongoose
White-tailed Mongoose
Aard-wolf
Serval
Rock Hyrax
Common Zebra
Hippopotamus
Masai Giraffe
Coke's Hartebeest
Bush Duiker
Klipspringer Hell's Gate
Steinbok
Kirk's Dik-dik
Defassa Waterbuck
Bohor Reedbuck
Chanler's Reedbuck
Impala
Thomson's Gazelle
Grant's Gazelle
Bushbuck
African Buffalo Hell's Gate
African Hare
Porcupine
Striped Ground Squirrel
Bush Squirrel
Spring Hare Numerous on Crescent Island
African Mole Rat

BIRDS

Masai Ostrich
Great-crested Grebe
Black-necked Grebe
Little Grebe
White-necked Cormorant
Long-tailed Cormorant
African Darter
White Pelican
Pink-backed Pelican
Grey Heron
Black-headed Heron
Goliath Heron
Purple Heron
Great White Egret
Yellow-billed Egret
Black Heron Rare visitor
Little Egret
Buff-backed Heron or **Cattle Egret**
Squacco Heron
Night Heron
Little Bittern
Dwarf Bittern
Hamerkop
White Stork
European Black Stork Rare visitor
Abdim's Stork
Open-bill Stork
Saddle-bill Stork Rare visitor
Marabou Stork
Wood Ibis or **Yellow-billed Stork**
Sacred Ibis
Hadada Ibis
Glossy Ibis
African Spoonbill
Greater Flamingo
Lesser Flamingo Flamingos are spasmodic visitors only
Maccoa Duck
White-backed Duck
African Pochard
European Shoveler
Yellow-billed Duck
African Black Duck
Garganey Teal
Cape Wigeon Rare visitor
Hottentot Teal
Red-billed Duck
European Pintail
Fulvous Tree Duck
Pygmy Goose Uncommon
Knob-billed Duck
Egyptian Goose
Spur-winged Goose
Secretary Bird
Ruppell's Vulture
White-backed Vulture
Lappet-faced Vulture
White-headed Vulture
Egyptian Vulture
Hooded Vulture
Peregrine
Lanner
European Hobby
European Kestrel
African Kestrel Hell's Gate
Greater or **White-eyed Kestrel**
Lesser Kestrel
European Black Kite
African Black Kite
Black-shouldered Kite
Bat Hawk
Verreaux's Eagle
Steppe Eagle
Tawny Eagle
Martial Eagle Rare visitor
Long-crested Eagle
Brown Harrier Eagle
Black-chested Harrier Eagle
Lesser Spotted Eagle
Bateleur
African Fish Eagle
Lammergeyer Hell's Gate
Steppe Buzzard
Augur Buzzard
Little Sparrow Hawk
Gabar Goshawk
Montagu's Harrier
Pallid Harrier
European Marsh Harrier
African Marsh Harrier
Harrier Hawk
Osprey
Hildebrandt's Francolin Hell's Gate
Yellow-necked Spurfowl
Cape Quail
Harlequin Quail
Helmeted Guinea-fowl
Kaffir Rail
Black Crake
Purple Gallinule
Moorhen
Red-knobbed Coot
Crowned Crane
African Jacana or **Lily-trotter**
Ringed Plover
Little Ringed Plover
Kittlitz's Plover
Three-banded Plover
Caspian Plover
Crowned Plover
Black-winged Plover
Spurwing Plover
Blacksmith Plover
Avocet
Black-winged Stilt
Painted Snipe
European Common Snipe
Great Snipe
African Snipe

Curlew Sandpiper
Little Stint
Temminck's Stint Rare visitor
Ruff
Common Sandpiper
Green Sandpiper
Wood Sandpiper
Marsh Sandpiper
Greenshank
Black-tailed Godwit
Temminck's Courser
Pratincole
Lesser Black-backed Gull
Grey-headed Gull
Gull-billed Tern
White-winged Black Tern
Whiskered Tern
African Skimmer
Speckled Pigeon
Red-eyed Dove
Ring-necked Dove
Laughing Dove
Emerald-spotted Wood Dove
Tambourine Dove
Green Pigeon
European Cuckoo
African Cuckoo
Red-chested Cuckoo
Black Cuckoo
Emerald Cuckoo
Didric Cuckoo
Klaas' Cuckoo
Blue-headed Coucal
White-browed Coucal
Fischer's Lovebird Common
European Roller
Lilac-breasted Roller
Rufous-crowned Roller
Broad-billed Roller
Pied Kingfisher
Giant Kingfisher
Malachite Kingfisher
Pygmy Kingfisher
Grey-headed Kingfisher
Striped Kingfisher
European Bee-eater
Madagascar Bee-eater
Blue-cheeked Bee-eater
White-throated Bee-eater
Little Bee-eater
White-fronted Bee-eater
Crowned Hornbill
Ground Hornbill
African Hoopoe
Green Wood Hoopoe
Scimitar-bill
Abyssinian Scimitar-bill
African Marsh Owl
Pearl-spotted Owlet
Spotted Eagle Owl
Verreaux's Eagle Owl
European Nightjar
Dusky Nightjar
Long-tailed Nightjar
Speckled Mousebird
Red-fronted Barbet
Red-fronted Tinkerbird
Greater Honeyguide
Scaly-throated Honeyguide
Lesser Honeyguide
Nubian Woodpecker
Cardinal Woodpecker
Bearded Woodpecker
Grey Woodpecker
Red-breasted Wryneck
Nyanza Swift
Mottled Swift
Little Swift
White-rumped Swift
Horus Swift
Rufous-naped Lark
Red-capped Lark
African Pied Wagtail
Wells' Wagtail
Blue-headed Wagtail and races
Richard's Pipit
Yellow-throated Longclaw
Black-lored Babbler
Yellow-vented Bulbul
White-eyed Slaty Flycatcher
Chin-spot Flycatcher
Paradise Flycatcher
Olive Thrush
Schalow's Wheatear
Anteater Chat
White-browed Robin Chat
Robin Chat
Greater Swamp Warbler
Red-faced Crombec
Brown Tit-warbler
Grey-capped Warbler
Pectoral-patch Cisticola Hell's Gate
Winding Cisticola
Rattling Cisticola
Black Cuckoo Shrike
Drongo
Grey-backed Fiscal
Lesser Grey Shrike
Fiscal Shrike
White-breasted Tit
Black-headed Oriole
Wattled Starling
Blue-eared Glossy Starling
Red-wing Starling
Superb Starling
Red-billed Oxpecker
Malachite Sunbird
Bronzy Sunbird
Golden-winged Sunbird
Mariqua Sunbird
Variable Sunbird
Amethyst Sunbird
Scarlet-chested Sunbird
Collared Sunbird
Grey-headed Social Weaver
Rufous Sparrow
Chestnut Sparrow
Speke's Weaver
Chestnut Weaver
Black-necked Weaver
Spectacled Weaver
Holub's Golden Weaver
Reichenow's Weaver
Red-headed Weaver
Red-billed Quelea
Yellow Bishop
White-winged Widow-bird
Bronze Mannikin
Quail Finch
Green-winged Pytilia
African Fire Finch
Red-billed Fire Finch
Yellow-bellied Waxbill
Waxbill
Crimson-rumped Waxbill
Red-cheeked Cordon-bleu
Purple Grenadier
Indigo-bird
Pin-tailed Whydah
Brimstone Canary
Yellow-rumped Canary
Streaky Seed-eater
Golden-breasted Bunting
Cinnamon-breasted Rock Bunting

FERGUSON'S GULF, LAKE TURKANA (RUDOLF). Ferguson's Gulf, some 64km (40 miles) north-east of Lodwar, Turkana, on the western shores of Lake Turkana possesses an extremely rich avifauna. This is the one locality in Kenya where, in the spring, one may observe Black-tailed Godwits and Spotted Redshanks in full breeding plumage. Between March and early May it is also an exceptional locality for the northwards movement of European passage migrants. Vast numbers of various races of Blue-headed and Yellow Wagtails move through in waves, together with huge flocks of Marsh Sandpipers and other waders. Birds of prey are abundant in the locality: in some years Swallow-tailed Kites are very common, even breeding in colonies in isolated groups of acacia trees between the Gulf and Lodwar.

Central Island in Lake Turkana may be reached from Ferguson's Gulf. This island with its crater lakes is the nesting area of large colonies of water-birds (and of crocodiles) and Lesser Flamingos are reputed to breed there also. African Skimmers nest in April/May on the black lava sand beaches.

Mammals are not well represented but the general region is rich in many species of bats, including the rare Mouse-tailed Bat: it is not at all unlikely that new species remain to be discovered.

Some of the special birds which occur in the Ferguson's Gulf area include:

Reef Heron
Taita Falcon
Fox Kestrel
Swallow-tailed Kite
Bat Hawk
Osprey Nests on Central Island
Heuglin's Bustard
Senegal Stone Curlew
Spotted Redshank
Black-tailed Godwit
Cream-coloured Courser
Pratincole
Caspian Tern Nests on Central Island
Little Tern
African Skimmer
Abyssinian Roller
Carmine Bee-eater
Jackson's Hornbill
Abyssinian Ground Hornbill
Star-spotted Nightjar
Curly-crested Helmet Shrike
Pygmy Sunbird
Shining Sunbird
Somali Sparrow
Yellow-crowned Bishop

SOKOKE-ARABUKU FOREST. The coastal Sokoke Forest runs parallel to the coast-line north of Mombasa from above Kilifi to Gedi. It is the home of two outstandingly interesting and rare mammals – the Zanzibar or Aders' Duiker and the Yellow-rumped Elephant Shrew – and of many rare and local birds. Amongst these is Morden's Owlet (*Otus ireneae*), also known as the Sokoke Scops Owl, discovered not many years ago and a species smaller even than the African Scops Owl with finely vermiculated underparts.

Other special birds which occur in the Sokoke-Arabuku forest are:

Southern Banded Harrier Eagle
Fischer's Turaco
Green Barbet
Green Tinkerbird
Golden-tailed Woodpecker
Boehm's Spinetail
Mottled-throated Spinetail
African Pitta
Sokoke Pipit
Scaly Babbler
Little Yellow Flycatcher
Spotted Ground Thrush
East Coast Akalat
Retz's Red-billed Shrike
Chestnut-fronted Shrike
Zanzibar Puff-back Shrike
Four-coloured Bush Shrike
Nicator
Amani Sunbird
Plain-backed Sunbird
Clarke's Weaver

TANZANIA

Tanzania possesses seven principal National Parks, the Ngorongoro Conservation Area which includes the famous Ngorongoro Crater, and a number of Game Reserves of which some may in future be designated National Parks.

Best known among Tanzania's faunal reserves is the Serengeti National Park of 14,500sq km (5,600sq miles), perhaps the most famous game area in the world. Lake Manyara National Park is noted for its birdlife and for tree-climbing lions. The Arusha National Park, sited between Mounts Kilimanjaro and Meru, has the small but beautiful Ngurdoto Crater where the wildlife exists without disturbance from man. Two more recently created sanctuaries are the Mikumi National Park, within easy reach of Dar-es-Salaam; and the Ruaha National Park, a vast region of over 12,950sq km (5,000sq miles) where Greater Kudu are common. These two parks are as yet relatively undeveloped, but their future potential is very great and Ruaha may well become the premier National Park in East Africa.

LAKE MANYARA NATIONAL PARK

Although Lake Manyara National Park covers an area of only 318sq km (123sq miles), its terrain is so diverse that its mammal and bird lists are most impressive. The Park includes the northern and most of the western parts of the lake and its shores with a westward expansion to the top of the Rift Valley wall where the Lake Manyara Hotel is sited. Large areas of ground-water forest with giant fig and mahogany trees alternate with acacia woodland and more open places, all well watered. A network of roads and tracks gives the visitor maximum game and bird viewing opportunities. The tree-climbing Lions of Manyara – like the tree-climbing Lions of Ishasha in the Ruwenzori National Park, Uganda – are famous for this feature of lion behaviour, which may also be observed in Ngorongoro and Serengeti. In Manyara it is probably due to a combination of the need to avoid dense undergrowth and a search for cool shade. Probably the lions have also found that in an arboreal resting place the torment of biting flies is less.

In the Ruwenzori National Park a different explanation must be sought: there the lions apparently climb trees as vantage points in order to see over the tall grass.

Numbers of Elephant are resident in the Park. Buffalo are common and herds of 300–400 have been recorded. Black Rhinoceros are very uncommon. Leopards occur in most places and it is not unusual to come across them in the early morning or late evening: like the lions, they may be seen resting in trees.

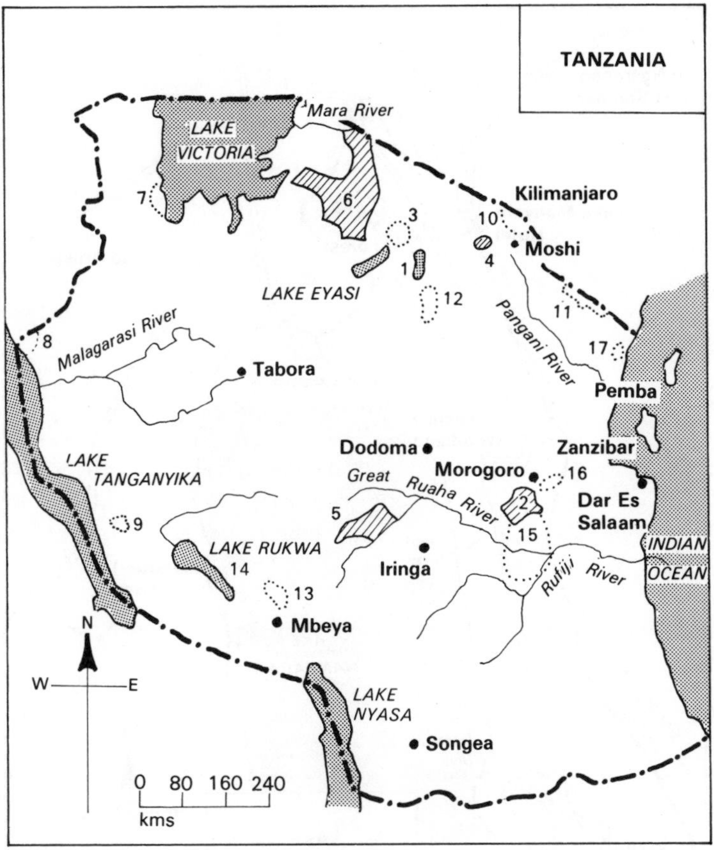

1 Lake Manyara NP	7 Biharamolo GR	13 Poroto Mountains
2 Mikumi NP	8 Gombe Stream GR	14 Rukwa Valley
3 Ngorongoro CA	9 Katavi Plain GR	15 Selous GR
4 Arusha NP	10 Kilimanjaro NP	16 Uluguru mountains
5 Ruaha NP	11 Mkomazi GR	17 Eastern Usambara Mountains
6 Serengeti NP	12 Tarangire NP	

Manyara is noted for its wealth of birdlife. At times the lake is visited by many thousands of Lesser Flamingos, together with a sprinkling of the larger species. Maccoa Ducks and White-backed Ducks are resident, and the beautiful little Pygmy Goose is sometimes observed. The Chestnut-banded

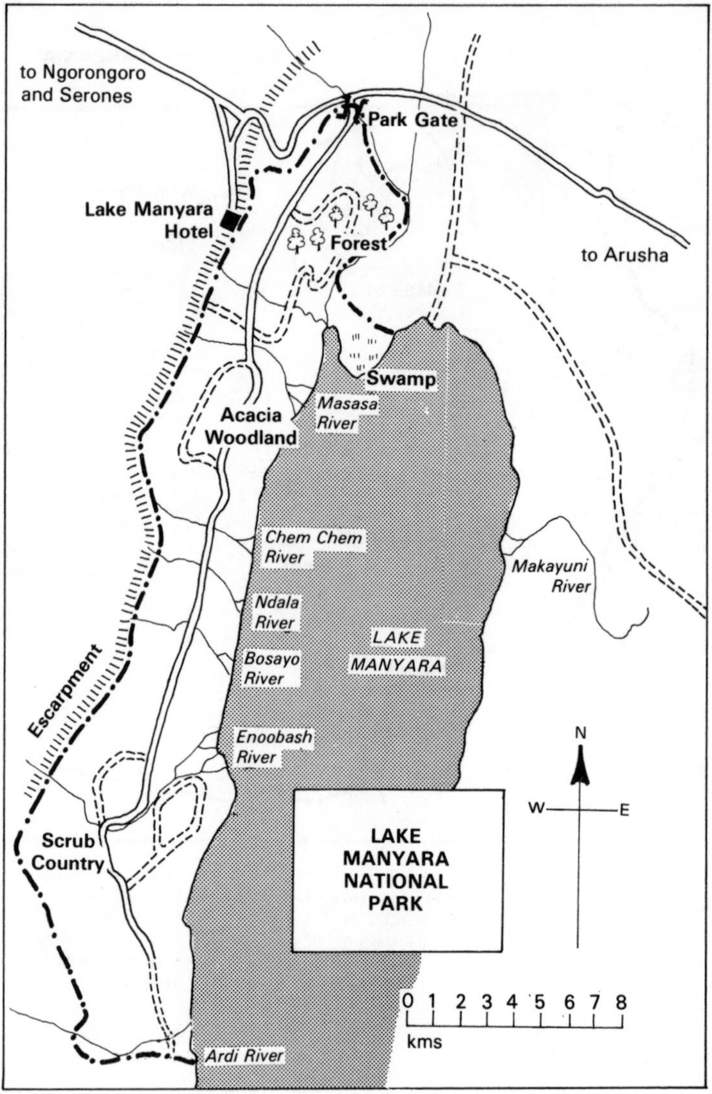
to Ngorongoro
and Serones
Park Gate
Lake Manyara
Hotel
Forest
to Arusha
Swamp
Masasa
River
Acacia
Woodland
Chem Chem
River
Makayuni
River
Ndala
River
LAKE
MANYARA
Bosayo
River
Escarpment
Enoobash
River
N
W
E
Scrub
Country
LAKE
MANYARA
NATIONAL
PARK
0 1 2 3 4 5 6 7 8
kms
Ardi River

Sand Plover, a bird with a very restricted distribution in East Africa, is found on mudflats and sandy areas. Over 30 different birds of prey have been recorded in the Park, including the Palm-nut Vulture and Ayres' and Crowned Hawk Eagles.

Lake Manyara National Park is 107km (67 miles) south-west of Arusha via the Great North Road; at Nakuyuni a right turn leads after 40km (25 miles) to the village of Mto-wa-Mbu: the Park entrance is a little over a mile past the village. Accommodation is available at the Lake Manyara Hotel, sited on the top of the Rift Wall with spectacular views over the lake. Official camping sites are available near the Park boundary.

MAMMALS OF LAKE MANYARA NATIONAL PARK

Spectacled Elephant Shrew
Giant White-toothed Shrew
Straw-coloured Fruit Bat
Epauletted Fruit Bat
White-bellied Tomb Bat
Hollow-faced Bat
False Vampire Bat
Yellow-winged Bat
Lander's Horseshoe Bat
Lesser Leaf-nosed Bat
Banana Bat or **African Pipistrelle**
Yellow-bellied Bat
Angola Free-tailed Bat
White-bellied Free-tailed Bat
Greater Galago
Bush Baby
Black-faced Vervet Monkey
Sykes' Monkey
Olive Baboon
Black-backed Jackal
Side-striped Jackal
Bat-eared Fox
Zorilla
Ratel or **Honey Badger**
Clawless Otter
African Civet
Small-spotted Genet
Large-spotted Genet
African Palm Civet
Marsh Mongoose
Dwarf Mongoose
Black-tipped Mongoose
Banded Mongoose
Spotted Hyaena
Lion
Leopard
Ant Bear
Tree Hyrax
Rock Hyrax
African Elephant
Black Rhinoceros
Common Zebra
Hippopotamus
Warthog
Masai Giraffe
Coke's Hartebeest
Red Duiker
Bush Duiker
Klipspringer
Suni
Kirk's Dik-dik
Common Waterbuck
Bohor Reedbuck
Impala
Bushbuck
African Buffalo
African Hare
Cane Rat
Porcupine
Striped Ground Squirrel
Bush Squirrel
African Dormouse

BIRDS OF LAKE MANYARA NATIONAL PARK

Masai Ostrich
Great-crested Grebe
Little Grebe
Long-tailed Cormorant
White Pelican
Pink-backed Pelican
Grey Heron
Black-headed Heron
Goliath Heron
Purple Heron
Great White Egret
Yellow-billed Egret
Black Heron
Little Egret
Buff-backed Heron or **Cattle Egret**
Squacco Heron
Green-backed Heron
Night Heron
Dwarf Bittern
Hamerkop
White Stork
European Black Stork Rare visitor
Abdim's Stork
Open-bill Stork
Saddle-bill Stork
Marabou Stork
Wood Ibis or **Yellow-billed Stork**
Sacred Ibis
Hadada Ibis
Glossy Ibis
African Spoonbill
Greater Flamingo
Lesser Flamingo
Maccoa Duck
White-backed Duck
African Pochard
European Shoveler
Yellow-billed Duck
African Black Duck On streams

Garganey Teal
Cape Wigeon
Hottentot Teal
Red-billed Duck
European Pintail
Pygmy Goose
Knob-billed Duck
Egyptian Goose
Spur-winged Goose
Secretary Bird
Ruppell's Vulture
White-backed Vulture
Nubian or **Lappet-faced Vulture**
White-headed Vulture
Egyptian Vulture
Hooded Vulture
Lanner
European Hobby
African Hobby
European Kestrel
Lesser Kestrel
Pygmy Falcon
Cuckoo Falcon Rare
European Black Kite
African Black Kite
Black-shouldered Kite
Steppe Eagle Uncommon winter visitor
Tawny Eagle
Wahlberg's Eagle
Ayres' Hawk Eagle
Martial Eagle
Crowned Hawk Eagle
Long-crested Eagle
Lizard Buzzard
Black-chested Harrier Eagle
Bateleur
African Fish Eagle
Palm-nut Vulture
Steppe Buzzard
Augur Buzzard
Little Sparrow Hawk
Ovampo Sparrow Hawk Rare
Great Sparrow Hawk
Shikra
African Goshawk
Gabar Goshawk
Pale Chanting Goshawk
Montagu's Harrier
Pallid Harrier
European Marsh Harrier
African Marsh Harrier
Harrier Hawk
Osprey
Crested Francolin
Hildebrandt's Francolin
Red-necked Spurfowl
Yellow-necked Spurfowl
Cape Quail
Harlequin Quail
Helmeted Guinea-fowl
Crested Guinea-fowl
African Crake
Black Crake
Purple Gallinule
Moorhen
Lesser Moorhen
Red-knobbed Coot
Crowned Crane
Black-bellied Bustard
Hartlaub's Bustard
Spotted Stone Curlew
Water Dikkop
African Jacana
Ringed Plover
Little Ringed Plover
White-fronted Sand Plover
Chestnut-banded Sand Plover
Kittlitz's Plover
Three-banded Plover
Caspian Plover
Crowned Plover
Blacksmith Plover
Long-toed Lapwing
Avocet
Black-winged Stilt
Painted Snipe
European Common Snipe
Great Snipe
African Snipe
Curlew Sandpiper
Little Stint
Sanderling Rare visitor
Ruff
Terek Sandpiper Uncommon
Common Sandpiper
Green Sandpiper
Wood Sandpiper
Redshank Rare visitor
Spotted Redshank Rare visitor
Marsh Sandpiper
Greenshank
Black-tailed Godwit Uncommon visitor
Curlew
Whimbrel
Temminck's Courser
Two-banded Courser
Pratincole
Lesser Black-headed Gull
Grey-headed Gull
Gull-billed Tern
White-winged Black Tern
Whiskered Tern
African Skimmer
Button Quail
Yellow-throated Sandgrouse
Speckled Pigeon
Olive Pigeon
Bronze-naped Pigeon
Red-eyed Dove
Mourning Dove
Ring-necked Dove
Laughing Dove
Namaqua Dove
Tambourine Dove
Emerald-spotted Wood Dove
Lemon Dove
Green Pigeon
European Cuckoo
African Cuckoo
Red-chested Cuckoo
Black Cuckoo
Great Spotted Cuckoo
Levaillant's Cuckoo
Black and White Cuckoo
Emerald Cuckoo
Didric Cuckoo
Black Coucal
White-browed Coucal
Schalow's Turaco
Violet-crested Turaco
Bare-faced Go-away-bird
Brown Parrot
Fischer's Lovebird
Yellow-collared Lovebird
European Roller
Lilac-breasted Roller
Rufous-crowned Roller
Broad-billed Roller
Pied Kingfisher
Giant Kingfisher
Malachite Kingfisher
Pygmy Kingfisher
Woodland Kingfisher
Brown-hooded Kingfisher
Grey-headed Kingfisher
Striped Kingfisher
European Bee-eater
Madagascar Bee-eater
Cinnamon-chested Bee-eater
Little Bee-eater
White-fronted Bee-eater
Silvery-cheeked Hornbill
Grey Hornbill
Red-billed Hornbill
Von der Decken's Hornbill
Crowned Hornbill
Ground Hornbill
African Hoopoe

Green Wood Hoopoe
Scimitar-bill
Cape Grass Owl
African Marsh Owl
Pearl-spotted Owlet
Spotted Eagle Owl
Verreaux's Eagle Owl
European Nightjar
Plain Nightjar
Speckled Mousebird
Blue-naped Mousebird
Narina's Trogon
White-headed Barbet
Spotted-flanked Barbet
Red-fronted Barbet
Red-fronted Tinkerbird
Levaillant's Barbet
Red and Yellow Barbet
D'Arnaud's Barbet
Greater Honeyguide
Scaly-throated Honeyguide
Lesser Honeyguide
Zambesi Honeyguide
Nubian Woodpecker
Cardinal Woodpecker
Bearded Woodpecker
Grey Woodpecker
Little Swift
Palm Swift
African Pitta
Redwing Bush Lark
Flappet Lark
Fischer's Sparrow Lark
Red-capped Lark
African Pied Wagtail
Mountain Wagtail
Wells' Wagtail
Blue-headed Wagtail and races
Sandy Plain-backed Pipit
Richard's Pipit
Pangani Longclaw
Rosy-breasted Longclaw
Arrow-marked Babbler
Northern Pied Babbler
Yellow-vented Bulbul
Fischer's Greenbul
Yellow-bellied Greenbul
European Spotted Flycatcher
Dusky Flycatcher
Ashy Flycatcher
Grey Tit-Flycatcher
Chin-spot Flycatcher
Paradise Flycatcher
European Rock Thrush
European Common Wheatear
Pied Wheatear
Capped Wheatear
Cliff Chat
White-browed Robin Chat
Red-capped Robin Chat
Spotted Morning Warbler
Red-backed Scrub Robin
White-winged Scrub Robin
Sprosser
Blackcap Warbler
Lesser Swamp Warbler
Black-breasted Apalis
Red-faced Crombec
Grey Tit-warbler
Grey-backed Camaroptera
Rattling Cisticola
Winding Cisticola
Croaking Cisticola
Tawny-flanked Prinia
European Swallow
Wire-tailed Swallow
Mosque Swallow
Striped Swallow
African Sand Martin
Banded Martin
African Rock Martin
Black Rough-wing Swallow
Black Cuckoo Shrike
Drongo
Straight-crested Helmet Shrike
White-crowned Shrike
Lesser Grey Shrike
Long-tailed Fiscal
Grey-backed Fiscal
Red-backed Shrike
Red-tailed Shrike
Magpie Shrike
Slate-coloured Boubou
Black-backed Puff-back
Brown-headed Tchagra
Sulphur-breasted Bush Shrike
White-breasted Tit
African Golden Oriole
European Golden Oriole
Black-headed Oriole
Pied Crow
White-naped Raven
Wattled Starling
Violet-backed Starling
Blue-eared Glossy Starling
Red-wing Starling
Hildebrandt's Starling
Superb Starling
Yellow-billed Oxpecker
Red-billed Oxpecker
Yellow White-eye
Bronzy Sunbird
Beautiful Sunbird (black-bellied race)
Golden-winged Sunbird
Variable Sunbird
Amethyst Sunbird
Scarlet-chested Sunbird
Collared Sunbird
Kenya Violet-backed Sunbird
Buffalo Weaver
White-headed Buffalo Weaver
Rufous-tailed Weaver
Grey-headed Sparrow
Yellow-spotted Petronia
Masked Weaver
Vitelline Masked Weaver
Golden-backed Weaver
Chestnut Weaver
Spectacled Weaver
Grosbeak Weaver
Red-headed Weaver
Red-billed Quelea
Cardinal Quelea
Red Bishop
Black Bishop
Fan-tailed Widow-bird
Red-collared Widow-bird
Rufous-backed Mannikin
Peters' Twin-spot
Green-winged Pytilia
Jameson's Fire Finch
Red-billed Fire Finch
Waxbill
Crimson-rumped Waxbill
Red-cheeked Cordon-bleu
Indigo-bird
Pin-tailed Whydah
Steel-blue Whydah
Fischer's Straw-tailed Whydah
Paradise Whydah
Streaky Seed-eater

MIKUMI NATIONAL PARK

Mikumi National Park, a faunal reserve of some 1,165sq km (450sq miles), is situated 294km (183 miles) from Dar es Salaam astride the macadamised main road to Iringa. Picturesque wooded hills form a border to the Mkata River flood plains, one of the main sections of the Park and the haunt of many Elephant and Buffalo. There are also areas of brachystegia woodlands, broken by glades and transient watercourses. Game animals and birds are abundant.

The mammals most frequently encountered are Lion, Hippopotamus, Masai Giraffe, Common Zebra, Impala, Warthog and Wildebeest. Present though less common are Greater Kudu, Black Rhinoceros, Cheetah, Leopard, Common Waterbuck, Bohor Reedbuck, Lichtenstein's Hartebeest and Sable Antelope.

Birdlife is extremely varied, many colourful and interesting species occurring in Mikumi National Park which are not found in the more northern Parks. Species of special note include White-backed Night Heron, Dickinson's Kestrel (in brachystegia woodlands), Bronze-winged Courser, Delalande's Green Pigeon, Violet-crested Turaco, Brown-necked Parrot, Racquet-tailed Roller, Boehm's Bee-eater, Pale-billed Hornbill, Spotted-throated Woodpecker, Angola Rock Thrush, White-headed Black Chat, White-breasted Cuckoo Shrike, Ashy Starling and Shelley's Double-collared Sunbird which frequents a red-flowered Loranthus parasitic on brachystegia trees.

Mikumi is most accessible from Dar-es-Salaam – an easy three and a half hours' drive. It may also be reached from Iringa, 217km (135 miles) along the Iringa-Morogoro road. There is a permanent lodge at Mikumi, adjacent to the main road and airstrip, and there are also a youth hostel and camp sites.

MAMMALS OF MIKUMI NATIONAL PARK

Spectacled Elephant Shrew
Epauletted Fruit Bat
Hollow-faced Bat
Lesser Leaf-nosed Bat
Yellow-bellied Bat
White-bellied Free-tailed Bat
Bush Baby
Black-faced Vervet Monkey
Yellow Baboon
Hunting Dog
Black-backed Jackal
Bat-eared Fox
Ratel
Small-spotted Genet
Large-spotted Genet
Dwarf Mongoose
Banded Mongoose
Spotted Hyaena
Cheetah
Serval
Lion
Leopard
Ant Bear
Rock Hyrax
African Elephant
Black Rhinoceros
Common Zebra
Hippopotamus
Warthog
Masai Giraffe
Wildebeest
Red Duiker
Bush Duiker
Common Waterbuck
Bohor Reedbuck
Impala
Sable Antelope
Bushbuck
Greater Kudu
African Buffalo
African Hare
Cane Rat
Porcupine
Striped Ground Squirrel
Bush Squirrel
Spring Hare
African Dormouse

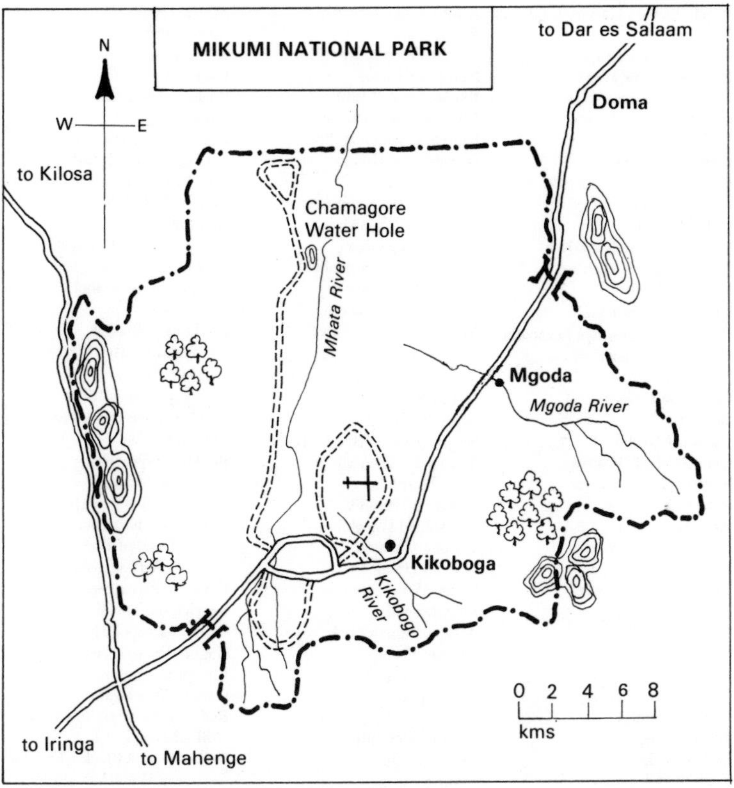

BIRDS OF MIKUMI NATIONAL PARK

Long-tailed Cormorant
White Pelican
Pink-backed Pelican
Black-headed Heron
Goliath Heron
Yellow-billed Egret
Black Heron
Little Egret
Buff-backed Heron or **Cattle Egret**
Squacco Heron
Green-backed Heron
White-backed Night Heron
Hamerkop
White Stork
Open-bill Stork
Saddle-bill Stork
Marabou Stork
Wood Ibis or **Yellow-billed Stork**
Sacred Ibis
Hadada Ibis
African Spoonbill
Red-billed Duck
Pygmy Goose
Egyptian Goose
Knob-billed Duck
Secretary Bird
White-backed Vulture
European Hobby Mainly spring migrant
Red-necked Falcon
European Kestrel
Lesser Kestrel
Dickinson's Kestrel
Cuckoo Falcon
African Black Kite
Black-shouldered Kite
Tawny Eagle
Wahlberg's Eagle
Martial Eagle
Lizard Buzzard

Black-chested Harrier Eagle
Bateleur
African Fish Eagle
Little Sparrow Hawk
Ovampo Sparrow Hawk
Great Sparrow Hawk
Shikra
Gabar Goshawk
Dark Chanting Goshawk
Montagu's Harrier
Pallid Harrier
European Marsh Harrier
African Marsh Harrier
Harrier Hawk
Coqui Francolin
Shelley's (Greywing) Francolin
Red-necked Spurfowl
Harlequin Quail
Helmeted Guinea-fowl
Black Crake
Crowned Crane
Black-bellied Bustard
Spotted Stone Curlew
Water Dikkop
African Jacana
Little Ringed Plover
Kittlitz's Plover
Three-banded Plover
Crowned Plover
Blacksmith Plover
Painted Snipe
Ruff
Common Sandpiper
Green Sandpiper
Wood Sandpiper
Greenshank
Temminck's Courser
Bronze-winged Courser
Pratincole
Red-eyed Dove
Ring-necked Dove
Laughing Dove
Namaqua Dove
Tambourine Dove
Emerald-spotted Wood Dove
Delalande's Green Pigeon
European Cuckoo
African Cuckoo
Red-chested Cuckoo
Levaillant's Cuckoo
Black and White Cuckoo
Emerald Cuckoo
Didric Cuckoo
White-browed Coucal
Violet-crested Turaco
Bare-faced Go-away-bird
Brown-necked Parrot
Brown Parrot
Yellow-collared Lovebird
European Roller
Racquet-tailed Roller
Lilac-breasted Roller
Rufous-crowned Roller
Broad-billed Roller
Pied Kingfisher
Half-collared Kingfisher
Malachite Kingfisher
Pygmy Kingfisher
Grey-headed Kingfisher
Striped Kingfisher
European Bee-eater
Madagascar Bee-eater
Southern Carmine Bee-eater
White-throated Bee-eater
Boehm's Bee-eater
Little Bee-eater
Swallow-tailed Bee-eater
Trumpeter Hornbill
Grey Hornbill
Crowned Hornbill
Pale-billed Hornbill
Ground Hornbill
African Hoopoe
Green Wood Hoopoe
Scimitar-bill
African Marsh Owl
African Wood Owl
African Scops Owl
Pearl-spotted Owlet
Verreaux's Eagle Owl
European Nightjar
Freckled Nightjar
Plain Nightjar
White-tailed Nightjar
Pennant-wing Nightjar
Long-tailed Nightjar
Speckled Mousebird
Narina's Trogon
Black-collared Barbet
Spotted-flanked Barbet
Red-fronted Barbet
Whyte's Barbet
Red-fronted Tinkerbird
Levaillant's Barbet
Red and Yellow Barbet
Greater Honeyguide
Lesser Honeyguide
Little Spotted Woodpecker
Golden-tailed Woodpecker
Cardinal Woodpecker
Spotted-throated Woodpecker
Bearded Woodpecker
Mottled Swift
Little Swift
White-rumped Swift
Palm Swift
Boehm's Spinetail
Flappet Lark
Red-capped Lark
African Pied Wagtail
Blue-headed Wagtail and races
Long-billed Pipit
Richard's Pipit
Yellow-throated Longclaw
Arrow-marked Babbler
Yellow-vented Bulbul
Brownbul
Fischer's Greenbul
European Spotted Flycatcher
Ashy Flycatcher
Pale Flycatcher
South African Black Flycatcher
Silverbird
Boehm's Flycatcher
Black and White Flycatcher
Yellow-bellied Flycatcher
Chin-spot Flycatcher
Black-throated Wattle-eye
White-tailed Crested Flycatcher
Paradise Flycatcher
Kurrichane Thrush
Ground-scraper Thrush
Angola Rock Thrush
European Common Wheatear
Capped Wheatear
Red-tailed or Familiar Chat
Cliff Chat
White-headed Black Chat
European Whinchat
White-browed Robin Chat
Red-capped Robin Chat
Spotted Morning Warbler
Red-backed Scrub Robin
Blackcap Warbler
European Willow Warbler
Barred Wren Warbler
Rattling Cisticola
Croaking Cisticola
Tawny-flanked Prinia
African Moustached Warbler
European Swallow
Angola Swallow
Blue Swallow
Wire-tailed Swallow
Red-rumped Swallow
Striped Swallow
Grey-rumped Swallow
African Sand Martin

Banded Martin
Black Cuckoo Shrike
White-breasted Cuckoo Shrike
Drongo
Square-tailed Drongo
Straight-crested Helmet Shrike
Retz's Red-billed Shrike
White-crowned Shrike
Northern Brubru
Souza's Shrike
Red-backed Shrike
Red-tailed Shrike
Magpie Shrike
Slate-coloured Boubou
Tropical Boubou
Black-backed Puff-back
Black-headed Tchagra
Brown-headed Tchagra
Blackcap Tchagra
Sulphur-breasted Bush Shrike
Grey-headed Bush Shrike
Nicator
Black Tit
Cinnamon-breasted Tit
African Penduline Tit
European Golden Oriole
African Golden Oriole
Black-headed Oriole
Pied Crow
White-naped Raven
Wattled Starling
Violet-backed Starling
Blue-eared Glossy Starling
Lesser Blue-eared Starling
Ruppell's Long-tailed Starling
Ashy Starling
Superb Starling
Red-billed Oxpecker
Yellow White-eye
Little Purple-banded Sunbird
Mariqua Sunbird
Shelley's Double-collared Sunbird
Variable Sunbird
Southern Double-collared Sunbird
Amethyst Sunbird
Scarlet-chested Sunbird
Olive Sunbird
Collared Sunbird
Violet-backed Sunbird
Spotted Creeper
White-headed Buffalo Weaver
White-browed Sparrow Weaver
Grey-headed Sparrow
Yellow-throated Petronia
Layard's Black-headed Weaver
Masked Weaver
Golden-backed Weaver
Black-necked Weaver
Spectacled Weaver
Holub's Golden Weaver
Grosbeak Weaver
Red-headed Weaver
Red-billed Quelea
Red-headed Quelea
Cardinal Quelea
Red Bishop
Black-winged Bishop
Yellow Bishop
Fan-tailed Widow-bird
Yellow-mantled Widow-bird
White-winged Widow-bird
Red-collared Widow-bird
Bronze Mannikin
Rufous-backed Mannikin
Magpie Mannikin
Grey-headed Silverbill
Urungu Seed-cracker
Quail Finch
Peters' Twin-spot
Green-winged Pytilia
Jameson's Fire Finch
Red-billed Fire Finch
Yellow-bellied Waxbill
Waxbill
Zebra Waxbill
Angola Cordon-bleu
Red-cheeked Cordon-bleu
Purple Grenadier
Indigo-bird
Pin-tailed Whydah
Fischer's Straw-tailed Whydah
Paradise Whydah
Yellow-fronted Canary
Brimstone Canary
Streaky-headed Seed-eater
Three-streaked Bunting
Golden-breasted Bunting
Cinnamon-breasted Rock Bunting

NGORONGORO CRATER CONSERVATION AREA

The Ngorongoro Conservation Area of 6,475sq km (2,500sq miles) was established in 1959. Previously, most of the area and the famous Ngorongoro Crater had formed part of the now contiguous Serengeti National Park. The dual purpose of the Conservation Area is to conserve the region's natural resources and also to safeguard the interests of the indigenous Masai inhabitants, who continue to reside there with their herds of cattle.

The Ngorongoro Crater is one of the most spectacular game haunts in Africa: it is also one of the biggest craters or more correctly calderas in the world, over 14.5km (9 miles) across, 610–760m (2,000–2,500ft) deep and covering 264sq km (102sq miles). The approach road at 2,286m (7,500ft) skirts the rim of the crater affording many breathtaking scenic views over the crater floor thousands of feet below.

Entry into the crater is by way of the Lerai Descent, an extremely steep and winding road down the slopes of the crater wall – negotiable only by four-

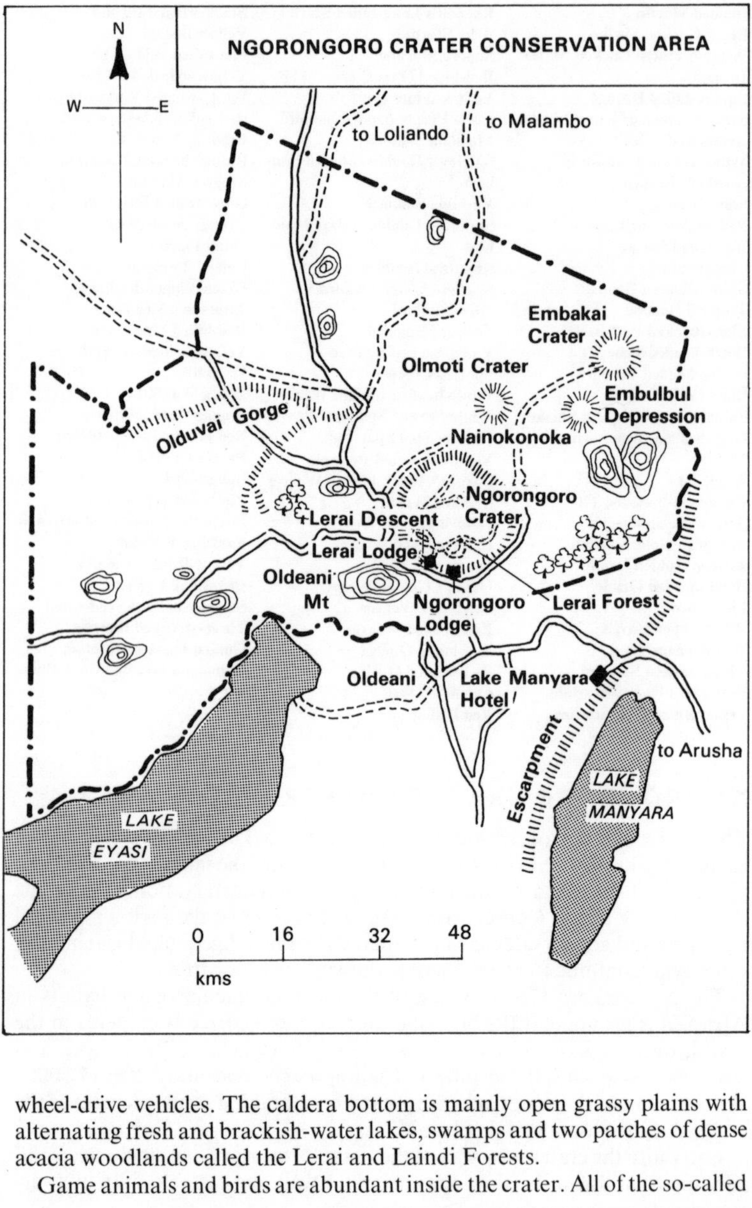

wheel-drive vehicles. The caldera bottom is mainly open grassy plains with alternating fresh and brackish-water lakes, swamps and two patches of dense acacia woodlands called the Lerai and Laindi Forests.

Game animals and birds are abundant inside the crater. All of the so-called

'Big Five' may be seen – Elephant, Lion, Black Rhinoceros, Hippopotamus and Buffalo. Other species encountered are Cheetah, Eland, Grant's and Thomson's Gazelles, Common Zebra, Wildebeest, a super-abundance of Spotted Hyaena, Hunting Dog, and, if one is lucky, Leopard.

Among the notable birds are Lammergeyer, Verreaux's Eagle and Egyptian Vulture, which make their home in the highest cliffs of the crater wall; the beautiful Rosy-breasted Longclaw, which appears on the plains after rains; and flocks of Lesser and Greater Flamingos which are spasmodic visitors to the crater lakes. The European Black Stork is sometimes seen; usually one or two winter in the crater.

In the highland forest on the crater rim two sunbirds are specially noticeable, the long-tailed Golden-winged Sunbird and the smaller Eastern Double-collared Sunbird. At dusk the Abyssinian Nightjar is often seen or heard – the call is a long-drawn-out 'Pee-oo-wee'.

From Arusha the distance to the Crater Lodge is 180km (112 miles); the road passes the entrance to Lake Manyara National Park, thence on to the Mbulu Plateau, through the farming country of Keratu and Oldeani and into the highland forest to the rim of the crater. From Seronera, headquarters of the Serengeti National Park, to the crater is 140km (87 miles), first over miles of open plains and light acacia woodlands and then into the hill country west of the crater. This road passes famous Olduvai Gorge, where remains of prehistoric man were discovered.

Accommodation is available at the two Ngorongoro Crater Lodges, situated at nearly 2,670m (8,000ft) on the crater rim, near the Lerai entrance road, and the Ngorongoro Wildlife Lodge. Other accommodation includes Ngorongoro Forest Hotel, Ngorongoro Safari Lodge at Keratu 40km (25 miles) eastwards towards Manyara National Park, three camp sites in the crater and one on the crater rim.

MAMMALS OF NGORONGORO CRATER CONSERVATION AREA

Rousette Fruit Bat
Epauletted Fruit Bat
Hollow-faced Bat
False Vampire Bat
Lesser Leaf-nosed Bat
Yellow-bellied Bat
Angola Free-tailed Bat
Black-faced Vervet Monkey
Olive Baboon
Hunting Dog
Golden Jackal
Black-backed Jackal
Side-striped Jackal
Bat-eared Fox
Ratel or **Honey Badger**
African Civet
Small-spotted Genet
Large-spotted Genet
Marsh Mongoose
Dwarf Mongoose
Banded Mongoose
Spotted Hyaena
Cheetah
African Wild Cat
Serval
Lion
Leopard
Rock Hyrax
Tree Hyrax
African Elephant
Black Rhinoceros
Common Zebra
Hippopotamus
Giant Forest Hog In forest on crater rim
Warthog
Masai Giraffe
Coke's Hartebeest
White-bearded Gnu or **Wildebeest**
Bush Duiker
Klipspringer
Common Waterbuck
Bohor Reedbuck
Impala
Thomson's Gazelle
Grant's Gazelle
Bushbuck
Eland
African Buffalo
African Hare
Porcupine
Bush Squirrel
Giant Rat

BIRDS OF NGORONGORO CRATER CONSERVATION AREA

Masai Ostrich
Little Grebe
Long-tailed Cormorant
White Pelican
Pink-backed Pelican
Grey Heron
Black-headed Heron
Goliath Heron
Great White Egret
Yellow-billed Egret
Little Egret
Buff-backed Heron or **Cattle Egret**
Squacco Heron
Hamerkop
White Stork
European Black Stork
Abdim's Stork
Open-bill Stork
Saddle-bill Stork
Marabou Stork
Wood Ibis or **Yellow-billed Stork**
Sacred Ibis
Hadada Ibis
African Spoonbill
Greater Flamingo
Lesser Flamingo
White-backed Duck
African Pochard
European Shoveler
Yellow-billed Duck
African Black Duck
Garganey Teal
Hottentot Teal
Red-billed Duck
Cape Wigeon
European Teal Rare visitor
European Pintail
Fulvous Tree Duck
Knob-billed Duck
Egyptian Goose
Spur-winged Goose
Secretary Bird
Ruppell's Vulture
White-backed Vulture
Nubian or **Lappet-faced Vulture**
White-headed Vulture
Egyptian Vulture
Hooded Vulture
Peregrine
Lanner
European Kestrel
Lesser Kestrel
European Black Kite
African Black Kite
Black-shouldered Kite
Verreaux's Eagle
Steppe Eagle
Tawny Eagle
Martial Eagle
Long-crested Eagle
Black-chested Harrier Eagle
Bateleur
African Fish Eagle
Lammergeyer
Steppe Buzzard
Augur Buzzard
Gabar Goshawk
Montagu's Harrier
Pallid Harrier
European Marsh Harrier
African Marsh Harrier
Yellow-necked Spurfowl
Helmeted Guinea-fowl
Crowned Crane
Kori Bustard
Little Ringed Plover
Kittlitz's Plover
Three-banded Plover
Caspian Plover
Crowned Plover
Senegal Plover
Blacksmith Plover
Avocet
Black-winged Stilt
Painted Snipe
European Common Snipe
African Snipe
Curlew Sandpiper
Little Stint
Ruff
Common Sandpiper
Green Sandpiper
Wood Sandpiper
Marsh Sandpiper
Greenshank
Temminck's Courser
Pratincole
White-winged Black Tern
Red-eyed Dove
Ring-necked Dove
Laughing Dove
Namaqua Dove
Emerald-spotted Wood Dove
Green Pigeon
European Cuckoo
African Cuckoo
Red-chested Cuckoo
Black Cuckoo
Great-spotted Cuckoo
Didric Cuckoo
White-browed Coucal
White-bellied Go-away-bird
Lilac-breasted Roller
Pied Kingfisher
Malachite Kingfisher
Pygmy Kingfisher
Grey-headed Kingfisher
Striped Kingfisher
European Bee-eater
Little Bee-eater
Grey Hornbill
Crowned Hornbill
African Hoopoe
Green Wood Hoopoe
Scimitar-bill
African Marsh Owl
Pearl-spotted Owlet
Spotted Eagle Owl
Verreaux's Eagle Owl
European Nightjar
Plain Nightjar
Abyssinian Nightjar
Long-tailed Nightjar
Speckled Mousebird
Nubian Woodpecker
Cardinal Woodpecker
Brown-backed Woodpecker
Nyanza Swift
Mottled Swift
Fischer's Sparrow Lark
Red-capped Lark
African Pied Wagtail
Blue-headed Wagtail and races
Richard's Pipit
Yellow-throated Longclaw
Rosy-breasted Longclaw
Yellow-vented Bulbul
European Spotted Flycatcher
Grey Flycatcher
White-eyed Slaty Flycatcher
South African Black Flycatcher
Chin-spot Flycatcher
Black-throated Wattle-eye
Paradise Flycatcher
European Rock Thrush
Little Rock Thrush
European Common Wheatear
Isabelline Wheatear
Pied Wheatear
Schalow's Wheatear

Capped Wheatear
Cliff Chat
Anteater Chat
Stonechat
European Whinchat
Robin Chat
European Willow Warbler
Black-breasted Apalis
Grey-backed Camaroptera
Rattling Cisticola
Winding Cisticola
Tawny-flanked Prinia
European Swallow
Angola Swallow
Red-rumped Swallow
Striped Swallow
Grey-rumped Swallow
European Sand Martin
African Sand Martin
Banded Martin
African Rock Martin
Black Rough-wing Swallow
Black Cuckoo Shrike
Drongo
White-crowned Shrike
Northern Brubru
Grey-backed Fiscal
Lesser Grey Shrike
Fiscal Shrike
Long-tailed Fiscal
Red-backed Shrike
Red-tailed Shrike
Magpie Shrike
Slate-coloured Boubou
Tropical Boubou
Black-headed Tchagra
Sulphur-breasted Bush Shrike
White-breasted Tit
Black-headed Oriole
Pied Crow
Cape Rock
White-naped Raven
Wattled Starling
Blue-eared Glossy Starling
Red-wing Starling
Superb Starling
Red-billed Oxpecker
Bronzy Sunbird
Golden-winged Sunbird
Mariqua Sunbird
Variable Sunbird
Eastern Double-collared Sunbird
Scarlet-chested Sunbird
Collared Sunbird
White-browed Sparrow Weaver
Rufous-tailed Weaver
Grey-headed Social Weaver
Rufous Sparrow
Yellow-spotted Pretonia
Speckle-fronted Weaver
Masked Weaver
Chestnut Weaver
Red-billed Quelea
Cardinal Quelea
Red Bishop
Yellow Bishop
Fan-tailed Widow-bird
White-winged Widow-bird
Bronze Mannikin
Cut-throat
Quail Finch
Green-winged Pytilia
Red-billed Fire Finch
Waxbill
Red-cheeked Cordon-bleu
Purple Grenadier
Indigo-bird
Pin-tailed Whydah
Paradise Whydah
Yellow-fronted Canary
Brimstone Canary
Yellow-breasted Seed-eater
Streaky Seed-eater
Golden-breasted Bunting
Cinnamon-breasted Rock Bunting

ARUSHA NGURDOTO CRATER NATIONAL PARK

Considering that the Arusha National Park embraces an area of only 52sq km (20sq miles) and is less than half an hour's drive from Arusha, it is remarkable for its range of habitats – a miniature volcanic crater, highland rain forest, acacia woodland and a string of crater lakes – and for the range of game animals and birds which occur there. In addition on a clear day there are spectacular views of both Mount Kilimanjaro and Mount Meru from strategically placed lookouts on Ngurdoto Crater rim.

Game animals in great quantity will not be seen in this Park, but Black Rhinoceros, Elephant, Buffalo, Masai Giraffe and other animals live in the crater and may be viewed through binoculars from the several ideally placed vantage points around the rim. The crater itself, one and a half miles across, is a sanctuary within a sanctuary, open only to the wild creatures which inhabit it and where man is completely excluded.

The Momela crater lakes at the northern end of the Park are visited by herds of Elephant, Masai Giraffe, the odd Black Rhinoceros and other animals, and it is here that Bushbuck sometimes emerge from cover in the early morning and late evening.

In the forested parts of the Park, Black and White Colobus and Blue

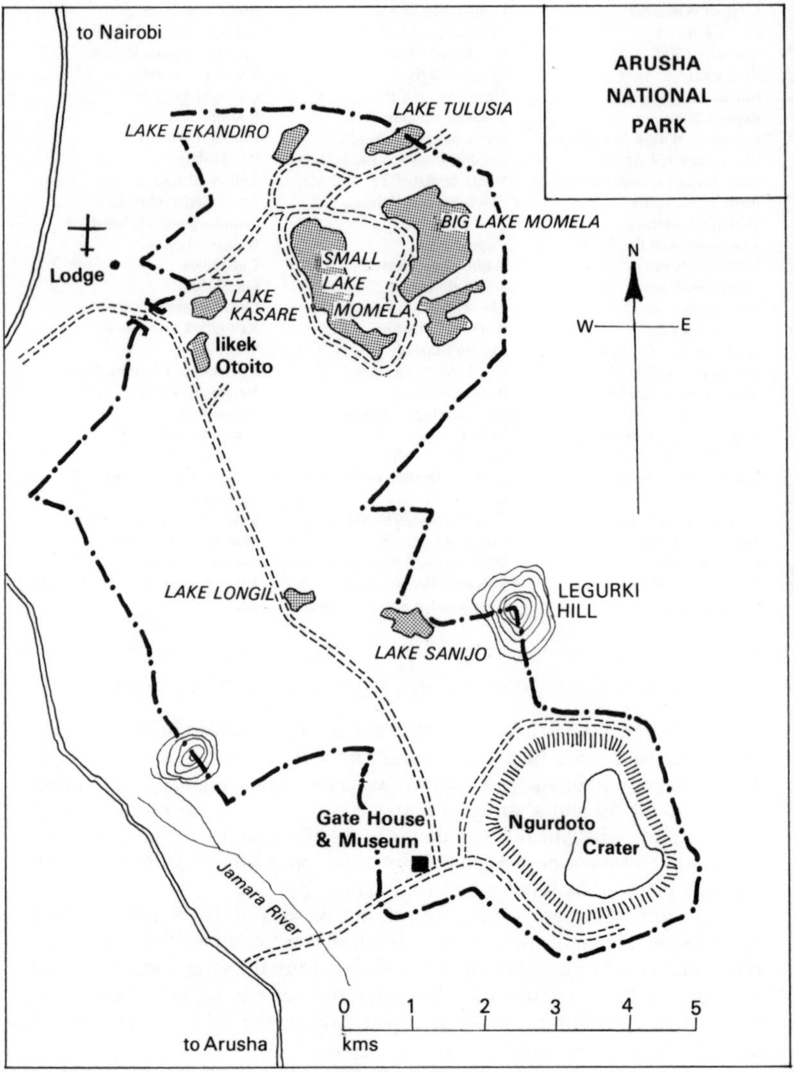

Monkeys are often observed, and if one is fortunate the Crowned Hawk Eagle – ogre of the monkey population – may also be seen.

Greater and Lesser Flamingos and a host of other water-birds occur on the

Momela lakes and offer many photographic opportunities. The beautiful Narina's Trogon is found in the forests, but is shy and often overlooked, and is best located by its call – a series of soft coos all on one note. The African Broadbill and the deep green Broad-ringed White-eye are other interesting birds found in this forest habitat.

To reach Arusha National Park from Arusha one follows the main Arusha-Moshi road for 20km (12 miles), there turning left into a signposted gravel road towards Ngare Nanyuki; and after 14.5km (9 miles) a short branch road to the right leads to the Park's crater gate. If travelling from Nairobi one takes a signposted turning to the left 38km (24 miles) before Arusha, from then on following signboards which lead to the Momela Gate. For those wishing to spend some days in the Park, accommodation is provided at the Momela Game Lodge and at the Mount Meru Game Sanctuary at nearby Usa River. There are also camp sites in the Park.

MAMMALS OF ARUSHA NATIONAL PARK

Giant White-toothed Shrew
Rousette Fruit Bat
Epauletted Fruit Bat
White-bellied Tomb Bat
Hollow-faced Bat
False Vampire Bat
Yellow-winged Bat
Banana Bat
Yellow-bellied Bat
Angola Free-tailed Bat
White-bellied Free-tailed Bat
Greater Galago
Bush Baby
Black-faced Vervet Monkey
Blue Monkey
Olive Baboon
Black and White Colobus
Black-backed Jackal
Side-striped Jackal
Zorilla
African Civet
Large-spotted Genet
African Palm Civet
Marsh Mongoose
Black-tipped Mongoose
Spotted Hyaena
Serval
Leopard
Ant Bear
Tree Hyrax
Rock Hyrax
African Elephant
Black Rhinoceros
Common Zebra
Hippopotamus
Giant Forest Hog
Warthog
Bush Pig
Masai Giraffe
Red Duiker
Blue Duiker
Bush Duiker
Suni
Kirk's Dik-dik
Common Waterbuck
Bohor Reedbuck
Impala
Bushbuck
African Buffalo
African Hare
Porcupine
Bush Squirrel
Giant Rat
Kenya Mole Rat

BIRDS OF ARUSHA NATIONAL PARK

Great-crested Grebe
Little Grebe
Long-tailed Cormorant
White Pelican
Pink-backed Pelican
Grey Heron
Black-headed Heron
Purple Heron
Great White Egret
Yellow-billed Egret
Buff-backed Heron or **Cattle Egret**
Squacco Heron
Night Heron
Little Bittern
Hamerkop
White Stork Spasmodic visitor
Saddle-bill Stork
Marabou Stork
Wood Ibis or **Yellow-billed Stork**
Sacred Ibis
Hadada Ibis
African Spoonbill
Greater Flamingo
Lesser Flamingo
Maccoa Duck
White-backed Duck
African Pochard
European Shoveler
Yellow-billed Duck
Garganey Teal
Cape Wigeon
Hottentot Teal
Red-billed Duck
European Pintail
White-faced Tree Duck
Fulvous Tree Duck
Knob-billed Duck

Egyptian Goose
Spur-winged Goose
White-backed Vulture
Peregrine
Lanner
European Kestrel
Cuckoo Falcon
African Black Kite
Black-shouldered Kite
Ayres' Hawk Eagle
Martial Eagle
Crowned Hawk Eagle
Long-crested Eagle
Bateleur
African Fish Eagle
Palm-nut Vulture
Mountain Buzzard
Augur Buzzard
Little Sparrow Hawk
Great Sparrow Hawk
African Goshawk
Gabar Goshawk
Harrier Hawk
Shelley's (Greywing) Francolin
Hildebrandt's Francolin
Scaly Francolin
Helmeted Guinea-fowl
Black Crake
Moorhen
Lesser Moorhen
Red-knobbed Coot
Crowned Crane
African Jacana or **Lily Trotter**
Ringed Plover
Little Ringed Plover
Kittlitz's Plover
Three-banded Plover
Crowned Plover
Black-winged Plover
Blacksmith Plover
Avocet
Black-winged Stilt
European Common Snipe
African Snipe
Curlew Sandpiper
Little Stint
Ruff
Common Sandpiper
Green Sandpiper
Wood Sandpiper
Marsh Sandpiper
Greenshank
Olive Pigeon
Bronze-naped Pigeon
Red-eyed Dove
Ring-necked Dove
Tambourine Dove
Emerald-spotted Wood Dove
Lemon Dove
Green Pigeon
Red-chested Cuckoo
Black Cuckoo
Levaillant's Cuckoo
Black and White Cuckoo
Emerald Cuckoo
Didric Cuckoo
Klaas' Cuckoo
White-browed Coucal
Green Coucal or **Yellowbill**
Hartlaub's Turaco
European Roller
Broad-billed Roller
Malachite Kingfisher
Brown-hooded Kingfisher
Striped Kingfisher
European Bee-eater
Little Bee-eater
Cinnamon-chested Bee-eater
White-fronted Bee-eater
Silvery-cheeked Hornbill
Crowned Hornbill
African Hoopoe
Green Wood Hoopoe
Scimitar-bill
African Wood Owl
Spotted Eagle Owl
European Nightjar
Abyssinian Nightjar
Speckled Mousebird
Narina's Trogon
White-headed Barbet
Brown-breasted Barbet
Spotted-flanked Barbet
White-eared Barbet
Greater Honeyguide
Lesser Honeyguide
Nubian Woodpecker
Cardinal Woodpecker
Bearded Woodpecker
Grey Woodpecker
Mottled Swift
African Broadbill
Rufous-naped Lark
Red-capped Lark
African Pied Wagtail
Blue-headed Wagtail and races
European Grey Wagtail
Richard's Pipit
Tree Pipit
Pangani Longclaw
Northern Pied Babbler
Abyssinian Hill Babbler
Yellow-vented Bulbul
Fischer's Greenbul
Dusky Flycatcher
Cape Puff-back Flycatcher
Chin-spot Flycatcher
Paradise Flycatcher
European Rock Thrush
European Common Wheatear
Capped Wheatear
Stonechat
White-browed Robin Chat
Red-backed Scrub Robin
White-starred Bush Robin
European Whitethroat
Blackcap Warbler
European Willow Warbler
Yellow-throated Woodland Warbler
Fan-tailed Warbler
Black-headed Apalis
Black-breasted Apalis
Red-faced Crombec
Grey-backed Camaroptera
Hunter's Cisticola
Tawny-flanked Prinia
African Moustached Warbler
European Swallow
Wire-tailed Swallow
Red-rumped Swallow
Mosque Swallow
Striped Swallow
Black Rough-wing Swallow
Black Cuckoo Shrike
Grey Cuckoo Shrike
Drongo
Square-tailed Drongo
Straight-crested Helmet Shrike
Retz's Red-billed Shrike
Fiscal Shrike
Red-backed Shrike
Red-tailed Shrike
Tropical Boubou
Black-backed Puff-back
Black-headed Tchagra
Brown-headed Tchagra
Black-fronted Bush Shrike
Red-throated Tit
European Golden Oriole
African Golden Oriole
Black-headed Oriole
Wattled Starling
Violet-backed Starling
Waller's Chestnut-wing Starling
Red-winged Starling
Kenrick's Starling
Superb Starling

Red-billed Oxpecker
Broad-ringed White-eye
Malachite Sunbird
Bronzy Sunbird
Beautiful Sunbird
Golden-winged Sunbird
Variable Sunbird
Amethyst Sunbird
Scarlet-chested Sunbird
Olive Sunbird
Collared Sunbird
Speke's Weaver
Chestnut Weaver
Golden Palm Weaver
Taveta Golden Weaver
Spectacled Weaver
Reichenow's Weaver
Grosbeak Weaver
Red-headed Weaver
Red-billed Quelea
Cardinal Quelea
Yellow Bishop
Red-naped Widow Bird
Bronze Mannikin
Rufous-backed Mannikin
Grey-headed Negro Finch
Jameson's Fire Finch
Yellow-bellied Waxbill
Waxbill
Crimson-rumped Waxbill
Pin-tailed Whydah
Streaky Seed-eater
Thick-billed Seed-eater
African Citril
Golden-breasted Bunting

RUAHA NATIONAL PARK

The Ruaha National Park, gazetted in 1964, is a vast, still comparatively unexplored game and bird sanctuary covering 12,950sq km (5,000sq miles); it is only a little smaller than the better-known Serengeti National Park. Mainly on account of its geographical position this most outstanding Park is at present little visited although it is readily accessible by air, being less than four hours' flying time from Nairobi. A landing strip suitable for light aircraft exists at Park headquarters at Msembe: or one can fly to Iringa and motor the remaining 113km (70 miles) to the Park.

The Ruaha National Park lies between two large rivers, the Njombe and the Ruaha: the latter flows for 160km (100 miles) along the entire eastern border, first through rugged gorges and rocky broken country then through lush plains where it is flanked by palm thickets and tall acacia woodland. During the dry season, from June to November, there is a concentration of game along the river, herds of Elephant, Giraffe, Buffalo and Impala and numerous Greater Kudu. Crocodiles may be seen basking on the many sandbanks.

The hinterland varies from mountains to undulating plateau country at an altitude around 914m (3,000ft). There are stretches of brachystegia woodland, the home of Roan and Sable Antelope and Lichtenstein's Hartebeest, and bush country where Lesser Kudu occur. There are also areas of open grassland, an abundance of rocky hills and in the south the zoologically unexplored massif of Ngalambulwa Mountain which rises to 1,600m (5,250ft).

Three main areas have so far been opened up for game viewing, the really spectacular Ruaha River drive of great scenic beauty where Greater Kudu are common and tame, the Mdonya woodlands circuit where Sable and Roan Antelope and Lichtenstein's Hartebeest may be encountered, and the Mbage-Mwagusi track for Elephants.

Access roads to other areas of special interest are under construction or being planned. Among the special facilities available at Ruaha – which should be introduced in other National Parks – are the several photographic hides and tree-houses strategically placed to overlook habitual game watering points.

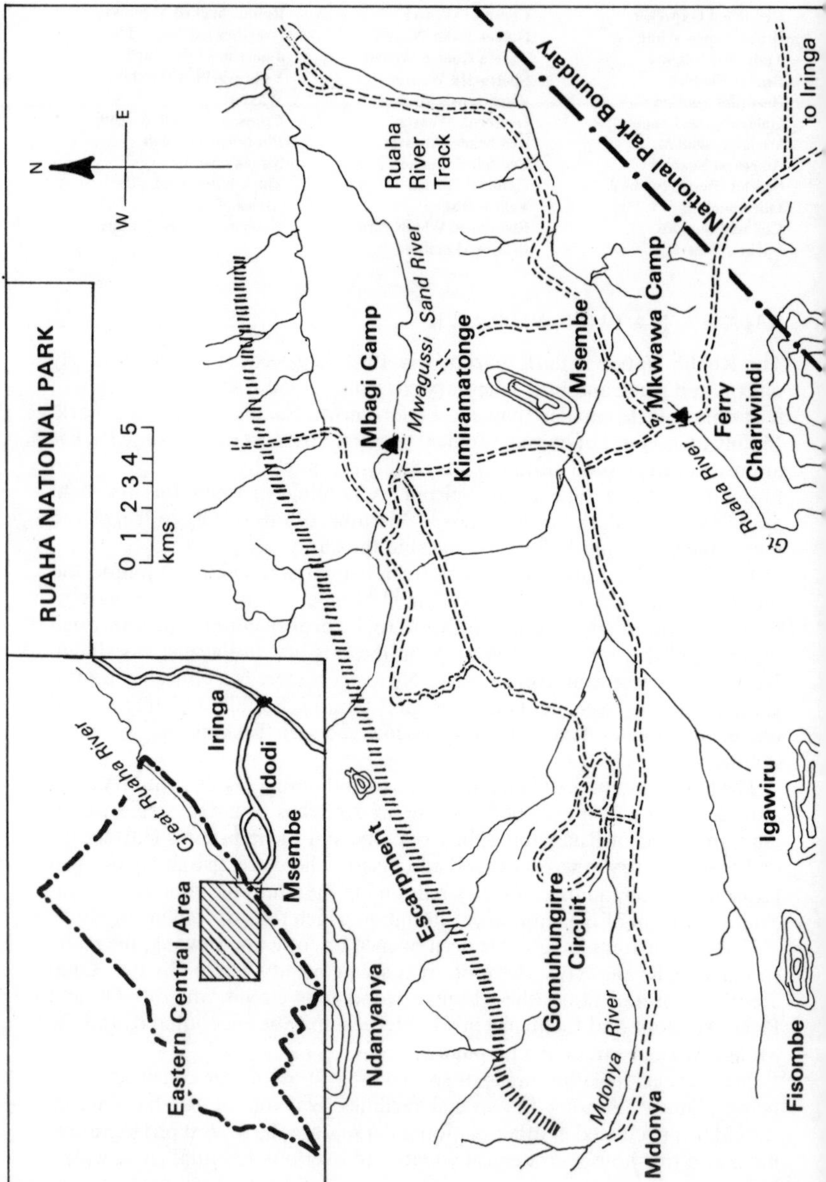
RUAHA NATIONAL PARK
N
W
E
0 1 2 3 4 5
kms
Eastern Central Area
Iringa
Idodi
Msembe
Great Ruaha River
Ruaha River Track
National Park Boundary
to Iringa
Mbagi Camp
Mwagussi Sand River
Kimiramatonge
Msembe
Mkwawa Camp
Ferry
Chariwindi
Gt Ruaha River
Escarpment
Ndanyanya
Gomuhungirre Circuit
Mdonya River
Mdonya
Igawiru
Fisombe

Perhaps Ruaha's greatest charm is the fact that it is a completely unspoiled African wilderness. Its future potential is very great and of all the East African faunal preserves it is the Park of the future. To visit it before it has been further developed is a unique experience.

There is an impressive array of game animals in the Ruaha National Park. It is the largest Elephant sanctuary in Tanzania, and it is the only East African Park where one may be certain of seeing and photographing Greater Kudu. Among the carnivora Lion, Leopard, Cheetah, Hunting Dog, Spotted Hyaena and Bat-eared Fox are all possibles.

Bird life is abundant and the Park is one of the few places in Africa where the rare raptorial Eleonora's Falcon may be encountered: migrating flocks have been recorded in December and January. The brachystegia woodland is the home of Dickinson's Kestrel, Violet-crested Turaco, Pale-billed Hornbill and Racquet-tailed Roller. Along the more heavily wooded sections of the Ruaha River is found the giant Pel's Fishing Owl.

The Park is reached from Iringa, 112km (70 miles), via Mloa (by-passing Idoli), and across the Ruaha River by ferry within the Park at Ibuguziwa. From Dar-es-Salaam to the Park is 621km (386 miles), by way of Morogoro and Iringa. Do-it-yourself rondavel accommodation is available near Park headquarters. Camping is permitted in demarcated areas in the Park.

MAMMALS OF RUAHA NATIONAL PARK

Rousette Fruit Bat
Epauletted Fruit Bat
White-bellied Tomb Bat
Hollow-faced Bat
False Vampire Bat
Yellow-winged Bat
Lesser Leaf-nosed Bat
Giant Leaf-nosed Bat
Banana Bat
Yellow-bellied Bat
Angola Free-tailed Bat
White-bellied Free-tailed Bat
Greater Galago
Bush Baby
Black-faced Vervet Monkey
Blue Monkey
Yellow Baboon
Hunting Dog
Black-backed Jackal
Side-striped Jackal
Bat-eared Fox
Ratel or **Honey Badger**
African Civet
Small-spotted Genet
Large-spotted Genet
African Palm Civet
Marsh Mongoose
Dwarf Mongoose
Large Grey Mongoose
Aard-wolf Rare
Spotted Hyaena
Cheetah
Caracal
African Wild Cat
Serval
Lion
Leopard
Ant Bear
Tree Hyrax
Rock Hyrax
African Elephant
Black Rhinoceros
Common Zebra
Hippopotamus
Warthog
Masai Giraffe
Lichtenstein's Hartebeest
Bush Duiker
Klipspringer
Kirk's Dik-dik
Common Waterbuck
Bohor Reedbuck
Impala
Grant's Gazelle
Sable Antelope
Roan Antelope
Bushbuck
Greater Kudu
Lesser Kudu
Eland
African Buffalo
African Hare
Cane Rat
Porcupine
Bush Squirrel
Spring Hare
African Dormouse

BIRDS OF RUAHA NATIONAL PARK

Little Grebe
Long-tailed Cormorant
African Darter
White Pelican
Pink-backed Pelican
Black-headed Heron
Goliath Heron
Great White Egret
Yellow-billed Egret
Little Egret
Buff-backed Heron or Cattle Egret
Green-backed Heron
Hamerkop
White Stork
European Black Stork
Woolly-necked Stork
Abdim's Stork
Open-bill Stork
Saddle-bill Stork
Marabou Stork
Wood Ibis or Yellow-billed Stork
Sacred Ibis
Hadada Ibis
African Black Duck
Red-billed Duck
Knob-billed Duck
Egyptian Goose
Spur-winged Goose
Secretary Bird
White-backed Vulture
Hooded Vulture
Lanner
European Hobby
Eleonora's Falcon
Red-necked Falcon
European Kestrel
Lesser Kestrel
Grey Kestrel
Dickinson's Kestrel
Cuckoo Falcon
European Black Kite
African Black Kite
Black-shouldered Kite
Bat Hawk
Tawny Eagle
Wahlberg's Eagle
African Hawk Eagle
Martial Eagle
Crowned Hawk Eagle
Long-crested Eagle
Lizard Buzzard
Brown Harrier Eagle
Black-chested Harrier Eagle
Southern Banded Harrier Eagle
Bateleur
African Fish Eagle
Palm-nut Vulture
Little Sparrow Hawk
Ovampo Sparrow Hawk
Great Sparrow Hawk
Shikra
African Goshawk
Gabar Goshawk
Dark Chanting Goshawk
Montagu's Harrier
Pallid Harrier
European Marsh Harrier
Harrier Hawk
Coqui Francolin
Shelley's Francolin
Hildebrandt's Francolin
Red-necked Spurfowl
Harlequin Quail
Helmeted Guinea-fowl
Crested Guinea-fowl
Black Crake
Moorhen
African Finfoot
Crowned Crane
Jackson's Bustard
Black-bellied Bustard
Spotted Stone Curlew
Water Dikkop
African Jacana
Kittlitz's Plover
Three-banded Plover
Crowned Plover
Senegal Plover
Blacksmith Plover
White-headed Plover
Wattled Plover
Long-toed Lapwing
Painted Snipe
African Snipe
Ruff
Common Sandpiper
Green Sandpiper
Wood Sandpiper
Greenshank
Temminck's Courser
Bronze-winged Courser
Pratincole
African Skimmer
Button Quail
Yellow-throated Sandgrouse
Speckled Pigeon
Olive Pigeon
Red-eyed Dove
Mourning Dove
Ring-necked Dove
Laughing Dove
Namaqua Dove
Tambourine Dove
Emerald-spotted Wood Dove
Delalande's Green Pigeon
European Cuckoo
African Cuckoo
Red-chested Cuckoo
Black Cuckoo
Levaillant's Cuckoo
Black and White Cuckoo
Emerald Cuckoo
Didric Cuckoo
Klaas' Cuckoo
Black Coucal
White-browed Coucal
Livingstone's Turaco
Violet-crested Turaco
Go-away-bird
Bare-faced Go-away-bird
Brown-necked Parrot
Brown Parrot
Yellow-collared Lovebird
European Roller
Racquet-tailed Roller
Lilac-breasted Roller
Rufous-crowned Roller
Broad-billed Roller
Pied Kingfisher
Giant Kingfisher
Half-collared Kingfisher
Malachite Kingfisher
Pygmy Kingfisher
Brown-hooded Kingfisher
Grey-headed Kingfisher
Striped Kingfisher
European Bee-eater
Madagascar Bee-eater
Southern Carmine Bee-eater
White-throated Bee-eater
Boehm's Bee-eater
Little Bee-eater
White-fronted Bee-eater
Swallow-tailed Bee-eater
Trumpeter Hornbill
Grey Hornbill
Red-billed Hornbill

Crowned Hornbill
Pale-billed Hornbill
Ground Hornbill
African Hoopoe
Green Wood Hoopoe
Scimitar-bill
African Marsh Owl
African Scops Owl
White-faced Scops Owl
Pearl-spotted Owlet
Spotted Eagle Owl
Verreaux's Eagle Owl
Pel's Fishing Owl
European Nightjar
Fiery-necked Nightjar
Freckled Nightjar
Plain Nightjar
Gaboon Nightjar
Pennant-wing Nightjar
Blue-naped Mousebird
Red-faced Mousebird
Narina's Trogon
Black-collared Barbet
Black-backed Barbet
Spotted-flanked Barbet
Whyte's Barbet
Red-fronted Tinkerbird
Yellow-fronted Tinkerbird
Golden-rumped Tinkerbird
Levaillant's Barbet
D'Arnaud's Barbet
Greater Honeyguide
Lesser Honeyguide
Bennett's Woodpecker
Little Spotted Woodpecker
Golden-tailed Woodpecker
Cardinal Woodpecker
Bearded Woodpecker
Olive Woodpecker
Mottled Swift
Little Swift
White-rumped Swift
Horus Swift
Palm Swift
Boehm's Spinetail
African Broadbill
African Pitta
Rufous-naped Lark
Flappet Lark
Chestnut-backed Sparrow Lark
Fischer's Sparrow Lark
Red-capped Lark
African Pied Wagtail
Long-billed Pipit
Richard's Pipit
Yellow-throated Longclaw
Fulleborn's Longclaw
Rosy-breasted Longclaw
Arrow-marked Babbler
Yellow-vented Bulbul
Fischer's Greenbul
Yellow-bellied Greenbul
European Spotted Flycatcher
Ashy Flycatcher
Grey Flycatcher
South African Black Flycatcher
Boehm's Flycatcher
Yellow-bellied Flycatcher
Chin-spot Flycatcher
Black-throated Wattle-eye
Blue Flycatcher
White-tailed Crested Flycatcher
Paradise Flycatcher
Kurrichane Thrush
Ground-scraper Thrush
Angola Rock Thrush
European Common Wheatear
Capped Wheatear
Red-tailed Chat
Cliff Chat
White-headed Black Chat
Sooty Chat
Stonechat
White-browed Robin Chat
Red-capped Robin Chat
Robin Chat
Morning Warbler
Red-backed Scrub Robin
Blackcap Warbler
European Sedge Warbler
Lesser Swamp Warbler
European Willow Warbler
Barred Wren Warbler
Fan-tailed Warbler
Red-faced Crombec
Grey Tit-warbler
Yellow-bellied Eremomela
Green-cap Eremomela
Grey-backed Camaroptera
Wing-snapping Cisticola
Pectoral-patch Cisticola
Rattling Cisticola
Winding Cisticola
Croaking Cisticola
Tawny-flanked Prinia
African Moustached Warbler
European Swallow
Angola Swallow
Blue Swallow
Wire-tailed Swallow
Red-rumped Swallow
Mosque Swallow
Striped Swallow
Grey-rumped Swallow
European Sand Martin
African Sand Martin
Banded Martin
African Rock Martin
Black Rough-wing Swallow
Eastern Rough-wing Swallow
White-headed Rough-wing Swallow
Black Cuckoo Shrike
White-breasted Cuckoo Shrike
Grey Cuckoo Shrike
Drongo
Square-tailed Drongo
Straight-crested Helmet Shrike
Retz's Red-billed Shrike
White-crowned Shrike
Black-browed Brubru
Grey-backed Fiscal
Lesser Grey Shrike
Uhehe Fiscal
Souza's Shrike
Red-backed Shrike
Magpie Shrike
Slate-coloured Boubou
Tropical Boubou
Black-backed Puff-back
Black-headed Tchagra
Brown-headed Tchagra
Blackcap Tchagra
Sulphur-breasted Bush Shrike
Black-fronted Bush Shrike
Grey-headed Bush Shrike
Nicator
Grey Tit
Black Tit
Cinnamon-breasted Tit
African Penduline Tit
European Golden Oriole
African Golden Oriole
Black-headed Oriole
Pied Crow
Wattled Starling
White-winged Babbling Starling
Violet-backed Starling
Blue-eared Starling
Lesser Blue-eared Starling
Ruppell's Long-tailed Starling
Ashy Starling
Red-wing Starling
Superb Starling
Yellow-billed Oxpecker
Red-billed Oxpecker
Yellow White-eye

Bronzy Sunbird
Beautiful Sunbird (black-bellied race)
Copper Sunbird
Little Purple-banded Sunbird
Mariqua Sunbird
Variable Sunbird
Southern Double-collared Sunbird
Amethyst Sunbird
Scarlet-chested Sunbird
Olive Sunbird
Collared Sunbird
Spotted Creeper
White-headed Buffalo Weaver
White-browed Sparrow Weaver
Grey-headed Sparrow
Swahili Sparrow
Yellow-throated Petronia
Layard's Black-headed Weaver
Masked Weaver
Golden-backed Weaver
Dark-backed Weaver
Spectacled Weaver
Golden Weaver
Holub's Golden Weaver
Bertram's Weaver
Grosbeak Weaver
Red-headed Weaver
Red-billed Quelea
Red-headed Quelea
Cardinal Quelea
Red Bishop
Black-winged Bishop
Yellow Bishop
Fan-tailed Widow-bird
Yellow-mantled Widow-bird
White-winged Widow-bird
Red-collared Widow-bird
Bronze Mannikin
Rufous-backed Mannikin
Magpie Mannikin
Grey-headed Silverbill
Quail Finch
Locust Finch
Parasitic Weaver
Peters' Twin-spot
Green-backed Twin-spot
Orange-winged Pytilia
Green-winged Pytilia
African Fire Finch
Jameson's Fire Finch
Red-billed Fire Finch
Yellow-bellied Waxbill
Waxbill
Zebra Waxbill
Fawn-breasted Waxbill
Lavender Waxbill
Southern Cordon-bleu
Red-cheeked Cordon-bleu
Purple Grenadier
Indigo-bird
Pin-tailed Whydah
Paradise Whydah
Broad-tailed Paradise Whydah
Yellow-fronted Canary
Brimstone Canary
Streaky-headed Seed-eater
Three-streaked Bunting
Golden-breasted Bunting
Cinnamon-breasted Rock Bunting

SERENGETI NATIONAL PARK

Serengeti, the largest and best known of Tanzania's National Parks, covers an area of over 14,500sq km (5,600sq miles). Its northern boundary abuts Kenya's Masai Mara Game Reserve, whilst its western extension known as the 'corridor' reaches to within 8km (5 miles) of Lake Victoria.

In this world-famous wildlife sanctuary there still exists the greatest and most spectacular concentration of game animals found anywhere in the world.

Most of the Serengeti is vast open plains with lofty rocky outcrops giving character to the landscape. There are also acacia and savannah woodland and scrub, forested and well-treed rivers, and the occasional swamp and small lake. In altitude Serengeti varies between 914 and 1,828m (3,000–6,000ft): Park headquarters at Seronera is at 1,524m (5,000ft).

In addition to its vast herds of Wildebeest, Common Zebra, Thomson's Gazelle and other plains game, Serengeti is renowned for its Lion population. It is not at all unusual to see 40 or more lions in a single day, including several superbly maned old males. Leopards are relatively numerous and are to be found during the daytime resting in trees along the Seronera River.

During May, June and July, or sometimes earlier, there is a remarkable migration of game animals, chiefly Zebra and Wildebeest, away from their usual haunts on the central plains and into the corridor. The animals converge and then move westwards, six to ten abreast in winding columns

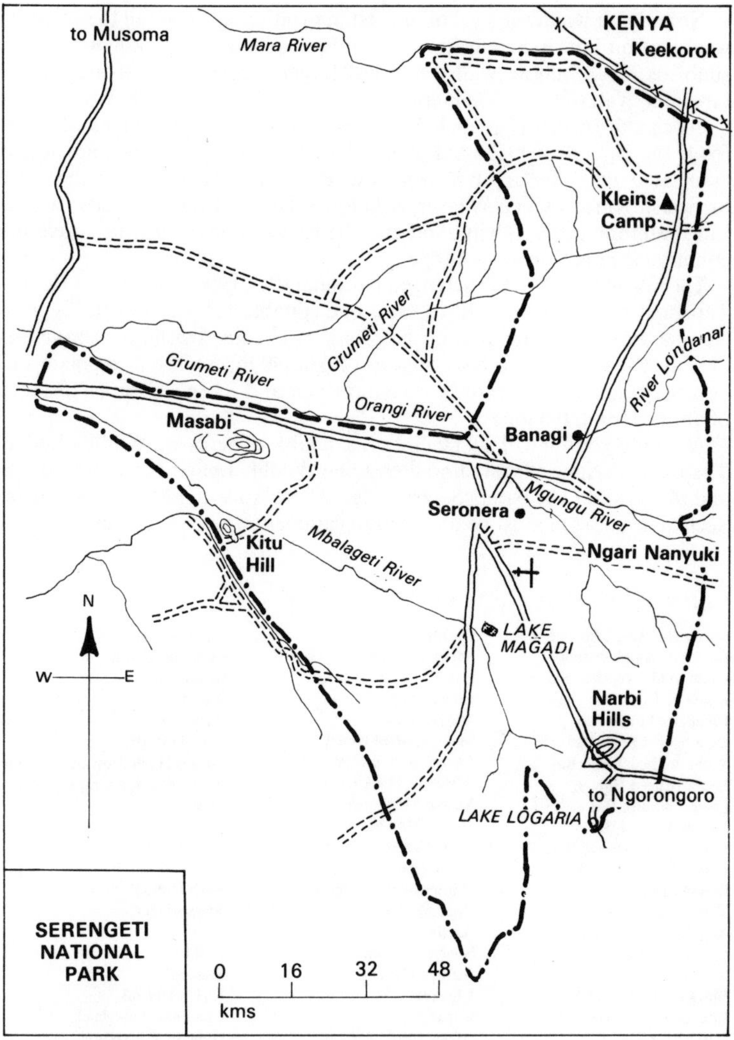

several miles long. This movement has its following of carnivora, ready to dispose of the weaklings and stragglers.

The remarkable 'robertsi' race of Grant's Gazelle with extremely wide-branched horns is found in the western sector of the Park. Other interesting animals include all three species of Jackal, Striped Hyaena and Aard-wolf.

Nobody, at whatever level of interest in ornithology, can fail to notice the wealth of bird life in Serengeti. Colourful rollers, bee-eaters, kingfishers and sunbirds are common, whilst amongst larger species birds of prey, game birds and waterfowl are well represented.

Species of special note include the extremely local Grey-breasted Spurfowl, the rare Brown-chested Wattled Plover which is sometimes found associated with flocks of Senegal Plover on the open plains, the large brownish Rufous-tailed Weaver, Schalow's Turaco which inhabits riverine forest and the Little Tawny Pipit and the Red-throated Tit which are quite common around Seronera Lodge.

The normal route to the Serengeti National Park, when the present Kenya-Tanzania restrictions are lifted, and one suitable for saloon cars, is from Arusha via Lake Manyara and Ngorongoro. From Arusha to Seronera is 318km (198 miles); from Ngorongoro 145km (90 miles). It is also possible to visit Serengeti from Keekorok via Sand River and Klein's Camp, a distance of about 153km (95 miles).

Accommodation with all facilities is available at Seronera Wildlife Lodge. There are also nine official camp sites, Lobo Wildlife Lodge, between Seronera and Mara, and Lake Nduta Safari Lodge. There is also a YMCA at Seronera. Special permission must be obtained to camp elsewhere in the Park.

MAMMALS OF SERENGETI NATIONAL PARK

Spectacled Elephant Shrew
East African Hedgehog
Giant White-toothed Shrew
Rousette Fruit Bat
Epauletted Fruit Bat
Pale-bellied Fruit Bat
White-bellied Tomb Bat
Hollow-faced Bat
False Vampire Bat
Yellow-winged Bat
Lander's Horseshoe Bat
Lesser Leaf-nosed Bat
Banana Bat
Yellow-bellied Bat
Angola Free-tailed Bat
Greater Galago
Bush Baby
Black-faced Vervet Monkey
Blue or **Sykes' Monkey**
Patas Monkey
Olive Baboon
Black and White Colobus
Hunting Dog
Golden Jackal
Black-backed Jackal
Side-striped Jackal
Bat-eared Fox
Zorilla
African Striped Weasel
Ratel or **Honey Badger**
Clawless Otter
African Civet
Small-spotted Genet
Large-spotted Genet
African Palm Civet
Marsh Mongoose
Dwarf Mongoose
Large Grey Mongoose
Black-tipped Mongoose
White-tailed Mongoose
Banded Mongoose
Aard-wolf
Spotted Hyaena
Striped Hyaena
Cheetah
Caracal
African Wild Cat
Serval
Lion
Leopard
Ant Bear
Tree Hyrax
Rock Hyrax
African Elephant
Black Rhinoceros
Common Zebra
Hippopotamus
Warthog
Bush Pig
Masai Giraffe
Coke's Hartebeest or **Kongoni**
White-bearded Gnu or **Wildebeest**
Topi
Red Duiker
Blue Duiker
Bush Duiker
Klipspringer
Suni
Oribi
Steinbok
Kirk's Dik-dik
Common Waterbuck
Defassa Waterbuck
Bohor Reedbuck
Chanler's Reedbuck Recorded Banagi Hill
Impala
Thomson's Gazelle
Grant's Gazelle Western race *robertsi* in western corridor;

nominate race elsewhere
Roan Antelope
Fringe-eared Oryx
Bushbuck
Lesser Kudu
Eland
African Buffalo
African Hare
Cane Rat
Porcupine
Bush Squirrel
Spring Hare
African Dormouse
Giant Rat
Kenya Mole Rat

BIRDS OF SERENGETI NATIONAL PARK

Masai Ostrich
Great-crested Grebe
Little Grebe
Long-tailed Cormorant
African Darter
White Pelican
Pink-backed Pelican
Black-headed Heron
Goliath Heron
Great White Egret
Yellow-billed Egret
Little Egret
Buff-backed Heron or **Cattle Egret**
Squacco Heron
Green-backed Heron
Little Bittern
Hamerkop
White Stork
European Black Stork
Woolly-necked Stork
Abdim's Stork
Open-bill Stork
Saddle-bill Stork
Marabou Stork
Wood Ibis or **Yellow-billed Stork**
Sacred Ibis
Hadada Ibis
African Spoonbill
Greater Flamingo
Lesser Flamingo
Maccoa Duck
African Pochard
Yellow-billed Duck
African Black Duck
Garganey Teal
Cape Wigeon
Hottentot Teal
Red-billed Duck
White-faced Tree Duck
Fulvous Tree Duck
Knob-billed Duck
Egyptian Goose
Spur-winged Goose
Secretary Bird
Ruppell's Vulture
White-backed Vulture
Nubian or **Lappet-faced Vulture**
White-headed Vulture
Egyptian Vulture
Hooded Vulture
Lanner
European Hobby
Greater or **White-eyed Kestrel**
European Kestrel
African Kestrel
Lesser Kestrel
Pygmy Falcon
European Black Kite
African Black Kite
Black-shouldered Kite
Bat Hawk
Verreaux's Eagle
Steppe Eagle
Tawny Eagle
Wahlberg's Eagle
African Hawk Eagle
Ayres' Hawk Eagle
Martial Eagle
Long-crested Eagle
Lizard Buzzard
Brown Harrier Eagle
Black-chested Harrier Eagle
Bateleur
African Fish Eagle
Steppe Buzzard
Augur Buzzard
Little Sparrow Hawk
Shikra
Gabar Goshawk
Pale Chanting Goshawk
Dark Chanting Goshawk
Montagu's Harrier
Pallid Harrier
European Marsh Harrier
Harrier Hawk
Coqui Francolin
Crested Francolin
Shelley's Francolin
Red-necked Spurfowl
Grey-breasted Spurfowl
Cape Quail
Harlequin Quail
Helmeted Guinea-fowl
Crested Guinea-fowl
African Crake
Black Crake
Crowned Crane
Kori Bustard
Jackson's Bustard
White-bellied Bustard
Black-bellied Bustard
Hartlaub's Bustard
Spotted Stone Curlew
Water Dikkop
African Jacana
Ringed Plover
Chestnut-banded Sand Plover
Kittlitz's Plover
Three-banded Plover
Caspian Plover
Crowned Plover
Senegal Plover
Black-winged Plover
Blacksmith Plover
Brown-chested Wattled Plover
Wattled Plover
Avocet
Black-winged Stilt
Painted Snipe
European Common Snipe
Great Snipe
African Snipe
Curlew Sandpiper
Little Stint
Ruff
Common Sandpiper
Green Sandpiper
Wood Sandpiper
Marsh Sandpiper
Greenshank
Curlew
Temminck's Courser
Two-banded Courser
Heuglin's Courser
Bronze-winged Courser
Grey-headed Gull
Gull-billed Tern
White-winged Black Tern
African Skimmer
Button Quail
Chestnut-bellied Sandgrouse
Black-faced Sandgrouse

Yellow-throated Sandgrouse
Speckled Pigeon
Red-eyed Dove
Mourning Dove
Ring-necked Dove
Laughing Dove
Namaqua Dove
Tambourine Dove
Emerald-spotted Wood Dove
Green Pigeon
European Cuckoo
African Cuckoo
Red-chested Cuckoo
Great-spotted Cuckoo
Levaillant's Cuckoo
Black and White Cuckoo
Emerald Cuckoo
Didric Cuckoo
Klaas' Cuckoo
Black Coucal
White-browed Coucal
Schalow's Turaco
Hartlaub's Turaco
Ross's Turaco
Eastern Grey Plantain-eater
Bare-faced Go-away-bird
Brown Parrot
Fischer's Lovebird
European Roller
Lilac-breasted Roller
Broad-billed Roller
Pied Kingfisher
Giant Kingfisher
Malachite Kingfisher
Pygmy Kingfisher
Woodland Kingfisher
Grey-headed Kingfisher
Striped Kingfisher
European Bee-eater
Madagascar Bee-eater
Blue-cheeked Bee-eater
White-throated Bee-eater
Little Bee-eater
Blue-breasted Bee-eater
Black and White-casqued Hornbill
Grey Hornbill
Red-billed Hornbill
Von der Decken's Hornbill
Crowned Hornbill
Ground Hornbill
European Hoopoe
African Hoopoe
Green Wood Hoopoe
Violet Wood Hoopoe
Scimitar-bill
Abyssinian Scimitar-bill
Barn Owl
African Marsh Owl
African Wood Owl
African Scops Owl
Pearl-spotted Owlet
Barred Owlet
Spotted Eagle Owl
Verreaux's Eagle Owl
European Nightjar
Dusky Nightjar
Pennant-wing Nightjar
Long-tailed Nightjar
Speckled Mousebird
Blue-naped Mousebird
Narina's Trogon
Double-toothed Barbet
White-headed Barbet
Spotted-flanked Barbet
Red-fronted Barbet
Red-fronted Tinkerbird
D'Arnaud's Barbet
Greater-Honeyguide
Lesser Honeyguide
Wahlberg's Honeyguide
Nubian Woodpecker
Little Spotted Woodpecker
Cardinal Woodpecker
Bearded Woodpecker
Grey Woodpecker
Mottled Swift
Little Swift
White-rumped Swift
Horus Swift
Palm Swift
Rufous-naped Lark
Flappet Lark
Fawn-coloured Lark
Fischer's Sparrow Lark
Red-capped Lark
Short-tailed Lark
African Pied Wagtail
Blue-headed Wagtail and races
Sandy Plain-backed Pipit
Richard's Pipit
Little Tawny Pipit
Red-throated Pipit
Striped Pipit
Yellow-throated Longclaw
Rosy-breasted Longclaw
Arrow-marked Babbler
Black-lored Babbler
Rufous Chatterer
Yellow-vented Bulbul
European Spotted Flycatcher
Dusky Flycatcher
Ashy Flycatcher
Pale Flycatcher
Grey Flycatcher
South African Black Flycatcher
Silverbird
Chin-spot Flycatcher
Wattle-eye
Paradise Flycatcher
European Rock Thrush
European Common Wheatear
Capped Wheatear
Cliff Chat
Sooty Chat
White-browed Robin Chat
Red-backed Scrub Robin
White-throated Robin
Garden Warbler
Blackcap Warbler
Great Reed Warbler
European Sedge Warbler
European Willow Warbler
Black-breasted Apalis
Fan-tailed Warbler
Buff-bellied Warbler
Red-faced Crombec
Banded Tit-warbler
Yellow-bellied Eremomela
Grey-backed Camaroptera
Pectoral-patch Cisticola
Rattling Cisticola
Croaking Cisticola
Tiny Cisticola
Winding Cisticola
Tawny-flanked Prinia
African Moustached Warbler
European Swallow
Angola Swallow
Wire-tailed Swallow
Red-rumped Swallow
Mosque Swallow
Striped Swallow
Banded Martin
African Rock Martin
Black Rough-wing Swallow
Black Cuckoo Shrike
Drongo
Straight-crested Helmet Shrike
White-crowned Shrike
Northern Brubru
Grey-backed Fiscal
Lesser Grey Shrike
Fiscal Shrike
Red-backed Shrike
Red-tailed Shrike
Magpie Shrike
Black-headed Gonolek

Slate-coloured Boubou
Tropical Boubou
Black-backed Puff-back
Black-headed Tchagra
Sulphur-breasted Bush Shrike
Grey-headed Bush Shrike
White-breasted Tit
Red-throated Tit
African Penduline Tit
Black-headed Oriole
Cape Rook
White-naped Raven
Wattled Starling
Violet-backed Starling
Blue-eared Glossy Starling
Ruppell's Long-tailed Starling
Ashy Starling
Hildebrandt's Starling
Superb Starling
Yellow-billed Oxpecker
Red-billed Oxpecker
Malachite Sunbird
Bronzy Sunbird
Beautiful Sunbird (black-bellied race)
Golden-winged Sunbird
Little Purple-banded Sunbird
Mariqua Sunbird
Variable Sunbird
Scarlet-chested Sunbird
Green-headed Sunbird
Olive Sunbird
Collared Sunbird
Violet-backed Sunbird
Kenya Violet-backed Sunbird
Buffalo Weaver
White-headed Buffalo Weaver
White-browed Sparrow Weaver
Rufous-tailed Weaver
Grey-headed Social Weaver
Rufous Sparrow
Swahili Sparrow
Chestnut Sparrow
Yellow-spotted Petronia
Speckle-fronted Weaver
Masked Weaver
Vitelline Masked Weaver
Chestnut Weaver
Black-necked Weaver
Spectacled Weaver
Holub's Golden Weaver
Vieillot's Black Weaver
Grosbeak Weaver
Red-headed Weaver
Red-billed Quelea
Red-headed Quelea
Cardinal Quelea
Red Bishop
Black-winged Bishop
Black Bishop
Yellow Bishop
Fan-tailed Widow-bird
Yellow-mantled Widow-bird
White-winged Widow-bird
Bronze Mannikin
Black and White Mannikin
Grey-headed Silverbill
Grey-headed Negro Finch
Cut-throat
Quail Finch
Green-winged Pytilia
African Fire Finch
Jameson's Fire Finch
Red-billed Fire Finch
Yellow-bellied Waxbill
Waxbill
Black-cheeked Waxbill
Red-cheeked Cordon-bleu
Blue-capped Cordon-bleu
Purple Grenadier
Indigo-bird
Pin-tailed Whydah
Steel-blue Whydah
Fischer's Straw-tailed Whydah
Paradise Whydah
Yellow-fronted Canary
White-bellied Canary
Brimstone Canary
Streaky Seed-eater
Golden-breasted Bunting
Cinnamon-breasted Rock Bunting

TARANGIRE NATIONAL PARK

The Tarangire National Park covers an area of 1,360sq km (525sq miles) of park-like country with scattered baobab trees alternating with open acacia woodland, open bush, plains, swamps and rivers and stands of palm trees. Big game and birds are abundant. Among the larger mammals Lion, Elephant, Black Rhinoceros and Buffalo are common.

Tarangire is reached via the Great North Road, turning left after passing through Makuyuni, and is some 112km (70 miles) south of Arusha. Accommodation with all facilities is at the Tarangire Lodge and Tented Camp.

MAMMALS OF TARANGIRE NATIONAL PARK

Epauletted Fruit Bat
Rousette Fruit Bat
White-bellied Tomb Bat
Hollow-faced Bat
False Vampire Bat
Yellow-winged Bat
Banana Bat
Yellow-bellied Bat
Angola Free-tailed Bat
White-bellied Free-tailed Bat
Bush Baby
Black-faced Vervet Monkey
Olive Baboon
Hunting Dog (rare)
Golden Jackal
Black-backed Jackal
Bat-eared Fox
Ratel or Honey Badger
African Civet
Small-spotted Genet
Marsh Mongoose

Dwarf Mongoose
Large Grey Mongoose
White-tailed Mongoose
Banded Mongoose
Aard-wolf
Spotted Hyaena
Cheetah
Caracal
African Wild Cat
Serval
Lion
Leopard
Rock Hyrax
African Elephant
Black Rhinoceros
Common Zebra
Warthog
Masai Giraffe
Bush Duiker
Steinbok
Kirk's Dikdik
Common Waterbuck
Bohor Reedbuck
Impala
Grant's Gazelle
Fringe-eared Oryx
Coke's Hartebeest
White-bearded Gnu or Wildebeest
Bushbuck
Lesser Kudu
Eland
African Buffalo
African Hare
Cane Rat
Porcupine
Striped Ground Squirrel
Unstriped Ground Squirrel
Bush Squirrel
Spring Hare

BIRDS OF TARANGIRE NATIONAL PARK

Masai Ostrich
Little Grebe
White Pelican
Pink-backed Pelican
White-necked Cormorant
Long-tailed Cormorant
African Darter
Dwarf Battern
African Little Bittern
Night Heron
Squacco Heron
Cattle Egret
Green-backed Heron
Great White Egret
Little Egret
Grey Heron
Black-headed Heron
Goliath Heron
Purple Heron
Hamerkop
White Stork
Abdim's Stork
Saddle-bill Stork
Open-bill Stork
Marabou
Yellow-billed Stork
Sacred Ibis
Hadada Ibis
African Spoonbill
Fulvous Tree Duck
White-faced Tree Duck
Egyptian Goose
Spur-winged Goose
Knob-billed Duck
Yellow-billed Duck
Red-billed Duck
Nubian or Lappet-faced Vulture
White-headed Vulture
White-backed Vulture
Hooded Vulture
Pallid Harrier
Montagu's Harrier
European Marsh Harrier
African Marsh Harrier
Harrier Hawk
Bateleur
Black-chested Harrier Eagle
Brown Harrier Eagle
Great Sparrow Hawk
Shikra
Little Sparrow Hawk
Gabar Goshawk
Lizard Buzzard
Grasshopper Buzzard
Augur Buzzard
Steppe Buzzard
Long-crested Eagle
Martial Eagle
African Hawk Eagle
Tawny Eagle
Wahlberg's Eagle
Fish Eagle
African Black Kite
Black-shouldered Kite
Bat Hawk
Osprey
Pygmy Falcon
Lanner
European Hobby
Red-necked Falcon
Lesser Kestrel
European Kestrel
Secretary Bird
Coqui Francolin
Crested Francolin
Shelley's Francolin
Red-necked Spurfowl
Harlequin Quail
Helmeted Guinea-fowl
Button Quail
Crowned Crane
African Crake
Black Crake
Moorhen
Red-knobbed Coot
African Finfoot
Kori Bustard
White-bellied Bustard
African Lily-trotter
Painted Snipe
Long-toed Lapwing
Blacksmith Plover
Crowned Plover
Wattled Plover
Ringed Plover
Kittlitz's Plover
Three-banded Plover
Greenshank
Marsh Sandpiper
Wood Sandpiper
Green Sandpiper
Common Snipe
Curlew Sandpiper
Little Stint
Ruff
Black-winged Stilt
Avocet
Water Dikkop
Spotted Stone Curlew
Violet-tipped Courser
Pratincole
White-winged Black Tern
Chestnut-bellied Sandgrouse
Black-faced Sandgrouse
Speckled Pigeon
Red-eyed Dove
Mourning Dove

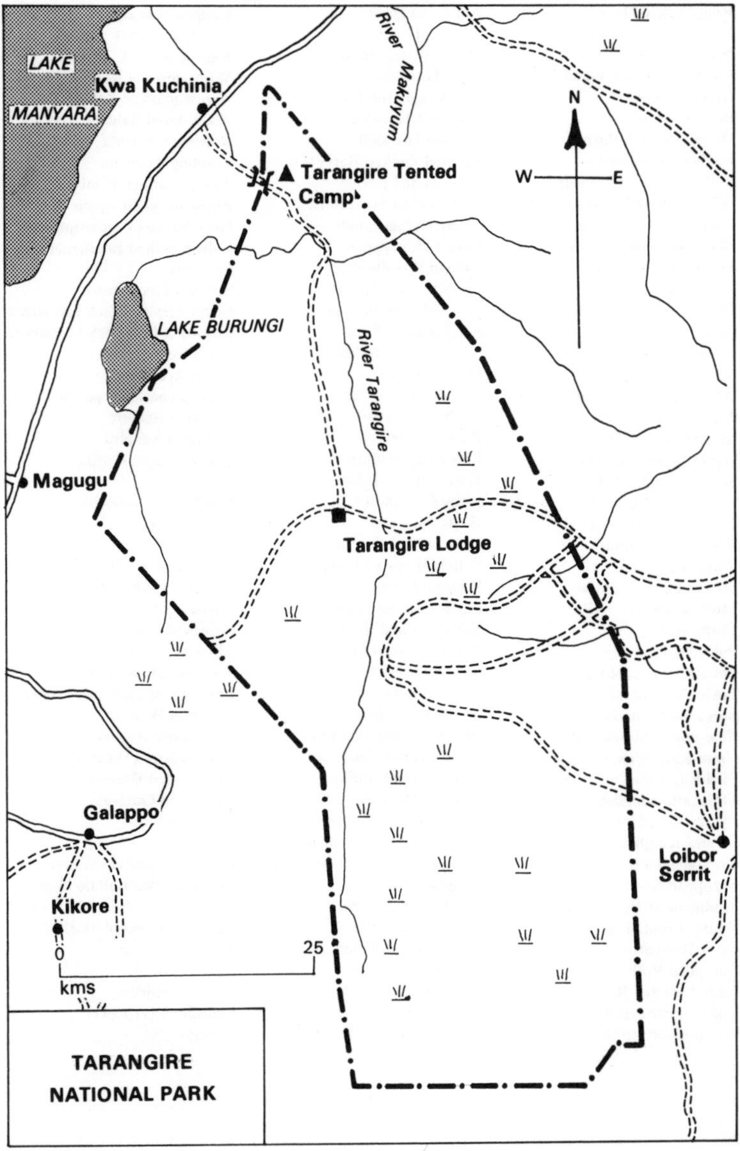
LAKE MANYARA
Kwa Kuchinia
River Makuyum
N
W
E
Tarangire Tented Camp
LAKE BURUNGI
River Tarangire
Magugu
Tarangire Lodge
Galappo
Kikore
0
25
kms
Loibor Serrit
TARANGIRE NATIONAL PARK

Ring-necked Dove
Laughing Dove
Namaqua Dove
Emerald-spotted Wood Dove
Green Pigeon
Brown Parrot
Orange-bellied Parrot
Fischer's Lovebird
Yellow-collared Lovebird
White-bellied Go-away-bird
Great Spotted Cuckoo
Black and White Cuckoo
Levaillant's Cuckoo
African Cuckoo
European Cuckoo
Didric Cuckoo
Emerald Cuckoo
Blue-headed Coucal
White-browed Coucal
African Barn Owl
African Scops Owl
White-faced Scops Owl
Spotted Eagle Owl
Verreaux's Eagle Owl
Pearl-spotted Owlet
European Nightjar
Plain Nightjar
Mozambique Nightjar
Mottled Swift
Little Swift
Palm Swift
Mottled-throated Spinetail
Boehm's Spinetail
Speckled Mousebird
Blue-naped Mousebird
Giant Kingfisher
Pied Kingfisher
Malachite Kingfisher
Pygmy Kingfisher
Striped Kingfisher
Grey-headed Kingfisher
European Bee-eater
Madagascar Bee-eater
White-throated Bee-eater
Little Bee-eater
European Roller
Lilac-breasted Roller
Rufous-crowned Roller
Broad-billed Roller
European Hoopoe
African Hoopoe
Green Wood Hoopoe
Grey Hornbill
Red-billed Hornbill
Crowned Hornbill
Ground Hornbill
Spotted-flanked Barbet
Red-fronted Barbet
Red-fronted Tinkerbird
Greater Honeyguide
Lesser Honeyguide
Nubian Woodpecker
Cardinal Woodpecker
Bearded Woodpecker
Singing Bush Lark
Northern White-tailed Lark
Flappet Lark
Fawn-coloured Lark
Fischer's Sparrow Lark
Banded Martin
European Swallow
Wire-tailed Swallow
Striped Swallow
Wells' Wagtail
African Pied Wagtail
Yellow-throated Longclaw
Pangani Longclaw
Black Cuckoo Shrike
Yellow-vented Bulbul
White-crowned Shrike
Straight-crested Helmet Shrike
Retz's Red-billed Shrike
Northern Brubru
Brown-headed Tchagra
Black-headed Tchagra
Rosy-patched Shrike
Tropical Boubou
Slate-coloured Boubou
Grey-headed Bush Shrike
Sulphur-breasted Bush Shrike
Magpie Shrike
Red-backed Shrike
Red-tailed Shrike
Lesser Grey Shrike
Long-tailed Fiscal
Common Wheatear
Pied Wheatear
Isabelline Wheatear
Capped Wheatear
Red-tailed Chat
European Rock Thrush
White-browed Robin Chat
Arrow-marked Babbler
Black-lored Babbler
Rattling Cisticola
Winding Cisticola
Tawny-flanked Prinia
Black-breasted Apalis
Grey-backed Camaroptera
Yellow-bellied Eremomela
Crombec
Spotted Flycatcher
South African Black Flycatcher
Chin-spot Puff-back Flycatcher
Paradise Flycatcher
White-breasted Tit
Scarlet-chested Sunbird
Mariqua Sunbird
Beautiful Sunbird
Green-winged Pytilia
Waxbill
Red-billed Firefinch
Quail-finch
Cut-throat
Grey-headed Silverbill
Pin-tailed Whydah
Paradise Whydah
Grosbeak Weaver
Masked Weaver
Vitelline Masked Weaver
Layard's Black-headed Weaver
Chestnut Weaver
Spectacled Weaver
Black-necked Weaver
Red-headed Weaver
Red-billed Quelea
Yellow Bishop
Red Bishop
Red-billed Buffalo Weaver
White-headed Buffalo Weaver
White-browed Sparrow Weaver
Lesser Blue-eared Starling
Superb Starling
Ashy Starling
Wattled Starling
Red-billed Oxpecker
Drongo

KILIMANJARO NATIONAL PARK

Kilimanjaro National Park covers an area of 1,864sq km (720sq miles) of Africa's highest mountain, extending from 1,824m (6,000ft) to the summit at 5,894m (19,340ft). At lower altitudes the Park consists of mountain rain forest, giving way to scrub – there is no bamboo zone on Kilimanjaro – then alpine moorland and finally icefields.

Easiest access to the mountain is from Marangu on the southern slopes, whence the Marangu mountain track, passable for four-wheel-drive vehicles, leads to the upper edge of the forest at 3,895m (9,500ft). There are huts on the mountain for mountain climbers and hotels at Marangu.

The most interesting mammal in the mountain forest is Abbot's Duiker, an extremely local and uncommon antelope restricted to a few mountain forests in northern Tanzania. In addition Elephant, Buffalo, Black Rhinoceros, Eland, Leopard, Black and White Colobus and Blue Monkey occur in the Park.

Of special note among Kilimanjaro birds in the alpine zone are Lammergeyer, Mountain Chat and Scarlet-tufted Malachite Sunbird; among forest species the following warrant enumeration:

Green Ibis
Cuckoo Falcon
Rufous-breasted Sparrow Hawk
Hartlaub's Turaco
Cinnamon-breasted Bee-eater
Silvery-cheeked Hornbill
Narina's Trogon
Bar-tailed Trogon
White-eared Barbet
Olive Woodpecker
Black-fronted Bush Shrike
Abbot's Starling
Kenrick's Starling
Broad-ringed White-eye
Malachite Sunbird
Tacazze Sunbird
Golden-winged Sunbird
Eastern Double-collared Sunbird
Olive Sunbird
Dark-backed Weaver
Abyssinian Crimson-wing
Oriole Finch

Game Reserves

Variety is the keynote of Tanzania's Game Reserves which range in terrain from lakeshore to wooded savannah and grassland. In each there exist species of animals and birds not to be encountered elsewhere in the country.

For the visitor prepared to disregard the nuisance of tsetse flies a visit to the Biharamulo Game Reserve in north-western Tanzania is a very well-worth-while safari. An expedition to the Chimpanzee Reserve on the Gombe Stream, accessible only by fisherman's boat from Kigoma, is also something of an adventure.

Farther afield the Katavi Plain Reserve, south of the Ugalla River game country, has the atmosphere of unspoiled Africa; but again tsetse flies may be a little troublesome. Finally there is the Mkomazi Game Reserve adjoining the Tsavo National Park.

BIHARAMULO GAME RESERVE

The Biharamulo Game Reserve is an area of 1,166sq km (450sq miles) on the south-western shores of Lake Victoria, east of the Mwanza-Bukoba road in north-western Tanzania. It was established in 1959. A rich mammal and bird fauna is present but for the visitor the area has the inconvenience of being spasmodically troubled by tsetse fly.

This Reserve comprises thickly wooded, undulating country ranging in altitude from 1,127m (3,700ft) at lake-shore to 1,524m (5,000ft) inland. It is mainly covered with heavy brachystegia and acacia woodlands, interspersed with more open areas, the home of Lichtenstein's Hartebeest, Sable Antelope, Southern Reedbuck and Sharpe's Grysbok. Crocodile and Hippopotamus occur in the lake-shore section.

Bird life is abundant and there are many unusual and rare species, including the following:

Rufous-bellied Heron
Grey Kestrel
Bat Hawk
Ring-necked Francolin
White-spotted Pygmy Crake
Long-toed Lapwing
Bronze-winged Courser
Afep Pigeon
Blue-breasted Kingfisher
Black-billed Barbet
Red-faced Barbet
Snowy-headed Robin Chat
Lesser Blue-eared Starling
Splendid Starling
Red-chested Sunbird
Copper Sunbird
Green-throated Sunbird
Blue-throated Brown Sunbird
Orange Weaver
Slender-billed Weaver
Weyn's Weaver
Black-bellied Seed-cracker

GOMBE STREAM GAME RESERVE

The Gombe Stream Game Reserve on the north-eastern shore of Lake Tanganyika, north of Kigoma, was established in 1945 mainly for the protection of the Chimpanzee population which exists there. It comprises 158sq km (61sq miles) of lake-shore and precipitous mountain country, well watered and with dense forest. Access is by boat from Kigoma. In addition to the Chimpanzees there are Red Colobus, Buffalo, Defassa Waterbuck, Bushbuck and Leopard.

Among the notable birds recorded from the Gombe Stream Reserve are:

African Hobby
Grey Kestrel
Bat Hawk
Palm-nut Vulture
Forbes' Plover
Afep Pigeon
Yellow-bill or **Green Coucal**
Shining-blue Kingfisher
Blue-breasted Kingfisher
Double-toothed Barbet
Hairy-breasted Barbet
Grey-throated Barbet
Yellow-spotted Barbet
Yellow-billed Barbet
African Broadbill
Equatorial Akalat
Splendid Starling
Purple-headed Starling
Red-chested Sunbird
Superb Sunbird
Green-throated Sunbird
Northern Brown-throated Weaver
Red-headed Malimbe
Red-headed Blue-bill

KATAVI PLAIN GAME RESERVE

The Katavi Plain Game Reserve of 1,864sq km (720sq miles) lies between the Ugalla River and the south-eastern shores of Lake Tanganyika in south-western Tanzania; it was established in 1951. Extensive open grassy plains alternate with brachystegia woodland, acacia bush country and lakes and swamps. The mammalian fauna includes large herds of Elephant and Buffalo besides Hippopotamus, Southern Reedbuck, Topi, Eland, Roan Antelope, Defassa Waterbuck, Common Zebra, Lion and Leopard.

The area is rich in water-birds and birds of prey. The following species of special note have been recorded:

Black Heron
Rufous-bellied Heron
Dwarf Bittern
Pygmy Goose
Dickinson's Kestrel
Forbes' Plover
Go-away-bird
Brown-necked Parrot
Boehm's Bee-eater
Swallow-tailed Bee-eater
Pale-billed Hornbill
Fiery-necked Nightjar
Pennant-wing Nightjar
Red-faced Mousebird
Black-backed Barbet
African Pitta
Blue Swallow
White-breasted Cuckoo Shrike
White-winged Babbling Starling
Yellow-throated Petronia
Tanzania Masked Weaver

MKOMAZI GAME RESERVE

Mkomazi Game Reserve, an area of 3,496sq km (1,350sq miles) in north-eastern Tanzania, adjoins a portion of the southern boundary of Kenya's Tsavo National Park: in effect it is a southern extension of that Park. The country is very arid, open plains and thornbush with isolated rocky hills.

The fauna includes Elephant, Black Rhinoceros, Buffalo, Lion, Leopard, Lesser Kudu, Gerenuk and Fringe-eared Oryx.

Bird life is more in evidence than big game and the following species are noteworthy:

Red-necked Falcon
Pygmy Falcon
Wahlberg's Eagle
Martial Eagle
Lizard Buzzard
Brown Harrier Eagle
Grasshopper Buzzard
Ovampo Sparrow Hawk
Shikra
Buff-crested Bustard
Heuglin's Courser
Button Quail
Carmine Bee-eater
Trumpeter Hornbill
Silvery-cheeked Hornbill
Yellow-billed Hornbill
Donaldson-Smith's Nightjar
Brown-breasted Barbet
Retz's Red-billed Shrike
Four-coloured Bush Shrike
Golden-breasted Starling
Hunter's Sunbird
Kenya Violet-backed Sunbird
Dark-backed Weaver
Paradise Whydah

Other Faunal Localities

In addition to the National Parks and Game Reserves enumerated above, there exist in Tanzania a number of other zoologically important localities. Among these haunts of rare and little-known animals and birds are the following:

POROTO MOUNTAINS, MBEYA DISTRICT, SOUTHERN TANZANIA

This is a good locality for the ornithologist. The striking, long-tailed, yellow-shouldered Marsh Widow-bird is found in the marshy hollows in the valleys. Forest patches on these mountains and on adjacent Mount Rungwe possess a rich avifauna including:

African Hobby
Cuckoo Falcon
Ayres' Hawk Eagle
Southern Banded Harrier Eagle
Livingstone's Turaco
Half-collared Kingfisher
Green Barbet
Stierling's Woodpecker
Olive Woodpecker
Boehm's Spinetail
White-chested Alethe
Yellow-throated Woodland Warbler
Blue Swallow

THE RUKWA VALLEY, NORTH-WEST OF MBEYA, SOUTHERN TANZANIA

The famous game country of the Rukwa Valley is relatively inaccessible and can be visited only in the dry season and with sturdy four-wheel-drive vehicles.

Large herds of Puku exist in the area, alongside concentrations of Topi, Eland and Buffalo. Lichtenstein's Hartebeest, Southern Reedbuck, Impala, Elephant, Defassa Waterbuck, Roan Antelope, Greater Kudu, Common Zebra, Masai Giraffe, Hippopotamus and Lion also occur. Sitatunga are found in the swamps to the west of the Rukwa.

Two remarkable genetic mutations have been reported from the Rukwa Valley, albino giraffe and a dark-coloured zebra marked with spots instead of stripes.

Bird life abounds in the Rukwa Valley and some 400 different species have been recorded. Amongst the more important are:

Black Heron
White-backed Night Heron
Rufous-bellied Heron
Glossy Ibis Nests in colonies
Pygmy Goose
Red-necked Falcon
Kaffir Rail
Wattled Crane
Boehm's Bee-eater
Anchieta's Sunbird
Tanzania Masked Weaver
Quail Finch

THE SELOUS GAME RESERVE

The Selous Game Reserve is a southern extension of the Mikumi National Park, covering some 54,490sq km (21,000sq miles), and is predominantly an elephant reserve. The area is mainly brachystegia woodlands with grassy flood-plains and some dense forest patches: much of it is inaccessible.

In addition to Elephant there are Hippopotamus, Buffalo, Wildebeest, Lichtenstein's Hartebeest, Sable Antelope, Greater Kudu, Eland, Lion and Leopard. Bird life is similar to that found in the Mikumi National Park.

Accommodation is available at a Safari Camp at Mbuyu. Foot safaris accompanied by armed rangers are permitted. Visits should be made between June and November; at other times some areas of the Reserve are liable to flooding.

ULUGURU MOUNTAINS, MOROGORO DISTRICT, EASTERN TANZANIA

The forests of the Uluguru Mountains, immediately south of Morogoro, support a varied avifauna, including three species which occur nowhere else. These are Mrs Moreau's Warbler (*Scepomycter winifredae*), 10cm (4in), a thickset olive-grey warbler with a chestnut head and chest; the Black-cap Shrike (*Malaconotus alius*), 20cm (8in), a heavy bush shrike, green above, yellowish-green below with a black cap and heavy black bill; and Loveridge's Sunbird (*Nectarinia loveridgei*). Other interesting species recorded from the Uluguru forests are:

African Black Duck
Ayres' Hawk Eagle
Southern Banded Harrier Eagle
Palm-nut Vulture
Rufous-breasted Sparrow Hawk
Crested Guinea-fowl
Bronze-naped Pigeon
Livingstone's Turaco
Half-collared Kingfisher
Usambara Nightjar
Bar-tailed Trogon
Olive Woodpecker
Sharpe's Akalat
White-chested Alethe
Green-headed Oriole
Uluguru Violet-backed Sunbird
Bertram's Weaver
Red-faced Crimson-wing
Oriole Finch

EASTERN USAMBARA MOUNTAINS, NORTH-EASTERN TANZANIA

The forests of the Eastern Usambara Mountains, in extreme north-eastern Tanzania, are readily accessible from Tanga and Amani. Among the few mammals occurring is the rare Abbot's Duiker which is sometimes seen in the early morning.

The locality boasts three endemic bird species, namely the Naduk Eagle Owl (*Bubo vosseleri*), 66cm (26in), a pale rufous-buff eagle owl with barred underparts and well-developed ear tufts; the Usambara Alethe (*Alethe montana*), 12.5cm (15in), a plump robin-like bird, olivaceous brown above, greyish and white below, with a rufous streak from the base of the bill to above the eye; and the Usambara Weaver (*Ploceus nicolli*). Other notable birds are:

Cuckoo Falcon
Southern Banded Harrier Eagle
Palm-nut Vulture
Great Sparrow Hawk
Bronze-naped Pigeon
Lemon Dove
Fischer's Turaco
Half-collared Kingfisher
Trumpeter Hornbill
Silvery-cheeked Hornbill
Usambara Nightjar
Narina's Trogon
Bar-tailed Trogon
White-eared Barbet
Green Barbet
Green Tinkerbird
Spot-throat
Mottled Spot-throat
Orange Ground Thrush
Sharpe's Akalat
White-chested Alethe
Square-tailed Drongo
Retz's Red-billed Shrike
Chestnut-fronted Shrike
Black-fronted Bush Shrike
Green-headed Oriole
Sharpe's Starling
Abbott's Starling
Kenrick's Starling
Banded Green Sunbird
Uluguru Violet-backed Sunbird
Amani Sunbird
Dark-backed Weaver
Red-headed Blue-bill, Usambara race
Red-faced Crimson-wing
Oriole Finch

UGANDA

Uganda possesses three national parks, the Rwenzori National Park in western Uganda between Lakes Edward and George; the Kabalega Falls National Park farther north, astride the Victoria Nile and bounded on the west by Lake Albert (Lake Mobutu Sesse Seko); and the Kidepo Valley National Park in the wilds of Karamoja on the border of Sudan in north-eastern Uganda.

Each of these National Parks lies within a distinct ecological region and each has a fauna complementing the others. The three together provide a remarkably complete cross-section of the wildlife of Uganda. In character they are quite unlike any other of East Africa's faunal preserves.

The Rwenzori National Park, immediately to the south of the snow-capped 'Mountains of the Moon' – the Rwenzori Range – is a region of lush green vegetation and rolling grassy plains, of great lakes and swamps and stretches of imposing tropical forests – outliers of the great forests of the Zaire. It includes the Kazinga Channel joining Lake Edward to Lake George, where in a launch one can approach to within feet of elephant and buffalo at the water's edge. To the north there is an extensive zone of old volcanic craters and crater lakes, with superb scenic views of the Rwenzori Mountains. In the Kigezi section – famous for its tree-climbing lions and herds of topi – the Ishasha River boundary abuts the Zaire Parc de Virunga, previously known as the Parc National Albert.

Kabalega Falls National Park has the attraction of the famous water-fall from which it derives its name. The launch trip on the Victoria Nile to the foot of the Falls is a highlight of a visit to East Africa; the river banks are lined with big game animals and some of the largest crocodiles in Africa bask on sand-bars in the river. Fishing is allowed in the Nile, both above and below the Falls, for Nile Perch which run up to 84kg (185lb) weight or more. Most of the Kabalega is open rolling grasslands, with areas of savannah woodland, an isolated forest where chimpanzees are found, and forest strips along the river.

Uganda's third Park, the Kidepo Valley National Park, is situated in what used to be one of the most inaccessible and wild parts of the country, north-eastern Karamoja. An extensive road construction programme now enables anyone to visit this supremely beautiful country of wide sand rivers, forests of borassus palms and rugged mountain terrain, all unusually rich in mammals and birds.

It must be stressed that on account of recent political upheavals in Uganda the status of certain mammals, such as Rhinoceros and Elephant, is at present uncertain. Uganda's National Parks, Game Reserves and Animal

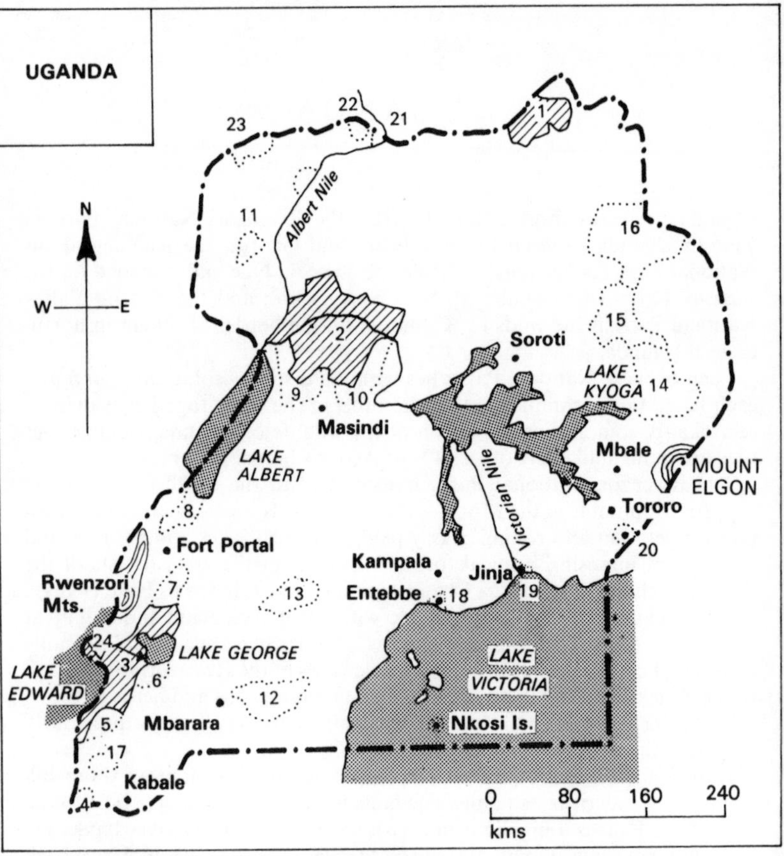

1 Kidepo Valley NP
2 Kabalega Falls NP
3 Rwenzori NP
4 Kigezi Mountain Gorilla GR
5 Kigezi GR
6 Kyambura GR
7 Kibale Forest Corridor GR
8 Toro GR
9 Bugundu GR
10 Karuma GR
11 Ajai GR
12 Lake Mburo GR
13 Katonga GR
14 Pian Upe GR
15 Bokora Corridor GR
16 Matheniko Plains GR
17 Bwindi Impenetrable Forest Gorilla Sanctuary
18 Entebbe Sanctuary
19 Jinja Sanctuary
20 Malaba Sanctuary
21 Dufile Sanctuary
22 Otze Forest Sanctuary
23 Mount Kei Sanctuary
24 Kazinga Sanctuary

Sanctuaries suffered terribly from neglect and organised poaching during Idi Amin's reign in the 1970s. Some species, such as the White Rhino, have disappeared from Uganda entirely, and only a very few Black Rhinos remain, confined to the Kidepo National Park. Other animals have been drastically reduced in numbers by poaching and the encroachment of human habitation.

An ambitious programme for the rehabilitation of Uganda's National Parks, Game Reserves and Animal Sanctuaries is planned to commence in late 1981. Meanwhile all hunting in Uganda is banned until at least July 1984.

Since the situation is not static the reader may find it useful to check on the latest information with local sources:
Tourist information: Ministry of Tourism, P.O. Box 4241, Kampala, Uganda. *Game Information:* Chief Game Warden, Game Department, P.O. Box 4, Entebbe, Uganda. *Lodge Bookings:* Uganda Hotels, P.O. Box 7173, Kampala, Uganda.

KABALEGA FALLS NATIONAL PARK

Kabalega Falls National Park, an area of 4,033sq km (1,557sq miles) in north-western Uganda, is Uganda's largest faunal reserve. It was gazetted in April 1952, when it was known as Murchison Falls National Park. The Park, bounded on the west by Lake Albert (Lake Mobutu Sese Seko) and the Albert Nile, is bisected by the Victoria Nile. At the Kabalega Falls in the centre of the Park the Nile forces its way through a rock cleft some six metres wide, falling in a spectacular cascade to the lower reaches of the river below. The great feature of this sector of the Nile is its large crocodile population, in 1981 one of the largest concentrations of these reptiles still left in Africa.

Much of the Kabalega Falls Park is vast undulating grassy plains, over which remnants of the once famed Elephant herds wander still at will. The Elephant population which was 15,000 in 1973 had by mid-1980 been reduced by poaching to 860 beasts, but game wardens hope that they will increase slowly in the next five years. Locally there are areas of savannah woodlands, some isolated forest patches such as the Rabongo Forest where Chimpanzees may be found, and strips of riverine forest along some sections of the Victoria Nile.

The most developed part of the Park with the best network of motorable tracks is immediately west of Paraa, the Park Headquarters, and includes what is known as the Buligi Circuit. This track follows the shore of the Albert Nile to its confluence with the Victoria Nile, an area especially prolific in water birds and where the rare Whale-headed Stork has been recorded. Mammals also are abundant, especially Buffalo, Warthog, Waterbuck, Elephant, Uganda Kob, Jackson's Hartebeest and Oribi.

A road system opens more distant parts of the Park to visitors, expecially rewarding routes being the access road right to the edge of the Kabalega Falls on the south bank, and the road north of the Victoria Nile to Chobe just below the picturesque Karuma Falls. This extremely attractive section of the river is dotted with well-treed islets. The area is noted for its Rothschild's Giraffe and Black Rhinoceros.

The highlight of any visit to Kabalega Park is the 11-km (7-mile) launch

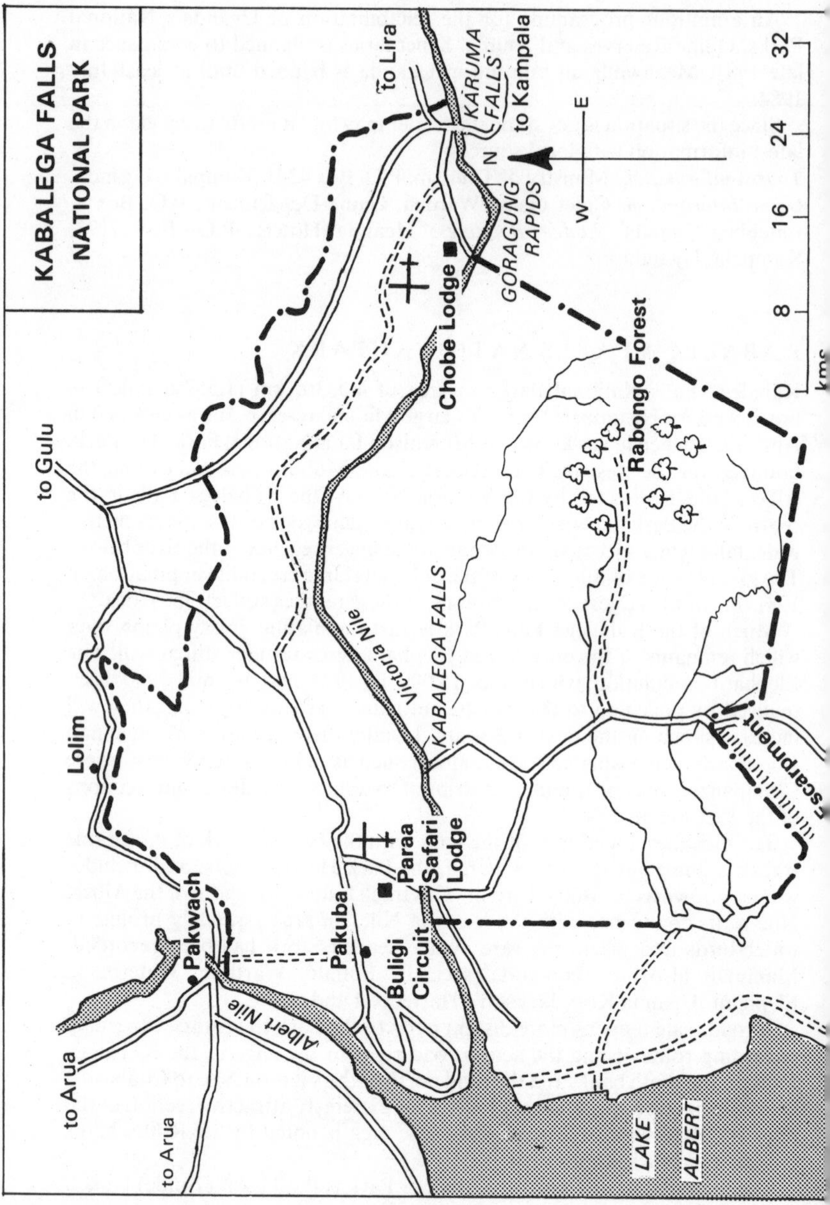
KABALEGA FALLS
NATIONAL PARK
to Gulu
to Lira
KARUMA FALLS
to Kampala
GORAGUNG RAPIDS
Chobe Lodge
Rabongo Forest
Victoria Nile
KABALEGA FALLS
Lolim
Paraa Safari Lodge
Pakuba
Pakwach
Buligi Circuit
Albert Nile
to Arua
to Arua
LAKE ALBERT
Escarpment
N
W
E
0
8
16
24
32
kms

trip from Paraa upstream to the foot of the Falls. Hippopotamus and Crocodiles are to be seen in abundance, and Elephant, Buffalo and occasionally the odd Black Rhinoceros line the water's edge, paying little heed to the boat and allowing a very near approach and unlimited photographic opportunities. There is a veritable bewilderment of bird life: it is not at all unusual to see 60 or more species on a single trip, ranging from stately Saddle-bill Storks and Goliath Herons to brilliant Malachite Kingfishers, Red-throated Bee-eaters and graceful Wattled Plovers.

Fishing is permitted in the waters of the Nile which lie within the Park and Nile Perch of up to 90kg (200lb) are to be caught. The most popular sections of the river for Nile Perch spinning are in the slack water at the foot of the Kabalega Falls and in pools below the Karuma Falls at Chobe.

Accommodation is available in a modern hotel in the Park, the Chobe Lodge to the north of the river below the Karuma Falls. The Paraa Safari Lodge on a northern bluff overlooking the Victoria Nile, another modern hotel, was badly damaged during the 1978–79 war but should reopen in 1982. Camping is allowed in specified places with permission from the Warden. Paraa Safari Lodge is 304km (190 miles) from Kampala, 88km (54 miles) from Masindi, on an all-weather road. From Gulu in the north-east the entrance is through Wangwar Gate, a distance of 56km (36 miles). From Arua west of the Nile, the Park is entered at the Pakwach bridge across the Albert Nile, 30km (18 miles) away. Recently built Pakuba Grand Lodge, opened in December 1977 is only 16km (10 miles) north-west of Paraa Lodge and 14km ($8\frac{1}{2}$ miles) south of Pakwach. Chobe Lodge is 270km (175 miles) direct from Kampala, or 338km (211 miles) if the road via Masindi is taken. The distance from Gulu to Chobe is 83km (52 miles). Landing strips suitable for light aircraft exist close to the three lodges.

MAMMALS OF KABALEGA FALLS NATIONAL PARK

East African Hedgehog
Giant White-toothed Shrew
Rousette Fruit Bat
Epauletted Fruit Bat
Pale-bellied Fruit Bat
White-bellied Tomb Bat
Hollow-faced Bat
False Vampire Bat
Yellow-winged Bat
Lander's Horseshoe Bat
Lesser Leaf-nosed Bat
Banana Bat
Yellow-bellied Bat
Angola Free-tailed Bat
White-bellied Free-tailed Bat
Black-faced Vervet Monkey
Red-tailed Monkey
Patas Monkey
Olive Baboon
Black and White Colobus
Chimpanzee
Lesser Ground Pangolin
Hunting Dog Mainly in north-west of Park
Black-backed Jackal
Zorilla
Ratel
Spotted-necked Otter
African Civet
Large-spotted Genet
Marsh Mongoose
Large Grey Mongoose
Black-tipped Mongoose
White-tailed Mongoose
Banded Mongoose
Spotted Hyaena
African Wild Cat
Serval
Lion
Leopard
Ant Bear
African Elephant
Hippopotamus
Warthog
Bush Pig
Rothschild's Giraffe
Jackson's Hartebeest
Red Duiker
Blue Duiker
Bush Duiker
Oribi
Uganda Kob
Defassa Waterbuck
Bohor Reedbuck
African Buffalo
African Hare
Bunyoro Rabbit
Cane Rat
Porcupine
Striped Ground Squirrel
Bush Squirrel
African Dormouse
Giant Rat

BIRDS OF KABALEGA FALLS NATIONAL PARK

Little Grebe
White-necked Cormorant
Long-tailed Cormorant
African Darter
White Pelican
Pink-backed Pelican
Grey Heron
Black-headed Heron
Goliath Heron
Purple Heron
Great White Egret
Little Egret
Buff-backed Heron or **Cattle Egret**
Squacco Heron
Night Heron
Little Bittern
Dwarf Bittern
Hamerkop
Whale-headed Stork
White Stork
Woolly-necked Stork
Abdim's Stork
Open-bill Stork
Saddle-bill Stork
Marabou Stork
Wood Ibis or **Yellow-billed Stork**
Sacred Ibis
Hadada Ibis
Glossy Ibis
African Spoonbill
Lesser Flamingo
European Shoveler
Garganey Teal
Red-billed Duck
European Pintail
White-faced Tree Duck
Fulvous Tree Duck
Pygmy Goose
Knob-billed Duck
Egyptian Goose
Spur-winged Goose
Secretary Bird
Ruppell's Vulture
White-backed Vulture
Nubian or **Lappet-faced Vulture**
White-headed Vulture
Hooded Vulture
Peregrine
Lanner
European Hobby
African Hobby
Sooty Falcon
Red-necked Falcon
European Kestrel
Lesser Kestrel
Grey Kestrel
European Black Kite
African Black Kite
Black-shouldered Kite
Bat Hawk
Steppe Eagle
Tawny Eagle
Wahlberg's Eagle
African Hawk Eagle
Martial Eagle
Long-crested Eagle
Lizard Buzzard
Brown Harrier Eagle
Black-chested Harrier Eagle
Banded Harrier Eagle
Grasshopper Buzzard
Bateleur
African Fish Eagle
Palm-nut Vulture
Augur Buzzard
Little Sparrow Hawk
Shikra
Gabar Goshawk
Pale Chanting Goshawk
Dark Chanting Goshawk
Montagu's Harrier
Pallid Harrier
European Marsh Harrier
African Marsh Harrier
Harrier Hawk
Osprey
Crested Francolin
Heuglin's Francolin
Cape Quail
Harlequin Quail
Blue Quail
Helmeted Guinea-fowl
African Crake
Black Crake
Allen's Gallinule
African Finfoot
Crowned Crane
Sudan Crowned Crane
Jackson's Bustard
Black-bellied Bustard
European Stone Curlew
Senegal Stone Curlew
Spotted Stone Curlew
Water Dikkop
African Jacana
Ringed Plover
Little Ringed Plover
White-fronted Sand Plover
Kittlitz's Plover
Caspian Plover
Senegal Plover
Spurwing Plover
White-headed Plover Rare
Wattled Plover
Blackhead Plover
Long-toed Lapwing
Black-winged Stilt
Painted Snipe
European Common Snipe
African Snipe
Curlew Sandpiper
Little Stint
Ruff
Common Sandpiper
Green Sandpiper
Wood Sandpiper
Spotted Redshank
Marsh Sandpiper
Greenshank
Black-tailed Godwit
Curlew
Whimbrel
Temminck's Courser
Pratincole
White-collared Pratincole
Egyptian Plover Single unconfirmed sight record
Gull-billed Tern
White-winged Black Tern
African Skimmer
Button Quail
Four-banded Sandgrouse
Speckled Pigeon
Red-eye Dove
Mourning Dove
Ring-necked Dove
Vinaceous Dove
Laughing Dove
Namaqua Dove
Black-billed Wood Dove
Bruce's Green Pigeon
Green Pigeon
European Cuckoo
African Cuckoo
Red-chested Cuckoo
Great Spotted Cuckoo
Levaillant's Cuckoo
Black and White Cuckoo
Emerald Cuckoo
Didric Cuckoo

Klaas' Cuckoo
Senegal Coucal
White-browed Coucal
White-crested Turaco
Eastern Grey Plantain-eater
Brown Parrot
Red-headed Lovebird
European Roller
Abyssinian Roller
Rufous-crowned Roller
Broad-billed Roller
Pied Kingfisher
Giant Kingfisher
Malachite Kingfisher
Pygmy Kingfisher
Woodland Kingfisher
Grey-headed Kingfisher
Striped Kingfisher
European Bee-eater
Madagascar Bee-eater
Blue-cheeked Bee-eater
Carmine Bee-eater
White-throated Bee-eater
Little Bee-eater
Cinnamon-chested Bee-eater
Blue-breasted Bee-eater
Red-throated Bee-eater
Swallow-tailed Bee-eater
Black and White-casqued Hornbill
Grey Hornbill
Crowned Hornbill
Abyssinian Ground Hornbill
European Hoopoe
Green Wood Hoopoe
Black Wood Hoopoe
African Marsh Owl
Pearl-spotted Owlet
Verreaux's Eagle Owl
Pel's Fishing Owl
European Nightjar
Plain Nightjar
Standard-wing Nightjar
Pennant-wing Nightjar
Long-tailed Nightjar
Speckled Mousebird
Blue-naped Mousebird
Double-toothed Barbet
Black-billed Barbet
White-headed Barbet
Spotted-flanked Barbet
Yellow-fronted Tinkerbird
Greater Honeyguide
Lesser Honeyguide
Nubian Woodpecker
Cardinal Woodpecker
Grey Woodpecker
Nyanza Swift
Scarce Swift
Alpine Swift
Little Swift
White-rumped Swift
Horus Swift
Palm Swift
Flappet Lark
European White Wagtail
African Pied Wagtail
Blue-headed Wagtail and races
Plain-backed Pipit
Richard's Pipit
Yellow-throated Longclaw
Brown Babber
Black-lored Babber
Yellow-vented Bulbul
Yellow-throated Leaflove
European Spotted Flycatcher
Swamp Flycatcher
Black Flycatcher
Silverbird
Yellow-bellied Flycatcher
Black-headed Puff-back Flycatcher
Wattle-eye Flycatcher
Blue Flycatcher
Paradise Flycatcher
African Thrush
European Rock Thrush
European Common Wheatear
Isabelline Wheatear
Pied Wheatear
Sooty Chat
European Whinchat
White-browed Robin Chat
Snowy-headed Robin Chat
Spotted Morning Warbler
Red-backed Scrub Robin
European Nightingale
European Sedge Warbler
European Willow Warbler
Crombec
Grey Tit-warbler
Green-backed Camaroptera
Grey-backed Camaroptera
Wing-snapping Cisticola
Rattling Cisticola
Winding Cisticola
Croaking Cisticola
Foxy Cisticola
Tawny-flanked Prinia
European Swallow
Angola Swallow
Ethiopian Swallow
Wire-tailed Swallow
Red-rumped Swallow
Mosque Swallow
Rufous-chested Swallow
Striped Swallow
European Sand Martin
African Sand Martin
White-headed Rough-wing Swallow
Red-shouldered Cuckoo Shrike
White-breasted Cuckoo Shrike
Grey Cuckoo Shrike
Drongo
Curly-crested Helmet Shrike
Northern Brubru
Grey-backed Fiscal
Lesser Grey Shrike
Fiscal Shrike
Red-backed Shrike
Emin's Shrike
Red-tailed Shrike
Woodchat Shrike
Yellow-billed Shrike
Black-headed Gonolek
Tropical Boubou
Puff-back Shrike
Black-headed Tchagra
Brown-headed Tchagra
Blackcap Tchagra
Sulphur-breasted Bush Shrike
Black Tit
European Golden Oriole
African Golden Oriole
Pied Crow
Piapiac
Wattled Starling
Violet-backed Starling
Blue-eared Glossy Starling
Lesser Blue-eared Starling
Purple Glossy Starling
Splendid Glossy Starling
Ruppell's Long-tailed Starling
Yellow-billed Oxpecker
Yellow White-eye
Red-chested Sunbird
Beautiful Sunbird
Pygmy Sunbird
Superb Sunbird
Copper Sunbird
Scarlet-chested Sunbird
Green-headed Sunbird
Collared Sunbird
Violet-backed Sunbird
Grey-headed Sunbird
Chestnut-crowned Sparrow Weaver

Grey-headed Sparrow
Chestnut Sparrow
Speckle-fronted Weaver
Black-headed Weaver
Masked Weaver
Little Weaver
Spectacled Weaver
Vieillot's Black Weaver
Compact Weaver
Red-headed Malimbe
Grosbeak Weaver
Red-billed Weaver
Red-billed Quelea
Red-headed Quelea
Cardinal Quelea
Red Bishop
Black-winged Bishop
Yellow-mantled Widow-bird
Bronze Mannikin
Brown Twin-spot
Cut-throat
Quail Finch
Green-winged Pytilia
African Fire Finch
Red-billed Fire Finch
Waxbill
Zebra Waxbill
Fawn-breasted Waxbill
Black-bellied Waxbill
Red-cheeked Cordon-bleu
Indigo-bird
Pin-tailed Whydah
Paradise Whydah
Yellow-fronted Canary
Yellow-rumped Seed-eater
Golden-breasted Bunting
Brown-rumped Bunting

RWENZORI NATIONAL PARK

With its landscape dominated by the snow-capped peaks of the mighty Rwenzori Range immediately to the north – the famed 'Mountains of the Moon' which rise to over 4,950m (16,500ft) – the Rwenzori National Park possesses a character all its own.

Originally established as the Queen Elizabeth National Park in April 1952 with an area of 1,986sq km (767sq miles), it lies in extreme western Uganda between Lake Edward and Lake George: its south-western and western borders at the Ishasha River and Kayanja adjoin the Zaire Parc du Virunga. The Park boasts a remarkable range of habitats – grassy plains, tropical forest, rivers, swamps, lakes and a zone of old volcanic craters, some of great beauty with wooded slopes and deep blue or green lakes hidden in their depths.

Throughout the Park game animals and birds still occur commonly, although there are some unexpected gaps. For instance there are no Impala, Roan, Rhinoceros, Giraffe, Zebra or Jackson's Hartebeest in the Park, and even more surprising, there are no crocodiles in Lakes George and Edward nor in the Kazinga Channel which connects the two lakes. Elephants, which were so abundant only a few years ago, by 1981 had been reduced by poaching to some 150 animals.

The Maramagambo Forest, south of the Kazinga Channel, divides the rolling park-like plains of the Kigezi section from the euphorbia-dotted grasslands of the north. Chimpanzees, Black and White Colobus, a few of the rare Red Colobus, Blue Monkey and Red-tailed Monkey may be seen from the main road which traverses the forest.

The Kigezi parkland – undulating grassy plains with isolated clumps of widely spaced trees – is famous for its lions which have developed a tree-climbing propensity. Here also are herds of Topi, Buffalo and Uganda Kob, and Giant Forest Hogs are not rare.

In the grassland valley bottoms drainage from surrounding slopes has created several sloughs, beloved by hippos and not infrequently the habitat

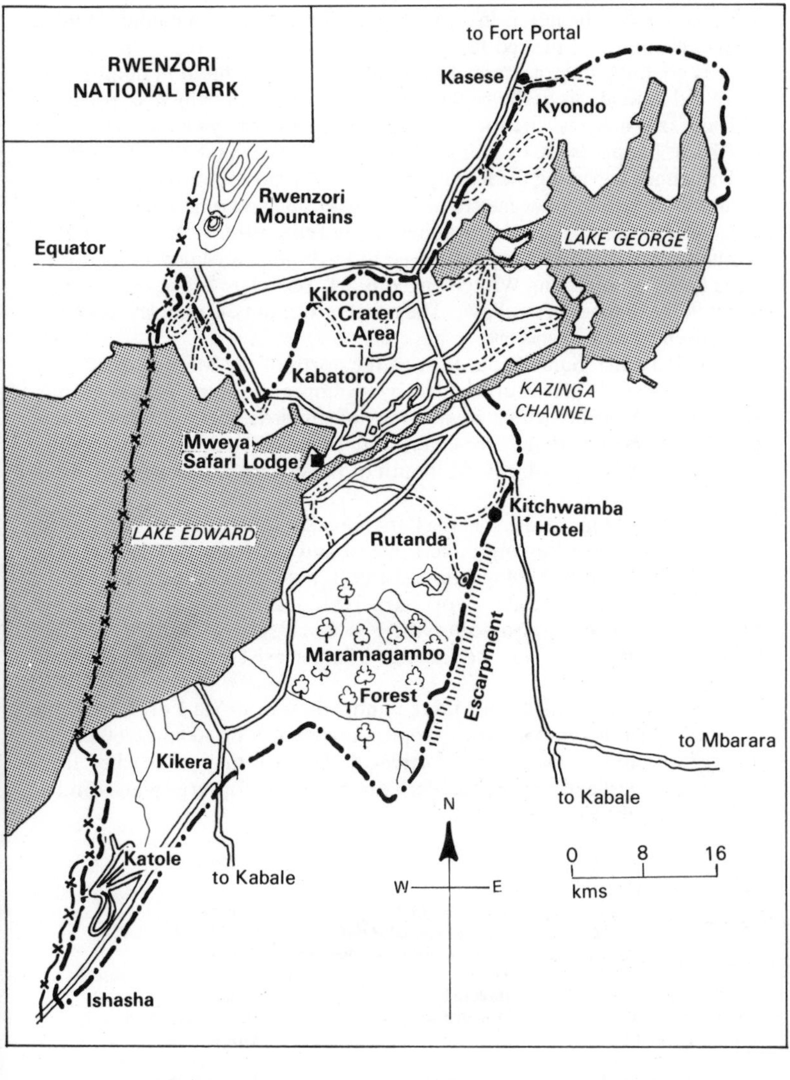

of the rare Whale-headed Stork. Elsewhere in the Park, this remarkably prehistoric-looking bird may be encountered on the shores of Lake George in the Kamulikwezi Circuit.

Large herds of Uganda Kob and Buffalo are still a feature of the Rwenzori

Park; certain of the latter, in their paler and more reddish colour, indicate inter-breeding with the red forest Buffalo of the Zaire. The Elephant previously roaming in large herds has been drastically reduced in number to a mere 150 individuals at the beginning of 1980. Exceptionally fine specimens of Defassa Waterbuck are found, some of the males carrying the finest horns in Africa. Leopards are by no means rare, but are shy and not often seen.

The launch trip along the Kazinga Channel is a most rewarding experience: to approach within a few metres of Buffalo, Hippo and other animals on the bank is unforgettable. Birds are abundant and colourful, Malachite and Pied Kingfishers abound and pay little heed to the human intruder. In the spring large flocks of migrating White-winged Black Terns hawk lake-fly above the water in the manner of swallows. The usual bird count on a single launch trip is between 60 and 70 species.

Near Rutanda Game Scout Post to the north of the Maramagambo are one or two small lakes surrounded by swamp and forest. This is an outstanding bird locality with a great variety of sunbirds, that most beautiful of the bee-eaters, the Black Bee-eater, and Blue-breasted and Shining-blue Kingfishers. For water-birds the mouth of the Nyamugasani River, Pelican Point, is outstanding.

Full hotel accommodation in the Park is available at Mweya Safari Lodge, built on a bluff overlooking Lake Edward and the Kazinga Channel. The Uganda Institute of Ecology responsible for wildlife research in all the National Parks and the Rwenzori Park Headquarters are also situated at Mweya. In the south-west sector there is a self-service camp at Ishasha. Official camping sites along the Kazinga Channel exist for those who wish to use them.

From Kampala, either via Masaka and Mbarara or via Fort Portal, the distance to the Rwenzori Park is approximately 420 or 460km (260 or 286 miles) respectively. The Kigezi portion of the Park may be reached from Kabale. The airfields serving the Park are at Kasese for large planes and at Mweya for light aircraft.

MAMMALS OF RWENZORI NATIONAL PARK

Otter Shrew May occur in streams in Maramagambo Forest
Straw-coloured Fruit Bat
Rousette Bat
Epauletted Fruit Bat
Pale-bellied Fruit Bat
Hammer-headed Fruit Bat
White-bellied Tomb Bat
Hollow-faced Bat
Yellow-winged Bat
Lander's Horseshoe Bat
Lesser Leaf-nosed Bat
Banana Bat
Yellow-bellied Bat
Angola Free-tailed Bat
White-bellied Free-tailed Bat
Potto
Bush Baby
Demidoff's Galago
Black-faced Vervet Monkey
Blue Monkey
Red-tailed Monkey
Olive Baboon
Black and White Colobus
Red Colobus
Chimpanzee
Lesser Ground Pangolin
Hunting Dog
Side-striped Jackal
Zorilla
African Striped Weasel
Ratel
Spotted-necked Otter
African Civet
Large-spotted Genet
African Palm Civet
Marsh Mongoose
Large Grey Mongoose
Black-tipped Mongoose
White-tailed Mongoose
Banded Mongoose

Spotted Hyaena
African Wild Cat
Serval
Golden Cat Not yet recorded but may occur
Lion
Leopard
Ant Bear
Rock Hyrax
African Elephant
Hippopotamus
Giant Forest Hog
Warthog
Bush Pig
Topi
Red Duiker
Yellow-backed Duiker
Blue Duiker
Bush Duiker
Uganda Kob
Defassa Waterbuck
Bohor Reedbuck
Bushbuck
African Buffalo
African Hare
Cane Rat
Porcupine
Striped Ground Squirrel
Bush Squirrel
Giant Forest Squirrel
Scaly-tailed Flying Squirrel
African Dormouse
Giant Rat

BIRDS OF RWENZORI NATIONAL PARK

Little Grebe
White-necked Cormorant
Long-tailed Cormorant
African Darter
White Pelican
Pink-backed Pelican
Grey Heron
Black-headed Heron
Goliath Heron
Purple Heron
Great White Egret
Yellow-billed Egret
Black Heron
Little Egret
Buff-backed Heron or **Cattle Egret**
Squacco Heron
Madagascar Squacco Heron
Green-backed Heron
Rufous-bellied Heron
Night Heron
Little Bittern
Dwarf Bittern
Hamerkop
Whale-headed Stork
White Stork
European Black Stork
Woolly-necked Stork
Abdim's Stork
Open-bill Stork
Saddle-bill Stork
Marabou Stork
Wood Ibis or **Yellow-billed Stork**
Sacred Ibis
Hadada Ibis
Glossy Ibis
African Spoonbill
Greater Flamingo
Lesser Flamingo
White-backed Duck
White-eyed Pochard
African Pochard
European Shoveler
Garganey Teal
Hottentot Teal
Red-billed Duck
European Teal
White-faced Tree Duck
Fulvous Tree Duck
Pygmy Goose
Knob-billed Duck
Egyptian Goose
Spur-winged Goose
Ruppell's Vulture
White-backed Vulture
Nubian or **Lappet-faced Vulture**
White-headed Vulture
Hooded Vulture
Peregine
Lanner
European Hobby
African Hobby
Sooty Falcon
European Kestrel
Grey Kestrel
Cuckoo Falcon
African Black Kite
Black-shouldered Kite
Honey Buzzard
Steppe Eagle
Tawny Eagle
Wahlberg's Eagle
Ayres' Hawk Eagle
Martial Eagle
Crowned Hawk Eagle
Long-crested Eagle
Lizard Buzzard
Brown Harrier Eagle
Black-chested Harrier Eagle
Beaudouin's Harrier Eagle
Grasshopper Buzzard
Bateleur
African Fish Eagle
Palm-nut Vulture
Steppe Buzzard
Mountain Buzzard
Augur Buzzard
Little Sparrow Hawk
Great Sparrow Hawk
Shikra
Gabar Goshawk
Montagu's Harrier
Pallid Harrier
European Marsh Harrier
African Marsh Harrier
Harrier Hawk
Osprey
Coqui Francolin
Red-wing Francolin
Scaly Francolin
Red-necked Spurfowl
Cape Quail
Harlequin Quail
Blue Quail
Helmeted Guinea-fowl
Crested Guinea-fowl
African Crake
Black Crake
Striped Crake
White-spotted Pygmy Crake
Moorhen
Crowned Crane
Black-bellied Bustard
Water Dikkop
African Jacana
Ringed Plover
Little Ringed Plover
White-fronted Sand Plover
Kittlitz's Plover

Three-banded Plover
Caspian Plover
Grey Plover
Crowned Plover
Senegal Plover
Spurwing Plover
Brown-chested Wattled Plover
Wattled Plover
Long-toed Lapwing
European Oystercatcher
Avocet
Black-winged Stilt
Painted Snipe
European Common Snipe
African Snipe
Curlew Sandpiper
Little Stint
Temminck's Stint
Sanderling
Ruff
Turnstone
Terek Sandpiper
Common Sandpiper
Green Sandpiper
Wood Sandpiper
Redshank
Spotted Redshank
Marsh Sandpiper
Greenshank
Black-tailed Godwit
Bar-tailed Godwit
Curlew
Whimbrel
Temminck's Courser
Bronze-winged Courser
Pratincole
Lesser Black-backed Gull
Grey-headed Gull
Gull-billed Tern
Caspian Tern
White-winged Black Tern
Whiskered Tern
African Skimmer
Button Quail
Black-rumped Button Quail
Olive Pigeon
Afep Pigeon
Red-eyed Dove
Ring-necked Dove
Laughing Dove
Namaqua Dove
Tambourine Dove
Blue-spotted Wood Dove
Western Lemon Dove
Green Pigeon
European Cuckoo
African Cuckoo
Red-chested Cuckoo
Black Cuckoo
Levaillant's Cuckoo
Black and White Cuckoo
Emerald Cuckoo
Didric Cuckoo
Klaas' Cuckoo
Black Coucal
Blue-headed Coucal
Senegal Coucal
White-browed Coucal
Yellow-bill or Green Coucal
Black-billed Turaco
Ross' Turaco
Great Blue Turaco
Eastern Grey Plantain-eater
Grey Parrot
Brown Parrot
Red-headed Lovebird
European Roller
Broad-billed Roller
Blue-throated Roller
Pied Kingfisher
Giant Kingfisher
Shining-blue Kingfisher
Malachite Kingfisher
Pygmy Kingfisher
Dwarf Kingfisher
Woodland Kingfisher
Blue-breasted Kingfisher
Grey-headed Kingfisher
Chocolate-backed Kingfisher
Striped Kingfisher
European Bee-eater
Madagascar Bee-eater
Blue-cheeked Bee-eater
White-throated Bee-eater
Little Bee-eater
Cinnamon-chested Bee-eater
Blue-breasted Bee-eater
Black Bee-eater
Black and White-casqued Hornbill
Grey Hornbill
Crowned Hornbill
African Hoopoe
Green Wood Hoopoe
Scimitar-bill
African Barn Owl
African Marsh Owl
African Wood Owl
Pearl-spotted Owlet
Spotted Eagle Owl
Verreaux's Eagle Owl
European Nightjar
White-tailed Nightjar
Gaboon Nightjar
Pennant-wing Nightjar
Long-tailed Nightjar
Speckled Mousebird
Blue-naped Mousebird
Narina's Trogon
Double-toothed Barbet
White-headed Barbet
Hairy-breasted Barbet
Spotted-flanked Barbet
Grey-throated Barbet
Yellow-fronted Tinkerbird
Lemon-rumped Tinkerbird
Yellow-throated Tinkerbird
Speckled Tinkerbird
Yellow-billed Barbet
Greater Honeyguide
Lesser Honeyguide
Scaly-throated Honeyguide
Thick-billed Honeyguide
Cassin's Honeyguide
Brown-eared Woodpecker
Buff-spotted Woodpecker
Little Spotted Woodpecker
Cardinal Woodpecker
Uganda Spotted Woodpecker
Grey Woodpecker
Yellow-crested Woodpecker
Red-breasted Wryneck
Alpine Swift
Little Swift
White-rumped Swift
Palm Swift
Mottled-throated Spinetail
African Broadbill
African Pitta
Green-breasted Pitta
Singing Bush Lark
Rufous-naped Lark
Flappet Lark
Red-capped Lark
European White Wagtail
African Pied Wagtail
Blue-headed Wagtail and races
Plain-backed Pipit
Richard's Pipit
Short-tailed Pipit
Yellow-throated Longclaw
Arrow-marked Babbler
Black-lored Babbler
Yellow-vented Bulbul
Red-tailed Greenbul
Bristle-bill
Fischer's Greenbul
Joyful Greenbul

Yellow-whiskered Greenbul
European Spotted Flycatcher
Dusky Flycatcher
Swamp Flycatcher
Ashy Flycatcher
Pale Flycatcher
Black Flycatcher
Black and White Flycatcher
Yellow-bellied Flycatcher
Chin-spot Flycatcher
Wattle-eye Flycatcher
Chestnut Wattle-eye
Jameson's Wattle-eye
Blue Flycatcher
Dusky Crested Flycatcher
Paradise Flycatcher
Black-headed Paradise Flycatcher
Kurrichane Thrush
African Thrush
European Common Wheatear
Sooty Chat
Stonechat
European Whinchat
White-browed Robin Chat
Blue-shouldered Robin Chat
Red-capped Robin Chat
Snowy-headed Robin Chat
Equatorial Akalat
Forest Robin
Fire-crested Alethe
Brown-chested Alethe
Red-backed Scrub Robin
Garden Warbler
Blackcap Warbler
European Sedge Warbler
Greater Swamp Warbler
European Willow Warbler
Uganda Woodland Warbler
Fan-tailed Warbler
Black-backed Apalis
Black-collared Apalis
Green-tailed Apalis
Black-throated Apalis
Grey-capped Warbler
Buff-bellied Warbler
Green Crombec
White-browed Crombec
Grey Tit-warbler
Green-cap Eremomela
Grey-backed Camaroptera
Wing-snapping Cisticola
Rattling Cisticola
Winding Cisticola
Croaking Cisticola
Tawny-flanked Prinia
White-chinned Prinia
African Moustached Warbler
European Swallow
Angola Swallow
Ethiopian Swallow
Wire-tailed Swallow
Red-rumped Swallow
Mosque Swallow
Rufous-chested Swallow
Striped Swallow
Grey-rumped Swallow
European Sand Martin
African Sand Martin
Banded Martin
African Rock Martin
Black Rough-wing Swallow
Red-shouldered Cuckoo Shrike
Velvet-mantled Drongo
Drongo
Square-tailed Drongo
Grey-backed Fiscal
Lesser Grey Shrike
Fiscal Shrike
Red-backed Shrike
Red-tailed Shrike
Black-headed Gonolek
Tropical Boubou
Puff-back Shrike
Pink-footed Puff-back Shrike
Black-headed Tchagra
Brown-headed Tchagra
Grey-green Bush Shrike
Nicator
Dusky Tit
Black-headed Oriole
Western Black-headed Oriole
Pied Crow
White-naped Raven
Piapiac
Wattled Starling
Violet-backed Starling
Blue-eared Glossy Starling
Splendid Glossy Starling
Purple-headed Glossy Starling
Ruppell's Long-tailed Starling
Stuhlmann's Starling
Yellow-billed Oxpecker
Yellow White-eye
Bronzy Sunbird
Red-chested Sunbird
Beautiful Sunbird
Superb Sunbird
Copper Sunbird
Little Purple-banded Sunbird
Variable Sunbird
Orange-tufted Sunbird
Olive-bellied Sunbird
Green-throated Sunbird
Scarlet-chested Sunbird
Green-headed Sunbird
Blue-throated Brown Sunbird
Olive Sunbird
Collared Sunbird
Grey-chinned Sunbird
Violet-backed Sunbird
Little Green Sunbird
Grey-headed Sunbird
Green Hylia
Grey-headed Sparrow
Black-headed Weaver
Masked Weaver
Little Weaver
Yellow-collared Weaver
Golden-backed Weaver
Northern Brown-throated Weaver
Orange Weaver
Dark-backed Weaver
Black-necked Weaver
Spectacled Weaver
Holub's Golden Weaver
Slender-billed Weaver
Vieillot's Black Weaver
Stuhlmann's Weaver
Compact Weaver
Brown-capped Weaver
Yellow-mantled Weaver
Crested Malimbe
Red-headed Malimbe
Grosbeak Weaver
Red-headed Weaver
Red-billed Quelea
Red-headed Quelea
Cardinal Quelea
Red Bishop
Black-winged Bishop
Yellow Bishop
Fan-tailed Widow-bird
Yellow-shouldered Widow-bird
Yellow-mantled Widow-bird
White-winged Widow-bird
Red-collared Widow-bird
Bronze Mannikin
Black and White Mannikin
Grey-headed Negro Finch
Chestnut-breasted Negro Finch
Red-headed Blue-bill
Black-bellied Seed-cracker
Quail Finch
Parasitic Weaver
Green-backed Twin-spot
Green-winged Pytilia

African Fire Finch
Red-billed Fire Finch
Waxbill
Zebra Waxbill
Fawn-breasted Waxbill
Black-crowned Waxbill
Red-cheeked Cordon-bleu
Indigo-bird
Pin-tailed Whydah
Yellow-fronted Canary
Brimstone Canary
Yellow-rumped Seed-eater
Golden-breasted Bunting
Cinnamon-breasted Rock Bunting

KIDEPO VALLEY NATIONAL PARK

The Kidepo Valley National Park, an area of 1,259sq km (486sq miles) in the remote north-eastern corner of Uganda, was established in March, 1962. Its 48-km (30-mile) long north-western boundary abuts the Sudan border. The Kidepo basin lies in mountainous country at an altitude of between 900 and 1,200m (3,000–4,000ft). It is encircled by wooded hills and dominated by Mount Morongole on its eastern flank and by the forested hogsback of Lotuke in the Sudan, peaks which rise to over 2,700m (9,000ft). Here exists some of the wildest and most magnificent scenery to be found in East Africa, relatively unsullied by civilisation.

The Park straddles the Kidepo and Narus Rivers and their tributaries, which during periods of rain flow northwards into the Sudan. For the greater part of the year most of the Kidepo Park water courses are dry, with the exception of the upper reaches of the Narus River which has some permanent surface water derived from the Napore Hills.

Much of the Park is arid savannah and acacia country with stands of borassus palms, broken by numerous sand rivers which make road construction difficult and which are often a barrier to anything other than four-wheel-drive vehicles. In the western section of the Park there is relatively more water, a greater abundance of wildlife and better developed roads.

The most rewarding time to visit the Kidepo Park is during the dry season, between December and early April. During the rainy seasons in April-May and July-August, travel is difficult and game difficult to locate on account of the long grass.

A number of game animals occur in the Kidepo National Park which are not found in either of the other Uganda National Parks. These include Lesser Kudu, usually found in the eastern sector of the Park, Bright's Gazelle (a race of Grant's Gazelle), Eland, Zebra, Roan Antelope, Klipspringer, Kirk's Dik-dik, Chanler's Mountain Reedbuck, Cheetah and Greater Kudu on the Morongole Massif.

Most numerous species are Jackson's Hartebeest, Oribi, Rothschild's Giraffe, Buffalo, Elephant, Bush Duiker, Eland, Common Zebra and Bright's Gazelle. Other species, such as Roan Antelope, the two Reedbuck, Klipspringer and Bushbuck are less common and more local. Lion, Leopard and Cheetah are present in small numbers. In January 1981 the game department reported that there were only ten Black Rhinoceros remaining in the park.

Bird life is abundant and varied, and the area is especially rich in birds of

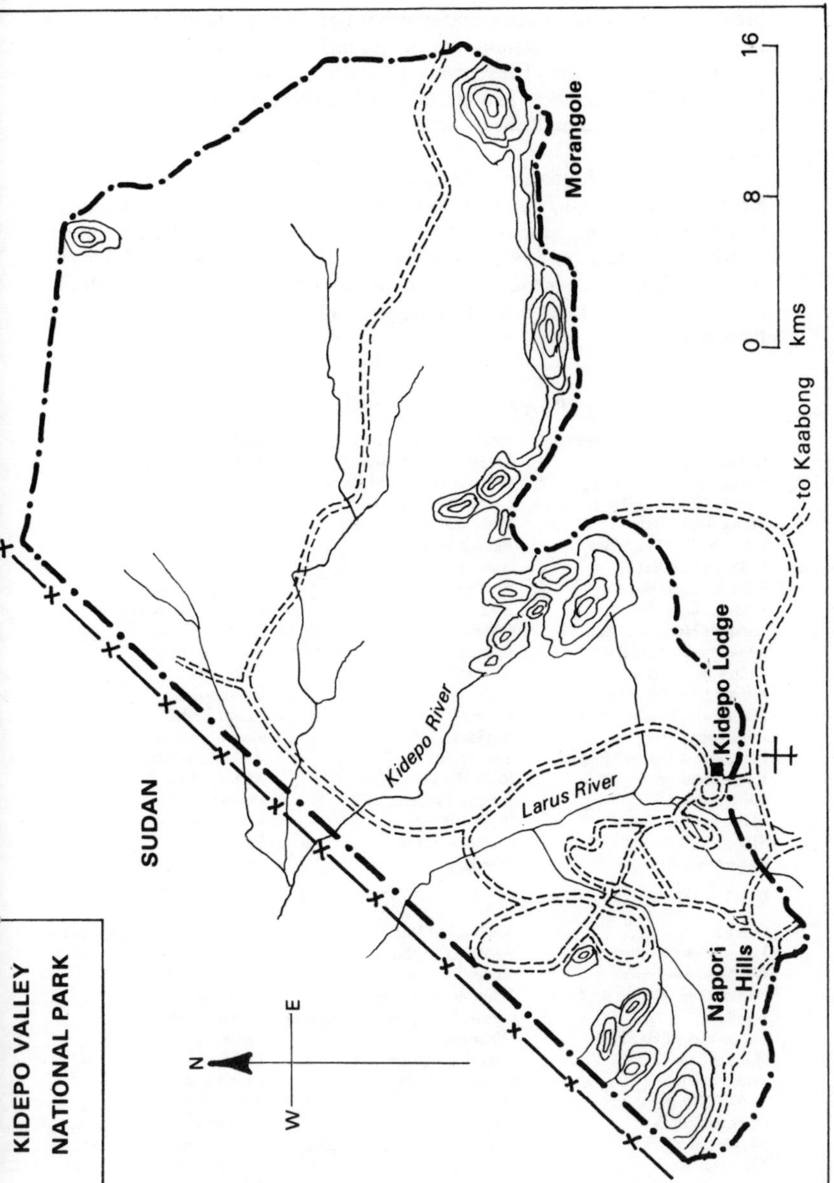
KIDEPO VALLEY
NATIONAL PARK
N
W
E
SUDAN
Kidepo River
Larus River
Napori
Hills
Kidepo Lodge
to Kaabong
Morangole
0
8
16
kms

prey, both resident species and northern migrants. Abyssinian Ground Hornbills are not uncommon and the remarkable Standard-wing Nightjar breeds in the Kidepo. Other specially noteworthy birds are Blue Quail, Stone Partridge, Four-banded Sandgrouse, White-crested Turaco, Rose-ringed Parakeet, Abyssinian Roller, Swallow-tailed Bee-eater, Fan-tailed Raven and Piapiac.

There are two alternative road routes to the Kidepo Park; one via Moroto, Kotido and Kaabong, and the other from Gulu via Kitgum, Rom and Karenga. A landing strip suitable for light aircraft exists at Kaalabi, and another near Kidepo Lodge and the Park Headquarters at Apoka Hill. Accommodation is available in a series of cool safari lodges of Italian design, operated on the self-service principle. A second lodge is being completed at Katurum.

MAMMALS OF KIDEPO VALLEY NATIONAL PARK

Spectacled Elephant Shrew
Rousette Fruit Bat
Epauletted Fruit Bat
Pale-bellied Fruit Bat
Mouse-tailed Bat
White-bellied Tomb Bat
Hollow-faced Bat
False Vampire Bat
Yellow-winged Bat
Lander's Horseshoe Bat
Lesser Leaf-nosed Bat
Yellow-bellied Bat
Angola Free-tailed Bat
Flat-headed Free-tailed Bat
Bush Baby
Black-faced Vervet Monkey
Patas Monkey
Olive Baboon
Black-backed Jackal
Side-striped Jackal
Bat-eared Fox
Small-spotted Genet
Large-spotted Genet
Percival's Dwarf Mongoose
Large Grey Mongoose
White-tailed Mongoose
Banded Mongoose
Aard-wolf
Spotted Hyaena
Striped Hyaena
Cheetah
Caracal
African Wild Cat
Lion
Leopard
Ant Bear
Tree Hyrax
Rock Hyrax
African Elephant
Black Rhinoceros
Common Zebra
Warthog
Rothschild's Giraffe
Jackson's Hartebeest
Bush Duiker
Klipspringer
Oribi
Kirk's Dik-dik
Defassa Waterbuck
Bohor Reedbuck
Chanler's Reedbuck
Bright's Gazelle
Roan Antelope
Bushbuck
Greater Kudu
Lesser Kudu
Eland
African Buffalo
African Hare
Porcupine
Unstriped Ground Squirrel
Bush Squirrel
African Dormouse

BIRDS OF KIDEPO VALLEY NATIONAL PARK

Ostrich
Long-tailed Cormorant
Black-headed Heron
Buff-backed Heron or **Cattle Egret**
Green-backed Heron
Hamerkop
White Stork
Abdim's Stork
Open-bill Stork
Saddle-bill Stork
Marabou Stork
Sacred Ibis
Knob-billed Duck
Secretary Bird
Ruppell's Vulture
White-backed Vulture
Nubian or **Lappet-faced Vulture**
White-headed Vulture
Egyptian Vulture
Hooded Vulture
Peregrine
Lanner
Taita Falcon Not yet recorded but probably occurs
European Hobby
Saker Sight records but not yet confirmed
Red-necked Falcon
European Kestrel
African Kestrel
Fox Kestrel
Lesser Kestrel
Grey Kestrel
Pygmy Falcon
Swallow-tailed Kite Not yet recorded but certain to occur
European Black Kite
African Black Kite

Black-shouldered Kite
Verreaux's Eagle
Steppe Eagle
Tawny Eagle
Wahlberg's Eagle
African Hawk Eagle
Booted Eagle
Martial Eagle
Long-crested Eagle
Lizard Buzzard
Brown Harrier Eagle
Grasshopper Buzzard
Bateleur
Palm-nut Vulture
Lammergeyer Not yet recorded but probably occurs
Steppe Buzzard
Long-legged Buzzard Sight record but not yet confirmed
Augur Buzzard
Little Sparrow Hawk
Shikra
Gabar Goshawk
Pale Chanting Goshawk
Dark Chanting Goshawk
Montagu's Harrier
Pallid Harrier
European Marsh Harrier
Harrier Hawk
Crested Francolin
Shelley's (Greywing) Francolin
Heuglin's Francolin
Yellow-necked Spurfowl
Harlequin Quail
Blue Quail
Stone Partridge
Helmeted Guinea-fowl
Black Crake
Kori Bustard
Jackson's Bustard
White-bellied Bustard
Black-bellied Bustard
Hartlaub's Bustard
Spotted Stone Curlew
African Jacana
Ringed Plover
Kittlitz's Plover
Caspian Plover
Spurwing Plover
Wattled Plover
Blackhead Plover
Green Sandpiper
Temminck's Courser
Bronze-winged Courser
Button Quail
Four-banded Sandgrouse
Speckled Pigeon
Red-eyed Dove
Mourning Dove
Ring-necked Dove
Vinaceous Dove
Laughing Dove
Namaqua Dove
Black-billed Wood Dove
Bruce's Green Pigeon
European Cuckoo
African Cuckoo
Red-chested Cuckoo
Black Cuckoo
Great Spotted Cuckoo
Black and White Cuckoo
Levaillant's Cuckoo
Didric Cuckoo
White-browed Coucal
White-crested Turaco
White-bellied Go-away-bird
Brown Parrot
Rose-ringed Parrakeet
European Roller
Abyssinian Roller
Rufous-crowned Roller
Broad-billed Roller
Grey-headed Kingfisher
Striped Kingfisher
Little Bee-eater
Swallow-tailed Bee-eater
Grey Hornbill
Red-billed Hornbill
Jackson's Hornbill
Abyssinian Ground Hornbill
European Hoopoe
Senegal Hoopoe
Green Wood Hoopoe
Abyssinian Scimitar-bill
African Scops Owl
White-faced Scops Owl
Pearl-spotted Owlet
Spotted Eagle Owl
Verreaux's Eagle Owl
European Nightjar
Freckled Nightjar
Plain Nightjar
Standard-wing Nightjar
Long-tailed Nightjar
Speckled Mousebird
Blue-naped Mousebird
Double-toothed Barbet
Black-billed Barbet
Spotted-flanked Barbet
D'Arnaud's Barbet
Greater Honeyguide
Nubian Woodpecker
Cardinal Woodpecker
Bearded Woodpecker
Nyanza Swift
Scarce Swift
Mottled Swift
Palm Swift
Flappet Lark
Redwing Bush Lark
African Pied Wagtail
Richard's Pipit
Yellow-throated Longclaw
Rufous Chatterer
Yellow-vented Bulbul
Dusky Flycatcher
Little Grey Flycatcher
Silverbird
Paradise Flycatcher
Olive Thrush
European Rock Thrush
European Common Wheatear
Isabelline Wheatear
Pied Wheatear
Cliff Chat
Sooty Chat
Spotted Morning Warbler
Barred Warbler
European Willow Warbler
Grey Wren Warbler
Fan-tailed Warbler
Black-breasted Apalis
Grey-capped Warbler
Buff-bellied Warbler
Crombec
Yellow-bellied Eremomela
Grey-backed Camaroptera
Rattling Cisticola
Foxy Cisticola
Winding Cisticola
Croaking Cisticola
Tawny-flanked Prinia
European Swallow
European Sand Martin
Banded Martin
African Rock Martin
White-headed Rough-wing Swallow
Black Cuckoo Shrike
Drongo
Curly-crested Helmet Shrike
White-crowned Shrike
Northern Brubru
Red-backed Shrike
Red-tailed Shrike
Black-headed Bush Shrike
Sulphur-breasted Bush Shrike
Grey-headed Bush Shrike

White-breasted Tit
Mouse-coloured Penduline Tit
African Golden Oriole
Fan-tailed Raven
Piapiac
Wattled Starling
Violet-backed Starling
Blue-eared Glossy Starling
Bronze-tail Starling
Lesser Blue-eared Starling
Ruppell's Long-tailed Starling
Superb Starling
Yellow-billed Oxpecker
Beautiful Sunbird
Pygmy Sunbird
Copper Sunbird
Mariqua Sunbird
Scarlet-chested Sunbird
White-headed Buffalo Weaver
White-browed Sparrow Weaver
Chestnut-crowned Sparrow Weaver
Grey-headed Social Weaver
Grey-headed Sparrow
Yellow-spotted Petronia
Speckle-fronted Weaver
Northern Masked Weaver
Masked Weaver
Chestnut Weaver
Black-necked Weaver
Spectacled Weaver
Red-headed Weaver
Red-billed Quelea
Cardinal Quelea
Red Bishop
Yellow Bishop
Black-winged Bishop
White-winged Widow-bird
Bronze Mannikin
Silverbill
Cut-throat
Green-winged Pytilia
Red-billed Fire Finch
Crimson-rumped Waxbill
Red-cheeked Cordon-bleu
Purple Grenadier
Pin-tailed Whydah
Paradise Whydah
Yellow-fronted Canary
White-bellied Canary
Yellow-rumped Seed-eater
Golden-breasted Bunting
Cinnamon-breasted Rock Bunting

Game Reserves and Animal Sanctuaries

In addition to the three National Parks Uganda possesses a number of Game Reserves and Animal Sanctuaries. Game Reserves hold status nearly equal to that of National Parks in that all human settlement, cultivation and stock grazing is prohibited. In an Animal Sanctuary all animal and bird life is also strictly protected, but there is no restriction on human activities such as cultivation of crops and grazing of domestic stock. Hunting in Game Reserves used to be allowed with the permission of the Chief Game Warden but now falls under the blanket ban on all hunting in Uganda, in effect until mid 1984.

AJAI GAME RESERVE (Formerly White Rhino Sanctuary)

The Ajai Game Reserve was originally gazetted as an animal sanctuary to protect the White Rhino, now extinct in Uganda due to poaching. Covering 158sq km (61sq miles) in the West Nile area about 32km (20 miles) from Arua, the reserve is named after a former tribal ruler of the area. During the rainy season April through July, the swamps in the Reserve flood, and game prospers unbothered by poachers or encroachment on Ajai 'Island'. Buffalo, Hippo, Warthog, Jackson's Hartebeest, Waterbuck and Bushbuck are found. The Ajai Reserve is one of Uganda's most scenic, but least visited areas because of its location – over 320km (200 miles) from Kampala.

ASWA LOLIM GAME RESERVE

The Aswa Lolim Game Reserve was an area of 102sq km (40sq miles) of savannah grasslands, adjoining the northern border of the Kabalega Falls National Park. It was degazetted by Amin in 1971 to make way for ranching projects which failed. Although no longer an official reserve, the Game Department reports conditions not greatly changed except for extensive poaching. It is still the seasonal breeding ground for Uganda Kob. A greatly reduced Elephant population, Jackson's Hartebeest, Bohor Reedbuck, Buffalo, Lion and Leopard occur and bird life is similar to that found in the Kabalega Falls National Park.

BOKORA CORRIDOR GAME RESERVE

The Bokora Corridor Game Reserve is 2,056sq km (794sq miles) in area and stretches from Napal mountain along the Karamoja-Teso border including most of the plain east of Labwor and south-west of Toror mountain. It is virtually a flat plain, a marginal land of no or little use for agriculture and settlement. Being a dry area a wide range of antelopes and other large mammals are found in the Reserve, but in smaller numbers than previously. The Reserve was gazetted to ensure that game could use the area unimpeded during their seasonal migrations. As its name implies it is a corridor through which the plains game migrates from the Matheniko plains to the Pian Upe Reserve and returns annually. Large mammals include Uganda Kob, Eland, Rothschild's Giraffe, Topi, Grant's Gazelle, Beisa Oryx, Jackson's Hartebeest, Roan Antelope, Oribi, Bohor Reedbuck, Spotted Hyaena and a few Lion and Leopard. Birdlife is abundant and varied.

KARUMA GAME RESERVE AND BUGUNDU GAME RESERVE

These two Reserves serve as buffers on the boundaries of Kabalega Falls National Park. Elephant, Lion, Buffalo, Kob, Hartebeest, Waterbuck, and most other animals found in Kabalega Falls National Park also occur in the two buffer Reserves.

Karuma Reserve covers 695sq km (268sq miles) to the south of the Victoria Nile adjoining Kabalega Falls Park. It is mostly open grassland with some forest in the south-west.

Bugundu Game Reserve occupies 510sq km (197sq miles) on the south-west boundary of Kabalega Falls Park, mostly savannah and semi-deciduous thicket. Both Reserves suffered heavily from poaching in the late 1970s, but diminished herds are already reviving after a year of intensified anti-poaching patrols begun in 1980. The Reserves have excellent future potential as they are among the least affected by human encroachment.

KATONGA GAME RESERVE

The 208sq km (80sq miles) Katonga Game Reserve takes its name from the Katonga River which flows immediately to its south. The Reserve is traversed by numerous tributaries of the Katonga. With plentiful water, there is diverse flora and fauna. Grassland species such as Waterbuck, Bushbuck, Bohor Reedbuck, Buffalo, Hippo and Warthog are found, and the reserve straddles the traditional elephant range which runs north to south through Uganda. Eland, Roan Antelope and Zebra used to occur but have mostly disappeared as illegal cattle grazing increased over the past decade. The Reserve is located 190km (118 miles) west of Kampala on the Kampala–Kasese railway. People wishing to visit this Reserve should first make enquiries at the Game Department, Entebbe.

KIBALE FOREST CORRIDOR GAME RESERVE

The 340sq km (131sq miles) Kibale Forest Corridor Game Reserve is located north-east of the Rwenzori National Park. It includes part of the Mpanga Forest (p.158). It was originally established in 1964 to allow the large herds of the Rwenzori Park additional habitat, and to serve as a migratory route to Game Reserves further north, and to Kabalega Falls National Park, for the huge herds of Elephants which once ranged along Uganda's western frontier.

The severe decline in animal populations during the 1970s has voided the Reserve's original purpose. The grasslands in the south of the reserve are now encroached upon by cultivation, and the evergreen forests in the north illegally exploited for timber.

Chimpanzees dwell in the north of the Reserve, as do Black and White and Red Colobus. Diminished herds of Elephant are still found, and Warthog, Buffalo, Uganda Kob, and Waterbuck are reported.

KIGEZI GAME RESERVE

The 333sq km (129sq miles) Kigezi Game Reserve adjoins the southern boundary of the Rwenzori National Park, and acts as a buffer zone between the Park and the thickly settled areas to the south and east. It contains open grasslands, park-like savannah woodland and forest, and carries small numbers of Elephant, Buffalo and Topi. Uganda Kob, Bushbuck, Giant Forest Hog and Defassa Waterbuck also occur. Bird life is abundant and similar to that of the adjoining Rwenzori Park.

KIGEZI MOUNTAIN GORILLA GAME RESERVE

The Kigezi Mountain Gorilla Game Reserve is situated on Mts Muhavura and Mgahinga in the Birunga volcanoes, extreme south-west Uganda. It covers 44sq km (17sq miles) of forested and bamboo-covered slopes. Accommodation and guides are available at the Travellers Rest Hotel at Kisoro: there is also a mountain camp on the saddle between Muhavura and

Mgahinga. A fairly strenuous three or four hours' climb up mountain footpaths is necessary to reach the gorilla habitat. The Game Department reported about 50 gorillas present in early 1981, but this may be exaggerated.

In addition to the chance of observing Gorillas the forest and bamboo-hypericum zone offer the possibility of seeing the rare Golden Monkey. Other animals which may be encountered are Buffalo, Leopard, Bushbuck, Giant Forest Hog, Blue Monkey and Black and White Colobus. Although relatively inaccessible, this Reserve, with its great forested volcanic cones and magnificent mountain lakes, is perhaps the most scenically impressive in the whole of Uganda. The general region has been called the 'Switzerland of Uganda'.

Birds are plentiful and the colourful Ruwenzori Turaco is common though more often heard than seen. Other specially interesting birds include:

Cuckoo Falcon
Mountain Buzzard
Great Sparrow Hawk
Handsome Francolin
Western Lemon Dove
Bar-tailed Trogon
Western Green Tinker-bird
Yellow-billed Barbet
African Broadbill
Mountain Illadopsis
Olive-breasted Mountain Greenbul
Mountain Yellow Flycatcher
Ruwenzori Puff-back Flycatcher
Blue Flycatcher
Abyssinian Ground Thrush
Brown-chested Alethe
White-starred Bush Robin
Cinnamon Bracken Warbler
Red-faced Woodland Warbler
Black-collared Apalis
Collared Apalis
Masked Apalis
Black-throated Apalis
Chestnut-throated Apalis
Grey-capped Warbler
White-browed Crombec
Luhder's Bush Shrike
Doherty's Bush Shrike
Stripe-breasted Tit
Waller's Chestnut-wing Starling
Slender-billed Chestnut-wing Starling
Scarlet-tufted Malachite Sunbird
Greater Double-collared Sunbird
Northern Double-collared Sunbird
Regal Sunbird
Green-headed Sunbird
Blue-headed Sunbird
Dark-backed Weaver
Strange Weaver
Brown-capped Weaver
Red-faced Crimson-wing
Abyssinian Crimson-wing
Dusky Crimson-wing
Shelley's Crimson-wing
Dusky Fire Finch
Yellow-bellied Waxwing
Black-headed Waxbill
Yellow-crowned Canary
Streaky Seed-eater
Oriole Finch

KITAGATA GAME RESERVE

This Reserve is in south-east Ankole, adjacent to the Uganda–Tanzania border. Although degazetted in 1974 it is now being considered for regazetting on account of the variety of game it still contains.

The habitat is dry shrubby grassland savannah inhabited by Eland, Roan Antelope, Impala, Common Zebra, Bushbuck, Bush Duiker, Bohor Reedbuck, Oribi, Lion and Leopard. The wetter areas towards the Kagera River have small numbers of Sitatunga and some Buffalo and Hippopotamus. Birdlife is very abundant.

KYAMBURA GAME RESERVE

Kyambura Game Reserve covers 156sq km (60sq miles) between the southern shore of Lake George and the north-east boundary of Rwenzori National Park, and serves as a buffer zone for the northern part of the Park. It contains several crater lakes and swamps. The once large concentrations of Hippopotamus in the Reserve have largely succumbed to poachers, but officials are confident that extensive anti-poaching programmes now underway will allow the populations to recover.

A forested area in the east is still zoologically little known. The Reserve still contains Elephants (in small numbers), Hippopotamus, Warthog, Giant Forest Hog, Uganda Kob, Bohor Reedbuck, Buffalo, Lion and Leopard. The birdlife is similar to that found in Rwenzori National Park.

LAKE MBURO GAME RESERVE

The Lake Mburo Game Reserve covers 541sq km (209sq miles) in south-western Uganda, a landscape from north to south of open plains, acacia grasslands, and marshy forests. The Reserve is bounded to the north by the main Kampala–Mbarara Road, to the east largely by Lake Kachera, to the west by the Ruizi River and the south by swampland and a chain of eleven lakes. It has attractive scenery with the hills interwoven with meandering shallow valleys. Two small lakes surrounded by wide swamps occur in it, areas of super-abundant birdlife. The northern parts are largely semi-open grasslands, while the southern areas include the lakes with largely swampy or forested shores.

Oribi, Zebra, and Topi inhabit the open plains of the north, but a greater concentration of wildlife occurs in the middle belt of acacia grassland. Here Impala, Oribi, Klipspringer, Warthog. Eland, Roan Antelopes and occasional Waterbuck are found. Many Buffalo occur in the southern marshes, and a few Lion and Leopard are found throughout the Reserve.

Lake Mburo's proximity to urban centres and easy access on the all weather tarmac Kampal–Mbarara road make the Reserve a likely candidate to become Uganda's fourth National Park within the next few years.

MATHENIKO PLAINS GAME RESERVE

The Matheniko Plains Game Reserve covers 1,605sq km (620sq miles) in north-east Karamoja abutting the Kenya frontier. It has been the traditional pasture for herds migrating from southern Karamoja, but war, drought, famine, and poaching have all taken their toll in recent years. At the beginning of 1981 the Game Department had not patrolled the area for over two years, and could not provide any estimates as to remaining herds.

PIAN UPE GAME RESERVE

Pian Upe Game Reserve is one of three which cover a vast area of Karamoja in north-eastern Uganda. The 2,314sq km (893sq miles) of its rolling plains of black cotton soil run from the Greek River in the south to Mt Napak (2,539m–8,330ft) on the boundary of Bokaora Corridor Game Reserve in the north. Roan Antelope, Bohor and Chanler's Reedbuck, Waterbuck, Rothschild's Giraffe, Hartebeest, Uganda Kob, Greater and Lesser Kudu, Lion, Leopard, and Cheetah are found in the Reserve. Most Eland, Topi, and Zebra migrate northwards when the rains begin between April and June, and return with drier weather at year's end. Oryx, Grant's Gazelle, and Baboon are also occasionally sighted.

Some of the most characteristic birds of the Reserve are:

Ostrich
Marabou Stork
Secretary Bird
Ruppell's Vulture
White-backed Vulture
Lanner
Wahlberg's Eagle
Tawny Eagle
Martial Eagle
Bateleur
Dark Chanting Goshawk
Stone Partridge
Buff-crested Bustard
Spotted Stone Curlew
Heuglin's Courser
Button Quail
White-bellied Go-away-bird
Brown Parrot
Rufous-crowned Roller
Grey-headed Kingfisher
Striped Kingfisher
European Bee-eater
White-throated Bee-eater
Red-billed Hornbill
Jackson's Hornbill
Abyssinian Scimitarbill
Nubian Woodpecker
Cardinal Woodpecker
Bearded Woodpecker
Mottled Swift
Spotted Morning Warbler
Curly-crested Helmet Shrike
Yellow-billed Shrike
Sulphur-breasted Bush Shrike
Lesser Blue-eared Starling
Beautiful Sunbird
Mariqua Sunbird
Buffalo Weaver
White-headed Buffalo Weaver
Paradise Whydah

TORO GAME RESERVE

The Toro Game Reserve, an area of 555sq km (214sq miles) at the southern end of Lake Albert, contains grassy lakeshore flats, swamps, steep forested escarpments and heavily wooded streams. A few Uganda Kob are still found here, estimated to number 1,500, and among other game animals are Hippopotamus, Bohor Reedbuck, Giant Forest Hog, Defassa Waterbuck, Lion and Leopard. Accommodation and guides are available at the Semliki Safari Lodge on the Wassa River.

In the main the bird life is similar to that found in the Kabalega Falls National Park. Specially interesting species, including some not found in the Kabalega Park, are:

African Hobby
Brown Harrier Eagle
Banded Harrier Eagle
Painted Snipe
White-naped Pigeon
White-thighed Hornbill
Wattled Black Hornbill
Pied Hornbill
Yellow-spotted Barbet
Hartlaub's Marsh Widowbird

BWINDI IMPENETRABLE FOREST GORILLA SANCTUARY

This sanctuary is 297sq km (115sq miles) of lowland rain forest and was gazetted to protect the Lowland Gorilla (*Gorilla gorilla graueri*) found there. A 1979 survey found six gorilla families with about 115 members, but noted that the population appeared to be declining. Game Wardens are sometimes available to take visitors to seek gorillas in their habitat, but it is advisable to check with the Game Department at Entebbe. Accommodation is available at the White Horse Inn in nearby Kabale. The sanctuary includes part of the Impenetrable Kayonza Forest (p.157).

ENTEBBE ANIMAL AND BIRD SANCTUARY

The 52sq km (20sq miles) of the Entebbe Animal and Bird Sanctuary encompass the township and famous botanical gardens of Entebbe on the shores of Lake Victoria.

In the swamp at the northern end of Entebbe Airport, Sitatunga may sometimes be seen in the early morning or late evening; and the Whale-headed Stork and Rufous-bellied Heron have also been recorded in this localiy.

The extensive botanical gardens which run down to the lake shore are extremely rich in birds, including many uncommon species. White-collared Pratincoles may often be seen perched on the Yacht Club jetty, amongst Grey-headed Gulls and Common Sandpipers. Grey Parrots visit flowering Erythrina trees in the early morning to feed on the nectar-rich blossoms. Sunbirds also favour these trees, including the aptly-named Superb Sunbird and the rare Orange-tufted Sunbird. The following are some of the characteristic and more interesting species likely to be encountered:

Little Grebe
White-necked Cormorant
Long-tailed Cormorant
African Darter
Grey Heron
Black-headed Heron
Goliath Heron
Great White Egret
Little Egret
Hamerkop
Abdim's Stork
Open-bill Stork
Hadada Ibis
Knob-billed Duck
Pygmy Goose
Egyptian Goose
Hooded Vulture
African Hobby
Bat Hawk
Long-crested Eagle
African Fish Eagle
Palm-nut Vulture
African Marsh Harrier
Harrier Hawk
Osprey
White-spotted Pygmy Crake
Crowned Crane
Water Dikkop
African Jacana
Long-toed Lapwing
Afep Pigeon
Blue-spotted Wood Dove
Green Pigeon
Red-chested Cuckoo
Emerald Cuckoo
Blue-headed Coucal
Ross's Turaco
Great Blue Turaco
Eastern Grey Plantain-eater
Red-headed Lovebird
Broad-billed Roller
Pied Kingfisher
Giant Kingfisher
Malachite Kingfisher
Pygmy Kingfisher
Woodland Kingfisher
Blue-breasted Kingfisher
Grey-headed Kingfisher
Striped Kingfisher
European Bee-eater
Madagascar Bee-eater
Blue-breasted Bee-eater
Little Bee-eater
Black and White-casqued Hornbill
Pied Hornbill
African Hoopoe
Double-toothed Barbet
Grey-throated Barbet
Yellow-spotted Barbet
Lemon-rumped Tinkerbird
Yellow-billed Barbet
Greater Honeyguide
Uganda Spotted Woodpecker
Little Swift
White-rumped Swift
Palm Swift
Bristle-bill
Yellow-throated Leaflove
Joyful Greenbul
Yellow-whiskered Greenbul
Swamp Flycatcher
Black and White Flycatcher
Wattle-eye Flycatcher
Blue Flycatcher
Paradise Flycatcher
Black-headed Paradise Flycatcher
Snowy-headed Robin Chat
Red-shouldered Cuckoo Shrike
Drongo
Grey-backed Fiscal

Black-headed Gonolek
Tropical Boubou
Puff-back Shrike
African Golden Oriole
Splendid Glossy Starling
Purple-headed Glossy Starling
Ruppell's Long-tailed Starling
Green White-eye
Bronzy Sunbird
Red-chested Sunbird
Copper Sunbird
Variable Sunbird
Olive-bellied Sunbird
Green-throated Sunbird
Scarlet-chested Sunbird
Green-headed Sunbird
Blue-throated Brown Sunbird
Olive Sunbird
Collared Sunbird
Grey-chinned Sunbird
Green Hylia
Black-headed Weaver
Yellow-collared Weaver
Golden-backed Weaver
Northern Brown-throated Weaver
Orange Weaver
Black-necked Weaver
Spectacled Weaver
Slender-billed Weaver
Vieillot's Black Weaver
Weyn's Weaver
Stuhlmann's Weaver
Brown-capped Weaver
Red-headed Malimbe
Grosbeak Weaver
Red-headed Weaver
Black-winged Bishop
Black Bishop
Yellow Bishop
Fan-tailed Widow-bird
Black-bellied Seed-cracker
Pin-tailed Whydah

JINJA ANIMAL AND BIRD SANCTUARY

This is another small sanctuary encompassing part of Jinja township and the mouth of the Victoria Nile, an area of about five square miles. Hippopotamus occur in the Nile and at night sometimes wander over the Jinja golf course.

Characteristic birds include:

White-necked Cormorant
African Darter
Black-headed Heron
Hamerkop
Hadada Ibis
African Hobby
Bat Hawk
Eastern Grey Plantain-eater
Brown Parrot
Pied Kingfisher
Woodland Kingfisher
Striped Kingfisher
Grey-headed Kingfisher
Double-toothed Barbet
Little Swift

KATWE BIRD SANCTUARY

This sanctuary, within Rwenzori National Park and around Katwe township, was created for bird protection because of the fishing and salt-mining activities permitted in the area. The birdlife does not differ from that of the Rwenzori National Park.

KAZINGA CHANNEL SANCTUARY

The Kazinga Channel Sanctuary, an area of approximately 207sq km (80sq miles), is 24km long, partly within the Rwenzori National Park and abuts its east-central border and part of the southern shores of Lake George. It consists of rough grasslands with scattered bush and small clumps of euphorbia and acacia trees.

Animals and birds are the same as those found in a similar habitat in the Park, Buffalo, Hippopotamus, Uganda Kob and Defassa Waterbuck are characteristic, and among birds the most noticeable are African Fish Eagle, Crowned Crane, various herons, egrets and storks and numerous weavers.

MALABA SANCTUARY

The Malabi Wildlife Sanctuary, not far south of Tororo, near the Kenya border, comprises an area of approximately 31sq km (12sq miles) of limestone hills, acacia woodland and swamp. The area is primarily of interest to ornithologists, and the following are some of the outstanding birds which occur:

White-backed Night Heron
Verreaux's Eagle Occurs on nearby Tororo Rock
Banded Harrier Eagle
Ross's Turaco
Eastern Grey Plantain-eater
Bare-faced Go-away-bird
Red-headed Lovebird
Broad-billed Roller
Blue-breasted Bee-eater
Ground Hornbill
Double-toothed Barbet
Black-billed Barbet
White-headed Barbet
Yellow-fronted Tinkerbird
Greater Honeyguide
Brown-backed Woodpecker
Blue Flycatcher
Blue Swallow
Black-headed Gonolek
Purple Glossy Starling
Splendid Glossy Starling
Copper Sunbird
Mariqua Sunbird
Variable Sunbird
Scarlet-chested Sunbird
Green-headed Sunbird
Red Bishop
Black-winged Bishop
Fan-tailed Widow-bird
Yellow-shouldered Widowbird
Yellow-mantled Widowbird
Hartlaub's Marsh Widowbird
Black-bellied Waxbill

WEST NILE WHITE RHINOCEROS SANCTUARIES

Four Sanctuaries in West Nile Province established for the protection of the White Rhinoceros together cover a total area of some 647sq km (250sq miles). They were Mount Kei Sanctuary in the north-west, Otze Forest and Dufile Sanctuaries in the north-east and Ajai's Sanctuary farther south.

The first three received little attention during the 1970s. The area has been heavily poached and torn by war. Sadly no White Rhino can now be found in Uganda.

The Ajai Sanctuary, now Ajai Game Reserve, does stand a strong chance of revival (see p.146).

Bird life in these sanctuaries is similar to that found in the Kabalega Falls National Park.

Other Important Faunal Areas

In addition to Uganda's National Parks, Game Reserves and Wildlife Sanctuaries there are four forest regions of great zoological importance, localities where animals and birds occur which are not found in the Parks and Reserves. Situated in western Uganda, these are the Budongo Forest, the Impenetrable Kayonza Forest and the Mpanga Forest, only parts of which are included within the reserves and sanctuaries already described, and the Bwamba Forest. The Zoka Forest and Nkosi Island also form unofficial sanctuaries.

BUDONGO FOREST

The Budongo Forest, part of which has been included in the recently established Budongo Game Reserve, lies between Masindi and Lake Albert and is easy of access. Accommodation is available at Masindi Hotel. The forest has been opened up by timber felling operations over many years and a network of forest roads and tracks greatly facilitates bird-watching.

Budongo Forest is famous for its Chimpanzees and is the most accessible locality in East Africa in which to see these apes. Other uncommon animals which live in the Budongo include the curious Scaly-tailed Flying Squirrel, the Tree Pangolin, Potto, Black-fronted Duiker, Blue Duiker, Black and White Colobus and Giant Forest Squirrel. Around the outskirts of the forest the local Bunyoro Rabbit is common and is often to be seen on roads at night.

The birdlife of the Budongo Forest is extremely rich and the following outstanding species have been recorded:

Cuckoo Falcon
Ayres' Hawk Eagle
Crowned Hawk Eagle
Crested Guinea-fowl
Forest Francolin
Nahan's Forest Francolin
White-spotted Pygmy Crake
Afep Pigeon
Western Lemon Dove
Black-billed Turaco
Ross's Turaco
Great Blue Turaco
Eastern Grey Plantain-eater
Grey Parrot
Broad-billed Roller
Blue-throated Roller
Shining-blue Kingfisher
Dwarf Kingfisher
Blue-breasted Kingfisher
Chocolate-backed Kingfisher
White-thighed Hornbill
White-headed Wood Hoopoe
African Wood Owl
White-tailed Nightjar
Narina's Trogon
Hairy-breasted Barbet
Yellow-spotted Barbet
Yellow-billed Barbet
Greater Honey-guide
Cassin's Honey-guide
Brown-eared Woodpecker
Buff-spotted Woodpecker
Yellow-crested Woodpecker
Mottled-throated Spinetail
Sabine's Spinetail
African Broadbill
Red-sided Broadbill
Green-breasted Pitta
Red-tailed Greenbul
Bristle-bill
Green-tailed Bristle-bill
Yellow-throated Leaflove
Spotted Greenbul
Chestnut-cap Flycatcher
Chestnut Wattle-eye
Jameson's Wattle-eye
Blue Flycatcher
Black-headed Paradise Flycatcher
Red-tailed Ant Thrush
Blue-shouldered Robin Chat
Snowy-headed Robin Chat
Equatorial Akalat
Forest Robin
Fire-crested Alethe
Brown-chested Alethe
Uganda Woodland Warbler
Black-capped Apalis
White-chinned Prinia
Banded Prinia
Grey Tit Warbler
Black-faced Rufous Warbler
Red-shouldered Cuckoo Shrike
Velvet-mantled Drongo
Square-tailed Drongo
Pink-footed Puff-back Shrike
Nicator
Dusky Tit
Splendid Glossy Starling
Purple-headed Glossy Starling
Stuhlmann's Starling
Superb Sunbird
Olive-bellied Sunbird
Green-headed Sunbird
Blue-throated Brown Sunbird
Grey-chinned Sunbird
Violet-backed Sunbird
Little Green Sunbird
Grey-headed Sunbird
Green Hylia
Dark-backed Weaver
Compact Weaver
Brown-capped Weaver
Yellow-mantled Weaver
Crested Malimbe
Red-headed Malimbe
Grey-headed Negro Finch
Red-headed Blue-bill
Black-bellied Seed-cracker
Red-faced Crimson-wing
Grey-headed Olive-back

BWAMBA FOREST

The low-lying Bwamba Forest, the average altitude 750m (2,460ft), lies at the southern end of the Semliki Valley, flanked on the east by the Ruwenzori Mountains. Ecologically it is part of the great Zaire Ituri Forest, and as such contains many species of birds and some mammals not found elsewhere in East Africa.

Habitats vary from almost impenetrable swamp forest to great stands of iron-wood trees and typical low altitude rain forest. The area is well-watered by streams from the Ruwenzori highlands.

Parts of the Bwamba Forest are accessible from Fort Portal, via the Buranga Pass at the northern end of the Ruwenzori Range, down the western escarpment to the hot springs at Mongiro and thence through the eastern edge of the forest to Bundibugyo. A few footpaths extend a short distance into the forest, but in most places elephant and buffalo trails afford the only feasible passage.

Elephant, Buffalo and Leopard are not uncommon, but are not often seen on account of the dense cover. Important among the smaller mammals are Otter Shrew, Potto, Bush Baby and Demidoff's Galago, Black Mangabey, Brazza Monkey, Red-tailed Monkey, Black and White Colobus, small numbers of Chimpanzee, Tree Pangolin, African Palm Civet, Golden Cat, Giant Forest Squirrel and Scaly-tailed Flying Squirrel.

Bird life in Bwamba is outstandingly rich and nearly 400 species have so far been recorded. Mixed bird parties in the tree-tops – a feature of these western Uganda forests – may contain upwards of thirty or forty species. Following is a list of some of the more interesting birds:

African Hobby
Grey Kestrel
Cuckoo Falcon
Bat Hawk
Crowned Hawk Eagle
Palm-nut Vulture
Western Little Sparrow Hawk
Long-tailed Hawk
Scaly Francolin
White-naped Pigeon Often found perched in trees around the hot springs at Mongiro
Western Lemon Dove
Black-billed Turaco
Ross's Turaco
Great Blue Turaco
Grey Parrot
Black-collared Lovebird
Broad-billed Roller
Blue-throated Roller
Giant Kingfisher
Shining-blue Kingfisher
White-breasted Kingfisher
Dwarf Kingfisher
Blue-breasted Kingfisher
Chocolate-backed Kingfisher
Black Bee-eater
White-tailed Hornbill
White-thighed Hornbill
White-crested Hornbill Sometimes associates with troops of Colobus monkeys, feeding on insects disturbed by the animals
Wattled Black Hornbill
Pied Hornbill
Black Dwarf Hornbill
Red-billed Dwarf Hornbill
Forest Wood Hoopoe
Fiery-necked Nightjar
Standard-wing Nightjar
Pennant-wing Nightjar
Narina's Trogon
Double-toothed Barbet
Hairy-breasted Barbet
Grey-throated Barbet
Yellow-throated Tinkerbird
Yellow-billed Barbet
Spotted Honeyguide
Cassin's Honeyguide
Green-backed Woodpecker
Brown-eared Woodpecker
Buff-spotted Woodpecker
Uganda Spotted Woodpecker
Yellow-crested Woodpecker
Elliot's Woodpecker
Scarce Swift
Alpine Swift
Mottled Swift
Mottled-throated Spinetail
Sabine's Spinetail
African Broadbill
Red-sided Broadbill
Green-breasted Pitta
Brown Illadopsis
Red-tailed Greenbul
White-tailed Greenbul

Leaflove
Honey-guide Greenbul
Xavier's Greenbul
Rufous Flycatcher
Shrike Flycatcher
Chestnut Wattle-eye
Jameson's Wattle-eye
Yellow-bellied Wattle-eye
Blue Flycatcher
Blue-headed Crested Flycatcher
White-tailed Crested Flycatcher
Black-headed Paradise Flycatcher
Kurrichane Thrush
Red-tailed Ant Thrush
Blue-shouldered Robin Chat
Red-capped Robin Chat
Snowy-headed Robin Chat
Equatorial Akalat
Akalat
Forest Robin
Fire-crested Alethe
Brown-chested Alethe
White-chinned Prinia
Banded Prinia
Black-faced Rufous Warbler
Velvet-mantled Drongo
Red-billed Shrike
Mackinnon's Grey Shrike
Luhder's Bush Shrike
Grey-green Bush Shrike
Nicator
Yellow-throated Nicator
Black-winged Oriole
Western Black-headed Oriole
Splendid Glossy Starling
Purple-headed Glossy Starling
Narrow-tailed Starling
Purple-breasted Sunbird
Superb Sunbird
Copper Sunbird
Olive-bellied Sunbird
Tiny Sunbird
Green-throated Sunbird
Scarlet-chested Sunbird
Green-headed Sunbird
Blue-throated Brown Sunbird
Grey-chinned Sunbird
Violet-backed Sunbird
Little Green Sunbird
Grey-headed Sunbird
Green Hylia
Yellow-mantled Weaver
Maxwell's Black Weaver
Crested Malimbe
Red-headed Malimbe
Gray's Malimbe
Red-bellied Malimbe
Grey-headed Negro Finch
Chestnut-breasted Negro Finch
White-breasted Negro Finch
Red-headed Blue-bill
Grant's Blue-bill
Black-bellied Seed-cracker
Green-backed Twin-spot
Black-crowned Waxbill

IMPENETRABLE KAYONZA BWINDI FOREST

The Impenetrable Kayonza Bwindi Forest of south-western Kigezi is a continuous belt of montane forest characterised by deep river gorges. It ranges in altitude from 1,220m (4,000ft) to over 2,590m (8,500ft). The low level rain forest is designated the Kayonza Forest: this merges into upland rain forest and bamboo, the Impenetrable Forest. This highland section has zoological affinities with the Rwenzori-Kivu faunistic zone.

Less than 30 years ago the region was inaccessible except on foot, but now a road linking Kabale with the Rwenzori National Park passes through the eastern edge affording some magnificent scenic views.

Among the interesting mammals which may be observed from this road are two rare primates, the Golden Monkey which lives in the high reaches, especially the bamboo zone, and at lower levels Hoest's Monkey. Gorillas exist in the remote western part of the forest, but are not likely to be seen by the casual visitor. Blue Monkey, Black and White Colobus and Red-tailed Monkey are common. The Golden Cat is reputed to occur but this has yet to be confirmed. Other interesting mammals are the fossorial Rwenzori Golden Mole, Otter Shrew, Hammer-headed Fruit Bat, Potto, Demidoff's Galago, African Striped Weasel, African Civet and Black-fronted Duiker: it is possible that the Yellow-backed Duiker also occurs in the Impenetrable Forest.

Birds are numerous and among the most noticeable are Rwenzori, Black-billed and Great Blue Turacos. Forest birds of prey are well represented including Cuckoo Falcon and Mountain Buzzard, whilst a great rarity, Cassin's Hawk Eagle, has been recorded. Other interesting birds include:

African Black Duck
Bat Hawk
Crowned Hawk Eagle
Rufous-breasted Sparrow Hawk
Great Sparrow Hawk
Handsome Francolin
Crested Guinea-fowl
Afep Pigeon
Pink-breasted Dove
Yellow-bill or Green Coucal
Giant Kingfisher
Shining-blue Kingfisher
Blue-breasted Kingfisher
Black Bee-eater
White-thighed Hornbill
White-headed Wood Hoopoe
Red-chested Owlet
Narina's Trogon
Bar-tailed Trogon
Western Green Tinkerbird
Yellow-billed Barbet
Greater Honeyguide
Thick-billed Honeyguide
Cassin's Honeyguide
Brown-eared Woodpecker
Yellow-crested Woodpecker
Elliot's Woodpecker
African Broadbill
Green Broadbill
African Pitta
Green-breasted Pitta
Mountain Yellow Flycatcher
Rufous Flycatcher
Shrike Flycatcher
Ruwenzori Puff-back Flycatcher
Chestnut Wattle-eye
Jameson's Wattle-eye
Blue Flycatcher
Dusky Crested Flycatcher
Grey-winged Robin Chat
Equatorial Akalat
Fire-crested Alethe
Brown-chested Alethe
Red-throated Alethe
Red-faced Woodland Warbler
Masked Apalis
White-browed Crombec
Black-faced Rufous Warbler
Doherty's Bush Shrike
Stripe-breasted Tit
Black-winged Oriole
Sharpe's Starling
Waller's Chestnut-wing Starling
Stuhlmann's Starling
Purple-breasted Sunbird
Northern Double-collared Sunbird
Regal Sunbird
Green-headed Sunbird
Blue-headed Sunbird
Grey-chinned Sunbird
Green Hylia
Strange Weaver
Black-billed Weaver
Brown-capped Weaver
Yellow-mantled Weaver
Crested Malimbe
Red-headed Malimbe
Red-headed Blue-bill
Red-faced Crimson-wing
Abyssinian Crimson Wing
Dusky Crimson-wing
Shelley's Crimson-wing
Dusky Fire Finch
Black-headed Waxbill
White-collared Olive-back
Yellow-crowned Canary

MPANGA FOREST

The Mpanga Forest, the northern margin of which abuts Fort Portal, is a vast tract of rain forest extending southwards almost to Lake George. In the Fort Portal section part of the forest has been opened up during timber felling operations and is easily accessible. The southern sector forms the Kibale Forest Corridor Game Reserve (p.148).

Elephant and Buffalo occur but it is the smaller mammals which are more frequently seen. The most interesting of these is the Red Colobus which is common: mixed troops of Red and Black and White Colobus are often seen in the tree tops along some of the older less frequented tracks. Chimpanzees are also quite numerous, but usually less fearless than they are in the Budongo Forest. Other interesting mammals include Potto, Demidoff's Galago, Tree Pangolin, African Civet, African Palm Civet, Giant Forest Squirrel and Scaly-tailed Flying Squirrel.

Bird life is less abundant than in the Bwamba and Budongo Forests, but these interesting species occur:

Cuckoo Falcon
Cassin's Hawk Eagle
Mountain Buzzard
Scaly Francolin
Nahan's Forest Francolin
Forest Francolin
Crested Guinea-fowl
Afep Pigeon
Western Lemon Dove
Black-billed Turaco
Ross's Turaco
Great Blue Turaco
Blue-throated Roller
Shining-blue Kingfisher
Blue-breasted Kingfisher
Blue-headed Bee-eater
Black Bee-eater
Pied Hornbill
Narina's Trogon
Bar-tailed Trogon
Hairy-breasted Barbet
Eastern Green Tinkerbird
Yellow-billed Barbet
Brown-eared Woodpecker
Buff-spotted Woodpecker
Yellow-crested Woodpecker
Elliot's Woodpecker
African Broadbill
Green-breasted Pitta
Jameson's Wattle-eye
Red-tailed Ant Thrush
Grey-winged Robin Chat
Blue-shouldered Robin Chat
Snowy-headed Robin Chat
Equatorial Akalat
Forest Robin
Fire-crested Alethe
Black-faced Rufous Warbler
Velvet-mantled Drongo
Square-tailed Drongo
Luhder's Bush Shrike
Splendid Glossy Starling
Narrow-tailed Starling
Superb Sunbird
Orange-tufted Sunbird
Green-throated Sunbird
Grey-chinned Sunbird
Grey-headed Sunbird
Green Hylia
Dark-backed Weaver
Black-billed Weaver
Brown-capped Weaver
Yellow-mantled Weaver
Red-headed Malimbe
White-breasted Negro Finch
Red-headed Blue-bill
Black-bellied Seed-cracker
Grey-headed Olive-back
White-collared Olive-back

ZOKA FOREST ELEPHANT SANCTUARY

The Zoka Forest, although not an officially gazetted sanctuary, used to form an elephant sanctuary. It covers approximately 207sq km (80sq miles) on the east side of the Albert Nile in East Madi, embracing the Zoka Forest and the country between the forest and the Nile.

Elephant and Black Rhinoceros used to occur in the forest, but by 1981 Elephants were few in number and the Black Rhino exterminated. On the surrounding plains Buffalo, Uganda Kob, Jackson's Hartebeest, Defassa Waterbuck, Oribi and Bohor Reedbuck may be found.

Plains and waterside birdlife is similar to that of the Kabalega Falls National Park, but the Zoka Forest remains ornithologically unexplored owing to its remoteness and general inaccessibility.

NKOSI ISLAND SITATUNGA SANCTUARY

Several of the Sesse group of islands in Lake Victoria, south of Entebbe, are famous as the haunt of the swamp-living antelope the Sitatunga. Today numbers have been reduced by poaching. Nkosi Island, a southern outlier of the group, has been established as a Sitatunga Sanctuary although not officially gazetted as such. A boat service to the Sesse Islands operates from Port Bell near Entebbe, and it is sometimes possible to hire a launch to visit the islands.

Many of the islands including Nkosi are forested and are margined by extensive areas of swamp. Bird life is abundant, perhaps the most characteristic species being the Grey Parrot: Whale-headed Storks occur locally in the swamps. Other special birds inhabiting these islands include:

Goliath Heron
Purple Heron
Night Heron
Rufous-bellied Heron
Saddle-bill Stork
Pygmy Goose
Bat Hawk
Crowned Hawk Eagle
African Fish Eagle
African Marsh Harrier
Kaffir Rail
White-spotted Pygmy Crake
Water Dikkop
Long-toed Lapwing
White-collared Pratincole
Afep Pigeon
Emerald Cuckoo
Blue-headed Coucal
Black-billed Turaco
Ross's Turaco
Great Blue Turaco
Eastern Grey Plantain-eater
Red-headed Lovebird
Broad-billed Roller
Giant Kingfisher
Blue-breasted Kingfisher
Blue-headed Bee-eater
Black and White-casqued Hornbill
Pied Hornbill
Double-toothed Barbet

PART 2

The Mammals of the National Parks of East Africa

The Mammals of the National Parks of East Africa

The essential purpose of this guide is to assist the user in identifying various living mammals in the field. This being so, characters given in the descriptions have been confined to the external appearance of the individual species. Details of anatomical and dental structure, of use only when one is handling a dead animal or a museum specimen, have been omitted.

Measurements given under each species indicate the total length, i.e. from tip of nose to end of tail. The tail length is also given when this may be of diagnostic value. In the case of larger mammals the height at shoulder is also given.

All the mammals you are likely to encounter have been described and illustrated, but no attempt has been made to define and figure all the many species in groups such as the shrews, bats and smaller rodents. These, after all, are of primary concern mainly to the specialist mammalogist, and are not likely to be seen by the average field naturalist visiting National Parks and Faunal Reserves.

The presentation of the groups is in systematic order, commencing with the Insectivores and finishing with the Rodents.

Insectivores: Insectivora

Five Families of the Order Insectivora are found in East Africa. These are:

Elephant Shrews (Macroscelididae)
A group of terrestrial mammals, ranging in length from 15–50cm (6–20in) with a long trunk-like, flexible snout. Differ from true shrews in having very large round eyes, upright ears, long hind legs and their generally much larger size. Mainly diurnal.

Fig. 1 Rufous Spectacled Elephant Shrew

Golden Moles (Chrysochloridae)
Small burrowing mammals, 10–11.5cm (4–4½in) in length, with cylindrical bodies and blunt-pointed muzzles; no visible tail; claws on forefeet well developed for digging. Fur soft and full with a characteristic metallic lustre. Golden moles may be distinguished from mole rats and other fossorial rodents by their lack of rodent-type incisor teeth.

Fig. 2 Rwenzori Golden Mole

Fig. 3 East African Hedgehog

Hedgehogs (Erinaceidae)
Plump terrestrial mammals, 15–20cm (6–8in) in length, with upperparts covered with sharp quills. Nocturnal; often appear after rains.

Otter Shrews (Potamogalidae)
Streamlined, aquatic insectivores, 20–61cm (8–24in) in length, with relatively broad and flattened heads and long powerful flat-sided tails which they use in swimming: feet not webbed. Mainly nocturnal.

Fig. 4 Otter Shrew

Fig. 5 Giant White-toothed Shrew

Shrews (Soricidae)
Small mouse-like insectivores, 6.5–20cm (2½–8in) in length, with long pointed snouts and soft velvety fur; eyes usually minute; ears small and rounded, often concealed in fur. The shrew family contains some of the smallest mammals in the world.

RUFOUS SPECTACLED ELEPHANT SHREW

Elephantulus rufescens **Fig. 1**

Identification: 25cm (10in), tail 11.5cm (4½in). A medium sized elephant shrew, greyish-brown above, tinged rufous on back and head; white below with a white patch above and below the eye. Progresses both by running and by jumping.

Distribution and Habitat: Widespread and locally common in the drier areas of East Africa: perhaps most abundant in northern Karamoja, Uganda.

Allied Species: The Short-snouted Elephant Shrew (*Nasilio brachyrhynchus*) is smaller, 21cm (8½in), tail 9cm (3½in), with a shorter snout. It occurs on open plains of southern Kenya, and has been recorded near Iringa, Tanzania. The Knob-bristled Forest Elephant Shrew (*Petrodromus sultan*) (Plate 5) is a giant edition of the Rufous Spectacled Elephant Shrew, 36cm (14in), tail 15cm (6in), with knob-tipped bristles on the ventral surface of the tail. It occurs in bush and forest along the Kenya coast, on the Teita Hills in south-eastern Kenya, and in eastern Tanzania, including Zanzibar and Mafia Islands.

YELLOW-RUMPED ELEPHANT SHREW

Rhynchocyon chrysopygus **Plate 5**

Identification: 51cm (20in), tail 20cm (8in). Hind legs and proboscis strongly developed. This is one of the larger elephant shrews, bright dark mahogany red, with a golden lower back and rump patch: tail black with white tip.

Distribution and Habitat: Coastal district of Kenya north of Mombasa. Inhabits coastal forests and dense bush. Usually shy and difficult to observe. Not uncommon in the Sokoke-Arabuku forest, Kenya coast. Mainly diurnal; solitary.

Allied Species: The Black and Red Elephant Shrew, *Rhynchocyon petersi*, lacks the yellow rump patch. It occurs in coastal forests of Kenya south of Mombasa, and in eastern Tanzania, including Zanzibar and Mafia Islands.

RWENZORI GOLDEN MOLE *Chrysochloris stuhlmanni* **Fig. 2**

Identification: 11.5cm (4½in). Two of the three fore-claws greatly developed for digging. Uniform deep brown with high metallic gloss; nose naked; no tail or external ears; eyes rudimentary.

Distribution and Habitat: Mountain forests of Rwenzori and Kigezi, western Uganda; Mount Elgon, western Kenya and Uganda, and the Livingstone Mountains, Poroto Mountains, Rungwe Mountain and Uzungura Mountains, Tanzania. Tunnels in soft forest soil, often near the surface, when its presence may be detected by the low ridges pushed up along the line of its burrows.

EAST AFRICAN HEDGEHOG *Erinaceus pruneri* **Fig. 3**

Identification: 18–23cm (7–9in). A short-legged plump animal with the crown and back covered with short, sharp quills, brown with white tips.

Forehead, side of face and underparts white; foreparts of face black. As a means of defence when disturbed the hedgehog curls itself into a spiny ball.
Distribution and Habitat: The hedgehog has a wide distribution in East Africa, but is extremely local and usually uncommon. An exception is the Nairobi district, Kenya, where it is abundant. Occurs in a variety of habitats from dry highland forest to arid bush country. Nocturnal and usually solitary: most in evidence after rains when plenty of insect food is available.

OTTER SHREW *Potamogale velox* **Fig. 4**

Identification: 51cm (20in), tail 20cm (8in). A short-limbed aquatic animal with a broad, flattened head and a powerful, vertically flattened tail: in general appearance much like a miniature otter. Above warm brown with very dense pale undercoat; underparts white.
Distribution and Habitat: In East Africa known only from Kakamega Forest, western Kenya, mountain streams on Ruwenzori range and in the Kalinzu Forest, south-western Kigezi, Uganda. Nocturnal and solitary: inhabits small fast-flowing rivers and streams. Very rarely encountered, but perhaps not very uncommon where it occurs.

GIANT WHITE-TOOTHED SHREW
Crocidura occidentalis **Fig. 5**

Identification: 23–25cm (9–10in), tail 9cm ($3\frac{1}{2}$in). Many species of White-toothed or Musk Shrews (so-called on account of their strong odour) occur in East Africa, the largest of which is the present species. It is uniform dark rufous brown. Shrews of the genus *Crocidura* may be distinguished from the related *Suncus* shrews by their white, not red-brown teeth. Both groups have the tail shorter than the head and body. Shrews of the semi-arboreal genus *Sylvisorex* have a tail longer than the head and body; those of the genus *Surdisorex*, Mole Shrews, two species of which occur in forest on Mount Kenya and the Aberdare range respectively, are short-tailed shrews with relatively large forefeet which are semi-fossorial in habits.
Distribution and Habitat: Widely distributed and locally common in East Africa. Favours edges of swamps and marshes where there is rank vegetation, but occurs also in damp woodlands and other habitats, often a long way from water. Usually solitary: diurnal and nocturnal.

BATS: Chiroptera

Bats are the only mammals which possess real wings and which are capable of sustained flight. They are almost exclusively nocturnal in their habits. The one East African exception is the semi-diurnal Yellow-winged Bat (*Lavia frons*) which roosts in acacia trees and thickets. During overcast and dull weather this bat sometimes forages for insect prey long before dusk.

East African bats are classified into two sub-orders, the Fruit Bats,

Megachiroptera, which possess large eyes and a claw on the second as well as the first finger (Fig. 6a) and the Insect-eating Bats, Microchiroptera, which have small or minute eyes and a claw on only the first finger (Fig. 6b).

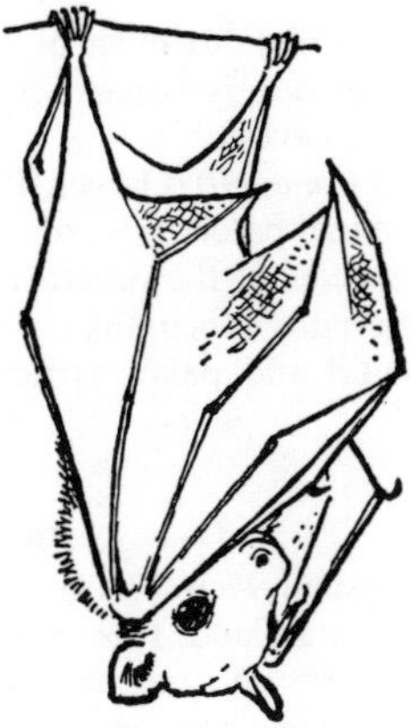

Fig. 6a Epauletted Fruit Bat

Fig. 6b Banana Bat or African Pipistrelle

FRUIT BATS

STRAW-COLOURED FRUIT BAT *Eidolon helvum* **Plate 1**

Identification: 23cm (9in), tail 1cm ($\frac{1}{2}$in), wingspan 76cm (30in). This is a large pale yellowish-brown fruit bat with orange-tawny tinge on foreneck: no white tufts at base of ears and no white 'epaulets' on shoulders. The Rousette Fruit Bats also lack ear tufts and epaulets, but are smaller and dark brown in colour.

Distribution and Habitat: This is a locally common species found in many localities in Uganda; in Kenya recorded from the coast and from Kakamega; and in north-eastern districts and Bukoba in Tanzania; occurs on both Pemba and Zanzibar. A highly gregarious species, roosting in trees. Sometimes many thousands occupy a single communal roost: one such exists in Kampala, Uganda, in a eucalyptus plantation inside the city boundary.

Allied Species: The Rousette Fruit Bat (*Rousettus aegyptiacus*) is smaller, 13cm (5in), uniform dark slate-brown. It occurs in coastal districts of Tanzania and Kenya and in Western Kenya. It is a colony rooster in caves.

EPAULETTED FRUIT BAT *Epomophorus wahlbergi* **Fig. 6a**

Identification: 14cm (5½in), wingspan 51cm (20in). A uniform buff-brown fruit bat with white tufts at the base of the ears and in the male a glandular sac, lined with white hairs, on each shoulder – the 'epaulets'. These epaulets are not always conspicuous as the bat can draw in the glandular pocket so that the white hairs are concealed.

Distribution and Habitat: Widespread but local throughout most of East Africa, including Zanzibar and Pemba Island. Gregarious, roosting in palms and other trees in small groups. Sometimes roosts in caves.

Allied Species: The Pale-bellied Fruit Bat (*Epomops franqueti*) is larger, 18cm (7in), wingspan 58cm (23in); and has a light abdominal patch. It is common in Uganda and north-western Tanzania. Other species of the genera *Epomophorus* and *Epomops* occur in East Africa, externally much alike. Their certain identification depends upon internal dental and palate structure characters.

HAMMER-HEADED FRUIT BAT
Hypsignathus monstrosus **Plate 1**

Identification: ♂ 27cm (10½in), ♀ 23cm (9in), wingspan 97cm (38in), 81cm (32in). This is the largest bat found on the African mainland. It is uniform brownish-grey with a slightly paler abdominal patch and inconspicuous white tufts at the base of the ears. The adult ♂ has a large, grotesque-looking head, with a monstrously developed nasal region, pendulous lips, swollen ruffles around the nose and a hairless split chin. Uniform dark grey colour and large size are best field characteristics.

Distribution and Habitat: Local and uncommon in Uganda; perhaps most frequent at Entebbe. Recorded from Kakamega Forest, Western Kenya. A forest bat, far less gregarious than most fruit bats. Usually seen at dusk when flighting to feeding areas.

INSECT-EATING BATS

East African insectivorous bats vary much in external appearance and are classified into eight families:

The **Mouse-tailed Bats** (Rhinopomidae) remarkable for their very long and slender tails extending outside the interfemoral membrane (Fig. 7).

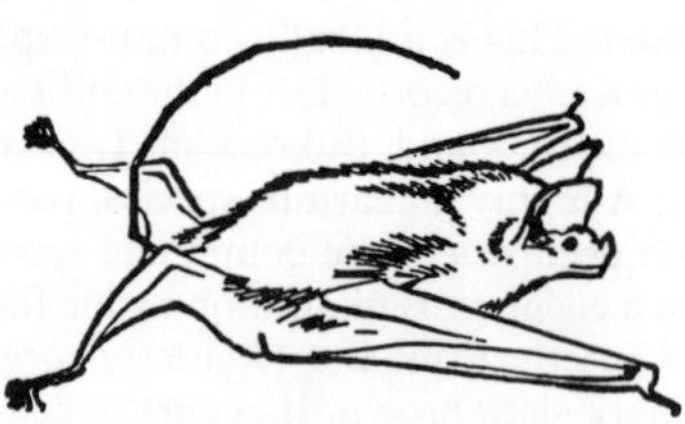

Fig. 7 Mouse-tailed Bat

The **Tomb** or **Sheath-tailed Bats** (Emballonuridae) in which the tail protrudes from the middle of the interfemoral membrane (Fig. 8).

Fig. 8 White-bellied Tomb Bat

The **Hollow-faced Bats** (Nycteridae) have long, soft grey or brown fur, large ears, a deep frontal groove and a long curiously bifid-tipped tail, enclosed in the interfemoral membrane (Fig. 9).

The **False Vampires** and **Yellow-winged Bats** (Megadermatidae) lack tails, but possess well developed interfemoral membranes. Ears large; fur long and soft (Fig. 10).

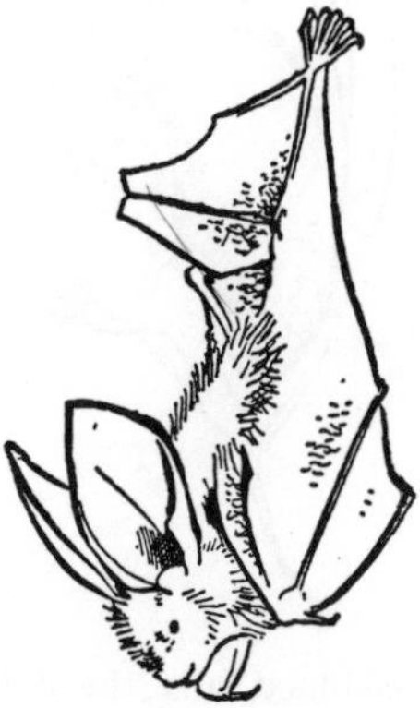

Fig. 9 Hollow-faced Bat

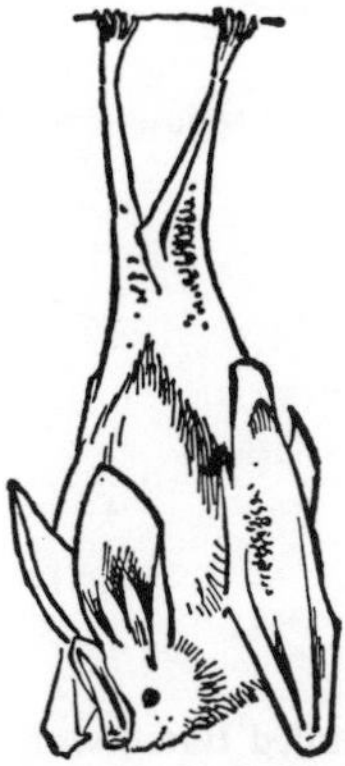

Fig. 10 Yellow-winged Bat

The **Horseshoe Bats** (Rhinolophidae) possess a simple tail enclosed in the interfemoral membrane and characteristic horseshoe-like nose leaves. The relatively large ears lack a tragus (Fig. 11).

The **Leaf-nosed Bats** (Hipposideridae) resemble the Horseshoe Bats but possess facial appendages of nose-leaf or trident shape (Fig. 12).

Fig. 11 Lander's Horseshoe Bat

Fig. 12 Nose-leaf forms: trident shape and normal nose-leaf

The **Mouse-eared** and **Pipistrelle Bats** and their allies (Vespertilionidae) represent the largest group. They are characterised by their short heads and small nostrils, without nose leaves or other complex structures: tail simple, enclosed in interfemoral membrane (Fig. 13).

Fig. 13 Mouse-eared Bat

Fig. 14 Angola Free-tailed Bat

The **Free-tailed Bats** (Molossidae) possess thick-skinned tails (the skin fits loosely over the vertebrae) which project well beyond the edge of the interfemoral membrane. Fur short and dense with a velvet-like lustre: heads thickset (Fig. 14).

MOUSE-TAILED BAT *Rhinopoma kardwickei* **Fig. 7**
Identification: 13cm (5in), tail 6.5cm ($2\frac{1}{2}$in), wingspan 23cm (9in). A creamy brown bat easily distinguished by its very long, slender tail which extends far beyond the poorly developed interfemoral membrane. Appears at dusk; flight slower than most insectivorous bats and less erratic.

Distribution and Habitat: In East Africa known from northern Turkana, Kenya, where it is recorded from Central Island and Ferguson's Gulf, Lake Rudolf, and at Lokomorinyang in the extreme north, and at Lake Baringo. Also occurs in north-eastern Karamoja, Uganda. Roosts in colonies in caves; hunts prey usually over water.

WHITE-BELLIED TOMB BAT *Taphozous mauritianus* **Fig. 8**
Identification: 11.5cm (4½in), tail 1cm (½in), wingspan 36cm (14in). Freckled grey above, white below; wings translucent white. Tail protrudes from centre of interfemoral membrane.
Distribution and Habitat: Wide ranging throughout East Africa outside forest areas. Roost singly or in small groups in palm trees or in houses, where they cling to walls below roofs. They are less attracted to dark roosting places than most bats. Flight direct and fast.

HOLLOW-FACED BAT *Nycteris hispida* **Fig. 9**
Identification: 10cm (4in), tail 5cm (2in), wingspan 22cm (8½in). A small greyish brown bat with long hair, large ears and a tail half the total length. The deep frontal groove, which gives this bat its name, is hidden by the nose-leaves. When resting hangs suspended by its feet.
Distribution and Habitat: Found locally throughout East Africa in all types of habitat. Roosts singly or in small groups in roofs of buildings, in hollow trees or in caves. Flight erratic but not very rapid.

FALSE VAMPIRE BAT *Megaderma cor* **Plate 1**
Identification: 7.5cm (3in), wingspan 33cm (13in). A grey, long-haired bat with very large ears and long oval nose-leaf; no tail. At rest hangs suspended by feet.
Distribution and Habitat: Found locally outside forest areas throughout East Africa. Roosts in colonies in caves and sometimes large hollow trees such as baobabs.

YELLOW-WINGED BAT *Lavia frons* **Fig. 10**
Identification: 9cm (3½in), wingspan 38cm (15in). A slate-grey, very long-furred bat with very large ears; wings yellowish-orange; no tail. At rest hangs suspended by its feet in acacia trees and bushes. Sometimes hunts by day in overcast weather. Orange wings render it most conspicuous when disturbed.
Distribution and Habitat: The Yellow-winged Bat has a wide distribution in East Africa in acacia woodland and bush country. Roosts singly, or in twos and threes, in thorn trees and bushes.

LANDER'S HORSESHOE BAT *Rhinolophus landeri* **Fig. 11**
Identification: 8cm (3in), tail 2½cm (1in), wingspan 28cm (11in). Two colour phases occur, the commoner which is uniform grey-brown and one which is bright cinnamon-rufous: muzzle with characteristic horseshoe leaf-nose: ears

sharp pointed, without tragus; the male has two patches of stiffened reddish hairs near the armpits. At rest hangs suspended by feet.
Distribution and Habitat: Widely distributed in East Africa, but uncommon and local. Roosts in caves and large hollow trees; often associated with Lesser Leaf-nosed Bat to which it bears a superficial resemblance.

LESSER LEAF-NOSED BAT *Hipposideros caffer* **Plate 1**
Identification: 8cm (3in), tail 2½cm (1in), wingspan 28cm (11in). Variable in colour, grey, brown or bright rufous-cinnamon: notched rounded ears without tragus: characteristic leaf-nose (fig. 12). At rest hangs by the feet.
Distribution and Habitat: Common and widespread in East Africa. Roosts in small groups or colonies in caves, buildings, hollow trees and animal burrows.

GIANT LEAF-NOSED BAT *Hipposideros commersoni* **Plate 1**
Identification: 14cm (5½in), tail 1cm (½in), wingspan 64cm (25in). One of the largest insectivorous bats in Africa. Relatively short-haired, pale brown with a broad Y-shaped darker band on upperparts. Ears rather narrow and pointed.
Distribution and Habitat: Locally common in coastal districts of Kenya and Tanzania: rare elsewhere. Found in colonies in caves and large hollow trees.

LONG-EARED LEAF-NOSED BAT
Hipposideros megalotis **Plate 1**
Identification: 8cm (3in), tail 2½cm (1in), wingspan, 25cm (10in). A small orange-buff, leaf-nosed bat with long ears. Has a resemblance to one of the *Nycteris* bats. At rest hangs suspended from its feet.
Distribution and Habitat: In East Africa known only from Naivasha, Nakuru, Elmenteita and the Kinangop plateau. Enters buildings and caves at night: daytime roosts not known, but probably roofs of buildings. This attractive bat is rare and little known.
Allied Species: The African Trident Bat (*Triaenops afer*) occurs in coastal districts of Kenya and Tanzania. It is a larger species than the Lesser Leaf-nosed Bat with a trident-shaped nose-leaf (Fig. 12).

AFRICAN MOUSE-EARED BAT *Myotis tricolor* **Fig. 13**
Identification: 10cm (4in), tail 4cm (1½in), wingspan 33cm (13in). A greyish bat with a distinct rufous tinge over upperparts; ears relatively long; muzzle without nose-leaves.
Distribution and Habitat: In Kenya known from the Rift Valley and Mount Elgon. Not recorded from Tanzania or Uganda. Roosts singly or in small colonies in holes in caves and in tree holes.

BANANA BAT or **AFRICAN PIPISTRELLE**
Pipistrellus nanus **Fig. 6b**
Identification: 7.5cm (3in), tail 2.5cm (1in), wingspan 23cm (9in). A dark

coloured little bat, deep rufous-brown on back; wings black. Ears small; muzzle simple. Appears during early dusk; flight very erratic.
Distribution and Habitat: Widespread and common in East Africa. More frequently seen than many small bats as it appears on the wing well before dark. Roosts singly or in small numbers, in unopened banana leaves or among banana fruits, and in holes in trees and buildings.

YELLOW-BELLIED BAT *Scotophilus nigrita* **Plate 1**
Identification: 13cm (5in), tail 5cm (2in), wingspan 33cm (13in). A rich brown bat with bright yellow or brownish-yellow underparts. Ears moderate; muzzle simple without nose-leaves. Wings, face and ears black.
Distribution and Habitat: Locally common in East Africa. Roosts in small groups in holes in trees and in roofs of houses.

ANGOLA FREE-TAILED BAT *Tadarida condylura* **Fig. 14**
Identification: 11.5cm (4½in), tail 4cm (1½in), wingspan 36cm (14in). Upperparts brown or grey-brown, sometimes pale rufous-brown, often speckled white; grey-brown below, often white in centre of abdomen; tufts of brown hairs between ears in ♂; wings grey-brown. Appears at dusk; flight extremely strong, direct and rapid.
Distribution and Habitat: Widespread and common in Kenya, but local in Uganda, and in Tanzania recorded in south-east and north. Roosts usually in roofs of buildings, sometimes in large colonies.

WHITE-BELLIED FREE-TAILED BAT
Tadarida limbata **Plate 1**
Identification: 10cm (4in), tail 2.5cm (1in), wingspan 31cm (12in). Above dark grey-brown; ♂♂ with tuft of long hairs between ears; below, chest and flanks grey-brown, belly white: wings white, sometimes greyish towards tips. Leaves roost at dusk; flight direct and very rapid.
Distribution and Habitat: A common and widely distributed bat in Kenya and Uganda; in Tanzania mainly in north-eastern and coastal districts; occurs on Zanzibar and Pemba. Roosts in colonies, generally in roofs of buildings, but sometimes in hollow trees and in cliffs.

FLAT-HEADED FREE-TAILED BAT
Platymops setiger **Plate 1**
Identification: 9cm (3½in), tail 2.5cm (1in), wingspan 25cm (10in). The striking feature of this group of bats is the marked flattening of the head and body, an adaptation which allows then to live in very narrow rock crevices. They are dark brown above; below warm pale brown with a dark brown stripe down each side: well developed gular sac present in both sexes.
Distribution and Habitat: Known only from Kenya, where recorded from Northern Turkana, Isiolo, West Suk, Lake Baringo, and Maktau and Simba River, Southern Kenya. These bats roost singly or in small scattered colonies

in rock fissures of rounded granite hills. They appear at dusk, their flight being direct and rapid.

GIANT FREE-TAILED BAT *Otomops martiensseni* **Plate 1**
Identification: 17cm ($6\frac{1}{2}$in), tail 4cm ($1\frac{1}{2}$in), wingspan 48cm (19in). Distinguished at once from all other African free-tailed bats by its large size and very large ears, 4cm ($1\frac{1}{2}$in) long. Above and below rich mahogany brown of various shades; narrowly edged white on the back.
Distribution and Habitat: The headquarters of this rare bat is in caves on Mount Suswa, Kedong Valley, Kenya: elsewhere it has been recorded from Nairobi and the Shimba Hills, Kenya, and in north-eastern Tanzania near Tanga. At Suswa large colonies exist in deep, remote caves. Flight exceptionally strong and direct.

POTTOS, GALAGOS, MONKEYS and GREAT APES: Primates

This order, the one in which man belongs, is divided into four groups in East Africa. These are the nocturnal pottos and galagos, and the diurnal monkeys and baboons and the great apes.

POTTO *Perodicticus potto* **Plate 5**
Identification: 46cm (18in), tail 7.5cm (3in). A thickset, arboreal mammal resembling a galago in general appearance but with a very short tail. Unlike the galagos its movements are slow and deliberate. Greyish-brown to rufous-brown, often with a grizzled appearance on back and flanks: fur soft and thick.
Distribution and Habitat: Locally not uncommon in the forests of Uganda, and also found in the Kakamega Forest, Western Kenya. Solitary, arboreal and nocturnal. Confined to areas of rain forest. Easily located at night with a powerful torch, when its eyes shine brightly in the torch beam.

GREATER GALAGO *Galago crassicaudatus* **Plate 2**
Identification: 64cm (25in), tail 28cm (11in). Arboreal, nocturnal primate with dense grey-brown fur and a long bushy tail: large oval ears and relatively pointed profile. Eyes large and round. Black and silver-grey forms occur in Western Kenya. The Bush Baby is a much smaller animal, 41cm (16in), with a relatively longer and thinner tail.
Distribution and Habitat: Widely distributed in Kenya and Tanzania, and on Pemba and Zanzibar; most abundant in coastal districts. Found in woodlands and coastal bush, and in cultivated areas where there are trees. Very noisy at night.

BUSH BABY *Galago senegalensis* **Plate 2**

Identification: 41cm (16in), tail 23cm (9in). A smaller, more slimly built animal than the Greater Galago with a rounder face and ears and eyes relatively larger. Fur thick and woolly, but tail thin at base, becoming bushy towards tip. Conspicuous white stripe down nose.

Distribution and Habitat: Widespread and common throughout most of East Africa, inhabiting a variety of habitats from coastal bush and acacia woodlands to forested areas. Like the Greater Galago nocturnal but less solitary; sometimes in small parties.

Allied Species: Demidoff's Galago (*Galago demidovi*) is a tiny species, 30cm (12in), tail 18cm (7in), with a longer profile, found in forests of Western Uganda. A single record for this species from Uluguru Mountains, Tanzania needs confirmation.

BLACK MANGABEY *Cercocebus albigena* **Plate 2**

Identification: 122–152cm (40–60in), tail 81–91cm (32–36in). An all blackish-brown monkey with the long hairs on the head forming an occipital crest. The hair on the tail instead of lying flat sticks out at right angles, imparting a very untidy appearance: a good field character.

Distribution and Habitat: Found locally in forests of Uganda and in the Bukoba district of north-western Tanzania. An arboreal species confined to forest.

Allied Species: The Tana Mangabey (*Cercocebus galeritus*) is a rare animal found in riverine forest along the Tana River in Kenya. It is smaller than the Black Mangabey and grey-brown in colour.

BLACK-FACED VERVET MONKEY
Cercopithecus aethiops **Plate 5**

Identification: 122–142cm (48–56in), tail 56–71cm (22–28in); ♀ smaller. A greyish monkey with an olive or yellowish tinge; whitish below; tail with black tip; face black with whitish cheek tufts and white bar above eyes.

Distribution and Habitat: Common and widespread in favourable areas throughout East Africa. It specially favours acacia woodland along streams, rivers and lakes. Both arboreal and terrestrial: diurnal. Gregarious, often in large troops.

BLUE or SYKES' MONKEY *Cercopithecus mitis* **Plate 5**

Identification: 140–158cm (55–62in), tail 86–96cm (34–38in); ♀♀ smaller. An extremely variable monkey of which many geographical races have been described. Those races called 'Blue Monkeys', of which *Cercopithecus mitis stuhlmanni* is a typical example, are deep blue-grey with the limbs, crown and end of tail black; eyebrow stripe whitish-grey. The 'Sykes' Monkeys', example *Cercopithecus mitis kolbi*, differ in having a distinct white throat and chest patch and the back more or less tinged rufous. Most distinct race is the rare and beautiful Golden Monkey, *Cercopithecus mitis kandti*, which has the entire back greenish-gold merging to orange on the flanks: crown, limbs and end of tail black.

Distribution and Habitat: This group of monkeys is widely distributed and common in forest areas throughout East Africa. 'Blue Monkeys' occur in Uganda, Western Kenya and Mount Kilimanjaro and elsewhere in Tanzania. 'Sykes' Monkeys' are found in Kenya east of the Rift Valley, in coastal districts of Kenya and Tanzania, and on Zanzibar. The Golden Monkey is confined, in East Africa, to mountain bamboo forest in south-western Kigezi, Uganda. The species is found in groups and is largely arboreal: diurnal.

Allied Species: The Brazza Monkey (*Cercopithecus neglectus*) is a pale blue-grey monkey with black limbs, an orange forehead band and a well-developed white beard. It is found in forests on Mount Elgon and the Cherengani Mountains, Western Kenya; and in forests near Busia and in the Bwamba Forest in Uganda. The semi-terrestrial Hoest's Monkey (*Cercopithecus l'hoesti*) is a large blackish species with white cheeks and throat. It is found in the Kayonza forest of south-western Kigezi, Uganda.

RED-TAILED or WHITE-NOSED MONKEY

Cercopithecus nictitans **Plate 5**

Identification: 116–142cm (46–56in), tail 61–71cm (24–28in); ♀♀ smaller. A dark, rich brown monkey, sometimes tinged olive above, with a conspicuous white nose and a bright chestnut-red tail; bare skin around eyes blue.

Distribution and Habitat: A common forest monkey in Uganda, Western Kenya and north-western Tanzania. This is essentially an arboreal species. Its long red tail and white nose are conspicuous in the field. Gregarious and diurnal.

PATAS MONKEY *Erythrocebus patas* **Plate 5**

Identification: 168–183cm (66–72in), tail 56–66cm (22–26in); ♀♀ smaller. The Patas Monkey or Red Hussar, as it is often called, is a mainly terrestrial animal. It is a long-legged monkey, bright ginger-red above and white below. Found in small troops: diurnal.

Distribution and Habitat: Locally distributed in bush and savannah country in northern Tanzania and Kenya (Nanyuki; Rumuruti; Eldoret-Kitale; Kongelai Escarpment, West Pokot), and more commonly in eastern and northern Uganda. A ground-dweller, this monkey uses trees and termite hills only as vantage points.

OLIVE BABOON *Papio anubis* **Plate 5**

Identification: 127–142cm (50–56in), tail 46cm (18in); ♀♀ smaller than ♂♂. This is a heavy, thickset baboon, greyish or olive brown, with a well-developed mane in old ♂♂; profile long and dog-like; tail carried in a loop, the base held upright. Gregarious and diurnal.

Distribution and Habitat: A common species in Kenya excepting eastern areas, western Tanzania and Uganda. Occurs in a variety of habitats from rocky bush and savannah country and acacia woodland to open plains in vicinity of trees or rocky outcrops. Terrestrial and arboreal.

YELLOW BABOON *Papio cynocephalus* **Plate 5**

Identification: 116–137cm (46–54in), tail 46–51cm (18–20in); ♀♀ smaller. This is a much lighter, slimmer built animal than the Olive Baboon, with conspicuously long legs. Colour yellowish olive-brown; profile shorter than that of Olive Baboon, and little trace of mane in old ♂♂. Gregarious; diurnal.
Distribution and Habitat: Locally common in eastern districts of Kenya and Tanzania. Inhabits bush country, baobab trees, rocky outcrops and woodland.

BLACK and WHITE COLOBUS *Colobus polykomos* **Plate 2**

Identification: 168–195cm (66–76in), tail 76–92cm (30–36in); ♀ smaller. The black and white colobus are divided into two groups of races, the *abyssinicus* section with short hair on the head, and the *angolensis* group with long hair (see Plate 2). General colour black with a white mantle and a more or less well developed bushy white termination of the tail. In the Kikuyu (Kenya) and Meru (Tanzania) races most of the tail is bushy and white. Gregarious, arboreal and diurnal. Colobus differ from other monkeys in lacking a thumb.
Distribution and Habitat: The Colobus is a forest monkey found from sea level to over 3,350m (11,000ft) in mountain forest. In Tanzania the *abyssinicus* group is found in Mount Kilimanjaro and Mount Meru forests; various races of the *angolensis* group elsewhere. In Kenya the *angolensis* type occurs in coastal forests and those of the *abyssinicus* in inland high country areas. In Uganda most of the colobus are of the short-haired *abyssinicus* section, except on Ruwenzori where a race of *angolensis* occurs.

RED COLOBUS *Colobus badius* **Plate 5**

Identification: 122–132cm (48–52in), tail 66–76cm (26–30in); ♀♀ a little smaller than ♂♂. This is a reddish-brown colobus, with a greyish cape and whitish underparts. Crown uniform deep reddish-brown; frontal band and tail blackish-brown.
Distribution and Habitat: This is a much rarer animal than the Black and White Colobus. It occurs in forests of western Uganda, western and north-western Tanzania, and in Kenya in some of the coastal forests and forests along the Tana River. On Zanzibar there exists a very distinct race which is coloured red, white and black, known as Kirk's Red Colobus (*Colobus badius kirkii*).

CHIMPANZEE *Pan troglodytes* **Plate 2**

Identification: Height *c.* 122cm (48in); tailless ape covered with black hair. Large protruding ears of human shape. The race found in East Africa is the

Long-haired Chimpanzee (*Pan troglodytes schweinfurthi*) which has long hair all over the body and a full cheek beard prominent in adult ♂♂.
Distribution and Habitat: Not uncommon in many forests in western Uganda; specially numerous in the Budongo Forest near Masindi. In Tanzania found east of Lake Tanganyika, from the Urundi border, south to the Mahari Mountains and Ubende. Chimpanzees occur usually in small groups or family parties; diurnal, arboreal and terrestrial.

MOUNTAIN GORILLA *Gorilla gorilla* **Plate 2**

Identification: Height *c.* 152cm (60in); ♀♀ smaller. A huge tailless ape covered with black hair. Old ♂♂ develop a high crown and heavy brow ridge and a silvery mantle. Body thickset with relatively short, weak legs but long and powerful arms. The race found in Uganda is the Mountain Gorilla (*Gorilla gorilla berengei*), which differs from the West African forest gorilla in its larger size and denser pelage. Diurnal.
Distribution and Habitat: In East Africa found only in the mountain forest and bamboo zone of the Bufumbiro volcanoes – Mgahinga, Muhavura and Sabinio – and the Impenetrable-Kayonza forests, Kigezi district, south-western Uganda. Occurs in small family groups; arboreal and terrestrial.

PANGOLINS: Pholidota

Pangolins, or Scaly Ant-Eaters as they are sometimes called, are an order of reptilian-looking mammals with small heads and long broad tails which have the upper surface of the body covered with horny, overlapping scales. They have no external ears and are toothless. Termites and ants form their diet which they pick up with their extremely long, sticky tongues. Forelimbs have large digging claws. When disturbed the animal rolls itself into a ball for protection.

LESSER GROUND PANGOLIN *Manis temmincki* **Plate 2**

Identification: 91–117cm (36–46in), tail 41–51cm (16–20in). Tail shorter than head and body; scales average 4cm ($1\frac{1}{2}$in) in width. Terrestrial, nocturnal and solitary.
Distribution and Habitat: Occurs throughout East Africa, but everywhere extremely uncommon and local. Most frequent in southern Tanzania. Inhabits open country, bush and light woodland. Sleeps during day in a hole in the ground. Strictly nocturnal and seldom observed.
Allied Species: The Tree Pangolin (*Manis tricuspis*) is a much smaller and more slender species, 51–61cm (20–24in) with a tail longer than the head and body, and scales less than 2.5cm (1in) wide. It is a semi-arboreal mammal found in rain forest in Uganda and western Kenya: nocturnal and solitary.

CARNIVORES: Carnivora

For purposes of field identification the carnivores may be divided into two groups: those with the general appearance dog-like, the jackals, foxes, hyaenas and aard-wolf; and those which are not dog-like, the cats, otters, mongooses and allies.

HUNTING DOG *Lycaon pictus* **Plate 7**

Identification: 122–127cm (48–50in), tail 38cm (15in), height at shoulder 61–76cm (24–30in). A rather long-legged, dog-like animal with massive jaws and very large, erect, rounded ears: tail bushy with white tip. Colour black with uneven rufous and white blotches: much individual variation in colour and markings. Diurnal; gregarious, hunting in small packs.
Distribution and Habitat: Locally distributed in small numbers throughout the big game areas of East Africa. Occurs both in open plains country and in sparse bush.

GOLDEN JACKAL *Canis aureus* **Plate 7**

Identification: 86cm (34in), tail 31cm (12in), height at shoulder 43–46cm (17–18in). A dusky yellowish or rufous-grey jackal with an ill-defined darker back which merges into the colour of the sides; underparts and legs yellowish or rufous-grey; ears sandy-rufous; tail reddish-brown with dark tip. The Side-striped Jackal has a longer, more slender muzzle, dark brown ears, a pale stripe on the side, and usually a white-tipped tail. The Black-backed (Silver-backed) Jackal has a well-defined blackish back, more or less streaked silvery-grey, in marked contrast to rufous flanks and legs.
Distribution and Habitat: Status imperfectly known owing to confusion with other species. Occurs locally in Kenya – recorded Laikipia, Naivasha, Loita Plains, Sotik and Mount Suswa – and known from Serengeti Plains and elsewhere in northern Tanzania. Probably occurs Karamoja district, Uganda. Frequents open plains and bush country; solitary or in pairs, nocturnal and sometimes diurnal.

BLACK-BACKED or SILVER-BACKED JACKAL
Canis mesomelas **Plate 7**

Identification: 86–96cm (34–38in), tail 31cm (12in), height at shoulder 41–43cm (16–17in). This is the jackal with a well-defined blackish back contrasting strongly with rufous sides: ears rufous: tail bushy with dark tip.
Distribution and Habitat: The commonest of the East African jackals, found in suitable habitats in Kenya, Uganda and Tanzania. Occurs in open plains and bush country and light woodlands; solitary or in pairs or family parties; diurnal and nocturnal.

SIDE-STRIPED JACKAL *Canis adustus* **Plate 7**

Identification: 86–96cm (34–38in), tail 30–36cm (12–14in), height at shoulder 46cm (18in). Uniform grizzled brownish-grey without dark 'saddle'; indistinct pale stripe on side of body; ears dark brown, not rufous; tail bushy, dark brown, usually with distinct white tip. Nocturnal, sometimes diurnal; solitary or in pairs.

Distribution and Habitat: Common and widespread in Tanzania; in Kenya much less common than Black-backed Jackal and very local; in Uganda found in area around Lake Victoria and in south-western Uganda. Found in both wooded and open plains country.

BAT-EARED FOX *Otocyon megalotis* **Plate 7**

Identification: 81cm (32in), tail 30cm (12in), height at shoulder 30–33cm (12–13in). Has field appearance of small, short-legged, greyish-brown jackal with enormous ears, black face and legs, and black tipped bushy tail.

Distribution and Habitat: Widely distributed in East Africa, but local and generally uncommon. Most frequent Serengeti Plains, northern Tanzania and localities in Rift Valley of Kenya. Nocturnal and diurnal. Often seen sunning themselves outside burrows in small groups or family parties. Frequents open country or sparse bush.

ZORILLA *Ictonyx striatus* **Plate 3**

Identification: 61cm (24in), tail 23cm (9in). General appearance skunk-like; above longitudinally striped black and white; long-haired, tail bushy; underparts and limbs black. Solitary or in pairs; nocturnal.

Distribution and Habitat: Widely distributed East Africa, but seldom seen because of its strictly nocturnal habits. Occurs in a variety of habitats – plains, woodlands and bush.

Allied Species: The African Striped Weasel (*Poecilogale albinucha*) is a smaller, shorter-legged and more slender animal, short-haired, with yellowish-white and black stripes. Of wide distribution but everywhere rare. Occurs in both wooded and forested areas. Nocturnal and diurnal (rarely). Found in pairs or small groups. Even less often observed than the Zorilla.

RATEL or HONEY BADGER *Mellivora capensis* **Plate 3**

Identification: 71–81cm (28–32in), tail 10cm (4in), height at shoulder 20cm (8in). A thickset, short-legged badger-like animal with small ears and a short, slightly bushy tail; pale grey above, whitish on crown and sides, black below. Solitary or in pairs; terrestrial, normally nocturnal.

Distribution and Habitat: Widespread in East Africa, but everywhere very uncommon and rarely observed. May be found in almost every type of habitat, including open plains and forested country.

CLAWLESS OTTER *Aonyx capensis* **Plate 3**

Identification: 152cm (60in), tail 63cm (25in), height at shoulder 18cm (7in).

A short-limbed aquatic animal, rich brown with a white chin and throat; small rounded ears and flattened tail; toes not webbed and clawless.
Distribution and Habitat: Widespread but local in suitable localities Kenya and Tanzania; much less frequent in Uganda where commoner in the west, its place being taken by the Spotted-necked Otter in Lake Victoria. Occurs in rivers, streams and swamps. Nocturnal and partially diurnal. Solitary or in family groups; shy and not often seen.
Allied Species: The Spotted-necked Otter (*Lutra maculicollis*) is a smaller species, 102cm (40in), tail 41cm (16in), with brown spots on its throat and fully-webbed feet. It occurs in Lake Victoria and other lakes in Uganda, being most numerous in Lake Bunyonyi in Kigezi.

AFRICAN CIVET *Civettictis civetta* **Plate 7**
Identification: 107cm (42in), tail 41cm (16in), height at shoulder 38cm (15in). A long-bodied, long-haired animal with a pronounced dorsal crest and long bushy tail: grey, with vertical blackish blotches and stripes; ears small and round, white tipped; all-black specimens are not uncommon.
Distribution and Habitat: Widely distributed in suitable areas throughout East Africa, including Zanzibar. Usually solitary; terrestrial; secretive and nocturnal: although not an uncommon animal it is infrequently observed. Occurs in most types of country from forest to open bush.

NEUMANN'S or SMALL-SPOTTED GENET
Genetta genetta **Plate 7**
Identification: 92cm (36in), tail 41cm (16in). A long-bodied spotted cat-like animal with a long banded tail. The species may be recognised by a dorsal crest of erectile hairs along the back. Terrestrial and arboreal.
Distribution and Habitat: Widely distributed over Kenya and Tanzania, but less common in Uganda. Occurs in a variety of habitats but most frequent in bush country and acacia woodland. Solitary, sometimes in pairs: nocturnal.

BUSH or LARGE-SPOTTED GENET *Genetta tigrina* **Plate 7**
Identification: 92–102cm (36–40in), tail 41–46cm (16–18in). Differs from Neumann's Genet in lacking the dorsal crest: a shorter-furred animal, usually with larger body spots. Melanistic examples are frequent: terrestrial and arboreal.
Distribution and Habitat: A common species throughout East Africa, including Uganda. Nocturnal and solitary. Occurs in a variety of habitats, favouring woodlands and forest areas.

AFRICAN PALM CIVET *Nandinia binotata* **Plate 7**
Identification: 92cm (36in), tail 46–51cm (18–20in). A thick-coated rufous-brown animal with a long bushy tail: indistinctly spotted dark brown; whitish spot on each side of shoulder; tail indistinctly ringed. Solitary, mainly arboreal and nocturnal.

Distribution and Habitat: An uncommon species throughout East Africa. Found in heavily wooded and forest areas, including both rain forest and montane forest.

MARSH MONGOOSE *Atilax paludinosus* **Plate 7**
Identification: 89cm (35in), tail 31cm (12in). A thickset dark reddish-brown or blackish-brown mongoose with long hair. In some lights looks completely black.
Distribution and Habitat: Found locally throughout East Africa. Occurs mainly in the immediate vicinity of water – marshes, swamps, lakes and rivers. Mainly nocturnal but sometimes appears in daylight: solitary; terrestrial.

DWARF MONGOOSE *Helogale undulata* **Plate 3**
Identification: 31–33cm (12–13in), tail 10cm (4in). A very small, short-tailed, reddish-brown mongoose of diurnal habits; gregarious in small packs; terrestrial.
Distribution and Habitat: Common species in Kenya and Tanzania: in Uganda place taken by similar but slightly larger Percival's Dwarf Mongoose (*Helogale percivale*), 38cm (15in). Inhabits bush country and savannah.

LARGE GREY MONGOOSE *Herpestes ichneumon* **Plate 3**
Identification: 122cm (48in), tail 43cm (17in). A large greyish-brown mongoose with a long relatively slender tail which terminates with a black tuft. Solitary; diurnal and nocturnal.
Distribution and Habitat: Occurs locally throughout East Africa. Frequents edges of lakes and swamps, woodlands and thick bush.

SLENDER or **BLACK-TIPPED MONGOOSE**
Herpestes sanguineus **Plate 3**
Identification: 71cm (28in), tail 36cm (14in). A slender, deep rufous-brown mongoose with a long black-tipped tail. Solitary; terrestrial; diurnal and nocturnal.
Distribution and Habitat: This is a common and widely distributed species found in a variety of habitats from woodlands to neglected cultivated ground.

WHITE-TAILED MONGOOSE *Ichneumia albicauda* **Plate 3**
Identification: 102cm (40in), tail 46cm (18in). A rather large, thickset grey mongoose with shaggy hair and a white tail. Examples occur in which the tail is grey like the rest of the body: solitary or in pairs; terrestrial; nocturnal.
Distribution and Habitat: This is a common species over much of East Africa. It occurs in wooded areas, bush and even on open plains.

BANDED MONGOOSE *Mungos mungo* **Plate 7**
Identification: 46cm (18in), tail 15cm (6in). This is a medium-sized greyish-brown mongoose with transverse dark bands along the body: occurs in small packs of up to a dozen or so; diurnal; terrestrial.
Distribution and Habitat: Widely distributed in East Africa, but local: inhabits bush country, open woodland and savannah.

AARD-WOLF *Proteles cristatus* **Plate 6**
Identification: 89–97cm (35–38in), tail 20cm (8in), height at shoulder 46–51cm (18–20in). In general appearance resembles a very small striped hyaena. Sandy rufous with vertical dark stripes, a dorsal mane and a bushy tail. Solitary or in pairs or family parties; terrestrial; nocturnal.
Distribution and Habitat: Of wide distribution throughout East Africa, but everywhere local, rare and seldom seen. It inhabits arid and semi-arid country and plains.

SPOTTED HYAENA *Crocuta crocuta* **Plate 6**
Identification: 140–165cm (55–65in), tail 31cm (12in), height at shoulder 69–91cm (27–36in). A large dog-like animal with a sloping back, large rounded ears and massive jaws. Varies in colour from reddish-brown to drab grey, with dark spots. Mainly nocturnal but may be seen during daytime and active at dawn and dusk. Solitary or gregarious; terrestrial. Produces eerie, wailing call at night.
Distribution and Habitat: A common animal throughout East Africa where conditions are favourable, but especially frequent in big game country. Habitat varied.

STRIPED HYAENA *Hyaena hyaena* **Plate 6**
Identification: 137cm (54in), tail 30cm (12in), height at shoulder 76cm (30in). Slighter in build than Spotted Hyaena, long-haired with dorsal mane and bushy tail; ears pointed and upright, not rounded; body grey or sandy grey with vertical black stripes. Mainly nocturnal but can be seen during day. Solitary, sometimes in pairs or even larger groups; terrestrial. Produces an eerie series of calls from moans to shrieks.
Distribution and Habitat: Wide distribution but everywhere very uncommon. Occurs in a variety of habitats, but favours dry, broken bush country. This is a much rarer animal than the Spotted Hyaena.

CHEETAH *Acinonyx jubatus* **Plate 6**
Identification: 214cm (84in), tail 76cm (30in), height at shoulder 71–81cm (28–32in). A lanky, small-headed, tawny yellow and black-spotted cat-type animal with an ill-defined short mane on the hindneck and shoulders. Stands higher than a leopard with rounded spots dotted over the body, not grouped in rosettes like a leopard's spots; tail ringed with black and has white tip. The cheetah is remarkable among the cats in being unable to retract its claws. Diurnal; solitary or in family groups; terrestrial.

Distribution and Habitat: Fairly widely distributed but uncommon in Kenya and Tanzania; in Uganda found only in Karamoja. Inhabits open plains country and dry, open bush. Probably much less common than leopard, but on account of its diurnal habits more often seen.

CARACAL *Felis caracal* **Plate 6**

Identification: 66–91cm (26–36in), tail 15cm (6in), height at shoulder 41–46cm (16–18in). A sleek red-brown cat with tufted ears and a short tail: some examples are tawny in colour and completely melanistic specimens have been recorded. Usually solitary; nocturnal, but sometimes observed by day; mainly terrestrial but can climb trees.

Distribution and Habitat: Widely distributed but nowhere common in Kenya and Tanzania: in Uganda confined to drier areas, being most frequent in Karamoja. Inhabits open woodlands and semi-arid bush country and plains country at the edge of bush.

AFRICAN WILD CAT *Felis lybica* **Plate 6**

Identification: 71–81cm (28–32in), tail 18cm (7in), height at shoulder 23cm (9in). Resembles a thickset broad-headed domestic tabby cat, but tail relatively shorter and body markings less distinct; backs of ears rufous. Solitary; nocturnal, but sometimes observed by day; terrestrial but partly arboreal.

Distribution and Habitat: Found throughout East Africa but not common. In the vicinity of human habitations often interbreeds with domestic cats. Inhabits a variety of country from wooded areas to semi-arid bush.

SERVAL *Felis serval* **Plate 6**

Identification: 102–122cm (40–48in), tail 20cm (8in), height at shoulder 46–51cm (18–20in). A large tawny-yellow, black-spotted cat with a short, black-ringed tail, long legs and large oval ears. A colour variety with very small black spots is known as the Servaline. All black melanistic examples are not infrequent, especially from high country in Kenya. Mainly nocturnal; terrestrial, but can climb trees; solitary.

Distribution and Habitat: Widespread in suitable areas in East Africa. Found in many different types of country but specially favours areas of scattered bush and tall grass and dry reedbeds near streams; also not uncommon on montane moorlands.

GOLDEN CAT *Felis aurata* **Plate 6**

Identification: 102cm (40in), tail 20cm (8in), height at shoulder 41cm (16in). A large, wild cat which may be either bright red-brown or grey-brown in general colour; usually with dark spots on flanks and underparts. Solitary; mainly terrestrial; nocturnal.

Distribution and Habitat: A rare animal in East Africa, found only in the Mau forest and Mt Elgon, western Kenya, and the forests of the Ruwenzori range and south-western Kigezi in western Uganda; perhaps most frequent on the alpine moorlands of the Ruwenzori Mountains. This is a forest species which is rarely encountered.

LION *Panthera leo* **Plate 6**
Identification: 228–280cm (90–110in), tail 76–81cm (30–32in), height at shoulder 102–114cm (40–45in); lionesses are smaller, averaging 86cm (34in) at shoulder. Largest of African cat family, tawny in colour with a black tail tuft. Adult ♂♂ develop manes which may be pale sandy-rufous to black. Usually gregarious; nocturnal and diurnal; normally terrestrial, but some – for example near Manyara, Tanzania and in the Ruwenzori Park, Uganda – do climb trees.
Distribution and Habitat: Found in suitable localities, mainly game areas in the National Parks and Reserves, throughout East Africa; but in much smaller numbers than formerly. Frequents lightly-wooded country, thickets, dry bush and broken rocky country and open plains.

LEOPARD *Panthera pardus* **Plate 6**
Identification: 204–230cm (80–94in), tail 86cm (34in), height at shoulder 61–71cm (24–28in). A more powerfully built and thickset animal than the cheetah with thicker, shorter legs and relatively larger head. Black spots tend to form rosettes; tail spotted and usually black at tip. Mainly nocturnal; terrestrial but to some extent arboreal; solitary.
Distribution and Habitat: Widespread but not common in suitable areas in East Africa. Far less often seen than the cheetah, although a commoner animal. Inhabits a wide variety of country from forest to rocky outcrops in arid bush: favours riverine forest and woodlands.

ANT BEAR: Tubulidentata

ANT BEAR or **AARDVARK** *Orycteropus afer* **Plate 2**
Identification: 122–137cm (48–54in), tail 43–61cm (17–24in), height at shoulder 38–41cm (15–16in). A grotesque, thickset animal with strong digging claws; greyish or reddish-brown in colour with very sparse bristly hairs; head narrow with an elongated snout; long pointed ears. Tail thick at base but tapering to a point. Feeds upon ants and termites which it sweeps up with its extremely long viscid tongue. Strictly nocturnal and although common, seldom seen; solitary; terrestrial.
Distribution and Habitat: Widespread in East Africa in localities where there are termite hills. Its diggings are often the only indication that the animal is present.

HYRAXES: Hyracoidea

Rabbit-sized animals without tails, dark brown or grey in colour, resembling gigantic guinea-pigs. They possess three toes on fore feet, four on hind feet, short ears and a narrow cream-coloured streak down the centre of the back, not always visible in the field. Species difficult to identify in field, when habitat – trees or rocks – is best guide to determination.

TREE HYRAX *Dendrohyrax arboreus* Plate 8

Identification: 41cm (16in). Tree Hyraxes vary from grizzled grey to deep brown in colour. They differ externally from the Rock Hyraxes in having longer and much softer fur. Both groups possess a dorsal line of pale cream-coloured fur. In general tree hyraxes live in trees and are nocturnal, whilst rock hyraxes live among boulders and are mainly diurnal. However the race of tree hyrax found in the Ruwenzori Mountains, Uganda, lives mainly among rocks. Occurs solitary, in pairs or in small groups; mainly nocturnal, drawing attention to its presence by its deep croaking and creaking calls and harsh strident screams: mainly arboreal.
Distribution and Habitat: Tree Hyraxes of this or closely related species are locally common in suitable areas over most of East Africa. They are specially numerous in the Mau Forest in the western Kenya highlands. They occur in forested country and woodland along streams and rivers.

ROCK HYRAX *Heterohyrax brucei* Plate 8

Identification: 38–46cm (15–18in). Thickset, tail-less animals looking like giant grey or brown guinea-pigs, often seen sunbathing on rocks and boulders. Much shorter-haired than tree hyrax and hair coarser and stiffer, not soft and silky. Dorsal patch of buff or rufous-buff hair present, but not always conspicuous. Gregarious, lives in colonies; mainly terrestrial, but able to climb trees. Mainly diurnal but feeds usually at night.
Distribution and Habitat: Wide ranging over East Africa where rocky out-crops, boulders and stony hills afford cover.

ELEPHANTS: Proboscidea

Remarkable for their great size and their trunks – an elongated nose – with which they convey food and water to their mouths, blow dust or water over themselves. Both sexes may grow tusks, but those of ♀♀ smaller than in ♂; tuskless elephants occur in both sexes.

AFRICAN ELEPHANT *Loxodonta africana* Plate 4

Identification: 280–356cm (9–11½ft) at shoulder: ♂♂ larger than ♀♀. Tusks of adult ♂♂ weigh 22–45kg (50–100lb) each, but much larger tusks have

been recorded. Gregarious in small or large herds, but bulls often solitary.
Distribution and Habitat: Occurs in all types of country from mountain forest to semi-arid bush and savannah country. Common in many National Parks and Game Reserves, and in other areas in East Africa. Very large tuskers occur on Marsabit Mountain in northern Kenya.

ODD-TOED UNGULATES: Perissodactyla

Ungulates are large hoofed mammals which feed on a vegetable diet. The present group includes the Rhinoceroses and Zebras.

BLACK RHINOCEROS *Diceros bicornis* **Plate 4**

Identification: 3.5m (11ft) in length from snout to base of tail, 168cm (5½ft) at shoulder; ♀♀ smaller. Front horns measure on average 50–89cm (20–35in), rear horns up to 53cm (21in), but larger measurements have been recorded. Differs from larger Square-lipped or White Rhinoceros in having a pointed and prehensile upper lip: feet relatively small, three toes on each foot. The Black Rhinoceros is mainly a browser, whilst the Square-lipped Rhinoceros is a grazer.
Distribution and Habitat: Generally but locally distributed in suitable localities in East Africa, but exterminated from much of its previous range. Inhabits many types of country from semi-arid bush to montane forest. Most frequent in the National Parks where it can receive protection. Weight from 1,000–2,540kg (1–1½ tons).

SQUARE-LIPPED or WHITE RHINOCEROS

Diceros simus **Plate 4**

Identification: 3.56–4.26m (11½–14ft) in length from snout to base of tail, 168–183cm (5½–6ft) at shoulder. Front horns measure on average 50–97cm (20–38in), rear horns up to 53cm (21in). Differs from much commoner Black Rhinoceros in its square-mouthed muzzle which has no prehensile upper lip; its enormous head; its front horn with an expanded square base and flat front surface; and its characteristic shoulder hump. When walking or resting the head is held low to the ground. After the Elephants the Square-lipped Rhinoceros is the largest of the land mammals, weighing about 3,550kg (3½ tons). The Square-lipped Rhinoceros is not white in colour, the name being derived from the Dutch '*weit*' – wide – referring to the wide square muzzle. Occurs solitary or in small groups.
Distribution and Habitat: In East Africa was found only in the West Nile district of north-western Uganda: present status uncertain. The species has been introduced successfully into the Kabalega National Park, where both species of Rhino may now be observed. The Square-lipped Rhinoceros is a more docile animal than the Black Rhinoceros, less likely to charge an intruder. It inhabits grassy savannah country and is a grazer.

GREVY'S ZEBRA *Equus grevyi* **Plate 4**
Identification: Height at shoulder 152cm (5ft). Mule-like; tallest and most beautiful of the zebras. Very narrow and close-set black or dark brown stripes on a white or cream ground; broad dorsal stripe; belly white, without stripes; mane thick and high extending on to the withers; ears large, rounded and heavily fringed. Gregarious, often associated with Burchell's Zebra and various antelopes.
Distribution and Habitat: Confined in East Africa to the northern districts of Kenya from the Tana River north-westwards to the eastern shores of Lake Turkana and northwards. Inhabits dry open plains and arid grass-bush country.

BURCHELL'S or COMMON ZEBRA *Equus burchelli* **Plate 4**
Identification: Height at shoulder 128cm (50in). Pony-like: stripes broad, especially on rump and hindquarters; ears relatively short and narrow; mane relatively short. Two distinct races of Burchell's Zebra occur in East Africa; Grant's Zebra in northern Kenya strikingly black and white without greyish 'shadow stripes' between the black and white stripes, and Boehm's Zebra in southern Kenya southwards which has 'shadow stripes'. Gregarious, in herds.
Distribution and Habitat: Widespread in Kenya and Tanzania, but much less common in Uganda, where confined mainly to Karamoja. Occurs on open grassy plains, savannah grasslands and semi-arid grass-bush.

EVEN-TOED UNGULATES: Artiodactyla

The Even-toed ungulates include the pigs, hippopotamus, giraffes and antelopes. All the members of this order have hoofs with an even number of toes. With the exception of the hippopotamus all are cloven-hoofed.

HIPPOPOTAMUS *Hippopotamus amphibius* **Plate 4**
Identification: Length 4.26m (14ft), height at shoulder 140cm (58in). A huge aquatic pig-like mammal with enormous head and broad square muzzle. General colour blackish-brown, merging to pink on sides of face and underparts. Gregarious as a rule, but old ♂♂ sometimes solitary.
Distribution and Habitat: Widespread and common in suitable inland waters and swamps throughout East Africa. Inhabits lakes, swamps and rivers with sufficient water. Especially abundant in the Ruwenzero and Kabalega Parks in Uganda; may be observed under ideal conditions in the crystal clear waters of Mzima Springs in the Tsavo National Park, Kenya.

GIANT FOREST HOG *Hylochoerus meinertzhageni* **Plate 8**
Identification: Length 122–127cm (48–50in), height at shoulder 81cm (32in). A very large, thickset pig, covered with coarse black hair; tusks well de-

veloped; boars possess extensive wart-like swellings below the eyes. The noticeable field character of this animal is its bulk, and when glimpsed in forest undergrowth, it can be mistaken for a young buffalo. Solitary or gregarious in small sounders and family groups; mainly nocturnal.
Distribution and Habitat: In Kenya occurs in small numbers in forests of Mount Kenya and Aberdare Mountains, and in forests of western districts; in Uganda it occurs in the Ruwenzori forests and in other forests in western Uganda; in Tanzania it is known from Mount Oldeani, and it probably occurs on Mount Meru. Inhabits highland and rain forest areas from 1,524 to 3,048m (5,000–10,000ft).

WARTHOG *Phacochoerus aethiopicus* **Plate 8**

Identification: 91–102cm (36–40in), height at shoulder 76cm (30in). Boars larger than sows. A naked-skinned, greyish wild pig with bristles down back of neck and shoulders. Large wart-like growths present on sides of face; tusks well developed. Holds its tail straight up when running or about to move. Gregarious, usually in family parties; old ♂♂ often solitary; diurnal.
Distribution and Habitat: Widespread and common in suitable areas throughout East Africa. Inhabits open plains and grasslands, savannah country and semi-arid grass-bush.

BUSH PIG *Potamochoerus porcus* **Plate 8**

Identification: 86–92cm (34–36in), height at shoulder 71–76cm (28–30in). Variable in general colour from bright rufous to dark rufous-brown with white dorsal mane. Tusks relatively short and knife-like; ears tipped with tufts of long hair. Gregarious or solitary; nocturnal. Although a common animal in many areas it is seldom seen owing to its nocturnal habits.
Distribution and Habitat: Wide ranging in East Africa and often common, but rarely seen. Inhabits highland and rain forest, riverine woodlands and dense bush from sea level to over 3,048m (10,000ft).

COMMON GIRAFFE *Giraffa camelopardalis* **Plate 8**

Identification: 4.56–5.48m (15–18ft), ♀♀ smaller than ♂♂. With their long neck and limbs and blotched markings giraffes are unmistakable. Two races of the Common Giraffe occur in East Africa, the Masai Giraffe, *Giraffa camelopardalis tippelskirchi* with two (sometimes three) horns on the head; yellowish-buff with jagged-edged pale or dark rufous markings and legs more or less spotted below the knees; and the Uganda or Rothschild's Giraffe, *Giraffa camelopardalis rothschildi*, a paler more thickset animal with less jagged markings, having three or five horns (one in front of normal horns and sometimes two extra ones behind) and legs usually unmarked below the knees.
Distribution and Habitat: The Masai Giraffe occurs in Kenya south-west of the Athi, southwards through Tanzania. The Rothschild's Giraffe is found in western Kenya in the Trans-Nzoia and Lake Baringo districts, extending

north-westwards to Karamoja and northern Uganda. Giraffes are found in open acacia woodland, desert grass-bush and scrub and coastal forest.

RETICULATED GIRAFFE *Giraffa reticulata* **Plate 8**

Identification: Height 4.56–5.18m (15–17ft), ♀♀ smaller than ♂♂. The most handsome of the giraffes, liver-red in colour marked with a network of white lines, quite different from the jagged blotches or rounded markings of the Common Giraffe. Often treated as a race of the Common Giraffe.

Distribution and Habitat: Found in the Northern Frontier region of Kenya, north of the Tana River. Giraffe occurring between the Tana and Athi Rivers are more or less intermediate in appearance between the Reticulated and Masai Giraffe and are probably of hybrid origin. The Reticulated Giraffe lives in dry acacia woodland, desert grass-bush and in forest on Mount Marsabit.

COKE'S HARTEBEEST or **KONGONI**

Alcelaphus buselaphus cokii **Plate 10**

Identification: Height at shoulder 122cm (48in). A long-faced, fawn-coloured, hump-shouldered antelope with a whitish rump; horns bracket-shaped, short and relatively thick; present in both sexes. On account of the existence in western Kenya of populations apparently of hybrid origin between Coke's and Jackson's Hartebeests these two antelopes are at present considered to be races of a single species, in spite of their very different general appearance.

Distribution and Habitat: Widespread and common in southern Kenya and in Tanzania. Occurs on open grassy plains and tree-grassland from sea level to 1,980m (6,500ft).

JACKSON'S HARTEBEEST

Alcelaphus buselaphus jacksoni **Plate 10**

Identification: Height at shoulder 132cm (52in). Typical hartebeest appearance: a larger animal than Coke's Hartebeest and quite different in colour, being uniform tawny-red not fawn. Horns on high pedicle, less bracket-shaped, more upright than in Coke's Hartebeest. In the closely related Lelwel Hartebeest, *Alcelaphus buselaphus lelwel*, the horns incline outwards at the tips and dark markings are present on the lower part of the legs.

Distribution and Habitat: Occurs commonly but locally in northern and eastern Uganda, and in western Uganda as far south as the Semliki Valley: in Kenya confined to areas near Lake Victoria: in Tanzania occurs south-west of Lake Victoria. Inhabits open plains and grasslands, and grasslands with scattered bush and trees. The Lelwel Hartebeest occurs in East Africa only in a small region of arid bush and grassland in extreme north-west Kenya.

LICHTENSTEIN'S HARTEBEEST

Alcelaphus lichtensteinii **Plate 10**

Identification: Height at shoulder 127–132cm (50–52in). Horn pedicle short, the horns much flattened and incurved. Rufous-tawny in colour with black markings on legs.

Distribution and Habitat: Found locally in Tanzania, north to Biharamulo and western Mwanza. Inhabits open plains and bush and wooded grasslands.

WHITE-BEARDED GNU or WILDEBEEST

Connochaetes taurinus **Plate 10**

Identification: Height at shoulder 132cm (52in). A rather thickset, ungainly-looking antelope with a humped back, buffalo-like horns and a lax, long-haired black mane and tail; dun-grey or brown with darker vertical stripes on body; distinct beard on throat, white in northern races, dark in race in southern Tanzania, the Nyasa Blue Wildebeest.

Distribution and Habitat: Locally abundant in southern Kenya and in Tanzania: not found in Uganda: inhabits open plains and tree-grasslands from 610–1,828m (2,000–6,000ft). Gregarious in large or small herds; bulls sometimes solitary. Often associated with zebra and sometimes other game animals.

HUNTER'S HARTEBEEST or HIROLA

Damaliscus hunteri **Plate 10**

Identification: Height at shoulder 107–117cm (42–46in). This species differs from the true hartebeest, which it somewhat resembles, in lacking a horn-pedicle: uniform pale rufous-fawn with white chevron on forehead and white tail tuft: horns with a simple curve, not unlike those of an impala.

Distribution and Habitat: A local and very uncommon species in eastern Kenya, from north of the Tana River to the Somali border. Inhabits desert grass-bush in small herds. In recent years a small number have been introduced into the Tsavo National Park, south of the species' normal range.

TOPI *Damaliscus korrigum* **Plate 10**

Identification: Height at shoulder 122–127cm (48–50in). A hartebeest-like robust antelope, rich deep rufous in colour with a satin-like sheen; blackish patches on limbs: stout ridged horns which curve backwards and upwards.

Distribution and Habitat: Local but usually common where it occurs. In Kenya found abundantly in the Mara Game Reserve, south-western Kenya. Also occurs in the coastal districts, mainly north of the Tana River; in the Northern Frontier east of Lake Turkana and rarely east of Mount Elgon. The closely related race, the Tiang (*Damaliscus korrigum tiang*) is recorded from northern Turkana, north-west of Lake Turkana. In Tanzania the Topi is widespread but local south to the Rukwa. In Uganda it occurs in the north-east and south-west of the country: abundant in the Kigezi section of the Ruwenzori Park. Inhabits open grassy plains, tree-grasslands, open coastal forest, bush and scrub. Gregarious, often in large herds.

ZANZIBAR or **ADERS' DUIKER** *Cephalophus adersi* **Plate 9**
Identification: Height at shoulder 35cm (14in). A tiny bright chestnut antelope with white underparts, a broad white band around upper part of hind leg to the rump, and white mottling on lower limbs; small horns present in both sexes.
Distribution and Habitat: Described from Zanzibar, but present status there unknown. Also occurs rarely in Sokoke-Arabuku Forest, Kenya coast, and in forest around Gedi ruins. Usually in pairs: at least partly nocturnal. Rare, shy and seldom observed.

HARVEY'S or **RED DUIKER** *Cephalophus harveyi* **Plate 9**
Identification: Height at shoulder 41–43cm (16–17in). Thickset bright mahogany-red antelope, black down the centre line of the face and on the hind legs: fore legs dark brown. Short horns, present in both sexes, extend backwards in line of head. Crest between horns bright red-brown; tail grizzled dark brown.
Distribution and Habitat: Widespread but local in East Africa, usually in localities below 2,668m (8,000ft) to sea level. Inhabits forested areas, riverine forest and areas which afford thick cover. In pairs or solitary; mainly crepuscular or nocturnal.
Allied Species: The Natal Red Duiker, *Cephalophus natalensis*, occurs in the Southern Province of Tanzania. It is a more uniformly coloured animal than the Red Duiker without the dark face marking. The classification of the red duikers found in East Africa is far from satisfactory and the group is in need of revision. Some authorities unite the Red Duiker and the Natal Red Duiker as one species; and the relationship between certain races of the former and the Black-fronted Duiker is not fully understood. It is not impossible that undescribed species of duikers await discovery in East Africa.

BLACK-FRONTED DUIKER *Cephalophus nigrifrons* **Plate 9**
Identification: Height at shoulder 48–51cm (19–20in). Larger and relatively longer-legged than Red Duiker. A uniform deep rufous-brown duiker with a black face and crest; tail tip white: lower part of limbs dark brown. Short horns, extending backwards in line with face, present in both sexes. Coat redder in western Uganda animals than those in Kenya.
Distribution and Habitat: Occurs above 2,668m (8,000ft) on Mount Kenya and Mount Elgon in Kenya, and on the Ruwenzori range and the mountains of south-western Kigezi, Uganda. Inhabits montane forest and bamboo zone, and also alpine moorlands where there is bush cover.

YELLOW-BACKED DUIKER *Cephalophus sylvicultor* **Plate 9**
Identification: Height at shoulder 86cm (34in). A very large, heavy, thickset duiker, blackish-brown in colour with a yellowish dorsal stripe from the middle of the back, broadening out over the rump to form a triangle. Horns

present in both sexes, extending straight back in line with the head; crest between horns reddish-brown. Holds head low when moving.
Distribution and Habitat: The Yellow-backed Duiker is a local and elusive species found in montane forest in western Uganda, and in the Mau Forest of the western Kenya highlands. Inhabits dense mountain forest and bamboo. Occurs singly or in family groups: mainly nocturnal and seldom seen.

ABBOT'S DUIKER *Cephalophus spadix* **Plate 9**
Identification: Height at shoulder 76cm (30in). Resembles a smaller edition of the Yellow-backed Duiker, but without the yellow dorsal stripe. Uniform dark brown or dark reddish-brown with small bare grey patch on rump above tail. Horns present in both sexes.
Distribution and Habitat: Known only from high altitude forests on Mount Kilimanjaro and other ranges in north-eastern Tanzania. Inhabits dense forest: shy and seldom observed: nocturnal.

BLUE DUIKER *Cephalophus monticola* **Plate 9**
Identification: Height at shoulder 33cm (13in). A hare-sized grey duiker tinged with brown on the back, face and limbs. Small horns set well back on the skull, pointing slightly upwards, almost hidden by tuft of hair. Horns present in both sexes in some races, absent from ♀♀ in others.
Distribution and Habitat: Widely distributed in East Africa, but local. Inhabits forests, thickets and dense coastal scrub. Occurs singly or in pairs: diurnal and nocturnal.

BUSH DUIKER *Sylvicapra grimmia* **Plate 9**
Identification: Height at shoulder 56–63cm (22–25in). A medium-sized grizzled-fawn or yellowish-fawn antelope with a dark stripe down centre of face. Horns present in ♂♂ only: rufous hair tuft between horns.
Distribution and Habitat: The Bush Duiker is widely distributed and often common throughout most of East Africa. Occurs in a variety of habitats from alpine moorlands and forest to woodlands, scrub and bush country. Solitary or in pairs: usually nocturnal, but partly diurnal.

KLIPSPRINGER *Oreotragus oreotragus* **Plate 9**
Identification: Height at shoulder 51–56cm (20–22in). A rather thickset, rough-coated yellowish olive-brown antelope associated with rocky outcrops. Horns present in both sexes in Masai race: in ♂♂ only in other races.
Distribution and Habitat: Locally distributed in Tanzania, in southern, central and western Kenya and in northern districts and Ankole in Uganda. Occurs on rocky hills and outcrops, often isolated: sometimes descends to adjacent flat ground. Occurs singly or in small parties.

SUNI *Nesotragus moschatus* **Plate 9**

Identification: Height at shoulder 30–33cm (12–13in). A tiny, graceful antelope brownish-grey with a white belly; horns ringed almost to tips, present in ♂ only; no tuft of hair on crown between horns.

Distribution and Habitat: Occurs locally in Kenya and the northern half of Tanzania. Inhabits coastal forest and bush, highland forest and scrub. Occurs singly or in pairs: mainly nocturnal.

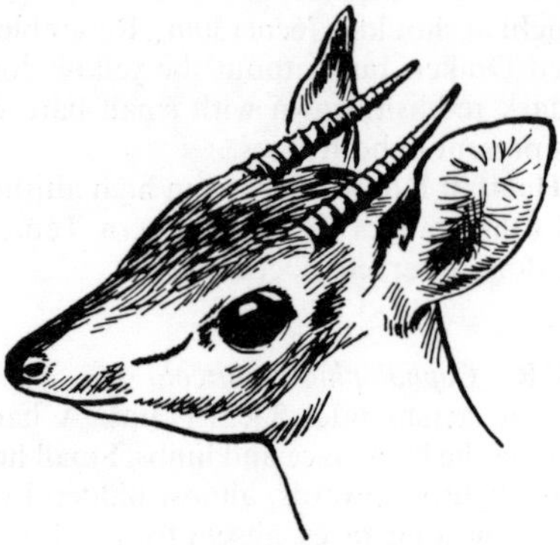

Fig. 15 Head and horns of Suni.

Allied Species: Livingstone's Suni, *Nesotragus livingstonianus*, is a larger animal, 35.5–38cm (14–15in) at shoulder, rufous-fawn, paler on sides; underparts white; lower part of limbs black. Occurs in thickets and forest-glades in southern region, Tanzania. Solitary or pairs: nocturnal; uncommon.

ORIBI *Ourebia ourebi* **Plate 9**

Identification: Height at shoulder 61cm (24in). A graceful small antelope with a relatively long neck and straight, upstanding horns in the ♂. Colour varies in different races from drab fawn-grey to bright rufous: bare black glandular patch below ear; short black-tipped tail and black knee tufts. Like the Duikers the Oribis are in need of revision. Some authors consider that there are several species of Oribi in East Africa: others that the various populations are local races of a single species.

Distribution and Habitat: In Kenya most numerous in western areas: occurs also in coastal districts, especially north of the Tana River, in south-western Kenya and the extreme north-west. In Tanzania found in the north, north-west and south. In Uganda plentiful locally in north and west, and especially abundant in the Kabalega National Park. Occurs singly, or in pairs and small groups, inhabiting grasslands, mixed grass and bush, coastal bush and forest and tree-grassland, from sea level to 2,668m (8,000ft). Diurnal.

STEINBOK *Raphicerus campestris* **Plate 11**

Identification: Height at shoulder 56cm (22in). A bright reddish-fawn antelope with very large ears: slender vertical horns present in ♂ only. No lateral hoofs.

Distribution and Habitat: In Kenya frequent in central, southern and coastal districts; widespread in Tanzania. Inhabits grasslands, open bush, coastal bush and forest and desert grass-bush from sea level to 2,668m (8,000ft). Occurs singly or in pairs and family parties; diurnal.

SHARPE'S GRYSBOK *Raphicerus sharpei* **Plate 11**

Identification: Height at shoulder 46–51cm (18–20in). Rich tawny-rufous in general colour with white streaking: sides of muzzle greyish-white, cheeks and sides of neck fawn: dark crescent-shaped mark on crown. Very large black-edged ears. Short vertical horns present in ♂ only. No lateral hoofs.

Distribution and Habitat: An uncommon little antelope restricted in East Africa to the southern region of Tanzania. Frequents thin bush and open hilly country: diurnal: solitary or in pairs.

KIRK'S DIKDIK *Rhynchotragus kirkii* **Plate 11**

Identification: Height at shoulder 36–41cm (14–16in). A small grizzled grey-brown antelope, yellowish-rufous on flanks to reddish-fulvous on limbs; elongated trunk-like nose with hair growing right up to the nostrils; extensive tuft of hair on crown; horns present in ♂ only.

Distribution and Habitat: Widely distributed in Kenya and Tanzania: in Uganda found in Karamoja and north-east Acholi. Inhabits desert grass-bush and scrub and coastal bush, and mixed grass-woodland. Occurs usually in pairs or family parties: diurnal.

GUENTHER'S DIKDIK *Rhynchotragus guentheri* **Plate 11**

Identification: Height at shoulder 36cm (14in). A slightly smaller and more uniformly grey animal than Kirk's Dikdik with a more elongated, trunk-like nose and less white around eye. Limbs fawn, not reddish. Horns present in ♂ only.

Distribution and Habitat: In East Africa confined to northern districts of Kenya from north of Lake Baringo and the Northern Uaso Nyiro River. Inhabits arid bush country and mixed grass-bush. Occurs singly or in pairs: diurnal.

UGANDA KOB *Adenota kob* **Plate 11**

Identification: Height at shoulder 92cm (36in). A relatively thickset antelope, bright red-brown with black and white markings on the face and legs, including a complete white ring around eye: horns, present in ♂ only, lyrate in shape.

Distribution and Habitat: The Uganda Kob is now confined mainly to the Kabalega and Ruwenzori National Parks and the Semliki Valley in western

Uganda, being far less common than previously outside these areas. In Kenya a few remain along the Nzoia River in western Kenya. No recent record of the species from Tanzania. Frequents open grassy plains and tree-grasslands: gregarious, in herds: diurnal.

PUKU *Adenota vardonii* **Plate 11**

Identification: Height at shoulder 99cm (39in). Similar in general appearance to Uganda Kob, but with no black markings on forelegs. Horns, present in ♂ only, lyrate in shape, shorter than those of Uganda Kob.

Distribution and Habitat: In East Africa restricted to the southern region of Tanzania, where it is generally uncommon and local. Frequents mixed grass and woodlands, flood plains, usually in vicinity of water. Gregarious in small or large herds; diurnal: sometimes associated with Impala.

COMMON WATERBUCK *Kobus ellipsiprymnus* **Plate 11**

Identification: Height at shoulder 122–137cm (48–54in). Robust, thickset antelope with shaggy grey-brown coat with a white ring round buttocks. Horns, heavily ringed, curve backwards, outwards and upwards: present in ♂ only. The Defassa Waterbuck differs only in having a double white patch on the buttocks instead of an elliptical white ring.

Distribution and Habitat: Widespread in suitable areas of south-central, south-eastern, north-eastern, northern and central districts of Tanzania. In Kenya found in eastern, central and southern districts. Both the Common and the Defassa Waterbuck occur on the southern and northern Uasio Nyiro rivers and on the Athi River including the Nairobi National Park, where apparently hybrid animals may be found. Occurs in riverine woodland and bush and well-watered tree-grassland. Gregarious in herds: diurnal.

DEFASSA WATERBUCK *Kobus defassa* **Plate 11**

Identification: Height at shoulder 122–137cm (48–54in). Robust thickset antelope with shaggy grey-brown to brown coat with double white patch on buttocks. Horns, heavily ringed, curve backwards, outwards and upwards. Distinguishable from Common Waterbuck only by white buttocks.

Distribution and Habitat: In Tanzania occurs in Bukoba district, the Serengeti plains and southwards to Rungwe, western Mbeya and Ufipa districts. In Kenya occurs in central south-western and western districts, and recorded from eastern Lake Turkana. In Uganda locally common, especially in Ruwenzori Park where finest heads in Africa are found. Inhabits grassy areas near water and riverine woodland. Gregarious, in herds, but bulls often solitary: diurnal.

BOHOR REEDBUCK *Redunca redunca* **Plate 11**

Identification: Height at shoulder 71–76cm (28–30in). A uniformly sandy-rufous antelope with a white belly and a bushy tail white below, conspicuous when the animal runs. Horns, present in ♂ only, sharply hooked forwards.

Reedbuck have a curious bare patch on each side of the head immediately below the ear.

Distribution and Habitat: Common locally in southern half of Kenya, and in Tanzania and Uganda. The Bohor Reedbuck favours marshy surroundings and areas of lush grass. Occurs singly or in small groups: during day lies down in tall grass or rushes, flushing only when nearly trodden on.

Allied Species: The Southern Reedbuck, *Redunca arundinum* (Plate 11) is a larger animal 91cm (36in) at the shoulder: horns of ♂ curved forwards without terminal hook. It is widespread in southern Tanzania, inhabiting flood plains and upland grasslands.

CHANLER'S MOUNTAIN REEDBUCK

Redunca fulvorufula **Plate 11**

Identification: Height at shoulder 71cm (28in). Similar to Bohor Reedbuck but greyer with sandy thighs and legs. ♂♂ have relatively short, sharply forward-hooked horns. Tail very bushy, greyish fawn above, white below.

Distribution and Habitat: Occurs locally, mainly in central and western districts of Kenya: in Uganda it is found locally in Karamoja: in Tanzania confined to hilly country in northern districts. Inhabits open grasslands on hills and mountains up to 3,658m (12,000ft). Diurnal, usually in small groups. Species best distinguished from Bohor Reedbuck by greyer colour and by habitat.

IMPALA *Aepyceros melampus* **Plate 10**

Identification: Height at shoulder 92–107cm (36–42in). A graceful rufous-fawn antelope, darker above with well-defined line of demarcation along flanks; white on abdomen. Rump white with a black streak on either side. Horns, in ♂ only, wide and lyre-shaped.

Distribution and Habitat: Common and widespread in south-western half of Kenya and widely distributed throughout Tanzania in suitable areas. In Uganda very uncommon and confined to Ankole and eastern Karamoja. Inhabits grass-woodland, riverine bush and arid grass-bush from near sea level to 1,981m (6,500ft). Gregarious in herds, but old ♂♂ often solitary. Diurnal and nocturnal.

THOMSON'S GAZELLE *Gazella thomsonii* **Plate 10**

Identification: Height at shoulder 64–69cm (25–27in). A rich rufous gazelle with a distinct blackish lateral stripe between the rufous flanks and white belly. White on rump ends below tail: tail black, constantly in motion. Horns curve upwards and backwards with tips vertical or curved slightly forward. Horns in ♀ slender and straighter. This is a smaller animal than Grant's Gazelle with less extensive white on buttocks.

Distribution and Habitat: Locally common or abundant central, southern and south-western Kenya and south through northern Tanzania to the Iringa district. Inhabits open grassy plains and scattered tree-grassland. Gregarious in herds, often associated with other plains game: diurnal.

GRANT'S GAZELLE *Gazelle granti* **Plate 10**
Identification: Height at shoulder 81–99cm (32–35in): ♀♀ smaller. Fawn or sandy-rufous in general colour with white belly: white of buttocks extends on to rump above tail. In Thomson's Gazelle white ends below tail. Lateral stripe variable (but more pronounced and darker in ♀♀), in some races dark and well-defined, in others indicated merely by darker tone along flanks. Both sexes carry horns, those of ♂ large and graceful, extending upwards and outwards, curving forward slightly at tips: those of ♀ smaller and thinner. Many races of Grant's Gazelle have been described. These include 'Roberts' Gazelle' from the Mwanza, western Masai and Musoma districts of Tanzania northwards to the Loita Plains, Kenya, in which the ♂'s horns, in extreme cases, grow outwards and downwards at the tips (see Plate 10, 8a): 'Bright's Gazelle' from northern Turkana, Kenya and north-eastern Karamoja, Uganda, which is small and pale without lateral stripes and with small almost parallel horns; and 'Peters' Gazelle', also a small race, from eastern districts of Kenya, including the northern section of the Tsavo National Park, in which the fawn body colour extends backwards in a band to the root of the tail; horns short, narrow and nearly straight.
Distribution and Habitat: Common throughout most of Kenya, except in south-west; in Tanzania widely distributed from Dodoma northwards and in Uganda occurs in Karamoja. Inhabits a variety of habitats from open plains and tree-grassland to arid grass-bush and desert scrub.

GERENUK *Litocranius walleri* **Plate 10**
Identification: Height at shoulder 91–104cm (36–41in). Rufous-fawn in general colour, white below. Neck very elongated; legs long. Only ♂♂ carry horns, which are massive and heavily ringed.
Distribution and Habitat: Ranges northwards from Pare and eastern Masai districts of northern Tanzania through eastern half of Kenya. Inhabits arid grass-bush country and semi-desert scrub from sea level to 1,219m (4,000ft). Occurs usually in pairs or small family groups: diurnal.

ROAN ANTELOPE *Hippotragus equinus* **Plate 12**
Identification: Height at shoulder 140–145cm (55–57in). A large grey to rufous-grey antelope with black and white facial markings; short mane on back of neck and long tufted ears. Thick, heavily ridged, scimitar-curved horns present in both sexes, but those of ♀ smaller.
Distribution and Habitat: Widespread in suitable areas of Tanzania; in Kenya extremely local and uncommon in Karamoja, Acholi and Ankole. Inhabits open wooded country and grass-woodlands. Occurs in small herds, sometimes associated with Eland and other game animals.

SABLE ANTELOPE *Hippotragus niger* **Plate 12**
Identification: Height at shoulder 127–137cm (50–54in). ♂♂ black or reddish-black with contrasting white underparts and white facial markings: ♀♀

chestnut-brown. Very long scimitar-curved horns present in both sexes. **Distribution and Habitat:** Widespread in suitable localities in Tanzania: in Kenya found only in the Shimba Hills, near Mombasa, Kenya coast. Gregarious, in small or large herds: inhabits open woodlands and tree-grasslands.

ORYX *Oryx beisa* **Plate 12**

Identification: Height at shoulder 122cm (48in). A thickset pale grey antelope, more or less tinged rufous, with black and white markings on the face; long, straight, rapier-like horns present in both sexes. Two well-defined races occur in East Africa, the Beisa Oryx (*Oryx beisa beisa*) (Plate 12) having pointed ears with no tuft of black hair at tips, and the Fringe-eared Oryx (*Oryx beisa callotis*) (Plate 12) which has a conspicuous fringe of black hair at the tips of its ears.

Distribution and Habitat: The Beisa Oryx inhabits Kenya north of the Tana River westwards to north-eastern Karamoja, Uganda. The Fringe-eared Oryx occurs south-east of the Tana River and south of the Aberdare Mountains, Kenya, southwards into northern Tanzania, where it is widespread in Masailand east of the Rift Valley. The Beisa Oryx inhabits arid, semi-desert bush and scrub: the Fringe-eared Oryx is found in similar country and in open grass-woodlands and grass country. Gregarious, in small or large herds: diurnal.

BONGO *Boocercus eurycerus* **Plate 12**

Identification: Height at shoulder 112–127cm (44–50in). ♀♀ smaller than ♂. A thickset bright chestnut antelope with the body marked with vertical white stripes. Open spiral horns present in both sexes, those of ♀ less massive.

Distribution and Habitat: In Kenya occurs in mountain forest on Mount Kenya, the Aberdares, the Mau Forest and the Cherengani Hills. In Uganda it is reputed to occur in hill forest on the Acholi-Sudan border. Bongo inhabit dense mountain forest and mixed bamboo forest. They are extremely shy animals which are seldom observed under ordinary circumstances. Occur in family parties as a rule, but bulls may be solitary. Now seen fairly frequently at the Ark, a lodge on the Aberdares, near Nyeri, Kenya.

SITATUNGA *Tragelaphus spekei* **Plate 12**

Identification: Height at shoulder 109–117cm (43–46in). The Sitatunga is an aquatic antelope, in general appearance resembling a shaggy-coated bushbuck, but unlike bushbuck tail not bushy. ♂♂ dark greyish-brown or brown, with a white chevron mark between eyes. ♀♀ are redder. Only the ♂ carries horns; these are longer and more twisted than those of the bushbuck, with yellowish tips. Has long, splayed-out hoofs, enabling it to move freely on the surface of boggy swamps.

Distribution and Habitat: Very uncommon and local in Kenya, known only from Saiwa Swamp National Park, Trans Nzoia and the papyrus swamps of Lake Victoria. In Uganda most frequent in the papyrus swamps surrounding

continued on p. 226

Plate 1 **BATS**

1 Straw-coloured Fruit Bat page 167
No white tufts at base of ears or on shoulders; yellowish-brown; gregarious, in trees.

2 Hammer-headed Fruit Bat ♂ 168
Large size, wingspan 91cm (36in); white tufts at base of ears; enlarged nasal region in ♂; dark grey.

3 Yellow-bellied Bat 173
Yellow or brownish-yellow underparts; simple muzzle without nose-leaf.

4 Long-eared Leaf-nosed Bat 172
Nose-leaf present; long ears; orange-brown or buff.

5 Giant Leaf-nosed Bat 172
Large size, wingspan 61cm (24in); short haired; narrow pointed ears; nose-leaf present.

6 Lesser Leaf-nosed Bat 172
Nose-leaf present; notched rounded ears.

7 False Vampire Bat 171
No tail; large ears; oval nose-leaf; grey wings.

8 White-bellied Free-tailed Bat 173
Tail free; wings white or greyish-white.

9 Flat-headed Free-tailed Bat 173
Body and head much flattened; tail free.

10 Giant Free-tailed Bat 174
Large size, wingspan 48cm (19in); large ears; upperparts rich mahogany-brown edged white.

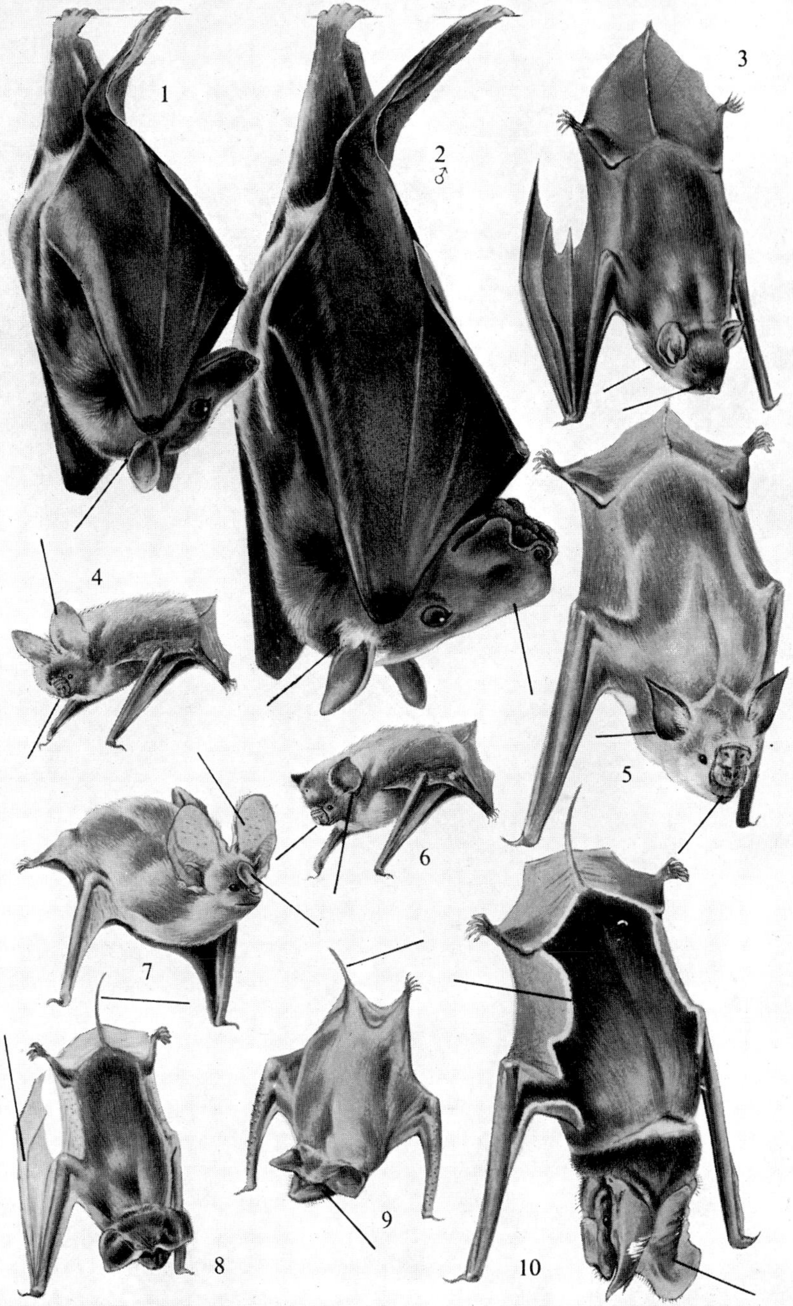

1
2 ♂
3
4
5
6
7
8
9
10

Plate 2 PRIMATES, AARDVARK and PANGOLIN

1 Bush Baby page 175
Size small, 41cm (16in); tail slender at base.

2 Greater Galago 174
Size large, 64cm (25in); tail thick and woolly.

3 Black Mangabey 175
Blackish-brown; tail appears dishevelled.

4a Black and White Colobus (*abyssinicus* group) 177
Black and white; no thumb; short hair on face.

4b Black and White Colobus (*angolensis* group) 177
Black and white; no thumb; long hair on face.

5 Chimpanzee 177
Height 122cm (48in); no tail.

6 Mountain Gorilla 178
Height *c*. 152cm (60in); no tail; high crown in ♂.

7 Ant Bear or **Aardvark** 185
Elongated snout; long pointed ears; strictly nocturnal.

8 Lesser Ground Pangolin 178
Tail shorter than head and body; length 91–117cm (36–46in).

Note: not drawn to scale.

1
2
3
4a
5
4b
6
7
8

Plate 3 MUSTELIDS, MONGOOSES, PORCUPINE

1 **Zorilla** page 180
61cm (24in); back striped black and white; tail bushy.

2 **Ratel** or **Honey Badger** 180
71–81cm (28–32in); pale grey back; black underparts

3 **Clawless Otter** 180
152cm (60in); throat unspotted; toes without claws.

4 **Dwarf Mongoose** 182
31–33cm (12–13in); tail short; reddish-brown.

5 **Large Grey Mongoose** 182
122cm (48in); tail tufted.

6 **Slender** or **Black-tipped Mongoose** 182
71cm (28in); black-tipped tail.

7 **White-tailed Mongoose** 182
102cm (40in); thick white (rarely pale grey) tail.

8 **Porcupine** 228
76–86cm (30–34in); long black and white quills.

1
2
3
4
5
6
7
8

Plate 4 BIG GAME, ZEBRAS

1 African Buffalo page 227
Massive bovine-type animal; thick downward-curving horns.

2 African Elephant 186
Great size, 280–356cm (9–11½ft) at shoulder; trunk and tusks.

3 White Rhinoceros 187
168–183cm (5½–6ft) at shoulder; square mouth, no prehensile upper lip.

4 Black Rhinoceros 187
152–168cm (5–5½ft) at shoulder; pointed and prehensile upper lip.

5 Common Zebra 188
Dark stripes very broad; ears relatively short and narrow.

6 Grevy's Zebra 188
Dark stripes narrow; ears large, rounded and heavily fringed.

7 Hippopotamus 188
Huge aquatic pig-like animal with broad square muzzle.

1
2
3
4
5
6
7

Plate 5 PRIMATES, ELEPHANT SHREWS

1 **Potto** page 174
Short tail. Arboreal; nocturnal. Length 46cm (18in).

2 **Yellow Baboon** 177
Relatively slim build; long legs. Length 116–137cm (46–54in).

3 **Olive Baboon** 176
Thickset build; legs relatively short and thick. Length 127–142cm (50–56in).

4 **Black-faced Vervet Monkey** 175
Black face. Length 122–142cm (48–56in).

5 **Blue Monkey** 175
Dark throat and chest; length 140–158cm (55–62in).

6 **Golden Monkey** 175
Orange back and thighs. Length 140–158cm (55–62in).

7 **Sykes' Monkey** 175
White chest patch. Length 140–158cm (56–62in).

8 **Red-tailed Monkey** 176
Copper-red tail; white nose. Length 116–142cm (46–56in).

9 **Patas Monkey** 176
Orange-red back and legs; largely terrestrial. Length 168–183cm (66–72in).

10 **Red Colobus** 177
Red-brown cap; no thumb. Length 122–132cm (48–52in).

11 **Yellow-rumped Elephant Shrew** 165
Golden rump patch. Length 51cm (20in).

12 **Knob-bristled Forest Elephant Shrew** 165
White eye-ring; knob-tipped bristles along underside of tail. Length 36cm (14in).

1
2
3
4
5
6
7
8
9
10
11
12

Plate 6 **CARNIVORES (1)**

1 Cheetah page 183
Body markings round black spots, not rosettes. Height at shoulder 71–81cm (28–32in).

2 Caracal 184
Dark tufted ears. Height at shoulder 41–46cm (16–18in).

3 African Wild Cat 184
Indistinct bands on body and limbs. Height at shoulder 23cm (9in).

4 Serval 184
Heavy black spots on body and limbs; short tail. Small-spotted and melanistic (black) forms occur. Height at shoulder 46–51cm (18–20in).

5 Golden Cat 184
Spotted belly. A grey form occurs. Height at shoulder 41cm (16in).

6 Lion 185
Well-developed mane in adult ♂; black tail tip. Height at shoulder 102–114cm (40–45in).

7 Leopard 185
Body markings in form of rosettes. Height at shoulder 61–71cm (24–28in).

8 Aard-wolf 183
Well-developed dorsal mane; black stripes on body. Height at shoulder 46–51cm (18–20in).

9 Spotted Hyaena 183
Sloping back; blackish-brown spots on body and limbs. Height at shoulder 69–91cm (27–36in).

10 Striped Hyaena 183
Shaggy; striped not spotted. Height at shoulder 76cm (30in).

1
2
3
4
5
6
♀
♂
7
8
9
10

Plate 7 CARNIVORES (2)

1 **Golden Jackal** page 179
Uniform colour; rufous ears; dark tail tip. Height at shoulder 43–46cm (17–18in).

2 **Side-striped Jackal** 180
Pale side stripe; dark ears; white tail tip. Height at shoulder 46cm (18in).

3 **Black-backed** or **Silver-backed Jackal** 179
Dark back; rufous ears; dark tail tip. Height at shoulder 41–43cm (16–17in).

4 **Hunting Dog** 179
Large rounded ears; variable colour pattern. Height at shoulder 61–76cm (24–30in).

5 **Bat-eared Fox** 180
Very large ears; dark tail tip. Height at shoulder 30–33cm (12–13in).

6 **African Civet** 181
Thick banded tail; dorsal crest. Melanistic examples occur. Height at shoulder 38cm (15in).

7 **Bush** or **Large-spotted Genet** 181
Large dark spots; no distinct dorsal crest. Melanistic examples occur. Length 92–102cm (36–40in).

8 **Neumann's** or **Small-spotted Genet** 181
Small dark spots; distinct dorsal crest. Length 92cm (36in).

9 **Banded Mongoose** 183
Distinct bands on body. Length 46cm (18in).

10 **Marsh Mongoose** 182
Large head; thick tail; uniform colour. Length 89cm (35in).

11 **African Palm Civet** 181
Thick long tail; pale spot on each side of shoulders. Length 92cm (36in).

1
2
3
4
5
6
7
8
9
10
11

Plate 8 PIGS, HYRAXES, GIRAFFES

1 Giant Forest Hog page 188
Covered with thick black hair; oval facial wart. Height at shoulder 81cm (32in).

2 Warthog 189
Grey, sparsely haired; carries tail upright when moving. Height at shoulder 76cm (30in).

3 Bush Pig 189
Body rufous or brown; white mane and whiskers. Height at shoulder 76cm (30in).

4 Tree Hyrax 186
Cream dorsal stripe; fur long and soft; occurs usually in trees. Length 41cm (16in).

5 Rock Hyrax 186
Cream dorsal stripe; fur short and harsh; occurs usually among rocks. Length 38–46cm (15–18in).

6 Masai Giraffe 189
Normally two horns; body and neck pattern broken; spotted shanks. Height 4.56–5.48m (15–18ft).

7 Rothschild's Giraffe 189
Normally three or five horns; body and neck pattern broken; unspotted shanks; thickset. Height 4.56–5.48m (15–18ft).

8 Reticulated Giraffe 190
Normally two horns; reticulated body and neck pattern. Height 4.56–5.18m (15–17ft).

1
2
3
4
5
6
7
8

Plate 9 ANTELOPES (1)

1 Zanzibar or **Aders' Duiker** page 192
White stripe across hindquarters; white spots on legs. Height at shoulder 35cm (14in).

2 Harvey's or **Red Duiker** 192
Body bright mahogany-red; blackish legs and face stripe; crown tuft rufous. Height at shoulder 41–43cm (16–17in).

3 Black-fronted Duiker 192
Body rufous-brown; dark legs; black face stripe. Height at shoulder 48–51cm (19–20in).

4 Blue Duiker 193
Grey or brown in general colour; legs sandy. Height at shoulder 33cm (13in).

5 Yellow-backed Duiker 192
Creamy-yellow rump patch. Height at shoulder 86cm (34in).

6 Suni 194
Horns ringed nearly to tips. Height at shoulder 30–33cm (12–13in).

7 Bush Duiker 193
Narrow dark face stripe; slender crest on crown. Height at shoulder 56–63cm (22–25in).

8 Abbot's Duiker 193
Uniform dark brown body. Height at shoulder 76cm (30in).

9 Klipspringer 193
Large ears; coarse greenish or yellowish-tinged fur. Inhabits rocky outcrops and hills. Height at shoulder 51–56cm (20–22in).

10 Oribi 194
Bare black patch below ears; black-tipped tail. Height at shoulder 61cm (24in).

1
2
3
4
5
6
7
8
9
10

Plate 10

ANTELOPES (2)

1 Coke's Hartebeest or **Kongoni** page 190
Short horn pedicle; general colour fawn. Height at shoulder 122cm (48in).

2 Jackson's Hartebeest 190
Long horn pedicle; general colour rufous. Height at shoulder 132cm (52in).

3 Lichtenstein's Hartebeest 190
Dark patch below shoulders; acutely back-angled horns. Height at shoulder 127–132cm (50–52in).

4 White-bearded Gnu or **Wildebeest** 191
Heavy mane and beard. Height at shoulder 132cm (52in).

5 Hunter's Hartebeest or **Hirola** 191
White chevron between eyes; lyrate horns. Height at shoulder 107–117cm (42–46in).

6 Topi 191
Black limb markings; general colour rich rufous. Height at shoulder 122–127cm (48–50in).

7 Impala 197
No black side stripe; lyrate horns. Height at shoulder 92–107cm (36–42in).

8 Grant's Gazelle 198
White on buttocks extends above tail. Height at shoulder 81–89cm (32–35in).

8a Head of Grant's Gazelle, race *robertsi* 198

9 Thomson's Gazelle 197
White on buttocks ends below root of tail. Height at shoulder 64–69cm (25–27in).

10 Gerenuk 198
Long and slender neck. Height at shoulder 91–104cm (36–41in).

1
2
3
4
5
6
7
8a,
8
9
10

Plate 11 **ANTELOPES (3)**

1 **Steinbok** page 195
Bright rufous upperparts and limbs; large ears. Height at shoulder 56cm (22in).

2 **Sharpe's Grysbok** 195
Rufous-fawn upperparts flecked with white; large ears. Height at shoulder 46–51cm (18–20in).

3 **Kirk's Dikdik** 195
Snout only slightly elongated; flanks and legs mainly rufous. Height at shoulder 36–41cm (14–16in).

4 **Guenther's Dikdik** 195
Snout greatly elongated; legs tinged pale rufous. Height at shoulder 36cm (14in).

5 **Uganda Kob** 195
White eye ring; black stripe on forelegs; horns ringed almost to tips. Height at shoulder 92cm (36in).

6 **Puku** 196
No black stripe on forelegs; ears tipped black; horns ringed almost to tips. Height at shoulder 99cm (39in).

7 **Common Waterbuck** 196
White ring on rump. Height at shoulder 122–137cm (48–54in).

8 **Defassa Waterbuck** 196
Buttocks white. Height at shoulder 122–137cm (48–54in).

9 **Chanler's Mountain Reedbuck** 197
Body colour greyish-rufous; forward curving horns relatively short; bare patch of skin below ears. Height at shoulder 71cm (28in).

10 **Bohor Reedbuck** 196
Body colour rufous not greyish; forward curving horns strongly hooked towards tips; bare patch of skin below ears. Height at shoulder 71–76cm (28–30in).

11 **Southern Reedbuck** 197
General colour yellowish-rufous; forward curving horns diverge upwards and outwards; bare patch of skin below ears. Height at shoulder 91cm (36in).

1
2
3
4
5
6
7
8
9
10
11

Plate 12 **ANTELOPES (4)**

1 Sable Antelope page 198
Long scimitar-curved horns; adult ♂♂ blackish, ♀♀ rufous-brown. Height at shoulder 127–137cm (50–54in).

2 Roan Antelope 198
Thick scimitar-curved horns; long tufted ears. Height at shoulder 140–145cm (55–57in).

3 Bongo 199
General colour bright chestnut-red with vertical white stripes; horns open spiral in shape. Height at shoulder 112–127cm (44–50in).

4 Beisa Oryx 199
Long straight horns; no ear tufts. Height at shoulder 22cm (48in).

5 Fringe-eared Oryx 199
Long straight horns; ears tufted. Height at shoulder 22cm (48in).

6 Greater Kudu 226
Open spiral horns; large ears; fringe of hair on throat. Height at shoulder 140–153cm (55–60in).

7 Lesser Kudu 226
No fringe of hair on throat. Height at shoulder 99–102cm (39–40in).

8 Sitatunga 199
Shaggy coat; spiral horns; very elongated hoofs. An aquatic antelope which inhabits swamps. Height at shoulder 109–117cm (43–46in).

9 Eland 227
Spiral horns; dewlap from throat. Height at shoulder 175–183cm (69–72in).

10 Bushbuck 226
♂♂ vary from rufous to black; ♀♀ rufous; spiral horns; high rump. Height at shoulder 79–92cm (30–36in).

♂
2
♀
1
3
4
5
6
7
8
9
♀
10
♂

1
2
3
4
5
6
7
8
9

Plate 13 **HARE, RABBIT and RODENTS**

1 **Bunyoro Rabbit** page 228
51cm (20in); short ears and legs.

2 **African Hare** 227
51cm (20in); long ears and legs.

3 **Cane Rat** 228
38–46cm (15–18in); coarse bristle-like hair.

4 **Spring Hare** 230
114cm (45in); hind legs very long; tail thick and bushy; progresses by kangaroo-like leaps.

5 **Scaly-tailed Flying Squirrel** 230
56cm (22in); fore and hind limbs connected by gliding membrane.

6 **Crested Rat** 230
38–41cm (15–16in); black and white with distinct flank stripe.

7 **Giant Rat** 231
69cm (27in); terminal third of tail white.

8 **Unstriped Ground Squirrel** 229
41cm (16in); rufous; no side stripe.

9 **Striped Ground Squirrel** 228
47–51cm ($18\frac{1}{2}$–20in); white flank stripe.

the Sese Islands and other localities fringing Lake Victoria and Lake George. In Tanzania local but widespread in suitable areas. Inhabits dense papyrus swamps: shy and difficult to observe. When alarmed often submerges below the surface, exposing only the nostrils above water. Occurs singly or in family parties.

BUSHBUCK *Tragelaphus scriptus* **Plate 12**

Identification: Height at shoulder 76–92cm (30–36in). A rufous-brown antelope with variable white spots and vertical stripes and a white band at base of neck: tail bushy, brown above, white below. ♂♂ of some races may be almost black with restricted white markings. Horns, present in ♂♂ only, spiral in form. Many races of bushbuck have been described, varying in size and general body colour and markings. When running bushbuck raise the tail showing the striking white underside.

Distribution and Habitat: Widely distributed in southern half of Kenya, extending northwards to Marsabit, Kulal and other isolated mountain forests. Widespread and common in Uganda and Tanzania. Inhabits forests, riverine thickets and bush where there is thick cover. Occurs singly or in small groups; shy: mainly nocturnal.

GREATER KUDU *Tragelaphus strepsiceros* **Plate 12**

Identification: Height at shoulder 140–153cm (55–60in). ♀♀ smaller than ♂♂. A large and majestic antelope, grey or fawn with several narrow white vertical stripes on the body, and, in the ♂, wide-spreading open spiral horns and a heavy fringe of hair along the throat to the chest; shoulders humped, tail bushy and ears very large. The Lesser Kudu is a much smaller animal without a throat fringe.

Distribution and Habitat: Widely distributed in Tanzania; much less common in Kenya where widely distributed but very local, most frequent on Matthews Range and on Mount Marsabit in Northern Frontier Province. In Uganda equally uncommon and confined mainly to Mount Moroto and other hills in north-eastern Karamoja. Inhabits woodland and thickets, especially in broken, hilly country in semi-desert bush. Gregarious, in small herds: ♂♂ often in separate groups or solitary.

LESSER KUDU *Strepsiceros imberbis* **Plate 12**

Identification: Height at shoulder 99–102cm (39–40in). A dark or light-grey antelope with vertical white stripes along the body; ears large. White patch on throat and white band across lower neck: tail bushy, dark above, white below. When running the tail is fanned and raised and is extremely conspicuous. Horns present in ♂ only; these grow in three graceful spirals. The Greater Kudu is a much larger animal with a well-developed neck fringe which is lacking in the Lesser Kudu.

Distribution and Habitat: In Kenya widespread and locally not uncommon in eastern and northern districts. In Uganda it is a much rarer animal, known from Karamoja. In Tanzania generally distributed in Masailand east of the Rift Valley. Inhabits arid bush country and coastal bush from sea level to 1,219m (4,000ft). Occurs in small parties or singly.

ELAND *Taurotragus oryx* **Plate 12**
Identification: Height at shoulder 175–183cm (69–72in); ♀♀ smaller. The largest of the antelopes, cattle-like in build with thick, spiralled horns present in both sexes. Rufous-fawn to fawn in general colour with narrow white stripes down flanks. Well-developed, tufted dewlap hangs below the neck.
Distribution and Habitat: Widely distributed in Kenya, mainly south of Lake Turkana. In Uganda found in Karamoja and parts of Acholi and Ankole. In Tanzania frequent in suitable areas. Inhabits open plains country, highland grassland, tree-grassland and semi-desert grass-bush. Gregarious, usually in small herds.

AFRICAN BUFFALO *Syncerus caffer* **Plate 4**
Identification: Height at shoulder 145–153cm (57–60in). A massive, blackish bovine-type animal with greatly developed downward spreading, widely curved horns, the bases of which meet on the forehead to form a heavy boss. Rufous-coloured beasts occur in western Uganda, especially in the Ruwenzori Park. These may be of hybrid origin between the present species and the Dwarf Forest Buffalo of Zaire.
Distribution and Habitat: Widely distributed and often common in suitable areas throughout East Africa. Inhabits a variety of habitats from forested country to open grassy plains and reed beds bordering rivers and swamps. Gregarious, often in large herds: old bulls sometimes solitary: nocturnal and diurnal.

HARES AND RABBITS: Lagomorpha

This familiar group is characterised by long, narrow ears, soft fur and short, woolly tails which are white below.

AFRICAN HARE *Lepus capensis* **Plate 13**
Identification: Length 51cm (20in), ear 7.5cm (3in). Above grizzled black and buff; nape, ears and legs rufous; tail dark brown above, sides and below white. There is need for a revision of the various species and races of hares described from East Africa.
Distribution and Habitat: Widely distributed in suitable localities throughout East Africa. Frequents more or less open ground, including grasslands, bush and sparse woodland. Solitary: nocturnal.

BUNYORO RABBIT *Pronolagus marjorita* **Plate 13**

Identification: Length 51cm (20in), ear 6.5cm (2½in). General colour grizzled buff; flanks buffy-yellow merging to white on belly. Distinguished from African Hare by much shorter ears and legs, and in having the sides of the tail grizzled brown, not white.

Distribution and Habitat: Locally not uncommon in north-western Uganda, including the Kabalega National Park. Can always be seen on the Masindi-Butiaba road after dark. Occurs in open grass-bush country: solitary: nocturnal.

RODENTS: Rodentia

The Rodents or Gnawing mammals may be recognised by their large chisel-like incisor teeth. With the exception of species such as the Porcupine and Spring Hare most members of this order are small or very small. It is not the intention of the present Field Guide to describe in detail the host of rats, mice and related small rodents found in East Africa – creatures seldom seen unless specially searched for and trapped. Only those species of special interest and the larger members of the order likely to be encountered in the National Parks have been described and illustrated.

CANE RAT *Thryonomys swinderianus* **Plate 13**

Identification: Length 38–46cm (15–18in), tail 7.5cm (3in). A heavy-looking, thickset rodent with coarse, bristle-like hair. Uniform brown: incisor teeth orange.

Distribution and Habitat: Locally common in suitable haunts in East Africa. Inhabits elephant grass and similar vegetation, including sugar-cane cultivation. Either solitary or in small parties: terrestrial: mainly nocturnal.

PORCUPINE *Hystrix galeata* **Plate 3**

Identification: Length 76–86cm (30–34in), tail 15cm (6in). Easily recognised by its covering of long black and white quills.

Distribution and Habitat: Common and widespread in East Africa, but owing to its nocturnal habits not often seen. Inhabits all types of country apart from swampy areas; favours rocky scrub-covered hills. Solitary; terrestrial and strictly nocturnal.

STRIPED GROUND SQUIRREL *Xerus erythropus* **Plate 13**

Identification: Length 47–51cm (18½–20in), tail 20cm (8in). Ground squirrels have abandoned the arboreal habits of the rest of the family and are terrestrial, living in burrows. Their fur is coarse and bristly. The present species may be recognised by the presence of a white longitudinal flank-stripe: general colour rufous brown.

Distribution and Habitat: Common and widespread in sandy bush country in

Kenya and in the vicinity of Lake Victoria, on Mount Elgon and in Bunyoro, Uganda. Inhabits arid bush country where a sandy soil exists: usually in pairs; terrestrial; diurnal.

UNSTRIPED GROUND SQUIRREL *Xerus rutilus* **Plate 13**
Identification: Length 41cm (16in), tail 20cm (8in). Easily distinguished by absence of conspicuous white flank stripe. General colour pinkish-rufous; paler below.
Distribution and Habitat: Widespread in Kenya in arid, sandy areas, being abundant locally in the Northern Frontier Province. In Tanzania frequent in north-eastern districts, and common in Karamoja, Uganda. Inhabits sandy, semi-desert bush country; solitary or in pairs; terrestrial; diurnal.

BUSH SQUIRREL *Paraxerus ochraceus* **Fig. 16**
Identification: Length 36cm (14in), tail 18cm (7in). A small olive-grey squirrel with a yellowish tinge on legs and underparts.
Distribution and Habitat: Widespread and locally common in Kenya and Tanzania. Inhabits bush and secondary growth at the edges of forest: seldom seen in large trees. Occurs usually in pairs: arboreal; diurnal.
Allied Species: The East African Red Squirrel, *Paraxerus palliatus*, with tail and underparts fiery orange-red, occurs in eastern districts of Kenya and Tanzania. It is most frequent in strips of riverine forest and coastal forests.

Fig. 16 Bush Squirrel

Fig. 17 Giant Forest Squirrel

GIANT FOREST SQUIRREL *Protoxerus stangeri* **Fig. 17**
Identification: Length 66cm (26in), tail 36cm (14in). Underparts blackish-brown speckled with buff; below reddish-buff; legs bright rufous; tail very bushy, blackish with pale bands.

Distribution and Habitat: An uncommon species inhabiting forests in the western Kenya highlands and Kakamega; in Uganda recorded from forests of Buganda, Toro and Busoga. Inhabits the tops of high forest trees, usually in pairs: diurnal.
Allied Species: The Sun Squirrel, *Heliosciurus rufobrachium*, closely resembles the Giant Forest Squirrel but is smaller, total length 48–51cm (19–20in), tail 25cm (10in). It occurs in forests on Mount Kenya and western areas of Kenya, and widely in Uganda.

SCALY-TAILED FLYING SQUIRREL

Anomalurus fraseri **Plate 13**

Identification: Length 56cm (22in), tail 25cm (10in). Scaly-tails may be recognised by the presence of a gliding membrane attached to fore and hind limbs which enables the animal to glide 15 or 18m (50 or 60ft) from one tree to another. The underside of the tail has an area of rough scales which assists the animal to obtain a better purchase on a tree trunk when climbing. Above dark grey; below creamy-white; fur soft and silky.
Distribution and Habitat: In Kenya found in the Kakamega Forest and on Mount Elgon. In Uganda recorded from forests in Buganda, Bunyoro and Toro. In Tanzania recorded from the eastern Usambara Mountains, and the Upper Ruvuma River. Inhabits dense rain forests: generally nocturnal but sometimes observed by day: solitary or in pairs.

SPRING HARE *Pedetes cafer* **Plate 13**

Identification: Length 114cm (45in), tail 53cm (21in). A pale rufous-brown animal with a bushy, black-tipped tail. Hind legs very long and adapted for jumping: forelegs short. Spring hares progress by rapid jumps in the manner of a kangaroo.
Distribution and Habitat: Widespread but local in Kenya and Tanzania. Inhabits grass plains and open bush country: gregarious, living in small colonies: nocturnal.

AFRICAN DORMOUSE *Graphiurus murinus* **Fig. 18**

Identification: Length 14–15cm ($5\frac{1}{2}$–6in), tail 7.5cm (3in). Small soft-furred rodent with long bushy tail, resembling a diminutive squirrel. General colour grey or buffy-grey, paler on the belly.
Distribution and Habitat: Widely distributed in East Africa. Inhabits hollow trees in wooded and forest areas: frequent in buildings. Usually solitary; arboreal and terrestrial; nocturnal.

CRESTED RAT *Lophiomys imhausi* **Plate 13**

Identification: Length 38–41cm (15–16in), tail 10cm (4in). A thickset animal, not in the least rat-like in spite of its name, covered with long, silky black and white fur; distinct whitish flank stripe and a conspicuous crest along the back and tail: ears nearly concealed in long fur.

Fig. 18 African Dormouse

Distribution and Habitat: Confined to forests of the Kenya Highlands, from Mount Kenya westwards to Mount Elgon. Uncommon and shy, and seldom observed. Slow moving, but both arboreal and terrestrial in its habits: nocturnal.

GIANT RAT *Cricetomys gambianus* **Plate 13**

Identification: Length 69cm (27in), tail 36cm (14in). A very large short-haired rat, brownish-grey in colour, with belly, feet and terminal third of the tail white; face pointed and oval ears prominent.

Distribution and Habitat: Widely distributed in Kenya, Tanzania and Uganda. Inhabits forests, wooded areas and dense bush. Occurs singly as a rule; terrestrial; nocturnal.

KENYA MOLE RAT *Tachyoryctes ibeanus* **Fig. 19**

Identification: Total length 18–20cm (7–8in), tail 2.5cm (1in). A thickset burrowing rodent, covered with rather long and soft, dense fur: reddish or golden brown, darker on belly: immature animals blackish-brown: incisor teeth bright orange. Many different species of *Tachyoryctes* have been described, most of which are probably conspecific with the present species.

Distribution and Habitat: This and closely related forms are locally distributed in the highlands of Kenya and northern Tanzania, and in Uganda. Their presence is betrayed by the mounds of earth which they throw up from their burrows.

Allied Species: The Mount Kenya Mole Rat, *Tachyoryctes rex*. from the

Fig. 19 Kenya Mole Rat

Fig. 20 Naked Mole Rat

alpine moorlands of Mount Kenya is a giant species 26–30cm (10–12in) in length.

NAKED MOLE RAT *Heterocephalus glaber* **Fig. 20**

Identification: Length 13cm (5in), tail 2.5cm (1in). This is one of the most remarkable rodents in the world, completely naked with just a few isolated hairs scattered over the body and on the tail: colour of skin pinkish-grey; incisor teeth white.

Distribution and Habitat: Confined to a few localities in eastern Kenya: it is perhaps most frequent in the Tsavo National Park, near Voi, and near Isiolo in the Northern Frontier Province. The Naked Mole Rat is completely fossorial, digging its burrows in sandy soil in semi-desert bush country. When digging it throws up puffs of fine earth resembling tiny geysers. Erupting every few moments to nearly a foot above the surface, these betray its whereabouts.

PART 3

The Commoner Birds of East Africa

Although there are a few regions in the world which possess more bird species than the three East African countries – for example Colombia and Ecuador in South America – few can surpass East Africa's wealth of species combined with accessibility of bird habitats. The total number of birds recorded from Kenya, Uganda and Tanzania is approximately 1,294, whilst Kenya alone has 1,030 different kinds.

Whatever the degree of interest the visitor may have in birds, no one can be other than impressed by their colour, beauty and abundance in East Africa. On a four weeks visit to Kenya at the peak of the spring migration, mid-March to mid-April, one can count on seeing well over 500 different kinds of birds. A six weeks safari throughout the three countries at the same time of year could produce a list of upwards of 800 species.

On the pages which follow is a selection of those birds most frequently encountered by the visitor to East Africa. All are to be found over a wide area, both in the National Parks and elsewhere.

The measurement given for each species in both centimetres and inches is taken from the tip of the bill to the end of the tail.

OSTRICH: Struthionidae

The largest living bird; flightless; two toes only on each foot.

OSTRICH *Struthio camelus* **Fig. 21**
Identification: 2–2.5m (7–8ft). Unmistakable for any other bird; adult ♂ black and white; ♀ and immatures greyish-brown. The Somali race ♂ has neck and thighs blue-grey; in north African and Masai races the neck and thighs are flesh-pink.
Voice: Usually silent; breeding ♂♂ utter deep booming call but this is seldom heard.
Distribution and Habitat: North African race, Sudan and north-eastern Ethiopia; Somali race, Somalia, eastern and southern Ethiopia and northern Kenya south to Voi. Masai race, southern Kenya and Tanzania. The ostrich is now extinct over much of its former range. Habitat, plains, open thorn-bush country and semi-desert. The Somali ostrich is still common in northern Kenya and Meru National Park. The Masai ostrich is found in Nairobi National Park, in Mara and on the Serengeti Plains, Tanzania.

Fig. 21 Ostrich ♂ foreground ♀ behind

GREBES: Podicipidae

Duck or teal-sized aquatic birds; slender pointed bills and tail-less appearance characteristic of family; expert divers; feet lobed, not webbed; sexes similar.

LITTLE GREBE *Podiceps ruficollis* **Plate 14**
Identification: 25cm (10in). A small, dark grebe with chestnut-red face and throat and pale green gape patch. Immatures much paler and lack chestnut on face and throat.
Voice: A loud and often prolonged trill.
Distribution and Habitat: Common throughout Africa in suitable localities. Occurs on fresh and brackish lakes, dams, ponds and slow-flowing rivers; rare on coast. Abundant on all the Rift Valley lakes in East Africa.
Allied Species: The Great Crested Grebe (*Podiceps cristatus*) is duck-sized, 45–57cm (18–20in), the adult with conspicuous chestnut and black frills on sides of head and a black tuft on each side of the crown. Occurs locally from Ethiopia southwards on both fresh and alkaline inland waters. The Black-necked Grebe (*Podiceps nigricollis*), 30cm (12in), is less common and is spasmodic in its appearances on fresh and brackish lakes and dams. It is slightly larger than the Little Grebe with a black head and neck with a patch of golden-chestnut plumes on each side of the crown; bill slender and slightly up-tilted.

PELICANS: Pelecanidae

Very large water birds with long, hook-tipped bills and a naked pouch suspended from the mandible and upper part of throat. Sexes similar.

WHITE PELICAN *Pelecanus onocrotalus* **Plate 14**
Identification: 152–180cm (60–70in). A white bird, except for black and grey flight feathers; in breeding plumage suffused salmon-pink. Immature pale buffish-brown, becoming whiter with successive moults. The Pink-backed Pelican is smaller and pale grey. White Pelicans are extremely gregarious, fishing in tightly-packed flotillas, all the birds submerging their heads and necks at the same moment. They rest on the shore in large groups and soar in flocks on thermal currents. The Pink-backed Pelican is more solitary.
Voice: Generally silent except for guttural croaking at nesting colonies.
Distribution and Habitat: Occurs commonly throughout Africa on large areas of inland water: uncommon on the coast. In East Africa vast numbers breed in the Rukwa swamps, southern Tanzania; also abundant on Lake Nakuru in Kenya and on lakes in western Uganda.

PINK-BACKED PELICAN *Pelecanus rufescens* **Plate 14**
Identification: 127–137cm (50–54in). Adults are pale grey with a shaggy nape crest; the vinous-pink rump is conspicuous only in flight. Immatures greyish-buff, best distinguished from juvenile White Pelicans by smaller size. Less gregarious than its larger relative, large flocks being uncommon. The Pink-backed Pelican is generally a solitary fisher, catching fish with a heron-like striking action but: often associates with White Pelicans when resting.
Voice: Silent except at breeding colonies, when it utters various croaking sounds.
Distribution and Habitat: A resident and local migrant on inland waters throughout Ethiopian region; uncommon on coast. In East Africa it is found on all the larger lakes, both alkaline and fresh-water.

CORMORANTS: Phalacrocoracidae

Dark-plumaged, moderately long-necked water birds with strong hook-tipped bills; small goose or duck-sized; swim and dive to capture food, mainly fish and frogs.

WHITE-NECKED CORMORANT
Phalacrocorax carbo **Plate 14**
Identification: 91cm (36in). A large blackish water-bird with white cheeks, foreneck and upper breast; eyes green. Immatures have entire underparts white, darkening with successive moults. After swimming it often perches with its wings held half open, a characteristic attitude of cormorants and darters. Differs from Long-tailed Cormorant in larger size, relatively shorter tail and in adults white neck and chest.
Voice: Various guttural croaks, uttered at the nest, otherwise silent birds.
Distribution and Habitat: Occurs commonly throughout eastern Africa, south to Zambia, Malawi and Rhodesia. Frequents lakes, dams and larger rivers. A gregarious breeder, it nests in colonies in trees, on rocky islands or in reed beds.

LONG-TAILED CORMORANT
Phalacrocorax africanus **Plate 14**
Identification: 56–61cm (22–24in). Distinguished from the White-necked Cormorant by smaller size, entirely black underparts of adult, red eyes and relatively longer tail. Immatures brownish-white below.
Voice: Normally silent but utters soft croaking sounds at nest.
Distribution and Habitat: Common throughout Africa in suitable localities, on inland waters and less frequently on the coast.
Allied Species: The Socotran Cormorant (*Phalacrocorax nigrogularis*) is bronzy-black, smaller than the White-necked Cormorant. It is restricted to coasts of the Red Sea and is an entirely marine species.

DARTERS: Anhingidae

Darters are large, long-necked, cormorant-like water birds with long tails. They differ from cormorants in having sharply pointed, not hooked bills. Darters swim low in the water with only the head and neck showing, giving a good imitation of a snake swimming: hence the name 'snake bird' often bestowed upon this species.

AFRICAN DARTER *Anhinga rufa* **Plate 14**
Identification: 96cm (38in). This bird resembles a long-necked, long-tailed cormorant but has slender, pointed bill. The neck has a characteristic 'kink', conspicuous both when bird is settled and in flight. Adults have chestnut necks with a white stripe down each side; underparts black. Immature much paler with buff-brown belly.
Voice: Normally silent except for croaking sounds uttered at nest.
Distribution and Habitat: Occurs throughout Africa in suitable localities; inhabits inland waters, favouring slow-flowing rivers and fresh and alkaline lakes. Common in East and Central Africa, especially on Kenya's Rift Valley lakes and lakes in western Uganda.

HERONS and EGRETS: Ardeidae

These are tall, graceful wading birds with lax plumage. In flight they carry the head well back on the shoulders with the neck curved: cranes, storks and spoonbills fly with the neck extended. Many species are gregarious, nesting in mixed colonies often with other water birds.

CATTLE EGRET *Ardeola ibis* **Plate 15**
Identification: 51cm (20in). A relatively short-legged and thickset white heron with yellowish or flesh-coloured legs; bill yellow or dull orange. Plumage white with buffy-orange crown, chest and mantle: in non-breeding birds and immatures plumage entirely white. Often associated with big game and cattle away from water, catching insects disturbed by the animals; gregarious.
Voice: Various croaking sounds at nesting colonies, otherwise silent.
Distribution and Habitat: Distributed throughout the Ethiopian region and common in East Africa. Frequents swamps and marshes, pasture land and lake and river margins: usually associated with large mammals from elephants to cattle.
Allied Species: The Squacco Heron (*Ardeola ralloides*) is also thickset, slightly smaller than a Cattle Egret, buffy-brown or vinous buff above and more or less streaked on neck and chest, appearing mainly white only when flying; the bird when settled appears uniformly coloured. Common in swamps, marshes

and lake-shore vegetation in East and Central Africa. The larger Night Heron (*Nycticorax nycticorax*), 61cm (24in), is a thickset grey and white heron with crown and upperparts greenish-black and large ruby-red eyes; immature pale brown with heavy buffish-white spots on upperparts and wing-coverts, streaked brown and white below. Locally common in many parts of East Africa frequenting swamps, lakes, rivers and coastal mangrove swamps; it keeps to thick waterside cover during the day, emerging at dusk to feed. The Little Egret (*Egretta garzetta*) 56–61cm (22–24in), is entirely white; bill black to blue-grey towards base; legs black with yellow toes. A common resident throughout East Africa it frequents marshes, swamps and coastal mudflats. The Black Heron (*Egretta ardesaica*) is the same size as the Little Egret and also has yellow toes but its plumage is slate-black. Most frequent coastal areas but also found on inland lakes; numerous on Lake Jipe, Kenya. The Rufous-bellied Heron (*Butorides rufiventris*) is similar but paler slate-grey with dark rufous wings and belly: uncommon on swamps and lakes in East Africa.

BLACK-HEADED HERON *Ardea melanocephala* Plate 15

Identification: 96cm (38in). A grey, black and white heron, slightly smaller than a Grey Heron from which it may be distinguished by its black crown and neck. Lack of rufous in plumage distinguishes it from Goliath and Purple Herons. Immature has crown and neck grey.

Voice: A loud nasal 'Kuark' and various croaking squarks at nest.

Distribution and Habitat: Resident throughout East Africa and often common. Frequents pasture-land in addition to inland and coastal waters, often feeding on rodents and large insects.

Allied Species: The slightly larger Grey Heron (*Ardea cinerea*) 102cm (40in), is easily recognised by its white crown and neck. Resident throughout East Africa on inland and coastal waters. Two large all white egrets also occur throughout East Africa, the Great White Egret (*Egretta alba*) 86–91cm (34–36in), and the Yellow-billed Egret (*Egretta intermedia*) 66cm (26in). The former may be recognised by its larger size and noticeably long bill, which may be yellow, black or parti-coloured; legs entirely black. The Yellow-billed Egret is smaller with a stumpy-looking yellow bill. It also has black legs. Great White Egrets occur on both inland and coastal waters whilst the Yellow-billed Egret is mainly found on inland waters.

GOLIATH HERON *Ardea goliath* Plate 15

Identification: 140–152cm (55–60in). The largest of all herons, its size and mainly chestnut head, neck and underparts distinguish it from all others. Immature is paler with greyish-white underparts.

Voice: A loud, deep 'arrk'.

Distribution and Habitat: Resident in small numbers throughout East Africa, found on both inland and coastal waters. Common on Lake Baringo, Kenya, nesting in a loose colony on Gibralter Island.

Allied Species: The Purple Heron (*Ardea purpurea*) 76–91cm (30–36in), is similar in plumage but is much smaller. At a distance it may be distinguished by its black crown. Immature mainly pale rufous-buff. A resident and winter visitor throughout East Africa, mainly found on inland waters.

HAMERKOP: Scopidae

A medium-sized brown bird, about the size of a cattle egret, with a superficial resemblance to both the herons and the storks. It flies with its neck extended. The Hamerkop is remarkable for its gigantic nest, a stick structure with a side entrance hole, built in a tree near water. It feeds largely on frogs and tadpoles.

HAMERKOP *Scopus umbretta* **Plate 16**
Identification: 56–61cm (22–24in). The entire plumage is dusky brown with a thick crest – the origin of the bird's name. Immature similar.
Voice: A series of shrill, piping whistles: at times when several birds are present the noise is considerable.
Distribution and Habitat: Resident throughout East Africa in suitable localities. Occurs on inland waters, favouring slowly running streams and rivers, lake margins and marshes.

STORKS: Ciconiidae

Storks are large, long-legged, long-necked birds with long, usually straight bills: necks are extended in flight, not drawn back as in the heron family.

MARABOU STORK *Leptoptilos crumeniferus* **Plate 15**
Identification: 152cm (60in). A very large stork, grey above with grey wings; white below with a white ruff at the base of a flesh-pink neck. Adults develop a large air-filled pouch which hangs from the front of the neck. Immature is similar but darker.
Voice: Generally silent except for bill rattling and short croaks and grunting sounds.
Distribution and Habitat: Resident throughout East Africa and common in areas where big game exists. Mainly a scavenger which associates with vultures at carrion; also occurs near open water where it feeds on frogs. It is an important destroyer of locusts and grasshoppers.
Allied Species: The Saddle-bill Stork (*Ephippiorhynchus senegalensis*) 168cm (66in), may be recognised by its even larger size, black and white plumage and massive black and red bill with a yellow saddle across the base of the upper mandible. Widely distributed in small numbers in East Africa, frequenting swamps and lakes.

YELLOW-BILLED STORK *Ibis ibis* **Plate 15**
Identification: 107cm (42in). A pinkish-white stork with black wings, a bare red face and a slightly decurved orange-yellow bill. Adults in breeding plumage have deep carmine tips to the mantle feathers and wing coverts. Immature duller and pale buff-grey.
Voice: Silent, but utters various guttural calls at nesting colonies.
Distribution and Habitat: Widespread in East Africa; frequents both inland waters and coastal areas.

IBISES and SPOONBILLS: Threskiornithidae

Ibises are characterised by their decurved bills: spoonbills lose this bill character when the nestling develops the spatulate tip. Ibises and spoonbills fly with the neck straight out, not drawn back like the herons.

SACRED IBIS *Threskiornis aethiopica* **Plate 15**
Identification: 76cm (30in). White plumage, naked black head and neck, and purple-black plumes on lower back render identification easy. Immature lacks plumes and head and neck are covered with mottled black and white feathers.
Voice: Generally silent but sometimes utters a harsh croak.
Distribution and Habitat: Resident throughout Ethiopian Region and common in East Africa. Frequents marshes, swamps, pasture land and flood plains.

HADADA IBIS *Hagedashia hagedash* **Plate 15**
Identification: 76cm (30in). The entire plumage is olive-grey, rather paler on underparts, head and neck. There is metallic green wash on back and wing coverts, but this is conspicuous only under good viewing conditions.
Voice: One of Africa's best known bird sounds, a loud, far-carrying 'har-har-har'.
Distribution and Habitat: A common resident in East Africa, frequenting swamps, marshes, lakes, flooded areas and farmland.
Allied Species: The Glossy Ibis (*Plegadis falcinellus*) 61cm (24in), is a more slender, dark-looking bird; plumage dark chestnut with a purple, green and bronze metallic wash. Immature and non-breeding birds are dark grey-brown, not chestnut. In East Africa a local resident on inland swamps and lakes, from October to March its numbers are augmented by northern migrants.

AFRICAN SPOONBILL *Platalea alba* **Plate 15**
Identification: 91cm (36in). Easily recognised by its long, spatulate bill, bare red face and legs and white plumage. Immature similar but with duller soft parts.

Voice: A double 'aark-ark' but normally silent.
Distribution and Habitat: Occurs locally in East Africa, frequenting both fresh water and brakish lakes, swamps and marshes.

FLAMINGOS: Phoenicopteridae

The flamingos are a group of long-legged, long-necked birds which occur in large flocks on brackish lakes. Their bills are characteristic, flattened above with the tip bent down at an angle: plumage mainly pink and white.

GREATER FLAMINGO *Phoenicopterus ruber* Plate 15

Identification: 142cm (56in). The plumage of the Greater Flamingo is white with a pink wash; wing-coverts and axillaries bright coral-red; flight feathers black; bill pink with a black tip. Immature greyish-white with a pinkish-grey bill. A much larger and paler bird than the Lesser Flamingo, from which it is easily distinguished by its pale pink bill.
Voice: A series of gruntings and murmurations, interspersed with goose-like honks.
Distribution and Habitat: Frequent on alkaline lakes in East Africa, especially those in the Rift Valley; uncommon visitor to coastal areas. Numbers augmented by northern migrants between October and April.

LESSER FLAMINGO *Phoenicopterus minor* Plate 15

Identification: 101cm (40in). The Lesser Flamingo has plumage of deep pink, much darker and brighter than Greater Flamingo; bill dark carmine-red with black tip. Immature paler and greyer with little or no pink in plumage. A much smaller and more richly coloured species than Greater Flamingo: its dark carmine bill is a good field character.
Voice: Deep murmurations and honks.
Distribution and Habitat: On alkaline lakes throughout East Africa, sometimes present in vast numbers on favoured lakes such as Nakuru and Elmenteita. Very infrequent in coastal areas.

DUCKS and GEESE: Anatidae

The Ducks and Geese are an easily recognised group of birds, characterised by webbed feet and their bill structure with its nail-like tip and row of lamellae along the edges. Wing pattern in flight is an important field character.

EGYPTIAN GOOSE *Alopochen aegyptiaca* Plate 15

Identification: 61cm (24in). The plumage of the Egyptian Goose is brown, paler below with a chestnut patch in centre of breast and chestnut around eye: contrasting white shoulders conspicuous in flight. Immature similar to adult but duller and chestnut breast patch small or lacking. Occurs in pairs or small flocks. Often alights in trees, usually over water.

Voice: A loud, strident honking.

Distribution and Habitat: Common throughout East Africa on all types of inland waters.

Allied Species: Other waterfowl common in East Africa include the African Pochard (*Netta erythrophthalma*), 38cm (15in), a diving duck of dark uniform plumage with a white patch in the wings in flight; the Yellow-billed Duck (*Anas undulata*) 48cm (19in), a dark Mallard-like duck with a conspicuous mainly yellow bill; the Red-billed Duck (*Anas erythrorhynchos*) 38cm (15in), identified by its red bill, blackish-brown cap which contrasts with pale cheeks and pinkish-buff speculum which is conspicuous in flight; the Cape Teal (*Anas capensis*) 36cm (14in), found on alkaline lakes, also with a red bill but crown pale, same colour as cheeks; speculum green bordered above and below by a white stripe; the Hottentot Teal (*Anas hottentota*) 28cm (11in), the smallest East African duck, dark brown with a blackish cap, sides of bill blue and with a wide white band in the wings which is conspicuou in flight. The Knob-billed Duck (*Sarkidiornis melanota*) ♂ 61cm (24in), ♀ 51cm (20in), is black and white, the ♂ with a large fleshy knob at the base of the bill: at close quarters the black upperparts are seen to have a metallic green and copper wash.

BIRDS OF PREY: Falconiformes

These include the Secretary Bird (*Sagittariidae*) of which only one species is known, a very distinct, terrestrial bird of prey; the Vultures, Eagles, Buzzards and Hawks (*Accipitridae*) and the Falcons (*Falconidae*).

SECRETARY BIRD *Sagittarius serpentarius* — Plate 16

Identification: 101cm (40in). A large, pale-grey, long-legged bird with black flight feathers and tibia and long central tail feathers, seen stalking about in open country. Its long crest feathers are conspicuous, raised like a halo by the bird whilst hunting. Immature similar but more buffy-grey.

Voice: Generally silent, but in breeding season produces remarkable croaks and even a lion-like cough.

Distribution and Habitat: Widely distributed but uncommon throughout East Africa on open plains, bush country and farmlands. Feeds largely on snakes and other reptiles.

WHITE-BACKED VULTURE *Gyps africanus* — Plate 16

Identification: 81cm (32in). Vultures are large or very large eagle-like birds with long wings, short tails and relatively small naked or down-covered heads: usually seen soaring and at carrion. The White-backed Vulture is a

large, dark or pale brown species with a white rump. Immature similar but lacks white rump. In flight distinguished by broad pale band along fore-edge of wings.
Voice: Harsh squarking croaks whilst feeding on carrion.
Distribution and Habitat: The commonest vulture, found throughout East Africa in open big game country, often congregating at lion kills. Roosts and nests in riverside trees, not on cliffs.
Allied Species: Ruppell's Vulture (*Gyps rueppellii*), 86cm (34in), has a dark back, feathers broadly edged creamy-white giving a spotted appearance. Nubian or Lappet-faced Vulture (*Torgos tracheliotus*) 101cm (40in), is a huge bird with an extremely massive bill; folds of naked skin on head and face purplish-grey. The least common species is the White-headed Vulture (*Trigonoceps occipitalis*) with a striking white head, white secondaries (in adult), a white belly and red bill; immature with head brown, best recognised by white belly. The Hooded Vulture (*Neophron monachus*) 66cm (26in), is entirely dark brown with a rounded tail and small slender bill. The Egyptian Vulture (*Neophron percnopterus*) 66cm (26in), is a small, mainly white species with a distinctive wedge-shaped white tail. Immature brown, distinguished from Hooded Vulture by tail shape.

BATELEUR *Terathopius ecaudatus* Plate 16

Identification: 61cm (24in). In all plumages the Bateleur can be identified by its remarkably short tail. On the wing the adult is unmistakable, with contrasting black underparts and white undersides of wings; back and tail chestnut, rarely rufous-buff. Immature dark brown, sometimes with a distinctly paler head.
Voice: A sharp, barking cry.
Distribution and Habitat: Widely distributed and common throughout East Africa, especially in the Northern Frontier Province of Kenya. Generally seen on the wing, soaring high overhead – a habit which may well explain its continued abundance! Occurs in semi-desert and open country, bush and savannah woodlands; less frequent in cultivated areas.

PALE CHANTING GOSHAWK *Melierax poliopterus* Plate 16

Identification: 48cm (19in). A very upright-standing pale grey hawk with a closely grey-barred belly. Legs long, orange; cere, at base of bill, yellow. Immature brownish-grey with heavy brown streaking on chest and rufous-brown barring on belly. Both adult and immature have a white rump, conspicuous in flight.
Voice: A sustained piping call which is reminiscent of the calls of some small hornbills.
Distribution and Habitat: A common resident of dry bush and acacia country in eastern Kenya and north-eastern Tanzania.
Allied Species: The Dark Chanting Goshawk (*Melierax metabates*) 48cm (19in), differs in its darker plumage, black and white barred rump and

orange-red cere. It occurs in western Kenya, Uganda and Tanzania in bush and wooded areas.

AUGUR BUZZARD *Buteo rufofuscus* **Plate 16**

Identification: 50–57cm (20–24in). This is probably East Africa's most frequently seen bird of prey. Easily recognised by its slate-grey upperparts, chestnut tail and greyish-white and black barring on the closed wing. Underparts variable, entirely white, white with a black throat and chest or entirely black. Immature has underparts whitish, streaked or blotched with black and the tail barred black and brown: immatures of the dark phase blackish-brown below, also with a barred tail. In flight the broad wings and chestnut tail are good field characters. The adult dark phase might be mistaken for a Bateleur but has a much longer tail.

Voice: A ringing, wild, far-carrying 'guang-guang'.

Distribution and Habitat: Common in the highlands of East Africa, usually above 914m (3,000ft). Frequents open moorland country, mountains, forest glades, inland cliffs and cultivated areas. Perches on telegraph poles and such-like vantage points. A most valuable bird as it preys almost entirely upon rodents: the birds seen near chicken runs are not hunting the fowls but the rats and mice attracted by the chicken food.

LONG-CRESTED EAGLE *Lophaetus occipitalis* **Plate 16**

Identification: 51–56cm (20–22in). A blackish-brown eagle with a long, lax crest; legs feathered brownish-white. In flight the pale bases of the flight feathers form a whitish patch towards the end of each wing. Immature similar but crest shorter. Often seen perched on telegraph poles. The black phase of the Augur Buzzard has yellow, unfeathered legs and lacks a crest.

Voice: Shrill series of whistles 'Kee, ee, ee, ee, ee, ee, ee'.

Distribution and Habitat: Common in many parts of East Africa from sea level to over 2,134m (7,000ft). Inhabits open park-like country, wooded areas, forest margins and cultivation. It feeds mainly upon rodents and other agricultural pests and is a most beneficial bird.

TAWNY EAGLE *Aquila rapax* **Plate 16**

Identification: 66–76cm (26–30in). A uniformly coloured brown eagle with a relatively short, rounded tail, legs feathered: plumages vary greatly from dark brown, rusty brown to pale brown. An uncommon plumage phase, most frequent in northern Kenya is pale brownish-cream. Immatures usually paler than adults with two pale wing bars in flight.

Voice: A raucous, yelping cry.

Distribution and Habitat: Resident locally throughout East Africa but most frequent in Kenya. Frequents cultivated areas, open big game and savannah country and mountains. Often associates with vultures at lion kills and around camps.

FISH EAGLE *Haliaeetus vocifer* **Plate 16**
Identification: 76cm (30in). The Fish Eagle is easily recognised by its distinctive colour pattern, white head, chest, back and tail, chestnut belly and shoulders and black wings. Immature is duller with black streaking on breast and some black on tail.
Voice: The far-carrying, wild, almost gull-like call is one of the characteristic sounds of the African wilds. When calling the bird throws its head backwards, even in flight.
Distribution and Habitat: In East Africa plentiful in suitable habitats – lakes, swamps, rivers and the coast.

BLACK KITE *Milvus migrans* **Plate 16**
Identification: 53–58cm (21–23in). A bird with brown to rusty-brown plumage the Black Kite has a conspicuously forked tail; bill yellow. Immature similar with traces of pale streaking on underparts. The European race of Black Kite, a common winter visitor, has a whitish-brown head and a black bill.
Voice: A high-pitched, wavering call.
Distribution and Habitat: A resident and local migrant throughout East Africa, frequenting savannah and open country, cultivated areas, towns, lakes and rivers and coastal areas. Often found in numbers when attracted by carrion or insect swarms.

BLACK-SHOULDERED KITE *Elanus caeruleus* **Plate 16**
Identification: 33cm (13in). A thickset, medium-sized hawk, pale grey above and white below, with a white, slightly forked tail and black 'shoulders'. Immature darker above with white tips to feathers of mantle and wing-coverts; below with rust-brown wash on breast. Frequently hovers and settles on telegraph wires and poles.
Voice: Usually silent, but sometimes utters a clear piping whistle.
Distribution and Habitat: A common species throughout East Africa, inhabiting savannah and open grasslands, cultivation, margins of lakes and rivers and also mountain moorland.

GAME BIRDS: Phasianidae

This family includes the quails, francolins, guinea-fowls and their allies. All are chicken-like, terrestrial birds with moderate or short tails: sexes usually similar in African species.

CRESTED FRANCOLIN *Francolinus sephaena* **Plate 17**
Identification: 25–28cm (10–11in). A bantam-sized francolin with distinctive white streaks on upperparts; below pale buff with mottling on the breast and

triangular chestnut spots on sides of neck; tail often carried cocked up over the back.
Voice: A very loud, far-carrying 'tee-dee-jee, tee, dee, jee' uttered over and over again: birds especially noisy at dusk and dawn.
Distribution and Habitat: In East Africa locally very common, inhabiting bush country, thick cover along dry water courses and semi-desert country.

YELLOW-NECKED SPURFOWL

Francolinus leucoscepus **Plate 17**

Identification: 33–36cm (13–14in). Spurfowls may be distinguished from francolins by their bare, unfeathered throats. The Yellow-necked Spurfowl is greyish-brown above, below buff-streaked darker brown; throat conspicuously bare, bright yellow to orange-red at base; bird stands high on its legs. In flight shows pale wing patch.
Voice: A loud, grating 'graark, grak, grak', especially vocal in the early morning and towards dusk.
Distribution and Habitat: This is the commonest francolin in East Africa in those areas where it occurs – north-eastern Uganda, Kenya and northern Tanzania. Frequents open bush country, margins of forest and woodland, and dry thornbush country.

HELMETED GUINEA-FOWL *Numida meleagris* **Plate 17**

Identification: 51–56cm (20–22in). General colour dark slate, spotted all over with white; head and neck sparsely feathered with a bony horn protruding from crown; blue and red, or blue wattles at base of bill. The Tufted Guinea-fowl which has a tuft of nasal bristles at the base of the bill, is now considered to be conspecific. Gregarious outside of the breeding season.
Voice: A loud cackling call, repeated frequently.
Distribution and Habitat: Locally common throughout East Africa in bush country, arid thorn-bush areas, neglected cultivation, open park-like country and savannah woodlands.

VULTURINE GUINEA-FOWL *Acryllium vulturinum* **Plate 17**

Identification: 58–61cm (23–24in). A most handsome long-tailed guinea-fowl with feathers of upper mantle and chest long and striped white, black and blue; breast cobalt-blue; head and neck bare, blue, with patch of downy chestnut feathers on nape; head small for the bird's size, imparting a vulturine appearance. Normally occurs in flocks.
Voice: A series of loud, shrill cackles and a loud 'kak, kak, kak, kak'.
Distribution and Habitat: A local but not uncommon bird in dry thorn-bush country and riverine acacia forest in eastern Kenya and north-eastern Tanzania. Numbers fluctuate, species at times uncommon, but in other more favourable years abundant.

CRANES: Balearicidae

The cranes are large, stately terrestrial birds, superficially resembling storks, from which they differ externally in having the nostrils in a long groove, and the hind toe short. Voices loud, trumpet or goose-like. Long neck and legs extended in flight. Gregarious outside breeding season.

CROWNED CRANE *Balearica regulorum* **Plate 17**

Identification: 100cm (40in). The Crowned Crane has upperparts of slate grey, paler on neck and underparts; wings appear mainly white in flight with black primaries and chestnut secondaries; crown with a black velvety cushion with a conspicuous tuft of straw-coloured bristle-like feathers behind; bare cheeks and neck wattles white and red.

Voice: A loud, honking call 'ah, aahow, ah, aahow', which has been likened to the honking of Canada geese. Call usually uttered in flight.

Distribution and Habitat: Locally common throughout East Africa in marshes, swamps, open plains, cultivated land and margins of rivers and lakes.

CRAKES, RAILS and COOTS: Rallidae

The Crakes and their allies are generally marsh or water-frequenting birds with rounded wings and apparently weak flight, with legs dangling. Tails short and often carried cocked up. Many species shy and skulking. Coots have heavy, thickset bodies and small heads with a white frontal shield: usually seen swimming and diving.

BLACK CRAKE *Limnocorax flavirostra* **Plate 17**

Identification: 20cm (8in). The plumage of the Black Crake is entirely slaty-black with contrasting yellow-green bill and pink legs. Immature browner with dusky bill and legs. Less skulking than most and often seen feeding among water-lily leaves at the edge of reed and papyrus beds.

Voice: A shrill 'r-r-r-r-r-r-r-r-r, yok' and various clucking sounds, not unlike the trill of a little grebe.

Distribution and Habitat: A common bird throughout East Africa where a combination of water and dense fringing vegetation exists. In the Amboseli National Park, Kenya these crakes are abundant and very tame.

RED-KNOBBED COOT *Fulica cristata* **Plate 17**

Identification: 40cm (16in). A large, thickset water bird, blackish-slate in colour: bill and frontal shield white with two dark red knobs at the base of the shield. Immature similar but bill and shield greyish-white and knobs not developed. Swims and dives well and has characteristic head bobbing motion whilst swimming. Flight laboured and weak with greyish legs dangling.

Voice: A harsh, deep sounding 'kwork' and various grunting calls.
Distribution and Habitat: Locally common in East Africa on lakes, ponds, swamps and dams where there is an abundance of aquatic vegetation and reed or papyrus beds.

BUSTARDS: Otididae

Large or very large terrestrial birds with three-toed feet and long necks; mainly buff or grey with fine dark vermiculations. Frequent open plains or desert or dry bush country. Gait a stately walk. Behaviour varies, sometimes very shy, running or crouching at the first sign of danger; at other times fearless of humans. Flight powerful with slow, deliberate wing strokes.

KORI BUSTARD *Otis kori* **Plate 17**

Identification: 76–101cm (30–40in). ♂ larger than ♀. The Kori Bustard has upperparts and neck vermiculated black and greyish-buff; top of head crested. Feathers of neck very lax giving the effect of a thick-necked bird. This bird is best identified by its large size, lack of chestnut at back of neck and lax neck feathers. ♂ has a distinctive breeding display, when neck is inflated like a balloon and the tail raised to lie along the back.
Voice: Less vocal than many other bustards, but at times utters a far carrying 'kah, kah, kah'.
Distribution and Habitat: Local in small numbers throughout East Africa, most frequent in Kenya. Inhabits open and semi-open plains and open bush.
Allied Species: Jackson's Bustard (*Neotis denhami*) 76cm (30in), differs from the Kori Bustard in the bright reddish-chestnut back to its neck. Occurs throughout East Africa, but far less common than Kori. The White-bellied Bustard (*Eupodotis senegalensis*) 61cm (24in), is a white-breasted bustard with a conspicuous blue-grey neck. Occurs locally on open plains and in semi-desert bush country. Its call is distinctive, a loud 'oo-warka, oo-warka'. The Buff-crested Bustard (*Eupodotis ruficrista*) 51cm (20in), has a black belly in both sexes and a thick drooping pinkish-buff crest. It is found in dry bush country and dry woodlands in East Africa, but is most plentiful in the arid bush of Kenya's Northern Frontier Province.

JACANAS or LILY-TROTTERS: Jacanidae

The Jacanas are long-legged water birds, somewhat resembling rails or plovers, with extremely long toes. Their enormous feet enable them to walk and feed on waterlily leaves and floating aquatic vegetation. Their nests are sodden platforms of water-weeds and their eggs, brown with black scrawls, are remarkable for their very high gloss.

AFRICAN JACANA *Actophilornis africana* **Plate 17**
Identification: 23–28cm (9–11in). A bright chestnut, plover-like bird with a large bluish head shield and bill, nearly always seen walking on floating vegetation. Immature similar but paler and duller.
Voice: A series of chittering call-notes.
Distribution and Habitat: Common in suitable areas throughout East Africa. Occurs on open water where there is an abundance of floating vegetation.

PLOVERS and ALLIES: Charadriidae

The Plovers are small or medium-sized birds of the wading bird type, although some species occur on dry plains. They are more thickset than the sandpipers and their allies, with thicker-looking necks and relatively larger and more thickset heads.

BLACKSMITH PLOVER *Vanellus armatus* **Plate 17**
Identification: 28cm (11in). A conspicuous species with contrasting black, white and pale grey plumage. The crown is white, there is a black patch on the mantle and the cheeks and underparts are black. Immature duller with buff edgings to feathers of upperparts.
Voice: A loud 'tik, tik, tik' call, resembling two pieces of metal being knocked together.
Distribution and Habitat: Found locally from southern Kenya southwards. Occurs on the shores of both fresh and alkaline lakes, swamps and rivers and on ploughed fields.
Allied Species: The Spurwing Plover (*Vanellus spinosus*) 27cm (10½in), differs from the Blacksmith Plover in having a pale greyish-brown back, without a black saddle, white cheeks and white sides to the neck. Locally common in Uganda and northern half of Kenya.

CROWNED PLOVER *Vanellus coronatus* **Plate 17**
Identification: 28cm (11in). The Crowned Plover is pale greyish-brown above; top of head black surrounded by a white ring; below, chin white merging to pale brown on breast, bordered by a black line; abdomen white; bill red with black tip, legs red. Immature similar.
Voice: A series of noisy, scolding whistles, frequently repeated.
Distribution and Habitat: A common species throughout East Africa, frequenting a variety of habitats from short grassy plains, edges of open water and grassy air-strips to cultivated ground.

BLACK-WINGED STILT *Himantopus himantopus* **Plate 17**
Identification: 38cm (15in). An unmistakable bird: in flight its very long pink legs trail 15–18cm (6–7in) beyond tail. Plumage black and white. Immature largely black and grey. Black undersides of sharply pointed wings conspicuous in flight.

Voice: A shrill, yelping 'Kyip, kyip, kyip'.
Distribution and Habitat: A local resident and abundant winter visitor to East Africa. Frequents both fresh and alkaline inland waters but uncommon on coast. In Kenya very common on Lakes Naivasha, Nakuru, Elmenteita and Magadi in Rift Valley.
Allied Species: The Avocet (*Recurvirostra avosetta*) 43cm (17in), is also a common resident and winter visitor, especially on alkaline lakes. Plumage black and white with thin black, upturned bill and blue-grey legs. Immature paler. Call, a loud 'kleep'.

GULLS and TERNS: Laridae

The Gulls and Terns are medium-sized or large swimming birds. Gulls are more robust and wider-winged with slightly hooked bills; tails square or rounded; gregarious. Terns are more slender and graceful and tails are usually forked; also gregarious.

GREY-HEADED GULL *Larus cirrocephalus* **Plate 17**

Identification: 40cm (16in). A pale grey gull with slightly darker grey head and red bill and legs; primaries black with white tips; breast white, with pale pink suffusion in freshly moulted birds. Non-breeding birds have head mainly white. Immature mottled brownish-grey on mantle.
Voice: A loud, laughing cackling call, but usually birds are silent.
Distribution and Habitat: Locally common throughout on inland waters, very uncommon on the coast. Frequents both fresh and alkaline lakes.
Allied Species: The Sooty Gull (*Larus hemprichii*) 46cm (18in), is the common gull along the East African coast. It is dark grey-brown above with a darker head and a white band on the hind neck; bill yellowish green with a black and red tip. Immature duller and paler with black tail band.

SANDGROUSE: Pterocididae

A family of thickset, pigeon-like, terrestrial birds: wings long and pointed, flight rapid. Legs short, feathered to base of toes. Most species are gregarious and inhabit arid regions; they come to drink at water in early morning or late evening, according to species.

CHESTNUT-BELLIED SANDGROUSE
Pterocles exustus **Plate 18**

Identification: 30cm (12in). Sexes unlike; ♂ with upperparts sandy-brown, ♀ streaked and barred buff and brown. ♂ and ♀ both possess long, narrow central tail feathers. White tips to inner flight feathers form a conspicuous white bar when bird is in flight. Gregarious; flights to water in early morning.

Voice: A guttural chuckling, rendered 'gutter, gutter, gutter, gutter, gutter, gutter'.
Distribution and Habitat: This is the commonest sandgrouse in most parts of Kenya and northern Tanzania. It inhabits semi-desert bush country, arid plains and open acacia bush.

BLACK-FACED SANDGROUSE *Pterocles decoratus* **Plate 18**
Identification: 25cm (10in). A stumpy-looking sandgrouse without long central tail feathers. Black pattern on face and throat of ♂ and broad white band across chest are good field characters. Less gregarious than Chestnut-bellied Sandgrouse: flights to water in early morning.
Voice: A series of chuckling whistles 'chucker-chucker-chucker'; also shorter guttural notes.
Distribution and Habitat: Common in dry thorn-bush areas and semi-desert scrub in Kenya and northern Tanzania. Specially common in Tsavo National Park, Amboseli and Samburu in Kenya.

DOVES and PIGEONS: Columbidae

These are medium-sized, plump birds with small rounded heads and the base of the bill swollen. Their flight is rapid. Many species have characteristic deep cooing calls. The terms 'dove' and 'pigeon' are used loosely to indicate size, the smaller species being called doves, the larger pigeons.

SPECKLED PIGEON *Columba guinea* **Plate 18**
Identification: 38cm (15in). This pigeon is easily recognised by its vinous chestnut back, grey, unspotted underparts, white spotted wings and, in flight, its pale blue-grey rump. The closely related Olive Pigeon has the underparts purplish-grey, thickly spotted white, and the bill and feet are yellow.
Voice: A deep guttural 'coo, coo – coo, coo'.
Distribution and Habitat: Locally common throughout East Africa. Inhabits open country, acacia woodland, cultivated areas and rocky hillsides and cliffs. In many places it breeds in human habitations like a domestic pigeon.
Allied Species: The Olive Pigeon (*Columba arquatrix*) 38cm (15in), is a forest species which is found in most parts of East Africa. It may be recognised by its bright yellow bill and legs and white-spotted underparts.

RED-EYED DOVE *Streptopelia semitorquata* **Plate 18**
Identification: 30cm (12in). This is the largest of the brownish-grey doves with a black collar on the hind-neck. It may be recognised by its size, conspicuous whitish-grey forehead and deep vinous-pink underparts. Immature similar but duller.
Voice: Its call-notes are distinctive, a deep 'coo, coo – co, co – co, co'.

Distribution and Habitat: Common over much of East Africa in a variety of habitats – semi-desert bush, forest margins and wooded areas, cultivation and gardens.

RING-NECKED DOVE *Streptopelia capicola* **Plate 18**
Identification: 25cm (10in). A greyish-brown dove with a black half-collar on the hind neck and a blackish-brown eye; greyish below, merging to white on the belly. It is a smaller and paler bird than the Red-eyed Dove from which it may also be distinguished by its white abdomen.
Voice: A constantly repeated three note call 'koo-kaa, kaa'.
Distribution and Habitat: A common resident throughout East Africa. Frequents semi-desert bush, thornbush country, woodlands and cultivated areas.
Allied Species: The Mourning Dove (*Streptopelia decipiens*) 27cm (10½in), is slightly larger, paler and pinker, and has a pinkish-white eye. It's call is a growling 'cooo-ah'. Common in acacia woodland and along rivers in arid areas.

LAUGHING DOVE *Streptopelia senegalensis* **Plate 18**
Identification: 24cm (9½in). A small dove with rusty coloured upperparts, much blue-grey in the wings and no black collar on the hind neck. Bases of feathers on fore-neck are black giving a mottled appearance. Chest pink, merging to white on belly; much white on tail.
Voice: A five-note call repeated several times 'coo, cook, cook, cou, cou'.
Distribution and Habitat: A common species throughout East Africa inhabiting both bush country and cultivated area.

NAMAQUA DOVE *Oena capensis* **Plate 18**
Identification: 20cm (8in). In all plumages this dove is easily identified by its small size and very long tail. ♂ has black on face and throat, which is lacking in the ♀. Immature similar to ♀ but with buff edging to feathers of upperparts and wing coverts.
Voice: Usually silent, but sometimes utters a soft 'koo-koo'.
Distribution and Habitat: Locally common in thorn-bush country and semi-desert areas in East Africa.

TURACOS: Musophagidae

The Turacos, Louries or Plantain-eaters, as they are variously called, are a group of medium or large-sized arboreal birds confined to Africa. The forest species are remarkable for their brightly coloured plumage and long tails; many possess crimson-red flight feathers. Most have loud, harsh calls.

SCHALOW'S TURACO *Tauraco schalowi* **Plate 18**
Identification: 41cm (16in). Plumage bright green with a long, attentuated,

narrowly white-tipped crest; flight feathers mainly crimson-red. Immature duller. Distinguished from the similar Livingstone's Turaco by its longer crest and violet-purple, not green glossed tail.
Voice: A deep, far-carrying 'kaa, kaa, kaa, kaa, kaaar' often repeated.
Distribution and Habitat: A common but local species in south-western Kenya and north-western Tanzania. Specially common in riverine forest in the Mara Game Reserve, Kenya. Inhabits open wooded country and strips of riverine forest. Often located by its loud call.
Allied Species: Livingstone's Turaco (*Tauraco livingstonei*) 41cm (16in), has a shorter crest and a green-glossed black tail. It occurs in wooded country and mountain and riverine forest in eastern and southern Tanzania.

HARTLAUB'S TURACO *Tauraco hartlaubi* **Plate 18**

Identification: 41cm (16in). This is the common forest Turaco of the Kenya highlands. Plumage violet-blue with a green belly and crimson flight feathers; crown and nape bluish-black with a round white patch above and in front of the eye, and a white streak below the eye. Immature duller.
Voice: A high-pitched 'gaw, gaw, gaw, gaw', frequently repeated.
Distribution and Habitat: A common but local resident in highland forests of Kenya, eastern Uganda and north-eastern Tanzania. Frequent in the forests around Nairobi, Kenya.
Allied Species: Ross's Turaco (*Musophaga rossae*) 51cm (20in), is a large violet-black species with a square crimson crest and flight feathers; face and bill orange-yellow. It occurs in forested areas and woodland in Uganda, western Kenya and western Tanzania.

WHITE-BELLIED GO-AWAY-BIRD
Corythaixoides leucogaster **Plate 18**

Identification: 51cm (20in). A grey, black and white dry country turaco. A conspicuous bird with its long tail, squared crest, grey chest and white belly. Usually in pairs or family parties.
Voice: A loud, bleating call 'aark, warrr' which has been rendered as 'go awayaaaa' or 'go-baaak' – hence the bird's common name.
Distribution and Habitat: A common but local resident in dry or relatively dry acacia country throughout Kenya, Uganda and northern Tanzania.

CUCKOOS and COUCALS: Cuculidae

The Cuckoos are medium-sized, slim birds with long tails. One of their characters is that their first and fourth toes are directed backwards. Most species are parasitic in their breeding habits, laying their eggs in the nests of foster parents. The Coucals and Green Coucals build their own nests and rear their own young.

RED-CHESTED CUCKOO *Cuculus solitarius* **Plate 19**
Identification: 30cm (12in). A dark slate-grey cuckoo with a rusty-brown patch on the throat and upper breast; chin grey; remainder underparts barred pale buff and black. Immature dark with black throat. This is a bird which is heard far oftener than seen.
Voice: Distinctive, shrill call of three notes – 'wip, wip, weeoo'. Often calls immediately before rains break and known locally as the 'rain-bird' – its call being rendered 'it will rain'.
Distribution and Habitat: A common bird throughout East Africa, frequenting open country, woodlands, forests, bush and cultivation.

WHITE-BROWED COUCAL *Centropus superciliosus* **Plate 19**
Identification: 40cm (16in). Coucals are heavily built, rather clumsy-looking birds with an awkward, floundering flight when flushed from cover. The impression is of a chestnut plumaged bird with a long, broad tail. The White-browed Coucal is distinguished by a wide whitish stripe over the eye and an earth-brown crown. Eye ruby-red and conspicuous at close quarters.
Voice: A distinctive bubbling call, likened to water being poured out of a bottle, which has given rise to a common name – 'water-bottle bird'.
Distribution and Habitat: Common in East Africa, inhabiting grassy bush country, rank undergrowth, coastal scrub and similar thick cover.

OWLS: Strigidae

Owls are mainly nocturnal birds of prey characterised by large heads, rather flattened faces and conspicuous 'facial discs', and forward facing eyes. Their plumage is soft and downy and flight noiseless: ear tufts present in many species; they have hooked bills and powerful claws.

PEARL-SPOTTED OWLET *Glaucidium perlatum* **Plate 20**
Identification: 20cm (8in). This owlet is distinguished by its lack of ear tufts and relatively long white-spotted tail; underparts white streaked dark brown. It is a species more frequently observed during the daytime than most owls and its whereabouts is often indicated by the presence of small birds engaged in mobbing.
Voice: A distinctive, low but far-carrying 'we-ooo, we-ooo', not unlike the call of the Water Dikkop.
Distribution and Habitat: Locally common in many parts of East Africa. Occurs in dry bush country, savannah, acacia and other types of woodland.
Allied Species: Other frequently encountered East African owls include the following: the African Scops Owl (*Otus scops*) 18cm (7in), has small ear tufts and its plumage is finely vermiculated pale grey, brown and white with black and white streaks on breast. Call a soft two-note 'ke-oo' run together to sound as one note. Most frequent in riverine acacia woodland. Verreaux's

Eagle Owl (*Bubo lacteus*) 61–66cm (24–26in), also has ear tufts; general colour finely vermiculated brownish-grey; underparts without heavy spotting; facial disc pale with a black stripe on each side. Call normally a mournful 'hu, hu, hu, hu, hu, hu' in ascending scale. Most frequent in acacia woodland, especially along rivers.

SWIFTS: Apodidae

In general appearance the swifts are swallow-like but structurally they are quite distinct from swallows, having flat skulls and a foot structure in which all the toes point forwards. They can be distinguished by the formation of their wings, which are more slender and scythe-like, their short tails and their manner of flight, which is rapid and direct, often gliding considerable distances without flapping wings.

LITTLE SWIFT *Apus affinis* Plate 21

Identification: 13cm (5in). A black swift with a square, not forked tail, a white patch on the rump and a whitish chin. Gregarious at all times and nests in colonies.
Voice: A shrill twittering call.
Distribution and Habitat: Common throughout East Africa, aerial, breeding on buildings in towns and country, below bridges and on cliffs.

MOUSEBIRDS: Coliidae

The mousebirds are a family endemic to Africa; their habit of climbing and running about amongst branches, with their long tails pointed downwards, gives them a rather rodent-like appearance. Their plumage is hair-like and lax, tail long and graduated, bill thick and finch-like; head crested. They have the ability to move the outer toes backwards or forwards. Usually found in small flocks or family parties.

SPECKLED MOUSEBIRD *Colius striatus* Plate 19

Identification: 36cm (14in). Upperparts of this bird are brown; head crested; sides of face greyish-white; chin and throat dusky, feathers with pale tips giving a speckled appearance; below tawny; tail long and graduated.
Voice: Short twittering calls and a harsher single or double 'tsssk'.
Distribution and Habitat: Common throughout East Africa. Inhabits forested and wooded areas, scrub and cultivation. Found in small flocks. At times destructive to growing vegetables and fruit trees.

BLUE-NAPED MOUSEBIRD *Colius macrourus* Plate 19

Identification: 36cm (14in). The plumage of this mousebird is greenish ash-

grey; tail feathers very long and slender; head crested with a turquoise-blue patch on nape. Base of bill and face crimson-red. Uniform colour, slender tail feathers and blue nape patch distinguish this species.
Voice: A loud clear whistle 'peeeeee, peeeeeeee'.
Distribution and Habitat: Locally common throughout East Africa in bush, scrub and arid areas. Occurs in small flocks.

KINGFISHERS: Alcedinidae

The Kingfishers are a distinct family of brightly coloured small or medium-sized birds. Not all species prey upon fish; some feed largely upon large insects and lizards and occur in habitats away from water.

PIED KINGFISHER *Ceryle rudis* **Plate 20**
Identification: 25cm (10in). This black and white kingfisher has upperparts spotted and barred black and white; below white with two or one (♀) incomplete black bands; head crested.
Voice: A sharp 'keek, keek'.
Distribution and Habitat: Common in suitable habitats both on inland waters and at the coast. Whilst hunting the Pied Kingfisher often hovers above water, plunging straight down to secure its prey.

MALACHITE KINGFISHER *Alcedo cristata* **Plate 20**
Identification: 13cm (5in). The Malachite Kingfisher's head is crested, its feathers cobalt-blue, barred black; upperparts ultramarine blue; throat white, cheeks and underparts rufous. This bird can be recognised by its elongated lax crest.
Voice: A sharp, but not very loud 'teep' when it flies.
Distribution and Habitat: Locally common throughout East Africa, frequenting permanent water where there is at least some fringing vegetation.
Allied Species: The smaller Pygmy Kingfisher (*Ceyx picta*) 10cm (4in), lacks the crest and its crown is ultramarine blue barred black, not contrasting with the colour of the back. Often encountered in scrub and woodland, sometimes away from water.

GREY-HEADED KINGFISHER *Halcyon leucocephala* **Plate 20**
Identification: 20cm (8in). This kingfisher's upperparts are black with contrasting cobalt-blue wing feathers, rump and tail; head and nape pale grey to whitish on throat and breast; abdomen dark chestnut; bill red. It is a dry country kingfisher which also occurs near water. The blue of the wings and tail are very conspicuous when the bird flies.
Voice: A weak, chattering 'ji, ji, ji-jeeee'.
Distribution and Habitat: Locally common in East Africa; frequents wooded areas, riverine acacias and relatively dry bush country.

BEE-EATERS: Meropidae

The Bee-eaters are medium-sized, slim birds of brilliant plumage; bills long and slightly decurved; legs short and wings sharply pointed.

LITTLE BEE-EATER *Merops pusillus* **Plate 19**
Identification: 15cm (6in). A small green bee-eater with a square tail, yellow throat, a blue-black foreneck stripe, a black eye-stripe and pale rufous underparts. Immature duller and more yellowish-green below.
Voice: Usually silent, but sometimes utters a single or double 'teeep' or 'tee-tsp'.
Distribution and Habitat: Common throughout East Africa in suitable localities, inhabiting open plains where there are bushes, coastal scrub, open woodlands and cultivation. Usually settles a metre or so above the ground.
Allied Species: The Cinnamon-chested Bee-eater (*Merops oreobates*) 20cm (8in), is like a large edition of the Little Bee-eater but with a wider black foreneck band and a deep chestnut chest and abdomen. This is a forest species, normally perching on bare tree branches high above the ground. It occurs locally in the highlands of Kenya, Uganda and northern and western Tanzania.

ROLLERS: Coraciidae

The Rollers are thickset, medium-sized, brightly plumaged birds with large heads and strong, slightly hooked bills. Most species occur singly or in pairs unless migrating, when they form loose flocks. They are usually observed perched on some vantage point, such as a telegraph pole or wires, a dead branch or termite hill from which they scan the ground for large insects and lizards which form their diet.

LILAC-BREASTED ROLLER *Coracias caudata* **Plate 19**
Identification: 41cm (16in). The outer tail feathers of this roller are elongated into long streamers: above olive-brown; rump and wing coverts ultramarine blue; throat and breast rich lilac, remainder underparts greenish-blue. Species easily recognised by lilac chest and tail streamers. Immature duller and without long tail feathers.
Voice: A series of harsh chattering notes.
Distribution and Habitat: Common throughout East Africa in woodlands, open bush country, cultivation and even open plains if there are isolated trees or telegraph poles or wires on which it can perch.

RUFOUS-CROWNED ROLLER *Coracias naevia* **Plate 19**
Identification: 33cm (13in). This is a large, thickset roller which lacks tail

streamers; entire underparts rufous with white streaks; above olive grey, rufous on crown and a white patch on the nape; wings and tail deep purple-blue, conspicuous when the bird flies.
Voice: Calls less harsh than most other rollers, a querulous 'kaak, kaak'.
Distribution and Habitat: Locally common in Uganda and Kenya, southwards to northern Tanzania. It occurs in woodland bush country with scattered trees and in cultivation. Single birds are the rule, but small parties occur when food supply (grasshoppers, etc.) is unusually plentiful.

HOOPOES: Upupidae

The hoopoes are a small group of medium-sized birds of unmistakable appearance. Plumage boldly barred pinkish-rufous, white and black with a conspicuous crest of erectile feathers. Feeds largely on the ground; ant-lion larvae are an important item of diet.

AFRICAN HOOPOE *Upupa epops africana* **Plate 20**

Identification: 28cm (11in). This hoopoe has pinkish-rufous plumage with black and white barred wings and tail, except for primaries which are black, a long, rufous, black-tipped erectile crest and curved bill. Its rather butterfly-like flight is comparatively slow and undulating. European and Senegal Hoopoes have a white bar across the primaries.
Voice: A low 'hoo-poo, hoo-poo'.
Distribution and Habitat: Locally common in East Africa, frequenting bush country, acacia and brachystegia woodland, cultivation and gardens.
Allied Species: The European and Senegal races of Hoopoe (*U.e. epops* and *U.e. sengalensis*) 28cm (11in), may be distinguished by the white bar across the primaries. The European bird is a winter visitor and passage migrant; the Senegal race occurs in northern Uganda, western Kenya and north-eastern Tanzania.

WOOD HOOPOES: Phoeniculidae

The Wood Hoopoes are medium-sized, slender birds with green, blue or purple-glossed black plumage, often spotted white. Tails long and graduated; bills decurved. Arboreal in habits, gregarious; noisy birds keeping up a constant chatter.

GREEN WOOD HOOPOE *Phoeniculus purpureus* **Plate 20**

Identification: 38–41cm (15–16in). A slender black-looking bird, highly glossed green, with a long graduated tail and a curved red bill and red legs. A white bar across the wings and white tips to tail feathers except central pair. Immature has a dusky bill. Occurs in noisy family parties, climbing over the

tree trunks and branches in the manner of woodpeckers, exploring cracks in the bark for insect larvae and pupae.
Voice: A series of harsh chattering cries.
Distribution and Habitat: Locally common in East Africa. Inhabits various types of woodland, especially riverine acacias.

HORNBILLS: Bucerotidae

The Hornbills are a very distinct group of birds of medium or large size characterised by their large curved bills which often possess casque-like structures on the culmens. The family has remarkable breeding habits, the ♀ during incubation sealing up the nesting hole, leaving only a narrow slit through which she and the young are fed by the ♂.

RED-BILLED HORNBILL *Tockus erythrorhynchus* Plate 20

Identification: 43–46cm (17–18in). Above, this hornbill is brownish-black with a white stripe down the back; wing coverts spotted white; underparts white; bill rather slender and slightly decurved, red with a dusky patch at base of lower mandible. (Von der Decken's Hornbill ♂ has a heavier red bill with an ivory tip; the ♀ has a black bill; wing coverts not white spotted.)
Voice: A continuous 'wot, wot, wot, wot, wot, wot, wot'.
Distribution and Habitat: Locally common throughout East Africa in dry bush country, open acacia woodland and along rivers where there are trees.
Allied Species: Von der Decken's Hornbill (*Tockus deckeni*) 43–50cm (17–20in), differs from the Red-billed Hornbill in having the wings black without white spots; bill in bright red with terminal third ivory-white; smaller and bill enitrely black. Common in bush and acacia woodland in eastern half of Kenya and northern Tanzania.

YELLOW-BILLED HORNBILL *Tockus flavirostris* Plate 20

Identification: 43–50cm (17–20in). A medium-sized hornbill with white underparts, conspicuously white-spotted black wings and a deep banana-yellow bill. The combination of wing and bill characters render this species easy to identify.
Voice: A yelping, piping note, 'ke, ke, ke, ke, ke, ke', repeated over and over again.
Distribution and Habitat: Local resident from Ethiopia and Somalia, south through Kenya and north-eastern Uganda to northern Tanzania. The species reappears again in Central Africa, being uncommon in Zambia and Malawi, but more frequent southwards. It is essentially a dry bush country bird in East Africa, being locally common in eastern and northern Kenya. In Central Africa it occurs in dry acacia and mopane woodland.

BARBETS: Capitonidae

The Barbets are related to the Woodpeckers and like those birds have the first and fourth toes directed backwards; birds thickset with short, heavy bills; extremely variable plumage characters. Barbets are mainly fruit eaters, and are often numerous in fruiting fig and other fruit-bearing trees.

RED-FRONTED BARBET *Lybius diadematus* Plate 19

Identification: 13cm (5in). This species is blackish above with yellow streaks; frontal half of crown bright red; eye stripe pale yellow; underparts yellowish-white, more or less spotted brown.
Voice: Harsh, loud three- or four-note whistles, often run together.
Distribution and Habitat: A locally common species in Kenya, Uganda and the northern half of Tanzania. Inhabits bush country, open woodland and stands of acacias along rivers.

RED-FRONTED TINKERBIRD *Pogoniulus pusillus* Plate 19

Identification: 9cm ($3\frac{1}{2}$in). The upperparts of this barbet are blackish, heavily streaked pale yellow or white; rump lemon yellow; forehead bright scarlet: below pale yellowish buff. Red forehead conspicuous in field. The Red-fronted Barbet which often occurs alongside this species is a much larger bird.
Voice: A slow, shrill trill.
Distribution and Habitat: Locally common in Kenya, Uganda and northern half of Tanzania. Inhabits bush country and acacia woodland. Feeds largely on fruits of parasitic mistletoe (Loranthus).

GOLDEN-RUMPED TINKERBIRD
Pogoniulus bilineatus Plate 19

Identification: 10cm (4in). This species has glossy black upperparts with a golden-yellow rump; white stripe above and below eye; black moustache stripe; underparts pale grey, greenish-yellow on belly.
Voice: A monotonous 'tink' uttered again and again with a few seconds interval between notes.
Distribution and Habitat: Common locally in forests of Uganda, Kenya and Tanzania. Occurs also in coastal woodland and scrub.

D'ARNAUD'S BARBET *Trachyphonus darnaudii* Plate 19

Identification: 15cm (6in). A barbet having brown upperparts with whitish spots on back, wings and tail; crown black spotted with yellow; sides of face yellow, spotted black; below pale yellow spotted with black on throat and breast. Some races have crown black and black on throat and chest.
Voice: Birds call in duet, two or more facing one another, tail cocked over the back and wagged from side to side, and uttering a loud four-note song 'doo, do, dee, dok' over and over again.

Distribution and Habitat: Locally common in Kenya and Uganda, southwards to south-western Tanzania. Inhabits dry bush country and open acacia woodland.

RED AND YELLOW BARBET
Trachyphonus erythrocephalus **Plate 19**

Identification: 23cm (9in). Another brightly plumaged 'ground barbet'. A striking pale yellow and red bird with upperparts, wings and tail heavily spotted with round white spots. Underparts bright pale yellow, washed with orange on chest; ♂ has a black stripe down centre of throat. Often seen perched on termite hills – a favoured nesting site.
Voice: A loud and unmistakable 'toogel-de-doogle' repeated many times, often by several birds in chorus.
Distribution and Habitat: A common species throughout Kenya south to north-eastern Tanzania. Frequents semi-arid bush country and open thorn-bush areas; favours localities where there are termite hills.

WOODPECKERS: Picidae

This is a family of chisel-billed, wood-boring birds with powerful feet (two toes directed backwards, two forwards) and stiff tails which act as supports in climbing tree trunks and branches: flight undulating. Woodpeckers nest in holes which they excavate in trees.

NUBIAN WOODPECKER *Campethera nubica* **Plate 20**

Identification: 18cm (7in). This woodpecker has greyish-olive upperparts which are spotted and indistinctly banded yellowish; crown and nape scarlet, ♀ with crown black with white spots; below creamy-white with round black spots on breast and flanks; shafts of tail feathers yellowish. The red nape and golden tail are conspicuous in the field: the distinctive round black spots on the breast are to be seen only with glasses when bird is settled.
Voice: A far-carrying 'cing, cing, cing, cing', almost a metallic, yaffling call, difficult to describe but not forgotten when once heard.
Distribution and Habitat: Common locally in Kenya, Uganda and the northern half of Tanzania. Frequents open bush, wooded savannah and acacia woodland.

LARKS: Alaudidae

A group of ground-loving song birds: often gregarious in non-breeding season. Hind claw often elongated and more or less straight. Build usually heavier and bills more robust than pipits and wagtails which are also terrestrial in their habits.

RUFOUS-NAPED LARK *Mirafra africana* **Plate 21**
Identification: 15–18cm (6–7in). A heavy, thickset lark. Rufous or greyish-brown above with black centres to feathers; nape more or less rufous; wings mainly rufous, conspicuous in flight; below rufous-buff with black streaking on chest; tail relatively short. Often perches on small bushes.
Voice: A clear whistle of four or five notes, 'cee-wee-wee, chee, wee' repeated several times.
Distribution and Habitat: Locally common throughout East Africa on open plains and grassy bush country.

FISCHER'S SPARROW LARK *Eremopterix leucopareia* **Plate 21**
Identification: 11cm (4½in). The gregarious sparrow larks are characterised by their heavy finch-like bills and blackish patch on the belly. Crown rufous edged dark brown; cheeks whitish; upperparts greyish-brown; below, throat and broad stripe down centre of belly blackish-brown, flanks buffish-brown.
Voice: A low 'tweet-ees' flock call. A brief warbling song when nesting, uttered from the ground.
Distribution and Habitat: Locally common in Kenya and Tanzania on short grass plains, open bush country and semi-desert.

SWALLOWS and MARTINS: Hirundinidae

Swallows and Martins are a well-marked group of birds which capture their insect food on the wing. They bear a superficial resemblance to swifts, but wing outline differs in being less slender and scythe-like. Their build is slim and their flight graceful, less direct and rapid than swifts. Many species possess long and slender outer tail feathers: feet very small; bill short with wide gape.

WIRE-TAILED SWALLOW *Hirundo smithii* **Plate 21**
Identification: 15cm (6in). The outer tail feathers of this swallow are long and wire thin; above glossy purplish-black with a rufous crown; below white. Easily distinguished by its chestnut crown and very slender tail streamers.
Voice: A soft twittering warble.
Distribution and Habitat: Locally common throughout East Africa. Normally occurs in pairs. Found near water and often associated with human habitations and bridges.

RED-RUMPED SWALLOW *Hirundo daurica* **Plate 21**
Identification: 18cm (7in). With long outer tail feathers, like the other swallows, this species has a glossy bluish-black crown and back with a rufous rump and rufous underparts; undertail coverts black.
Voice: Variable twittering notes.
Distribution and Habitat: Locally common throughout East Africa, frequent-

ing open country, the vicinity of lakes and rivers and cultivation. Often nests on buildings.

STRIPED SWALLOW *Hirundo abyssinica* **Plate 21**
Identification: 18cm (7in). This swallow is easily recognised by its black streaked underparts and its chestnut crown and rump; outer tail feathers thin and elongated.
Voice: Squeaky metallic notes, not unlike a violin being tuned; also a brief warbling song.
Distribution and Habitat: Common resident and local migrant throughout East Africa. May be encountered anywhere outside forest areas and often associated with human habitations and bridges.

WAGTAILS and PIPITS: Motacillidae

These are graceful, slender, terrestrial birds which run and walk. Pipits are generally brown above, usually streaked; like larks but more slender with thinner bills and more upright stance. Wagtails have long tails and strongly marked patterns.

AFRICAN PIED WAGTAIL *Motacilla aguimp* **Plate 21**
Identification: 20cm (8in). A black and white wagtail associated with human habitations. Above black with a white band over eye and a white patch on each side of the neck; below white with a black breast band; white stripe along side of wing.
Voice: Typical wagtail 'tssssp'; song not unlike that of a canary.
Distribution and Habitat: Common throughout East Africa and associated with human dwellings; also occurs along rivers and streams; very tame and confiding.

GOLDEN PIPIT *Tmetothylacus tenellus* **Plate 21**
Identification: 15cm (6in). This bird is a slightly mottled olive-green above, bright yellow with a black chest band below; wings and tail bright canary yellow. When perched it appears yellowish-green with no conspicuous field character, but immediately it flies its appearance changes and it looks as brightly yellow as a canary. ♀ duller. The Golden Pipit is remarkable among passerine birds in having the lower third of the tibia bare, as if it were a wading bird, in spite of the fact that it inhabits arid bush country.
Voice: A series of weak whistles.
Distribution and Habitat: Locally common in Kenya and north-eastern Tanzania. Inhabits dry bush country. It is fairly common in parts of Tsavo National Park, Kenya.

YELLOW-THROATED LONGCLAW

Macronyx croceus **Plate 21**

Identification: 20cm (8in). The Longclaws are a group of robust pipits with yellow or red on the underparts. This species has the underparts bright yellow with a black chest band; above streaky brown.
Voice: A rather drawn-out whistle 'tuewhee' uttered over and over again.
Distribution and Habitat: Locally common throughout East Africa in open woodland, grassy areas where there are bushes and in cultivation.

BULBULS: Pycnonotidae

A group of somewhat thrush-like birds of plain green, yellow, grey and brown plumage; tarsus short; arboreal in habits and most species are inhabitants of forest and woodland; food mainly fruits but with some insects; many are outstanding songsters.

YELLOW-VENTED BULBUL *Pycnonotus barbatus* **Plate 21**

Identification: 18cm (7in). A common garden bird through most of East Africa. Above greyish-brown, darker on head and chin, merging to pale brown on chest; belly white; undertail coverts pale yellow; head slightly crested. Yellow undertail coverts conspicuous. Upon alighting this bird has a habit of half raising its wings and uttering a brief warble.
Voice: A rapid, brief song 'too, dede, de, che, che' and a scolding alarm call.
Distribution and Habitat: A very common bird throughout East Africa. Occurs as a garden bird, in old cultivation, woodland, coastal scrub, open forest and in secondary growth especially Lantana thickets.

SHRIKES: Laniidae

Shrikes are conspicuously coloured, medium-sized birds with strong, hooked bills. Some perch on vantage points from which they can pounce on their prey; others, more skulking, feed among foliage of trees or bushes. Call-notes usually harsh but songs sometimes surprisingly musical.

WHITE-CROWNED SHRIKE *Eurocephalus rueppelli* **Plate 22**

Identification: 23cm (9in). This shrike has a dusky brown back with a contrasting white crown and rump; below white with a brown patch on each side of the breast. Immature has crown brown and back barred. Occurs in pairs or small family parties. Field appearance distinctive, white crown and rump conspicuous; flies with a stiff gliding flight with wings held rigid.
Voice: A harsh 'kaa, kaa, kaa' and various other whistling and chattering calls.
Distribution and Habitat: Locally common throughout East Africa in bush country, acacia woodland and dry thornbush areas.

BLACK-HEADED TCHAGRA *Tchagra senegala* **Plate 22**
Identification: 20cm (8in). A brownish bush shrike with chestnut-red wings, a black crown and a buffy-white eye-stripe; tail dark with white tips. Usually seen as it dives for cover into a bush, when red wings and white-tipped tail are noticeable.
Voice: A series of clear piping whistles and a churring alarm call.
Distribution and Habitat: Common throughout East Africa; inhabits semi-desert scrub, bush, wooded areas, gardens, neglected cultivation and undergrowth and bush along rivers.

TROPICAL BOUBOU *Laniarius aethiopicus* **Plate 22**
Identification: 23cm (9in). The upperparts, wings and tail of this bird are glossy black, with or without a white wing bar; below pinkish-white. Immature barred tawny on upperparts. Boubous are found in pairs. Their clear bell-like whistles draw attention to them.
Voice: Varied and remarkable duet between ♂ and ♀; one utters three rapid, clear bell-like whistles, answered immediately with a croaking 'kweee'. This second cry is uttered so instantaneously that the whole call appears to be made by one bird. The notes vary and different localities seem to have their own local variety of whistles and croaks. Birds also make a harsh churring call.
Distribution and Habitat: Common throughout East Africa, inhabiting thick cover in forests, woodland, riverine thickets, gardens, bush and coastal scrub. Sometimes feeds on the ground in dense cover. Well known in gardens in towns, where it has the popular name of 'bell-bird'.

BLACK-HEADED GONOLEK *Laniarius erythrogaster* **Plate 22**
Identification: 20cm (8in). The upperparts of this beautiful and unmistakable bird are jet black; underparts bright crimson-red; undertail coverts buff. Immature barred buff and black below. It has a rather skulking habit and normally keeps to dense bush cover.
Voice: A clear, two-note whistle 'wee-oooo', frequently repeated; also a harsher rasping call.
Distribution and Habitat: Locally not uncommon in Uganda, western Kenya and northern Tanzania. Occurs in bush country, often near water, thick tangled vegetation and neglected cultivation. It is a common bird around Kisumu, Kenya and Entebbe, Uganda, where it is a conspicuous species in gardens.

SLATE-COLOURED BOUBOU *Laniarius funebris* **Plate 22**
Identification: 18cm (7in). In the field this appears to be a completely black bird. Its entire plumage is dark slate shading to blackish on the head, wings and tail. Immature has indistinct tawny barring on upperparts. It is a skulker, keeping to thick cover, and best located by its call notes. Normally in pairs.

Voice: ♂ and ♀ duet, 'kok-oh-wee, kwik kwik'. Also various other whistles and churring notes and a harsh 'krrrr' alarm call.
Distribution and Habitat: A widespread resident throughout East Africa, normally below 1,524m (5,000ft). Inhabits dry bush country, keeping to thickets and stands of Salvadora bushes; also found in coastal scrub and woodland where thick cover exists.

FISCAL SHRIKE *Lanius collaris* **Plate 22**

Identification: 23cm (9in). This shrike is black above with a white V-shaped patch on back; below white; tail long and graduated, black broadly tipped white. Immature barred black and tawny above, lightly barred below. One of the commonest and best-known of East African birds, it frequently perches on telegraph wires.
Voice: A rather sharp, drawn-out 'cheeeee'; alarm call a clear whistle.
Distribution and Habitat: A widespread but local resident, often common. Inhabits cultivated areas, the vicinity of human habitations and lightly wooded country.
Allied Species: The Long-tailed Fiscal (*Lanius cabanisi*) 30cm (12in), has upperparts black merging to grey on lower back; tail very long, black. Common in many parts of central and eastern Kenya and eastern Tanzania. Inhabits bushy areas and coastal scrub. The Grey-backed Fiscal (*Lanius excubitorius*) 25cm (10in), has upperparts and crown pale grey; forehead and eye streak black; tail white with broad black tip. Locally common in Uganda, western Kenya and Rift Valley, south to central and western Tanzania. Frequents bush and acacia woodland.

THRUSHES AND ALLIES: Turdidae

A group of rather long-legged birds of upright stance: eyes inclined to be large and bills usually pointed and slender; juvenile plumages spotted. Many species spend much time on the ground and feed largely upon insects. Many are outstanding songsters.

STONECHAT *Saxicola torquata* **Plate 22**

Identification: 13cm (5in). The Stonechats resident in Africa are races of the well known British bird. ♂ has distinctive black head and throat, a white half collar, a white rump and a small white wing patch; a patch of deep chestnut on chest. ♀ tawny with small white wing patch; cinnamon below. Immature mottled buff above. This bird's flight is jerky, it perches on tops of bushes, fences and on telegraph wires.
Voice: A scolding 'tsk, tsk, tsk' and a softer clicking note; song a rapid warble.
Distribution and Habitat: Local, but often common, in areas above 914m (3,000ft) in Uganda, Kenya and Tanzania, the Stonechat frequents mountain

moorlands, cultivated areas, scattered bush in grassland and lush marshy country.

CAPPED WHEATEAR *Oenanthe pileata* **Plate 22**
Identification: 18cm (7in). Upperparts dark russet-brown with white rump; crown, sides of neck and ear-coverts black; forehead and stripe over eye white; underparts white with a broad black band across chest; flanks rufous. Immature has buff-spotted upperparts. Upright stance more marked than in most wheatears; broad black breast-band best field character.
Voice: One of the best African bird mimics, imitating the calls and songs of many other species of birds and other sounds. It has its own brief warbling song which is frequently repeated, and which is often uttered during display flight.
Distribution and Habitat: Widely distributed in Kenya, eastern Uganda and Tanzania. In some areas a partial migrant, it frequents open country from alpine moorlands and short-cropped grasslands to coastal flats. It is most attracted to grasslands which have been burned.

ANTEATER CHAT *Myrmecocichla aethiops* **Plate 22**
Identification: 20cm (8in). A thickset blackish-brown bird having something of the appearance of a starling, with a dull whitish patch in the wings, formed by the white bases of the flight feathers and seen only when the bird is flying. Often common at roadsides; tame and confiding.
Voice: Various piping and whistling calls and an attractive whistling song. Some birds are mimics of other birds' calls.
Distribution and Habitat: A local resident, sometimes common, in western and central Kenya and northern Tanzania. Numerous in the highlands and Rift Valley of Kenya. Inhabits open country with scattered bush and trees, also open acacia woodlands.

SPOTTED MORNING WARBLER *Cichladusa guttata* **Plate 23**
Identification: 16.5cm (6½in). A lightly built thrush-like bird, dull rufous-brown with a conspicuous cinnamon-red tail; below buff-white heavily spotted with black – shy and skulking, disappearing into thick cover when disturbed, when its red tail suggests a robin-chat.
Voice: An extremely variable, clear whistling song: the most vocal of birds in early morning and at dusk; also mimics the calls and songs of other birds. Alarm notes harsh and scolding.
Distribution and Habitat: Locally common in Uganda, Kenya to central Tanzania. Inhabits dry bush country, especially Salvadora thickets along dry river beds, palm scrub and dense coastal bush. It is a common bird of the semi-desert areas of northern Kenya.

WHITE-STARRED BUSH ROBIN *Pogonocichla stellata* **Plate 23**

Identification: 15cm (6in). A robin-like forest bird, brilliantly golden-yellow below with a slate-blue head and an olive-green mantle; a small white spot in front of each eye and a silvery white spot bordered with black at the base of the throat; tail yellow and black. Juvenile olive green, spotted dull yellow; immature green above with a few yellow spots, below pale mottled green. In East Africa it is typically a bird of bamboo forest. It often perches on the ground to feed on ants: much in evidence when safari ants are present.

Voice: A rather harsh 'tssst' or 'tsssp' and a two-note call. Song a high pitched flute-like warble.

Distribution and Habitat: A locally common resident in East Africa, in forest areas, often favouring bamboo and mixed bamboo and mountain forest.

ROBIN CHAT *Cossypha caffra* **Plate 23**

Identification: 16.5cm ($6\frac{1}{2}$in). A rather small robin chat with the habits of an English robin: often seen in gardens. Has well-marked white eye-stripe; may be recognised by orange-rufous throat and chest and contrasting grey belly. Immature spotted on back and chest. The White-browed Robin Chat has underparts entirely rufous. Usually shy and retiring, but becomes tame and confiding in gardens where it is protected. Feeds largely on ground, where it progresses by hopping, frequently raising and lowering the tail.

Voice: An outstanding warbling song; also a mimic of other birds' calls and songs.

Distribution and Habitat: Common in East Africa, inhabiting forests, woodland and scrub areas, thickets and gardens.

WHITE-BROWED ROBIN CHAT *Cossypha heuglini* **Plate 23**

Identification: 20cm (8in). Thrush-like but with relatively longer tail. Above olive-grey; crown and sides of face black with white eye-stripe; below orange-rufous; tail rufous except the central pair of feathers which are olive-brown. Immature spotted and mottled tawny-buff. A bird of thick undergrowth, feeding mainly on the ground; usually shy; occurs in gardens.

Voice: A loud purring 'pip, ir, eee'; song a series of sustained flute-like whistles of great beauty; sings especially at dusk and at dawn. Singing birds difficult to locate, may be ventriloquial. Often mimics other birds' calls, such as Red-chested and Black Cuckoos.

Distribution and Habitat: A locally common species over much of East Africa. Inhabits forests, woodlands where there is thick undergrowth, wooded gardens, scrub and dense coastal bush.

OLIVE THRUSH *Turdus olivaceus* **Plate 23**

Identification: 23cm (9in). Upperparts dark olive-brown, paler on throat and breast with dusky streaks on throat; belly bright rufous; bill and feet orange. Immature has black spotted underparts.

Voice: Typical thrush-type scolding call-notes and a loud warbling song.

Distribution and Habitat: Locally common throughout East Africa, inhabiting forests, well wooded areas, dense scrub, cultivation and gardens. A very common garden bird in the Kenya highlands.

BABBLERS and CHATTERERS: Turdoididae

A group of thrush-like and thrush-sized birds which occur in noisy parties in bush and acacia country. They have scaly legs and rounded wings: plumage usually dull grey, brown or rufous.

RUFOUS CHATTERER *Turdoides rubiginosus* **Plate 23**

Identification: 20cm (8in). A gregarious bird seen in small parties in thick undergrowth and thorn thickets; sandy-rufous in colour, slightly darker and browner on upperparts; eye creamy yellow, bill yellow. Draws attention by its noisy chattering.
Voice: A variety of chattering and bubbling calls and a plaintive whistle not unlike that of the Blue-naped Mousebird.
Distribution and Habitat: Locally common in eastern Uganda, Kenya to Tanzania. Frequents thick bush and tangled cover in arid and semi-arid areas; frequent in coastal bush in Kenya and Tanzania.

WARBLERS: Sylviidae

A large family of small, active insectivorous birds of generally slim build: related to thrushes and flycatchers but with slender bills and juvenile plumages unspotted. Many species, especially among the 'leaf warblers', *Phylloscopus*, and the Cisticolas lack distinctive markings and may appear confusingly alike. Voice, behaviour, habitat and distribution are important in their identification.

HUNTER'S CISTICOLA *Cisticola hunteri* **Plate 23**

Identification: 14cm (5½in). A dark-looking Cisticola, found in highland areas over 1,828m (6,000ft), which draws attention by its habit of singing in duets and trios. Two, three or more birds will form a group and start singing together. Above dark brown, slightly russet on the head, with ill-defined streaking; below grey, paler on the throat.
Voice: Sings in duet, a loud, clear, babbling warbling.
Distribution and Habitat: Found commonly in localities over 1,828m (6,000ft), in the Kenya highlands, on Mount Elgon in eastern Uganda and in northern Tanzania. Inhabits scrub and bush, often along forest margins. Occurs up to at least 3,962m (13,000ft).

RATTLING CISTICOLA *Cisticola chiniana* **Plate 23**

Identification: 13cm (5in). A characteristic bird of thornbush and acacia woodland, this species' mantle is streaked, dusky on brown or greyish-brown; crown rusty-brown, with indistinct streaking. It draws attention by its scolding call-notes.

Voice: A loud scolding 'chaaaaa – chaaaaa'.

Distribution and Habitat: Common over much of East Africa, a typical bird of acacia thickets and woodland; further south, in Tanzania, occurs in Brachystegia and open woodland.

TAWNY-FLANKED PRINIA *Prinia subflava* **Plate 23**

Identification: 13cm (5in). A uniform tawny-brown warbler with a long graduated tail and a white eye-stripe. Its actions are jerky, settling on grasses and bushes, frequently raising and lowering tail.

Voice: A loud churring 'chee, cheer' often repeated, and a brief piping song.

Distribution and Habitat: Common throughout East Africa, frequenting rank grass and other herbage, scrub along streams, edges of forest, regenerating bush in neglected cultivation, forest plantations and gardens.

BLACK-BREASTED APALIS *Apalis flavida* **Plate 23**

Identification: 11.5cm (4½in). The widely accepted name 'black-breasted' is unfortunate as species only has a small black patch in centre of chest and often in the ♀ even this is lacking. Upperparts green, merging to grey on forehead; below white with a wide greenish-yellow band across chest with a black patch or spot in centre; tail long and slender, green with yellow tips to outer feathers. Feeds among foliage of trees some distance above the ground.

Voice: A two-note soft churr and a brief warbling song.

Distribution and Habitat: Widely distributed and common in many places in East Africa. Frequents a variety of habitats from forest and woodland to thorn scrub and riverine acacias.

GREY-BACKED CAMAROPTERA
Camaroptera brevicaudata **Plate 23**

Identification: 10cm (4in). A rather short-tailed warbler with head, mantle and underparts grey, contrasting with green-edged wings and tail. A skulking bird inhabiting thick cover.

Voice: A drawn-out, bleating call 'squeeee', frequently repeated, which draws attention to the bird in spite of its skulking habits.

Distribution and Habitat: Common and widespread; inhabits thick undergrowth, bush and thickets from mountain forest to arid acacia scrub.

CROMBEC *Sylvietta brachyura* **Plate 23**

Identification: 8cm (3½in). Plump little warbler with an extremely short tail; silvery-grey above with a pale eye-stripe; dusky streak through eye; rufous below merging to white on throat and abdomen. Usually seen in pairs,

continued on p. 304

Plate 14 GREBE, PELICANS, CORMORANTS and DARTER

1 White Pelican page 236

1a 152–180cm (60–70in). Plumage white or pinkish-white;
1b adult from below.

2 Pink-backed Pelican 237

Smaller than White Pelican, 127–137cm (50–54in); plumage pale grey with pink rump; drooping crest.

3 African Darter 238

96cm (38in). Long pointed bill, not hooked at tip; conspicuous white neck stripe. Immature much paler and lacks white neck stripe.

4 White-necked Cormorant 237

4a Larger than Long-tailed Cormorant, 91cm (36in), with relatively short tail; fore-neck white;
4b immature white below.

5 Long-tailed Cormorant 237

Relatively small, 56–61cm (22–24in); plumage all black with long tail. Immature whitish below.

6 Little Grebe 236

6a Small, 25cm (10in); chestnut face and throat;
6b immature paler and lacks chestnut.

1b
2
1a
5
3
4b
4a
6b
6a

Plate 15 HERONS, HAMERKOP, STORKS and allies, FLAMINGOS and GEESE

1 Hamerkop page 240
56–61cm (22–24in). Plumage dark brown; crest characteristic, thick and blunt.

2 Sacred Ibis 241
76cm (30in). Naked black head and neck. Immature has head and neck feathered, mottled black and white.

3 Hadada Ibis 241
76cm (30in). Plumage grey with metallic green wash on wings and coverts. Distinctive 'ah ah ah' call.

4 Yellow-billed Stork 241
107cm (42in). Plumage bright pinkish-white with black wings and tail; face bare, bright red; bill yellow. Immature greyish.

5 African Spoonbill 241
91cm (36in). Spatulate bill; bare face and legs red. Immature similar but face and legs pinkish-grey.

6 Greater Flamingo 242
Large, 142cm (56in); bill pink with black tip; plumage white with slight pink flush and contrasting red wing coverts. Immature greyish-white with pale grey bill.

7 Lesser Flamingo 242
Smaller than Greater Flamingo, 101cm (40in); bill deep carmine-red; plumage deep pink all over. Immature brownish-grey with pinkish-grey bill.

8 Egyptian Goose 242
61cm (24in). Contrasting white shoulders, very conspicuous in flight. Immature similar to adult but duller.

9 Marabou Stork 240
Very large, 152cm (60in); heavy bill; neck pouch conspicuous when inflated.

10 Goliath Heron 239
Very large, 140–152cm (55–60in); rufous neck. Immature paler and sandier, whitish below.

11 Black-headed Heron 239
96cm (38in). Black crown and hind-neck.

12 Cattle Egret 238
51cm (20in). White with orange-buff crown, chest and dorsal plumes; bill and feet yellowish or flesh-coloured. Non-breeding and immature birds all white.

1
2
3
4
5
6
7
8
9
10
11
12

Plate 16 BIRDS OF PREY

1 Tawny Eagle page 245
66–76cm (26–30in). Uniform brown plumage, variable from pale brownish-cream to blackish brown; legs feathered.

2 Black-shouldered Kite 246
33cm (13in). Slightly forked tail; black shoulders; white underparts and tail. Immature with brownish wash on breast.

3 Fish Eagle 246
76cm (30in). White head, mantle, chest and tail. Immature brown with black streaked breast; some black on tail.

4 Augur Buzzard 245
4a,b 50–57cm (20–24in). Underparts variable, black, white with black neck or all white; chequered black and white wing patch in all plumages; tail rufous.
4c Immature, tail barred; below normally white with heavy dark streaks.
4d Adult in flight from below.

5 Bateleur 244
5a 61cm (24in). Very short chestnut tail. Immature uniform brown.
5b In flight from below.

6 Black Kite 246
53–58cm (21–23in). Forked tail; yellow bill.

7 Pale Chanting Goshawk 244
48cm (19in). Grey with white rump; cere yellow; legs orange-red. Immature greyish-brown, streaked on chest, barred on belly.

8 Long-crested Eagle 245
51–56cm (20–22in). Distinctive long crest; white wing patch conspicuous in flight from below.

9 White-backed Vulture 243
9a 81cm (32in). Wings, back and underparts uniform brown, not spotted; rump white. Immature lacks white rump and is streaky on underparts.
9b In flight from below white band along fore edge of wing.

10 Secretary Bird 243
101cm (40in). Mainly terrestrial; long central tail feathers; lax crest; black tibia.

1
2
3
4a
4b
4c
4d
5a
5b
6
7
8
9a
9b
10

Plate 17 GAME BIRDS, CRANE, CRAKE, COOT, BUSTARD, JACANA, PLOVERS and GULL

1 **Red-knobbed Coot** page 248
40cm (16in). Uniform blackish-grey; white bill and frontal shield with two dark red knobs.

2 **Black Crake** 248
20cm (8in). Uniform slate-black; bill yellow-green; legs pink. Immature brownish; bill and legs dull brown.

3 **Grey-headed Gull** 251
40cm (16in). Occurs mainly on inland waters. Pale grey and white gull with pale grey head. Non-breeding birds have white head. Immature mottled brownish on mantle.

4 **African Jacana** or **Lily-trotter** 250
23–28cm (9–11in). Bright chestnut plumage; bluish-white bill and frontal shield; very long toes. Immature paler and duller. Inhabits floating aquatic vegetation.

5 **Black-winged Stilt** 250
38cm (15in). Very long pink legs; plumage black and white; straight bill. Immature largely black and grey.

6 **Blacksmith Plover** 250
28cm (11in). White crown; black patch on back.

7 **Crowned Plover** 250
28cm (11in). White ring on crown; bill red with black tip; legs red.

8 **Crowned Crane** 248
100cm (40in). Straw-coloured upright crest and velvety black forehead; white and red face wattles.

9 **Crested Francolin** 246
25–28cm (10–11in). Chestnut neck spots; white streaks on upperparts; carries tail cocked up.

10 **Yellow-necked Spurfowl** 247
33–36cm (13–14in). Bare yellow throat.

11 **Kori Bustard** 249
Large, 76–101cm (30–40in); neck appears thick with lax feathers; hind-neck grey, no reddish-brown patch.

12 **Vulturine Guinea-fowl** 247
58–61cm (23–24in). Upper mantle and chest feathers long, striped black, white and blue; belly cobalt blue.

13 **Helmeted Guinea-fowl** 247
51–56cm (20–22in). Conspicuous bony helmet.

1
2
3
4
5
6
7
8
9
10
11
12
13

Plate 18 SANDGROUSE, PIGEONS and DOVES and TURACOS

1 **Black-faced Sandgrouse** page 252
1a 25cm (10in). Broad white band across chest;
1b black face pattern in ♂.

2 **Chestnut-bellied Sandgrouse** 251
2a,b 30cm (12in). Long pointed central tail feathers.

3 **Namaqua Dove** 253
3a Smallest African dove, 20cm (8in); long tail;
3b ♀ lacks black face and throat.

4 **Red-eyed Dove** 252
30cm (12in). Black collar on hind-neck; deep vinous-pink underparts.

5 **Mourning Dove** 253
27cm (10½in). Similar to Ring-necked Dove but paler and with pinkish-white eye.

6 **Ring-necked Dove** 253
25cm (10in). Black collar on hind-neck; pale grey and white underparts; eye blackish-brown.

7 **Laughing Dove** 253
24cm (9½in). No black collar on hind-neck; fore-neck mottled black.

8 **Hartlaub's Turaco** 254
41cm (16in). Crown bluish-black with white patch above and in front of eye.

9 **Schalow's Turaco** 253
41cm (16in). Long attenuated white-tipped crest.

10 **White-bellied Go-away-bird** 254
51cm (20in). Long crest and tail; white belly.

11 **Speckled Pigeon** 252
38cm (15in). Vinous-chestnut back, white spotted wings and pale grey rump.

♀ 1a
1b ♂
2a ♀
♂ 2b
3a
♂
3b
♀
4
5
6
7
8
9
10
11

Plate 19 CUCKOOS, MOUSEBIRDS, ROLLERS, BEE-EATER and BARBETS

1 **Red-chested Cuckoo** page 255
30cm (12in). Distinct rufous throat; characteristic call of three notes, 'wip, wip, weeoo'. Immature dark with blackish throat.

2 **White-browed Coucal** 255
40cm (16in). Clumsy-looking with floundering flight; chestnut wings and whitish eye-stripe.

3 **Lilac-breasted Roller** 258
41cm (16in). Long tail streamers; throat and breast rich lilac. Immature duller and without long tail streamers.

4 **Rufous-crowned Roller** 258
33cm (13in). No tail streamers; underparts rufous with white streaks; white nape patch.

5 **D'Arnaud's Barbet** 261
15cm (6in). Indistinctly spotted on upperparts. Some races have black crowns.

6 **Red and Yellow Barbet** 262
23cm (9in). Back with conspicuous round white spots; ♀ lacks black throat streak.

7 **Red-fronted Barbet** 261
13cm (5in). Red forehead; yellowish-white eye-stripe.

8 **Blue-naped Mousebird** 256
36cm (14in). Gregarious; long slender tail; blue patch on nape.

9 **Speckled Mousebird** 256
36cm (14in). Gregarious; long thick tail; crested; speckled chest.

10 **Red-fronted Tinkerbird** 261
Very small, 9cm ($3\frac{1}{2}$in); forehead bright red.

11 **Golden-rumped Tinkerbird** 261
10cm (4in). Conspicuous white head streaks; black above; golden-yellow rump.

12 **Little Bee-eater** 258
Small size, 15cm (6in); square tail; yellow throat. See text.

1
2
3
4
5
6
7
8
9
10
11
12

Plate 20 OWL, KINGFISHERS, HOOPOE, WOOD HOOPOE, HORNBILLS and WOODPECKER

1 Malachite Kingfisher page 257
13cm (5in). Conspicuous blue and black barred crest.

2 African Hoopoe 259
2a,b 28cm (11in). Long erectile crest; primaries black without white bar.

3 Green Wood Hoopoe 259
38–41cm (15–16in). Plumage glossed green; white spots on wings and tail; bill and feet red.

4 Pied Kingfisher 257
25cm (10in). Plumage black and white; head crested.

5 Grey-headed Kingfisher 257
20cm (8in). Belly deep chestnut-red.

6 Nubian Woodpecker 262
6a 23cm (9in). Red nape and golden-yellow tail shafts; round black spots on breast.
6b ♀ has white spotted forehead.

7 Pearl-spotted Owlet 255
20cm (8in). No ear tufts; relatively long, white-spotted tail.

8 Yellow-billed Hornbill 260
43–50cm (17–20in). Bill banana yellow; white spots on wing coverts; white bars on tail.

9 Red-billed Hornbill 260
43–46cm (17–18in). Bill red; white spots on wing coverts.

1
2a
2b
3
4
5
6b
♀
♂ 6a
7
8
9

Plate 21 SWIFT, LARKS, SWALLOWS, WAGTAIL and PIPIT and BULBUL

1 **Little Swift** page 256
13cm (5in). Conspicuous white rump; square tail.

2 **Red-rumped Swallow** 263
18cm (7in). Rufous underparts and rump; black under tail-coverts.

3 **Striped Swallow** 264
18cm (7in). Streaked underparts; rufous cap and rump.

4 **Wire-tailed Swallow** 263
15cm (6in). Very slender long outer tail feathers; rufous cap; white underparts.

5 **Yellow-vented Bulbul** 265
18cm (7in). Dark head; yellow under tail-coverts.

6 **Rufous-naped Lark** 263
15–18cm (6–7in). Conspicuous rounded rufous wings in flight; relatively short tail.

7 **Fischer's Sparrow Lark** 263
7a 11cm (4½in). Gregarious; small stumpy lark with heavy bill; crown tinged rufous;
7b black face mask in ♂.

8 **Golden Pipit** 264
8a 15cm (6in). In flight wings conspicuously bright canary-yellow; black chest band.
8b ♀ much duller.

9 **African Pied Wagtail** 264
20cm (8in). Plumage black and white; long tail and black breast-band.

10 **Yellow-throated Longclaw** 265
20cm (8in). Large robust pipit with yellow underparts and black chest band; often perches on bushes.

1
2
3
4
5
6
♀ 7a
♂ 7b
♀
8b
♂
8a
9
10

Plate 22 SHRIKES, THRUSHES and allies

1 White-crowned Shrike page 265
23cm (9in). Contrasting brown mantle and white crown and rump.

2 Capped Wheatear 268
18cm (7in). White rump; black chest band. Immature has buff-spotted upperparts and chest.

3 Anteater Chat 268
3a,b 20cm (8in). Blackish, starling-like bird, often seen along roads; whitish wing patch conspicuous in flight.

4 Black-headed Gonolek 266
20cm (8in). Brilliant red underparts and black upperparts. Immature barred black and buff below.

5 Stonechat 267
5a 13cm (5in). Conspicuous white neck, wing and rump patches; no eye-stripe. Immature mottled buff on upperparts and chest.
5b ♀ browner and duller.

6 Fiscal Shrike 267
23cm (9in). White V on back. Immature pale brown, lightly barred below.

7 Black-headed Tchagra 266
20cm (8in). Chestnut-red wings and black crown; conspicuous whitish eye-stripe.

8 Slate-coloured Boubou 266
18cm (7in). Plumage entirely slate-black; distinctive call, see text; skulker. Immature indistinctly barred above.

9 Tropical Boubou 266
23cm (9in). Pinkish-white underparts; usually in pairs; distinctive calls, see text. Immature barred tawny on upperparts.

1
2
3a
3b
4
5a
5b
♀
♂
6
7
8
9

Plate 23 THRUSHES and allies, BABBLERS and WARBLERS

1
2
3
4
5
6
7
8
9
10
11
12

Plate 24 FLYCATCHERS, TIT, WHITE-EYE, FINCHES and BUNTING

1 Paradise Flycatcher page 305
1a,b ♂ 30–36cm (12–14in); ♀ 20cm (8in). Long tail, shorter in ♀ and immature; black head and chestnut back.
1c In some areas ♂ has white phase.

2 Chin-spot Puff-back 305
2a 11cm (4½in). ♂ black chest band;
2b ♀ chestnut chest band and patch on throat.

3 Silverbird 304
20cm (8in). Grey back, wings and tail; rufous underparts.

4 Blue Flycatcher 305
14cm (5½in). Above caerulean-blue, paler below; very active, constantly fans tail.

5 Kikuyu White-eye 310
13cm (5in). Large white eye-ring; broad yellow forehead.

6 White-eyed Slaty Flycatcher 304
16.5cm (6½in). Grey plumage; large white eye-ring.

7 Yellow-rumped Seedeater 311
10cm (4in). Normally in small flocks; distinct yellow rump.

8 Streaky Seedeater 311
15cm (6in). Whitish eye-stripe; rump same colour as remainder of upperparts.

9 Brimstone Canary 311
15cm (6in). A rather stocky canary with a heavy pale bill and bright yellow underparts.

10 Golden-breasted Bunting 311
15cm (6in). Rufous back and golden-yellow breast.

11 White-breasted Tit 305
14cm (5½in). White belly; wing feathers edged white.

1a ♂
♀ 1b
1c
2b ♀
2a ♂
3
4
5
6
7
8
9
10
11

Plate 25 SUNBIRDS

1 **Golden-winged Sunbird** page 309
1a,b ♂ 23cm (9in); ♀ 15cm (6in). ♂ with long central tail feathers; wings and tail edged yellow in both ♂ and ♀.

2 **Bronze Sunbird** 309
2a ♂ 23cm (9in) with long central tail feathers; metallic bronze-green on upperparts and chest.
2b ♀ 14cm (5½in), yellow below with dusky streaks.

3 **Kenya Violet-backed Sunbird** 309
15cm (6in). ♂ metallic bluish-violet on upperparts, chin and tail; below white. ♀ grey and whitish with pale eye-stripe and violet-blue tail.

4 **Collared Sunbird** 310
10cm (4in). ♂ and ♀ metallic yellowish-green; ♂ with violet breast band. ♀ like ♂ but throat yellow or greyish.

5 **Tacazze Sunbird** 307
5a ♂ 23cm (9in) with long central tail feathers; metallic violet head, back and chest.
5b ♀ 14cm (5½in), grey with whitish streak on each side of throat.

6 **Scarlet-chested Sunbird** 306
15cm (6in). ♂ plumage mainly velvety blackish-brown; breast scarlet; chin metallic green. ♀ dusky, lacks pale eye-stripe.

7 **Malachite Sunbird** 308
♂ 23cm (9in) with long central tail feathers; plumage bright emerald green; pectoral tufts yellow. ♀ 13cm (5in), below yellowish, unstreaked.

8 **Amethyst Sunbird** 306
8a 13cm (5in). ♂ plumage mainly velvety black; throat rosy-purple, cap metallic green.
8b ♀ with pale eye-stripe, heavily streaked on underparts.

9 **Mariqua Sunbird** 307
14cm (5½in). ♂ metallic green with maroon breast band; see text. ♀ greyish with pale eye-stripe; dusky streaks on breast.

10 **Variable Sunbird** 306
10a 10cm (4in). ♂ plumage metallic blue-green; purplish breast patch; belly white, yellow or red in different races.
10b ♀ greyish, unstreaked below.

11 **Eastern Double-collared Sunbird** 307
11.5cm (4½in). ♂ metallic green with scarlet breast band; yellow pectoral tufts; bluish upper tail coverts. ♀ greyish-green, unstreaked below.

12 **Beautiful Sunbird** 308
12a ♂ 15cm (6in) with long central tail feathers; scarlet breast patch, bordered yellow.
12b Belly black in race east of Rift Valley.
12c ♀ 11.5cm (4½in), pale below with whitish eye-stripe.

13 **Red-chested Sunbird** 308
♂ 16cm (6½in) with long central tail feathers; plumage metallic bluish-green; deep red breast band. ♀ 13cm (5in), streaked on chest; pale eye-stripe.

♀ 1a
♂ 1b
♂ 2a
2b ♀
3
4
5a ♂
♀ 5b
6
7
8b ♀
8a ♂
9
10b ♀
10a ♂
11
♀ 12c
12b
12a ♂
13

Plate 26 WAXBILLS and allies, WEAVERS

1 Paradise Whydah page 314
1a ♂ 38–41cm (15–16in). Unmistakable tail; plumage black, chestnut and buff.
1b ♀ 13cm (5in). Buff streak down centre of crown; bill black.

2 Pin-tailed Whydah 314
♂ 30–33cm (12–13in). Plumage black and white with long black tail; bill red. ♀ 11.5cm (4½in). Pale band down centre of crown; bill red.

3 Cut-throat 313
11.5cm (4½in). ♂ with crimson-red band on throat. ♀ lacks red throat band.

4 Green-winged Pytilia 312
4a 13cm (5in). ♂ with green upperparts and wing-coverts, red face and dark red tail.
4b ♀ lacks red on face.

5 Bronze Mannikin 314
10cm (4in). Dusky head and bluish-white bill. Immature all brown.

6 Purple Grenadier 313
6a 14cm (5½in). ♂ deep blue on rump and upper tail coverts; bill red.
6b ♀ white spotted orange-buff below.

7 Common Waxbill 312
11.5cm (4½in). Red bill and red streak through eye. Immature duller.

8 Yellow-bellied Waxbill 312
9cm (3½in). Black and red bill; crimson rump.

9 Red-billed Buffalo Weaver 320
25cm (10in). Gregarious; ♂ black with wings margined white. ♀ and immature greyish-brown, below whitish with heavy streaks.

10 White-headed Buffalo Weaver 320
23cm (9in). Sexes alike; orange-red rump and under tail-coverts; head and underparts white.

11 Red-billed Firefinch 313
11a 10cm (4in). ♂ bill rosy-red; under tail-coverts pale brown.
11b ♀ duller.

12 Red-cheeked Cordon-bleu 313
13cm (5in). Plumage pale blue; ♂ with conspicuous crimson cheek patch. ♀ duller, lacks crimson face patch.

♀ 1b
♂ 1a
2
3
4b ♀
♂ 4a
5
7
♀ 6b
6a ♂
8
9
10
♀ 11b
♂ 11a
12

Plate 27 **WEAVERS**

1 Cardinal Quelea page 317
10cm (4in). Gregarious. ♂ has crimson-red head; bill dark grey.

2 Red-billed Quelea 317
13cm (5in). Extremely gregarious. Sparrow-like with red bill. ♂ has black face mask and is often flushed pink below.

3 Red-headed Weaver 317
15cm (6in). ♂ head and chest bright red; bill pink. ♀ has pink bill but lacks red on head and chest.

4 Grey-capped Social Weaver 321
13cm (5in). Sexes alike. Pale grey cap and short tail. Immature lacks grey cap.

5 White-browed Sparrow Weaver 321
15cm (6in). Gregarious and noisy. Conspicuous white rump and eye-stripe.

6 Reichenow's Weaver 315
15cm (6in). Black above, yellow below. ♂ with front half of crown yellow; ♀ with crown black.

7 Black-headed Weaver 316
18cm (7in). ♂ head and throat black, nape chestnut. ♀ olive-brown above, lightly streaked; yellowish-white below.

8 Taveta Golden Weaver 315
14cm (5½in). ♂ greenish-yellow with chestnut patch on nape and chestnut wash on throat. ♀ yellowish-olive above with indistinct dusky streaking.

9 Spectacled Weaver 317
15cm (6in). Upperparts green. ♂ with black patch around eye and black throat. ♀ similar but lacks black throat.

10 Golden Palm Weaver 315
15cm (6in). ♂ greenish-yellow with bright orange head; eye blackish-brown. ♀ greenish-yellow above, yellow below.

11 Chestnut Weaver 316
16.5cm (6½in). ♂ black head and chestnut back and belly. ♀ sparrow-like with tawny chest band.

12 Masked Weaver 315
14cm (5½in). ♂ front half of crown black. ♀ olive above, below yellowish to white on belly.

13 Vitelline Masked Weaver 316
14cm (5½in). ♂ with very narrow black frontal band. ♀ olive-yellow above, streaked dusky; yellowish below.

14 Speke's Weaver 316
15cm (6in). ♂ with yellow crown, black face mask and mottled black and yellow back. ♀ olive-brown above, slightly mottled; below whitish.

1
3
5
2
4
7
6
8
9
10
11
12
13
14

WEAVERS

1 Black-winged Bishop page 318
14cm (5½in). ♂ with black wings and tail. ♀ sparrow-like with yellowish eye-stripe.

2 West Nile Red Bishop 319
10cm (4in). ♂ has tail concealed by very long red upper tail-coverts. ♀ sparrow-like.

3 Red Bishop 319
13cm (5in). ♂ has pale brown wings and tail; upper tail-coverts short. ♀ sparrow-like.

4 Long-tailed Widow-bird 319
♂ 61–76cm (24–30in), with extremely long tail and red and buff shoulders. ♀ 15cm (6in). Sparrow-like, streaked dusky above and below.

5 Yellow Bishop 318
15cm (6in). ♂ black with bright yellow rump and shoulders. ♀ sparrow-like with contrasting yellowish-olive rump.

6 Red-collared Widow-bird 318
♂ Kenya Highlands race. 28–30cm (11–12in). Red absent or confined to crescent-shaped breast patch in other races. ♀ 13cm (5in). Sparrow-like.

7 Jackson's Widow-bird 320
7a ♂ 33–36cm (13–14in) with thick, black, decurved tail; brown shoulders. ♀ 14cm (5½in). Sparrow-like, streaked dusky above and below.
7b Display leap.

8 White-winged Widow-bird 318
♂ 18cm (7in). Black with moderately long tail and white wing-patch. ♀ 13cm (5in). Sparrow-like, brownish on chest.

1
2
3
4
5
6
7a
7b
8

Plate 29 STARLINGS, ORIOLES, DRONGOS and CROWS

**All crows drawn to a smaller scale.*

1 Black-headed Oriole page 324
23cm (9in). Black head and throat. Immature has yellow streaks on head and throat.

2 Golden-breasted Starling 323
30–36cm (12–14in). Long graduated tail; belly bright golden yellow; eye white.

3 Superb Starling 322
18cm (7in). Narrow white breast band; white below tail and under wings; eye creamy white.

4 Hildebrandt's Starling 322
18cm (7in). No white breast band and under tail-coverts rufous; eye bright orange-red.

5 Drongo 324
23–25cm (9–10in). Tail forked and 'fish-tailed'; eye red.

6 Ruppell's Long-tailed Starling 321
33–36cm (13–14in). Long graduated tail; metallic violet plumage and white eye.

7 Wattled Starling 323
21.5cm (8½in). ♂ in breeding plumage has distinctive bare black and yellow head and fleshy wattles; rump whitish. Non-breeding ♂, ♀ and immature with head feathered and no wattles.

8 Blue-eared Starling 321
23cm (9in). Plumage metallic green, merging to violet on belly; eye yellow.

9 Violet-backed Starling 322
9a ♂ 16.5cm (6½in). Upperparts and throat brilliant metallic violet-blue, changing to crimson-violet in certain lights; belly white.
9b ♀ and immature brown with white underparts with dark brown spotting.

10 Red-billed Oxpecker 323
18cm (7in). Associated with both big game and domestic animals; bill entirely red; yellow wattle around eye.

11 Cape Rook* 325
43cm (17in). Plumage entirely black; throat feathers lax.

12 Fan-tailed Raven* 325
46cm (18in). Tail very short; when perched wing tips extend beyond tail.

13 Pied Crow* 325
46cm (18in). White breast and white on hind neck.

14 White-naped Raven* 325
56cm (22in). Heavy white-tipped bill; white collar on hind-neck; black underparts.

1
2
3
4
5
6
7
8
♀
9b
9a
♂
10
11
12
13
14

climbing amongst branches of acacia trees and bushes in a manner reminiscent of a nuthatch.

Voice: A sharp two-note 'tic, tic' and a brief warbling song.

Distribution and Habitat: Locally common in Uganda and Kenya, southwards to north-eastern Tanzania. Inhabits dry bush, coastal scrub and acacia woodland.

Allied Species: The Red-faced Crombec (*Sylvietta whytii*) is larger, 10cm (4in), lacks the dusky eye streak and has more extensive rufous underparts. It occurs in bush and acacia woodland; locally common in East Africa, normally in wetter areas than the common Crombec.

FLYCATCHERS: Muscicapidae

This is a large family of small or medium-sized birds, usually with flattened bills and well-developed bristles at the gape: immatures spotted. Many species perch upright on some vantage point from which short erratic flights are made after insect prey. Some other species hunt insect food amongst foliage in the manner of warblers.

WHITE-EYED SLATY FLYCATCHER

Melaenornis fischeri **Plate 24**

Identification: 16.5cm ($6\frac{1}{2}$in). The upperparts of this flycatcher are slate-grey, paler below; a conspicuous white ring around eye. Immature has whitish spots on upperparts and breast mottled. The field appearance is of a plump-looking slaty-blue flycatcher with a white eye-ring. It often alights on the ground to pick up insects; very active at dusk when often observed on paths in woodland in the manner of a robin chat.

Voice: Usually silent: most vocal in evening when it utters a sharp sunbird-like 'tssk' and a short descending trill.

Distribution and Habitat: Locally common in wooded areas of East Africa. Occurs in highland forest, forest margins and scrub. A well-known garden bird.

SILVER BIRD *Empidornis semipartitus* **Plate 24**

Identification: 20cm (8in). A slim, rather long-tailed flycatcher, pale silver-grey above, bright rufous below. Immature spotted pale buff above, mottled black below. Usually found in pairs. Easily recognised by grey back and rufous underparts.

Voice: Usually silent, but ♂ has a soft warbling song.

Distribution and Habitat: A locally not uncommon bird. In Uganda, western Kenya and northern Tanzania. Occurs in bush country and acacia woodland.

CHIN-SPOT PUFFBACK *Batis molitor* **Plate 24**
Identification: 11cm (4½in). A small, rather stumpy black, grey and white flycatcher: ♂ with black band across chest, ♀ with a chestnut band and a patch of chestnut on the throat. Immature like ♀ but with buff speckling above and on chest. Occurs in pairs in trees. In flight produces a sharp 'brrrrp' with wings.
Voice: Clear whistles 'doo-dor-dee' and a louder double alarm note.
Distribution and Habitat: Common and widespread in East Africa. Frequents acacia woodland, forest edges, cultivation and gardens.

BLUE FLYCATCHER *Erannornis longicauda* **Plate 24**
Identification: 14cm (5½in). A very beautiful small blue flycatcher with a long graduated tail. Plumage caerulean blue, paler on throat and belly. Immature spotted buff on upperparts. Tame and confiding, readily identified by its colour and habit of constantly fanning its tail.
Voice: A brief, sunbird-like twittering song.
Distribution and Habitat: Locally not uncommon in Uganda, western Kenya and western Tanzania. Occurs in woodland and forest edges and in gardens.

PARADISE FLYCATCHER *Terpsiphone viridis* **Plate 24**
Identification: ♂ 30–36cm (12–14in); ♀ 20cm (8in). An unmistakable bird. The combination of a very long tail and chestnut, black and grey, or grey and white plumage is distinctive. In some parts of its range, especially in eastern Kenya, the white phase of plumage in the ♂ is commoner than the normal chestnut plumage. In the white phase the back, wings and tail are white not chestnut. ♀ is much shorter tailed and does not have a white plumage phase. Immature similar to ♀ but duller.
Voice: The call note is a sharp two- or three-note whistle; its song a subdued warbling.
Distribution and Habitat: Widespread and locally common. Inhabits wooded areas, forest, thick scrub, thornbush and acacia country, and gardens.

TITS: Paridae

A group of small rather plump birds of distinctive habits: extremely active and acrobatic when feeding, often hanging upside down while searching for insects in foliage and on bark. Frequently members of mixed bird parties.

WHITE-BREASTED TIT *Parus albiventris* **Plate 24**
Identification: 14cm (5½in). A black tit with contrasting white belly and wing feathers and coverts edged white. In pairs or family parties, in the tree-tops; very active and always on the move.
Voice: A sharp 'tss, tssee' or 'tss, tss, tee'; song a repeated warbling 'chee, chee, churr'.

Distribution and Habitat: Locally common throughout East Africa. Inhabits acacia woodland, forest margins, cultivation where there are trees, coastal bush and gardens.

SUNBIRDS: Nectariniidae

A very distinct family of small birds with slender curved bills and, in most species, brilliant metallic plumage in ♂♂. In some species ♂ has a dull, ♀-like non-breeding plumage. Some females are difficult to identify in the field and are best recognised by their associated males. Their flight is very erratic and rapid. Most visit flowering trees, such as *Erythrina*, in which they may be observed at close quarters. The best way in which some of the rarer forest species may be seen is to wait in the vicinity of a flowering tree for the birds to appear.

AMETHYST SUNBIRD *Nectarinia amethystina* **Plate 25**

Identification: 13cm (5in). A square-tailed, velvety black sunbird with a metallic green cap and a rosy-purple throat; ♀ olive-brown with whitish eye-stripe, heavily streaked on breast and flanks; immature like ♀ but with blackish throat. ♀ Scarlet-chested Sunbird has no pale eye-stripe, is browner and mottled below.
Voice: A variety of loud 'cheep' or 'tssp' calls and a loud warbling song.
Distribution and Habitat: Locally common in Kenya, mainly eastern districts, and Tanzania. Occurs in a variety of habitats from mountain forest to coastal scrub, and mangrove swamps, savannah and open woodlands, and gardens. Often attracted to flowering aloes and *Leonotis*.

SCARLET-CHESTED SUNBIRD
Nectarinia senegalensis **Plate 25**

Identification: 15cm (6in). A thickset, square-tailed, velvety, blackish-brown sunbird with a metallic green cap and chin and a vivid scarlet chest. ♀ brown without eye-stripe, heavily mottled below; immature like ♀ but throat dusky. ♀ Amethyst Sunbird has pale eye-stripe and is streaked below.
Voice: A variety of loud, clear notes – a descending 'tssp, teee, tee'; song a loud trilling warble.
Distribution and Habitat: A common and conspicuous sunbird throughout East Africa. Occurs along forest margins, woodland, savannah, bush, riverine acacias and gardens.
Allied Species: Hunter's Sunbird (*Nectarinia hunteri*) 15cm (6in), differs in having the chin velvety black, not metallic green, and a metallic violet rump. It occurs in arid bush country in eastern Kenya and north-eastern Tanzania.

VARIABLE SUNBIRD *Nectarinia venusta* **Plate 25**

Identification: 10cm (4in). ♂ plumage a metallic blue-green with broad

purplish-black chest patch; belly yellow with orange wash (white in birds from extreme northern Kenya; orange-red in those from south-western Uganda); pectoral tufts yellow and orange-red. ♀ and immature olive-grey, white or yellowish below, unstreaked. The similar Collared Sunbird is metallic yellowish-green and lacks the broad purplish chest patch.
Voice: Short 'tssp' calls and a longer churring call. Song a subdued warble.
Distribution and Habitat: Locally common throughout East Africa. Frequents bush country, gardens, edges of forests and rank vegetation along rivers. Attracted to flowers of *Leonotis* and to various flowering acacias.

EASTERN DOUBLE-COLLARED SUNBIRD
Nectarinia mediocris **Plate 25**
Identification: 11.5cm (4½in). ♂ plumage a metallic green; upper tail-coverts violet; narrow violet-blue line at base of throat, followed by bright red band across chest; belly olive; pectoral tufts yellow. ♀ and immature dusky olive-green, darker below.
Voice: A clear, sharp 'tssp, tssp, tssp', frequently uttered; a clear warbling song.
Distribution and Habitat: Locally common highland areas over 1,524m (5,000ft): Uganda (Mount Elgon), Kenya and Tanzania. Inhabits forests, scrub and gardens. Much attracted to flowers of *Leonotis* and red-hot pokers.
Allied Species: The Northern Double-collared Sunbird (*Nectarinia preussi*) is smaller, 10cm (4in), with a much broader and darker red breast band. It is also a highland forest species found in Uganda and western Kenya east to Mount Kenya.

MARIQUA SUNBIRD *Nectarinia mariquensis* **Plate 25**
Identification: 14cm (5½in). ♂ plumage a metallic coppery green with a maroon breast band and a blackish belly. ♀ greyish-brown with pale eye-stripe; below yellowish with dark breast streaks. Immature like ♀ but with black throat.
Voice: A clear loud 'tssp' and a soft warbling song.
Distribution and Habitat: Locally not uncommon in drier areas; occurs in savannah and acacia woodland, scrub and cultivation.
Allied Species: The Little Purple-banded Sunbird (*Nectarinia bifasciata*) 10cm (4in), closely resembles the Mariqua Sunbird but is smaller. It is found locally in East Africa, abundant only in the coastal areas of Kenya and Tanzania.

TACAZZE SUNBIRD *Nectarinia tacazze* **Plate 25**
Identification: ♂ 23cm (9in); ♀ 14cm (5½in). A large, thickset sunbird with long central tail feathers; appears black, changing in certain lights to brilliant metallic violet, glossed copper on head. ♀ olive-grey, paler below with whitish streak down each side of throat. Immature similar to ♀ but with

dusky throat. ♂ Bronzy Sunbird appears blackish but metallic upperparts and breast coppery-green, not violet; ♀ yellow below, streaked olive.
Voice: Loud single or double 'tsssp', and a sustained warbling song usually delivered from high in a tree.
Distribution and Habitat: Locally common in highland areas over 2,134m (7,000ft) in eastern Uganda, Kenya and northern Tanzania. Inhabits mountain forest and marshy glades, and in gardens and near human habitations at high altitudes. Much attracted to flowers of red-hot pokers.

RED-CHESTED SUNBIRD *Nectarinia erythroceria* **Plate 25**
Identification: ♂ 16cm (6½in); ♀ 13cm (5in). A long-tailed bluish-green sunbird with a dusky red breast band and a black belly; ♀ greyish-brown with chest streaks. Immature similar to ♀ but throat black. Occurs amongst rank vegetation near water.
Voice: Typical sunbird 'tssps' and a warbling song.
Distribution and Habitat: Locally common in western Kenya (around Lake Victoria), Uganda and north-western Tanzania. Occurs always in the vicinity of water – lake margins, swamps and gardens near water. Very common throughout Uganda.

BEAUTIFUL SUNBIRD *Nectarinia pulchella* **Plate 25**
Identification: ♂ 15cm (6in); ♀ 11.5cm (4½in). A small long-tailed sunbird, shining metallic green with a scarlet breast patch bordered on each side by yellow; belly black or metallic green. ♂ in non-breeding dress similar to ♀ but with retained metallic wing-coverts and long tail feathers. ♀ ash-grey with pale eye-stripe; below yellowish-white with trace of streaking on breast. Immature like ♀ but with black throat.
Voice: A sharp, clear 'tsp' and a soft warbling song.
Distribution and Habitat: Locally common in Uganda, Kenya, except extreme eastern districts, and Tanzania. Inhabits bush country, savannah, open woodland and stands of acacia. Much attracted to *Leonotis* flowers and the flowering tree *Delonix elata*.

MALACHITE SUNBIRD *Nectarinia famosa* **Plate 25**
Identification: ♂ 23cm (9in); ♀ 13cm (5in). The bright emerald-green of ♂ is unmistakable, with its long central tail feathers and yellow pectoral tufts, the latter conspicuous when bird displays. In non-breeding plumage pale brownish-grey, but retaining long tail and green wing coverts. ♀ and immature brownish-grey, paler, yellowish and unstreaked below. ♀ Golden-winged Sunbird has yellow edged wings and tail; ♀ Bronzy Sunbird is lightly streaked olive below.
Voice: A rapid 'chiii' or a harsher 'chee, chee'. Song a rapid, jingling warble, often of short duration.
Distribution and Habitat: Highland areas of Uganda, Kenya and Tanzania, usually over 1,828m (6,000ft). Favours bushy moorlands, montane grass-

lands where there are protea bushes, forest margins and glades and montane scrub.

Allied Species: The Scarlet-tufted Malachite Sunbird (*Nectarinia johnstoni*), ♂ 30cm (12in), ♀ 15cm (6in), with much longer tail streamers and red pectoral tufts in both sexes, is confined to alpine moorlands of Mount Kenya and the Aberdare range in Kenya, Mounts Kilimanjaro and Meru, the Crater Highlands in northern Tanzania, and the Ruwenzori Mountains and Birunga Volcanoes in western Uganda.

BRONZE SUNBIRD *Nectarinia kilimensis* Plate 25

Identification: ♂ 23cm (9in); ♀ 14cm (5½in). This is a black-looking sunbird with long central tail feathers which appear metallic bronze-green in a good light. ♀ olive-grey with dark ear-coverts and streaky yellowish underparts; immature similar but throat dusky. The Tacazze sunbird ♂ is metallic violet, not bronze-green and ♀ is unstreaked pale grey below.

Voice: A very distinct 'chee-choo, wee' usually uttered twice; also a brief warbling song.

Distribution and Habitat: Locally common in highlands of East Africa, normally above 1,219m (4,000ft). Occurs in wooded areas, gardens and mountain scrub. Much attracted to flowering *Erythrina* trees and *Crotolaria* bushes.

GOLDEN-WINGED SUNBIRD *Nectarinia reichenowi* Plate 25

Identification: ♂ 23cm (9in); ♀ 15cm (6in). ♂ plumage a brilliant metallic reddish-bronze and copper with yellow-edged wings and tail; long tailed: non-breeding ♂ has most of metallic plumage replaced by dull black. ♀ olive above, yellowish below, also with yellow-edged wings and tail; immature similar but darker below. The deep yellow edged flight and tail feathers distinguish this sunbird in all plumages.

Voice: A variety of liquid 'tweeps' and 'tsssps' and a warbling song.

Distribution and Habitat: Locally common in areas over 1,828m (6,000ft) in Uganda, Kenya and northern Tanzania. Inhabits moorlands, mountain bush and forest margins. Attracted to orange-flowered *Leonotis*. ♂♂ have a curious slow, zig-zag display flight among bushes when yellow-edged wings and tail are very conspicuous.

KENYA VIOLET-BACKED SUNBIRD

Anthreptes orientalis **Plate 25**

Identification: 15cm (6in). The *Anthreptes* group of sunbirds are distinguished by their short, only slightly curved bills. ♂ metallic violet above and on chin, rest of underparts white with pale yellow pectoral tufts. ♀ grey above with a white eye-stripe and a violet-black tail. Immature similar but yellowish below.

Voice: A rather loud 'tssp'; song a series of soft warbling notes.

Distribution and Habitat: Kenya and Tanzania, locally common in dry bush country and acacia woodland.

COLLARED SUNBIRD *Anthreptes collaris* **Plate 25**

Identification: 10cm (4in). A small rather thickset sunbird; metallic yellowish-green above and on throat, with a narrow violet breast band and yellow underparts. ♀ and immature are also metallic green on upperparts, but not on throat. The somewhat similar ♂ Variable Sunbird has the plumage bluish-green and a broad dark violet breast patch.
Voice: A weak 'tsssp', frequently uttered, and a soft warbling song.
Distribution and Habitat: A locally very common species in East Africa, frequenting forest and woodland, scrub, bush country and gardens: often abundant in coastal thickets.

WHITE-EYES: Zosteropidae

A group of small greenish or yellowish-green warbler-like birds with conspicuous white rings around their eyes. Gregarious, in flocks even during the nesting season. Often associated with mixed bird parties. The classification of these birds is still unsatisfactory: different populations vary greatly and the status of some races and species is uncertain.

KIKUYU WHITE-EYE *Zosterops kikuyuensis* **Plate 24**

Identification: 13cm (5in). The Kikuyu White-eye is bright green above with a broad bright yellow forehead; white eye-ring very large and conspicuous; below yellow on throat and centre of belly; flanks yellowish-green. Immature duller. The Kikuyu White-eye is sometimes classified as a race of an Ethiopian montane species, *Zosterops poliogastra*.
Voice: High-pitched piping flock call: song a soft clear warble.
Distribution and Habitat: A local species but common in its restricted range – the highlands of southern Kenya and some northern Tanzania highlands – Mount Hanang, Ngorongoro, Longido, Oldeani and Ufiome. In Kenya very common in forest on Aberdare Mountains and Mount Kenya, and in Nairobi district. Inhabits highland forest, bamboos and gardens.
Allied Species: Races of the Yellow White-eye and the Green White-eye are now considered to be conspecific and are classified under the name *Zosterops senegalensis*, 10–10.5cm (4–4½in). Best recognised by its very narrow white eye-ring and small yellow band on forehead. Widely distributed in East Africa. Frequents forests, scrub, cultivated areas and gardens.

BUNTINGS: Emberizidae

Mainly ground-feeding finch-like birds found singly, in pairs or in small parties. Distinguished from finches by bill structure, the cutting edge of the upper mandible being sinuated.

GOLDEN-BREASTED BUNTING

Emberiza flaviventris **Plate 24**

Identification: 15cm (6in). This bunting is best recognised by its rufous back, white-tipped outer tail feathers and golden-rufous breast; crown and sides of face black with a white stripe down centre of crown and a white band on each side of the face. Immature has buff streaks on crown and is duller.

Voice: A trilling 'zizi, zizi' and a bubbling song, 'tee, wee – cheee- te – tweee' repeated over and over again.

Distribution and Habitat: Locally common in East Africa, inhabiting dry forest, woodlands, bush and acacia country; usually single or in pairs.

FINCHES: Fringillidae

The finches are thick-billed, seed-eating birds which resemble weavers but have nine visible primaries only. Nests unlike those of weavers, open and cup-shaped.

YELLOW-RUMPED SEED-EATER

Serinus atrogularis **Plate 24**

Identification: 10cm (4in). A tawny-grey seed-eater with whitish underparts and a bright lemon-yellow rump which contrasts strongly with remainder upperparts when bird in flight. Found in pairs or small flocks.

Voice: Usual canary type song and a double 'tssp' call note.

Distribution and Habitat: Locally common through most of East Africa. Inhabits most types of woodland, open bush, grassland and cultivation.

BRIMSTONE CANARY *Serinus sulphuratus* **Plate 24**

Identification: 15cm (6in). A thickset greenish-yellow canary with a stout horn-grey bill and bright yellow underparts. Immature duller. Occurs in pairs or small parties. Similar looking weavers have black bills.

Voice: Rather harsh chirping calls and a varied but typical canary song.

Distribution and Habitat: Locally common through most of East Africa, inhabiting scattered bush in open country, mountain moorland, riverine thickets and vegetation near water, cultivation and gardens.

STREAKY SEED-EATER *Serinus striolatus* **Plate 24**

Identification: 15cm (6in). A tawny-brown bird with dark streaked upper-

parts and crown; whitish eye-stripe; below tawny-white or buff, streaked dark brown on throat, breast and flanks; immature duller. A common species best recognised by streaky plumage, the rump being the same colour as rest of upperparts and the white eye-stripe.
Voice: A high-pitched three-note call and a bubbling canary-like song.
Distribution and Habitat: Common in the highlands of Kenya, Uganda and northern Tanzania. Inhabits mountain moorlands, margins and glades in forest, bush, cultivation and gardens. A very common bird in the highlands of Kenya.

WAXBILLS and ALLIES: Estrildidae

Small seed-eating birds related to the weavers. Many are highly gregarious and feed largely on or near the ground. Many are well known cage birds.

GREEN-WINGED PYTILIA *Pytilia melba* **Plate 26**
Identification: 13cm (5in). A red-billed, green finch-like bird with a red face, throat, rump and tail; breast golden-orange. ♀ and immature lack red on face and throat and are vermiculated grey and white below. Shy, usually in pairs or family parties. When disturbed the birds dive into the nearest thicket, leaving a fleeting impression of a green bird with a red rump and tail.
Voice: Usually silent, but sometimes utters weak chirping calls.
Distribution and Habitat: Widely distributed in East Africa, locally common, but elusive and difficult to see. Inhabits bush country, coastal thickets, thorn scrub, neglected cultivation and rank grass and bush.

YELLOW-BELLIED WAXBILL *Estrilda melanotis* **Plate 26**
Identification: 9cm ($3\frac{1}{2}$in). A tiny greenish waxbill with a buff belly, grey head and chest, black tail and crimson rump; bill colour distinctive, upper mandible black, lower mandible red. Immature duller and bill dusky. Usually found in small flocks.
Voice: A weak 'swee, swee'.
Distribution and Habitat: Throughout East Africa, in rank undergrowth along forest margins and water, and in grassy areas generally.

COMMON WAXBILL *Estrilda astrild* **Plate 26**
Identification: 11.5cm ($4\frac{1}{2}$in). A pale brown waxbill with a conspicuous and vivid red bill and a red streak through the eye; red patch on belly; brown, not red, on the rump and tail: immature duller with dusky bill. In flocks in lush grass.
Voice: Constant weak twittering flock calls.
Distribution and Habitat: Common throughout East Africa; inhabits neglected cultivation, lush grasslands and dense waterside vegetation.
Allied Species: The Crimson-rumped Waxbill (*Estrilda rhodopyga*) 11.5cm

(4½in), differs in having a crimson rump and crimson edged tail and wing feathers and a dark slate bill. It is locally common over much of East Africa favouring marshes and lush vegetation along streams.

PURPLE GRENADIER *Uraeginthus ianthinogaster* **Plate 26**

Identification: 14cm (5½in). A cinnamon-brown waxbill with a relatively long black tail, cobalt blue rump and red bill; underparts violet-blue with some cinnamon-brown markings. ♀ has breast and belly brown with whitish spots and barring. Immature duller without white markings on underparts.

Voice: Usually silent; sometimes utters soft twittering notes.

Distribution and Habitat: Locally common in northern Uganda, Kenya and northern Tanzania in scrub, thickets and thornbush country.

RED-CHEEKED CORDON-BLEU

Uraeginthus bengalus **Plate 26**

Identification: 13cm (5in). A mainly azure-blue waxbill with crimson cheek patches; ♀ and immature duller and lack crimson on face. Seen in pairs or family parties; tame and confiding.

Voice: Weak call notes; song a soft 'ts, ts, tseee' repeated several times.

Distribution and Habitat: Common in Uganda, Kenya and the northern half of Tanzania. Frequents thornbush and acacia country, savannah, neglected cultivation and forest margins and found in gardens and around habitations. It feeds largely on the ground.

RED-BILLED FIREFINCH *Lagonosticta senegala* **Plate 26**

Identification: 10cm (4in). A small pinkish-red waxbill with a mainly rosy-red bill. ♀ and immature browner and duller. A tame and confiding little bird much at home around human habitations and in gardens. It is well known as the 'animated plum', a not inappropriate name.

Voice: A weak 'tweet, tweet' and a brief song.

Distribution and Habitat: Widespread and common throughout East Africa. Usually seen feeding on open or bare ground near human dwellings; also in scrub, thickets and riverine undergrowth.

CUT-THROAT *Amadina fasciata* **Plate 26**

Identification: 11.5cm (4½in). Small finch-like bird of speckled brown appearance, paler below with a rufous belly; ♂ with conspicuous crimson band across throat. Immature similar to ♀. Gregarious in small flocks; often associated with cordon-bleus and other waxbills.

Voice: Sparrow-like chirping calls.

Distribution and Habitat: Locally common in East Africa, inhabiting dry thornbush and acacia country; often noticed around waterholes and dams. Common in the arid northern districts of Kenya.

BRONZE MANNIKIN *Lonchura cucullata* **Plate 26**
Identification: 10cm (4in). A tame, gregarious little bird, feeding on grass seeds on the ground. Plumage is dusky above with an oily-green gloss, darker on head, throat and breast; rump and flanks vermiculated black and white; belly white; bill pale blue-grey. Immature uniform brown with black tail.
Voice: A sharp, low 'tik, tik'.
Distribution and Habitat: Common throughout East Africa. Found in bush country, coastal scrub, cultivation, grasslands, on the edges of swamps, lakes and rivers and among rank herbage.

PIN-TAILED WHYDAH *Vidua macroura* **Plate 26**
Identification: ♂ 30–33cm (12–13in), ♀ 11.5cm (4½in). A red-billed, black and white whydah with a long, narrow black tail. ♀ and immature streaky and sparrow-like with a buff band down centre of crown and a reddish bill. ♂ in non-breeding dress like ♀ but larger with much white in wings. Its flight is erratic and jerky; there is a characteristic display flight, the ♂ hovering and 'dancing' in the air over the ♀ perched below.
Voice: Various chirping calls and a sustained twittering song.
Distribution and Habitat: Common throughout East Africa. Inhabits all types of grassland and light bush and scrub and in cultivation. Usually in small parties, the ♂♂ greatly outnumbered by ♀♀ and young.

PARADISE WHYDAH *Vidua paradisaea* **Plate 26**
Identification: ♂ 38–41cm (15–16in), ♀ 13cm (5in). ♂ is unmistakable, recognised by its black, chestnut and buff plumage and remarkable tail. This whydah perches frequently on the tops of thorn trees and flies in a curious undulating, jerky manner. Non-breeding ♂ and ♀ sparrow-like with black bill and a broad whitish stripe down centre of crown. Immature dull tawny-brown with white belly.
Voice: A rather shrill, metallic 'teeet' call, but usually silent.
Distribution and Habitat: A local resident in suitable localities throughout East Africa, sometimes common. Inhabits bush and acacia country, and savannah woodlands.

WEAVERS and ALLIES: Ploceidae

One of the largest bird families in Africa. Most but not all are seed-eaters with short, heavy bills. They resemble true finches in general appearance but have ten, not nine primaries. Finches build open nests; weavers and allies build domed structures with a side, top or bottom entrance. Many species are highly gregarious, nesting in colonies. In some the ♂ has a ♀-like non-breeding plumage.

REICHENOW'S WEAVER
Ploceus baglafecht reichenowi **Plate 27**

Identification: 15cm (6in). Upperparts black; ♂ with front half of crown rich golden-yellow; ear-coverts black; ♀ has crown and ear-coverts black; underparts ♂ and ♀ bright yellow. Immature like ♀ but upperparts dusky olive with dark streaks. Usually seen in pairs or family parties, not gregarious.
Voice: Sparrow-like chirps and a brief chattering song.
Distribution and Habitat: Locally common in highlands over 1,219m (4,000ft) in Kenya and northern Tanzania. Inhabits the edges of forests, moorland scrub, wooded areas, cultivation and gardens.

GOLDEN PALM WEAVER *Ploceus bojeri* **Plate 27**

Identification: 15cm (6in). An entirely yellow weaver with a brilliant orange head; washed chestnut on chest; eye blackish-brown. ♀ greenish-yellow above with faint indication of streaking; below yellow. Normally gregarious.
Voice: A low-pitched weaver chattering.
Distribution and Habitat: Locally common in eastern Kenya and north-eastern Tanzania. One of the most noticeable weavers on the Kenya coast, breeding in colonies in coconut palms and in bushes in coastal scrub.

TAVETA GOLDEN WEAVER *Ploceus castaneiceps* **Plate 27**

Identification: 14cm (5½in). ♂ a bright yellow weaver with a greenish-yellow back and greenish wings and tail; chestnut patch on nape and chestnut wash on chest; ♀ yellowish-olive with dusky streaks on mantle; yellowish stripe above eye; below pale buffy-yellow.
Voice: A constant low chattering.
Distribution and Habitat: An extremely local species but often common where it does occur. Found in south-eastern Kenya and north-eastern Tanzania. Abundant around camps and park lodges in the Amboseli National Park, Kenya. Inhabits open acacia woodland where there is bushy undergrowth, and lush vegetation in the vicinity of water. Although the status of the Taveta is an uncommon species with a restricted distribution it is included here on account of its abundance in the Amboseli National Park.

MASKED WEAVER *Ploceus intermedius* **Plate 27**

Identification: 14cm (5½in). A mainly yellow weaver with an olive-green, indistinctly streaked mantle; face, throat and front half of crown black; rest of underparts yellow. ♀, non-breeding ♂ and immature have no black on head, upperparts more olive and a yellow stripe over eye; below yellowish to white on belly; feet blue-grey. Gregarious.
Voice: The usual chattering weaver calls at nesting colonies but less noisy than many other weavers.
Distribution and Habitat: Locally common and widespread in East Africa. In north of range generally a bird of thornbush country but also occurs in

acacia woodland and savannah: in the south it is commoner in the vicinity of swamps and wet areas.

VITELLINE MASKED WEAVER *Ploceus vitellinus* **Plate 27**
Identification: 14cm (5½in). ♂ resembles ♂ Masked Weaver but crown washed chestnut with very narrow black frontal band; black on throat restricted to chin. ♀, ♂ non-breeding and immature olive-yellow above with dark streaking on mantle; below yellowish; feet flesh-pink. This species is much less gregarious than the Masked Weaver and individual pairs often nest alone.
Voice: Soft chattering calls and a 'tssp' call note.
Distribution and Habitat: Locally common in Uganda and Kenya, south to northern half of Tanzania. A bird of thick bush, acacia woodland and arid thorn scrub.

SPEKE'S WEAVER *Ploceus spekei* **Plate 27**
Identification: 15cm (6in). Yellow with a dusky mottled back, a yellow crown and a contrasting black face and throat. ♀ and immature olive-brown above, slightly mottled; below white, washed yellowish-buff on throat and breast. Gregarious, breeds in colonies in acacia trees or in swamps.
Voice: Usual weaver chatter at nesting colonies and a sharp 'teep'.
Distribution and Habitat: Locally common in Kenya and northern Tanzania. Inhabits lightly wooded areas, cultivation, riverine acacias and vicinity human habitations. A common bird in the eastern highlands of Kenya, including Nairobi.

BLACK-HEADED WEAVER *Ploceus cucullatus* **Plate 27**
Identification: 18cm (7in). A thickset black-headed weaver with chestnut hind crown and nape; broad yellow collar on hind neck; mantle black and yellow; below, throat black, remainder underparts yellow with rufous wash on breast and flanks. ♀ and immature olive brown above, indistinctly streaked; yellowish white below. Gregarious, breeding in colonies. The eastern race from eastern Kenya and eastern Tanzania was previously recognised as a distinct species, Layard's Black-headed Weaver (*Ploceus nigriceps*). It is smaller, 16.5cm (6½in), and has the head and nape black without chestnut on crown or nape.
Voice: A noisy chatter at nesting colonies.
Distribution and Habitat: A common species throughout East Africa. Occurs in forested and cultivated areas, swamps and margins of lakes and rivers; nests usually in vicinity of human habitations. Abundant in many parts of Uganda.

CHESTNUT WEAVER *Ploceus rubiginosus* **Plate 27**
Identification: 16.5cm (6½in). ♂ very distinct, bright chestnut with black head and throat. ♀ and ♂ non-breeding are sparrow-like, brownish streaked black above, below tawny-buff to white on throat and belly. Immature similar but

tinged rufous. Very gregarious, breeding in dense colonies in acacia trees.
Voice: Usual weaver type chattering calls at nesting colonies.
Distribution and Habitat: A locally common bird in north-eastern Uganda, Kenya and northern half of Tanzania. Inhabits dry bush country and open acacia woodland, entering cultivation where wheat is grown during non-breeding season.

SPECTACLED WEAVER *Ploceus ocularis* **Plate 27**
Identification: 15cm (6in). A green-backed weaver with yellowish-green wings and tail, yellow underparts and a black patch around eye; ♂ has a black chin, ♀ an orange-rufous throat. Immature similar to ♀ but duller. Occurs singly or in pairs; shy.
Voice: A weak 'tss, tss, tss, tss' or a single metallic 'peeet'.
Distribution and Habitat: Local in small numbers in southern Uganda, Kenya and Tanzania. Inhabits forested areas, acacia woodland, riverine forest and rank bush and vegetation near streams and lakes. Visits blossoms of Erythrina trees when these are in flower.

RED-HEADED WEAVER *Anaplectes rubriceps* **Plate 27**
Identification: 15cm (6in). ♂ easily recognised by bright red head, mantle and chest, and in northern birds the black face; bill pink-red. ♀ greyish with red or yellowish edgings to wings and tail; bill pink. Immature like ♀ but duller and bill dusky. Not gregarious, occurs singly, in pairs or in family parties.
Voice: Usually silent, but utters a high-pitched chatter at nest.
Distribution and Habitat: Locally not uncommon and widely distributed in East Africa. Occurs in savannah woodland, scrub, brachystegia forest and riverine acacias. Frequents tree tops, creepers and bushes; mainly insectivorous.

CARDINAL QUELEA *Quelea cardinalis* **Plate 27**
Identification: 10cm (4in). A small, short-tailed sparrow-plumaged weaver with a crimson head and throat and a black bill. ♀ and immature lack the crimson head. Occurs in loose colonies of a dozen or so pairs, and in larger flocks in the non-breeding season.
Voice: A soft 'zeet, zeet' call note.
Distribution and Habitat: Widespread and locally common in East Africa. Inhabits open bush country where there is rank grass.

RED-BILLED QUELEA *Quelea quelea* **Plate 27**
Identification: 13cm (5in). A streaky, sparrow-like weaver with pink-red bill and legs; ♂ in breeding plumage has black face and is suffused pink on crown and breast. ♀, non-breeding ♂ and immature lack black face and pink suffusion. Extremely gregarious, sometimes in flocks numbering hundreds of thousands of birds. The Cardinal Quelea is smaller, the ♂ with crimson head and black, not pink bill.

Voice: A constant but low murmuration of chatter from flocks and breeding colonies.
Distribution and Habitat: Common, locally abundant, throughout East Africa. Inhabits dry thornbush, scrub and acacia country, at times entering cultivation when it is very destructive to wheat crops.

WHITE-WINGED WIDOW-BIRD
Euplectes albonotatus **Plate 28**
Identification: ♂ 18cm (7in), ♀ 13cm (5in). ♂ black with moderately long tail; white wing patch conspicuous in flight. ♀ and immature streaky, sparrow-like, best identified by associated ♂♂; ♂ in non-breeding dress like ♀ but retains white wing patch. Gregarious, found in scattered colonies when nesting and in flocks when not breeding.
Voice: Various brief twittering notes.
Distribution and Habitat: Locally common and widespread in East Africa. Inhabits rank tall grass and bushy grassland, usually on dry ground but sometimes in swampy hollows; much attracted to artificial dams in agricultural land. Common in the Kenya highlands where it is often associated with Yellow Bishops and Red-collared Widow-birds.

RED-COLLARED WIDOW-BIRD *Euplectes ardens* **Plate 28**
Identification: ♂ 28–30cm (11–12in), ♀ 13cm (5in). ♂ plumage black with crescent-shaped scarlet patch on upper breast. The Kenya Highlands, Kilimanjaro race has the crown and nape scarlet in addition to the red breast patch. Some birds in Uganda and southern Tanzania are all black, without the red breast patch. ♀, ♂ non-breeding and immature streaked black and tawny on upperparts; below, buff, washed yellow on throat and breast. Gregarious, nesting in loose colonies.
Voice: Various chirping calls and a metallic rasping song.
Distribution and Habitat: Widespread and locally common in East Africa. Inhabits mixed bush and grassland, margins of forest, lush vegetation near marshes and cultivation.

YELLOW BISHOP *Euplectes capensis* **Plate 28**
Identification: 15cm (6in). ♂ black with shoulders and rump bright yellow. ♀ and immature sparrow-like with an olive rump; ♂ non-breeding similar but retains yellow rump. Normally not gregarious, usually in pairs or single.
Voice: A series of brief cheeping and twittering calls.
Distribution and Habitat: Locally common and widespread in East Africa. Inhabits grassy bush country, savannah woodland, forest margins and overgrown neglected cultivation.

BLACK-WINGED BISHOP *Euplectes hordeaceus* **Plate 28**
Identification: 14cm (5½in). ♂ large red and black bishop with black wings and tail and buff or white under tail-coverts. ♀, non-breeding ♂ and immature

buff with dark streaked mantle, black wings and tail and yellowish eye-stripe. Black wings and tail distinguish this species from other red and black bishops. Not gregarious except in non-breeding flocks.

Voice: Various twittering calls, but often silent.

Distribution and Habitat: Widespread and locally common in East Africa. Inhabits areas of rank grass and bush, margins of swamps, maize and sugar-cane cultivation and riverine elephant grass.

RED BISHOP *Euplectes orix* **Plate 28**

Identification: 13cm (5in). One of the several species of brilliant red and black bishops. ♂ distinguished by pale brown wings and tail, orange-red under tail-coverts and black forehead. ♀, non-breeding ♂ and immature sparrow-like, streaky above. Nests in loose colonies; gregarious outside the nesting season, in flocks.

Voice: Various soft clicking notes.

Distribution and Habitat: Widespread in southern Uganda, western Kenya and locally in western Tanzania. Inhabits tall, rank grass, sugarcane and maize cultivation and rank herbage near water.

Allied Species: The Zanzibar Red Bishop (*Euplectes nigroventris*) 10cm (4in), is a very small species easily recognised by its entirely black underparts. It occurs in eastern Kenya and eastern Tanzania.

WEST NILE RED BISHOP *Euplectes franciscanus* **Plate 28**

Identification: 10cm (4in). ♂ differs from related species in having the crown of the head black as well as the forehead and the red upper and under tail-coverts very long, completely covering the tail. ♀ and non-breeding ♂ sparrow-like but with elongated tail coverts.

Voice: Soft chipping or clicking call notes.

Distribution and Habitat: Very common locally in northern Uganda and frequent in western Kenya, as far east as Lake Baringo. Occurs in rank grasslands and swampy areas along lake margins.

LONG-TAILED WIDOW-BIRD *Euplectes progne* **Plate 28**

Identification: ♂ 61–76cm (24–30in), ♀ 15cm (6in). This is one of the most striking of African birds, jet black with a neck ruff, a tail 60cm (2ft) or more long and bright red and buff shoulders. Flies slowly with slow, jerky wing-beats and tail spread, a few feet above nesting ground. ♀ and immature pale tawny, heavily streaked; non-breeding ♂ similar but larger and retains red shoulder patches. Forms flocks in non-breeding season when frequents and roosts in swamps and reed-beds.

Voice: Loud sharp chirping calls.

Distribution and Habitat: Local resident in the highlands of central and western Kenya, over 1,828m (6,000ft). Frequents open high level grasslands and moorland, the vicinity of dams and marshes and areas in cultivation.

JACKSON'S WIDOW-BIRD *Euplectes jacksoni* **Plate 28**
Identification: ♂ 33–36cm (13–14in), ♀ 14cm (5½in). ♂ black with olive-brown shoulders and a thick, long, decurved tail. ♀, non-breeding ♂ and immature tawny, streaked dark brown. When nesting, ♂♂ construct circular dancing rings on which they display by repeatedly springing three-quarters of a metre or more in the air. Forms large flocks in the non-breeding season.
Voice: A soft 'chee' uttered display and a brief clicking sound.
Distribution and Habitat: Local resident in highlands over 1,524m (5,000ft) in western and central Kenya and the Loliondo and Crater Highlands in northern Tanzania. Gregarious; found during breeding season in highland grasslands. Forms flocks in post-breeding period, when it visits cultivated areas.

RED-BILLED BUFFALO WEAVER *Bubalornis niger* **Plate 26**
Identification: 25cm (10in). ♂ a large thickset weaver, black except for white-edged flight feathers and white bases to feathers of body plumage. Bill dull, pale red with dusky tip. ♀ and immature with pale, dark streaked underparts. Gregarious, building large stick nests close together in baobab or acacia trees.
Voice: Very noisy birds, especially at nesting colonies, with a variety of loud, falsetto croaking and chattering calls.
Distribution and Habitat: Locally common north-eastern Uganda, north of Mt Elgon, Kenya and central and eastern Tanzania. Inhabits acacia woodland, savannah country, especially where there are baobab trees and in thornbush country.
Allied Species: The White-billed Buffalo Weaver (*Bubalornis albirostris*) 25cm (10in). ♂ differs only in the colour of the bill which is dull yellowish-white. ♀ very distinct, similar to ♂ with slaty-black underparts. The two species' ranges overlap in north-western Kenya. Ranges from northern and eastern Uganda to extreme north-western Kenya: in thornbush and savannah.

WHITE-HEADED BUFFALO WEAVER
Dinemellia dinemelli **Plate 26**
Identification: 23–25cm (9–10in). Sexes alike; large, thickset, white-headed weaver, brown and white, rather parrot-like in general appearance, with most conspicuous orange-red rump and under tail-coverts, especially noticeable during flight. Usually in pairs or small flocks; frequently feeds on ground and often associated with Superb Starlings. The Tanzanian race is larger and darker with a greyish-white bill.
Voice: A harsh, parrot-like call and a series of chattering notes.
Distribution and Habitat: Locally common in northern and eastern Uganda, Kenya and Tanzania. Inhabits acacia woodland, dry bush and thornbush scrub. One of the most conspicuous birds of the arid northern areas of Kenya.

WHITE-BROWED SPARROW WEAVER

Plocepasser mahali **Plate 27**

Identification: 15cm (6in). Sexes similar. Upperparts light brown, darker on crown with broad white eyebrow and white rump; below white. Immature similar. Gregarious in small flocks and nesting colonies.

Voice: Noisy birds especially at nesting colonies, uttering a 'chuk, chuk' call and various loud chatterings: ♂'s song not unlike that of Superb Starling.

Distribution and Habitat: A common but local species in Uganda, Kenya and northern and southern Tanzania. Found in dry bush and acacia country. Especially common in the arid Northern Frontier Province of Kenya.

GREY-CAPPED SOCIAL WEAVER

Pseudonigrita arnaudi **Plate 27**

Identification: 13cm (5in). Sexes similar; a rather short-tailed, greyish-brown weaver with a pale dove-grey cap. Immature browner with a buff cap. Gregarious, nesting in loose colonies.

Voice: A short piping call and a rather squeaky chatter.

Distribution and Habitat: Locally common Uganda, Kenya and northern and central Tanzania. Inhabits dry thornbush and acacia country and savannah. Feeds largely on ground.

STARLINGS: Sturnidae

A group of medium-sized, usually gregarious birds: many species possess brilliantly metallic plumage, greens, blues and purples predominating. Most are noisy and conspicuous.

BLUE-EARED STARLING *Lamprotornis chalybaeus* **Plate 29**

Identification: 23cm (9in). A thickset metallic green starling, golden or bluish in some lights, with a bright orange-yellow eye. Throat and chest metallic green like upperparts, merging to metallic violet on belly. Ear coverts bluish but not conspicuously so. Immature sooty black with green gloss. Often perches and feeds on the ground. Ruppell's Long-tailed Starling differs in having a white eye and a longer, graduated tail.

Voice: A variety of deep musical whistles and high-pitched chattering notes.

Distribution and Habitat: Common and widespread in East Africa, found both in highland and in lowland localities. Inhabits open park-like country, areas of cultivation, all kinds of woodland and the vicinity of human habitations.

RUPPELL'S LONG-TAILED STARLING

Lamprotornis purpuropterus **Plate 29**

Identification: 33–36cm (13–14in). This starling's tail is long and graduated; plumage metallic violet-blue with head and throat washed bronze; eye

creamy-white. Immature duller with dusky eye. Best recognised by long, graduated tail and white eye. Usually in pairs or small parties; often alights and feeds on the ground.
Voice: Various chattering calls and whistles.
Distribution and Habitat: Locally common Uganda and Kenya; in Tanzania mainly found in western districts. Inhabits bush and acacia country, savannah and open woodland, cultivation and gardens.

VIOLET-BACKED STARLING

Cinnyricinclus leucogaster **Plate 29**
Identification: 16.5cm ($6\frac{1}{2}$in). ♂ upperparts and throat brilliant violet-blue, changing in some lights to crimson-purple; belly pure white; eyes yellow. ♀ and immature quite different with mottled brown upperparts; below white streaked and spotted dark brown. A bird of the treetops, rarely seen on the ground. Appears when trees, especially figs, are in full fruit, disappears when crop is over; very gregarious.
Voice: A soft twittering whistle of three or four notes.
Distribution and Habitat: Distributed widely over East Africa but spasmodic in its appearance. Frequents forested and wooded areas, open park country with scattered trees and gardens where there are fruiting trees; also in dry country where there are fig trees.

HILDEBRANDT'S STARLING *Spreo hildebrandti* **Plate 29**

Identification: 18cm (7in). A starling of dark metallic violet-blue plumage with belly, under wings and under tail-coverts rufous; eye orange-red. Immature duller and browner. It differs from the Superb Starling in lacking white breast band, white under wing and white under tail. Its eye colour is also a good field character.
Voice: Various melodious whistles; song a series of drawn-out double whistles.
Distribution and Habitat: Locally common southern half of Kenya and northern Tanzania; commonest in the Ukamba country of Kenya. Inhabits bush and wooded savannah, riverine acacia belts and cultivation. Usually gregarious and like Superb Starling commonly feeds on the ground.

SUPERB STARLING *Spreo superbus* **Plate 29**

Identification: 18cm (7in). A plump, short-tailed starling; upperparts and chest metallic blue and green, head blackish; breast and belly bright rufous chestnut with a narrow white band across chest; under tail-coverts and below wings white; eyes pale yellow. Immature duller with dusky eyes. Hildebrandt's Starling has no white in its plumage and its eyes are orange-red. Feeds mainly on the ground, often below or near acacia trees; gregarious.
Voice: Various chattering and whistling notes; song a sustained warbling. Sometimes mimics other birds' calls.
Distribution and Habitat: Widespread and locally common in Kenya, Uganda and eastern Tanzania. Occurs in thornbush and acacia country and in the

vicinity of human dwellings. Gregarious and usually tame and fearless of man.

GOLDEN-BREASTED STARLING

Cosmopsarus regius **Plate 29**

Identification: 30–36cm (12–14in). The most beautiful of the East African starlings and the easiest to identify in the field. It is slim with long graduated tail; brilliant green-blue upperparts and throat, violet in some lights, and contrasting rich golden yellow belly; eyes white. Immature much duller. Gregarious, in small flocks; usually very shy and wild.

Voice: Various loud whistling and subdued chattering calls.

Distribution and Habitat: Locally common through eastern Kenya and in the northern half of eastern Tanzania. Inhabits dry bush and thornbush country; most numerous in Tsavo East National Park.

Allied Species: A closely related, long-tailed species, but very different in colour, is the Ashy Starling (*Cosmopsarus unicolor*) 30cm (12in), entirely brownish-grey with a slight greenish tinge on wings and tail. It is a bush country species found locally in Tanzania.

WATTLED STARLING *Creatophora cinerea* **Plate 29**

Identification: 21.5cm ($8\frac{1}{2}$in). A pale grey starling with a whitish rump and black wings and tail. In breeding season ♂'s head is bare of feathers, skin yellow and black; a large fleshy black wattle on forehead above bill and another smaller wattle in centre of crown; double large pendent wattles on throat. In non-breeding season wattles are absorbed and head becomes feathered. ♀ does not develop the bare skin and wattles. Immature resembles adult but browner. Gregarious, often in large flocks; breeds in colonies.

Voice: A soft, squeaky whistle; less noisy than many species of starlings.

Distribution and Habitat: Widely distributed throughout East Africa but erratic in its appearances. Movements appear to depend on the availability of an abundance of insect life. It inhabits thornbush and acacia woodland, open country and especially pasture, where it associates with horses, cattle and sheep or game animals, running between their feet and catching insects disturbed by the grazing animals.

RED-BILLED OXPECKER *Buphagus erythrorhynchus* **Plate 29**

Identification: 18cm (7in). This is a rather slim, ash-brown bird with a thick red bill and a yellow eye-ring. Oxpeckers are associated with large game animals and sometimes domestic stock, perching upon and climbing all over the animals searching for food – ticks and blood-sucking flies. Immature similar but with dusky bill and eye-wattle.

Voice: A hissing 'tsssssss' and a shrill chattering call, often uttered in flight.

Distribution and Habitat: Locally plentiful throughout East Africa but especially in National Parks and Reserves. Frequents open country and farmlands where associated with big game and domestic animals.

Allied Species: The Yellow-billed Oxpecker (*Buphagus africanus*) is larger, 20cm (8in), with a contrasting pale buff rump and a heavy, chrome yellow, red-tipped bill. It lacks the yellow eye wattle. Locally not uncommon but absent from many areas such as eastern Tanzania. Like the Red-billed Oxpecker it associates with big game and stock.

ORIOLES: Oriolidae

A group of active, thrush-sized birds, usually of brilliant yellow plumage, which inhabit tree-tops in woodland and forest. Calls, loud clear melodious whistles.

BLACK-HEADED ORIOLE *Oriolus larvatus* **Plate 29**

Identification: 23cm (9in). A bright yellow oriole with a black head and throat; wing feathers edged greyish-white; tail green with yellow tips to feathers except for the central pair. Montane forest birds from the Kenya highlands and south-western Uganda often have black and green tail feathers. The status of these birds is at present uncertain.
Voice: A series of liquid, melodious whistles.
Distribution and Habitat: Locally common over much of East Africa. Mainly a woodland savannah species, but also occurs in acacia stands, forest, scrub and thick bush, and in gardens. Keeps to the tree-tops.

DRONGOS: Dicruridae

Medium-sized black, shrike-like birds with hooked bills and more or less forked tails, the outer feathers curving outwards towards the tip, 'fish-tail' fashion. Feeding habits resemble those of some species of flycatchers – catching insects in flight and returning to same perch.

DRONGO *Dicrurus adsimilis* **Plate 29**

Identification: 23–25cm (9–10in). The Drongo's plumage is black, the tail forked and 'fish-tailed'; inner webs of flight feathers ashy, imparting a pale wash to the underside of wings when the bird flies; eye red. Immature has greyish tips to feathers of mantle and underparts.
Voice: Normally silent during the day but vocal during early morning and evening. A great variety of harsh, metallic calls and clear whistles.
Distribution and Habitat: Widespread and common through most of East Africa. Inhabits all types of woodland, forest margins, acacia and thornbush country and scrub. Especially common in coastal districts.

CROWS: Corvidae

The largest of the perching birds. The plumage of many species is black or black and white. Bills are usually heavy with nostrils covered by forward-pointing bristles. Omnivorous, feed mainly on ground.

PIED CROW *Corvus albus* **Plate 29**

Identification: 46cm (18in). A black crow with a white breast and a white collar on the hind neck. The White-naped Raven is larger, black above and below with a crescent-shaped white patch on the lower nape.
Voice: A deep, guttural croak.
Distribution and Habitat: Locally common over most of East Africa. Inhabits open country, cultivated areas, refuse dumps, the vicinity of human habitations and margins of rivers, lakes and swamps, and the sea coast.
Allied Species: The Indian House Crow (*Corvus splendens*) 38cm (15in), resembles a large slender Jackdaw. It is an introduced species now abundant along the Kenya and northern Tanzania coast and one of the most noticeable birds in Mombasa.

CAPE ROOK *Corvus capensis* **Plate 29**

Identification: 43cm (17in). The entire plumage of the Cape Rook is glossy black, slightly brownish on head; feathers of the throat long and lax; bill very slender. Closely resembles a European Rook but with its throat feathered.
Voice: A guttural, high-pitched 'kaaah'.
Distribution and Habitat: A local resident, sometimes common, Uganda, Kenya and northern Tanzania. Frequents open plains country with scattered trees, cultivated and pasture land and sometimes lightly wooded areas. Frequently perches and feeds on the ground.

FAN-TAILED RAVEN *Corvus rhipidurus* **Plate 29**

Identification: 46cm (18in). An all black raven with an extremely short tail, especially noticeable in flight. When perched wings extend far beyond end of tail. Nostril bristles very long.
Voice: A shrill, falsetto 'pruuk'.
Distribution and Habitat: Locally not uncommon in the arid areas of north-eastern Uganda and northern Kenya. Occurs in the vicinity of cliffs and gorges and is a common visitor to the vicinity of human habitations.

WHITE-NAPED RAVEN *Corvus albicollis* **Plate 29**

Identification: 56cm (22in). An entirely black raven with a heavy black, white-tipped bill and a white crescent-shaped patch on the base of the nape. Immature similar but browner.

Voice: A typical raven croak, deep and guttural.
Distribution and Habitat: Occurs locally through East Africa, frequenting cliffs, rocky hills and gorges; often in the vicinity of hunting camps and around human habitations where it acts as a scavenger.

Index of Places

in Part 1

Index of Mammals and Birds

in Parts 2 and 3

Numbers in **bold** type refer to pages facing illustrations